W9-CFU-516

Shelf Life

Supermarkets and the
Changing Cultures of Consumption

Supermarkets, in all their everyday mundanity, embody something of the enormous complexity of living and consuming in late twentieth-century western societies. *Shelf Life* explores the supermarket as a retail space and as an arena of everyday consumption in Australia. It historically situates and critically discusses the everyday food products we buy, the retail environments in which we do so, the attitudes of the retailers who construct such environments, and the diverse ways in which all of us undertake and think about supermarket shopping. Yet this book is more than narrative history. It engages with broader issues of the nature of Australian modernity, the globalisation of retail forms, the connection between consumption and self-autonomy, and the highly gendered nature of retailing and shopping. It interrogates also the work of cultural critics, and questions recent attempts to grasp what it means to consume and to be a 'consumer'.

Kim Humphery is currently a Senior Research Fellow at the Cooperative Research Centre for Aboriginal and Tropical Health in Darwin. He has taught politics and cultural theory at Melbourne University, Monash University and La Trobe University, and has completed extensive social research at La Trobe University, King's College London and the Northern Territory Department of Health. His numerous journal publications have appeared in *Arena, Labour History, Australian Historical Studies* and *Meanjin*.

Shelf Life

Supermarkets and the
Changing Cultures of Consumption

Kim Humphery

CAMBRIDGE
UNIVERSITY PRESS

PUBLISHED BY THE PRESS SYNDICATE OF THE UNIVERSITY OF CAMBRIDGE
The Pitt Building, Trumpington Street, Cambridge, United Kingdom

CAMBRIDGE UNIVERSITY PRESS
The Edinburgh Building, Cambridge CB2 2RU, UK   http://www.cup.cam.ac.uk
40 West 20th Street, New York, NY 10011–4211, USA   http://www.cup.org
10 Stamford Road, Oakleigh, Melbourne 3166, Australia

© Kim Humphery 1998

First published 1998

Printed in Australia by Australian Print Group

Typeset in Adobe New Aster 9/12pt

A catalogue record for this book is available from the British Library

National Library of Australia Cataloguing in Publication data
Humphery, Kim, 1958– .
Shelf life: supermarkets and the changing cultures of consumption.
Bibliography.
Includes index.
ISBN 0 521 62316 2.
ISBN 0 521 62630 7 (pbk.)
1. Supermarkets – Australia – History. 2. Supermarkets –
Social aspects – Australia. 3. Shopping – Australia –
History. 4. Shopping – Social aspects – Australia. 5.
Retail trade – Australia – History. 6. Retail trade –
Social aspects – Australia. 7. Consumers – Australia. I.
Title.
381.1480994

ISBN 0 521 62316 2 hardback
ISBN 0 521 62630 7 paperback

Contents

List of Illustrations   *vii*

Acknowledgements   *viii*

  Introduction   *1*

Part I: Emergent Cultures

  1 The Discovery of the Consumer   *21*

  2 Really Modern Retailing   *39*

Part II: New Worlds

  3 Engineering the Shop   *61*

  4 She Likes to Look   *79*

  5 Tomorrow's Shop Today   *100*

  6 Living the Transformation   *121*

Part III: Familiar Places

7   Magic Futures   *143*

8   Strangers in Paradise   *161*

9   Everyday Shopping   *178*

10 Towards the Exit   *203*

Notes   *213*

Bibliography   *245*

Index   *264*

Illustrations

Opening day at the Coles-Dickins New World supermarket, 1963   4
A British grocery store, 1906   31
Woolworths 'Bargain Basement', 1920s   37
An Australian grocery store, 1940s   40
Extract from *The Grocers' Assistant*, 1916   56
Shopping over the counter, 1958   62
Shopping off the shelf, 1954   62
An American Safeway supermarket, 1950s   70
Opening day at a Crofts store, 1951   88
A Crofts superette, c.1954   91
Coles New World supermarket, 1963   101
Interior of Coles New World supermarket, 1964   113
A 'mega-emporium', 1964   118
A McEwan's advertising handbill, 1953   134
Supermarket opening, 1963   138
Marketing brochure, Woolworths, 1991   158
A contemporary supermarket, 1997   183
From grocery to takeaway, 1995   204

Acknowledgements

There are many people to thank, and in many instances for things way beyond those connected with this particular project. Yet hours of scribbling away have convinced me that too many words simply rob gratitude of its clearest meaning. So with an economy of ink but much appreciation, I thank Stuart Macintyre for his engaged and insightful guidance during the long final stages of the thesis upon which this book is based, Dipesh Chakrabarty and Geoff Sharp for early assistance and encouragement, and Judy Brett, Paul James and, in particular, Dennis Altman for giving me opportunities to teach, research and learn. Thanks also to Gail Reekie, Peter Spearritt and Ruth Barcan for some excellent advice on redrafting the manuscript for publication. I am especially grateful to Phillipa McGuinness at Cambridge University Press, who showed constant faith in my ability to deliver a text – despite alarming indications to the contrary – and also to Sally Paxton, my copy-editor.

Much of the research for this book relied on the collections and generous assistance of staff at the British Library, London, the State Library of Victoria, the University of Melbourne Archives and the Benga Oral History Centre at Heritage Hill, Dandenong. I am especially indebted to Benga for facilitating the oral history and immensely grateful to all of the people who agreed to be interviewed for this study. Those interviews gave an invaluable insight into the meanings surrounding everyday shopping and proved to be one of the most enjoyable aspects of the research.

Over many years, and at various stages, a number of close friends have inspired, humoured, critiqued and supported me in relation to this project and with myriad other things. I am hardly going to do justice to these friendships in a sentence but I do want some people to know the depth of my gratitude. Thanks then to Mandy Brett, Julia Cabassi, Steve Cowden, Tim Jordan, Sue Miller and particularly Sandra Plant. To Alison Ravenscroft I owe a special debt not least for her warmth, constant advice and wonderful conversation. Lucy and Ivy Broadhead were a tangible presence throughout the writing of this book; so too were my sisters Gill, Jan and Rob and, in unfathomable ways, my late father Jim Humphery. I am, as ever, very deeply indebted to Mandy Paul for her conviction, her grasp of the world and our unbreakable friendship. Finally, and with all I have, I thank Sarah MacLean for her gentle intelligence, her enthusiasm and every moment of her company. To Nicky Humphery, my mother, I dedicate this book.

A note on the research. For useful information and illustrations I am grateful to Michael Collins (Australian Centre for Retail Studies), Greg Every (Coles Myer), Ken Henrick (Australian Supermarket Institute), Malcolm Taylor (Woolworths Limited), David Parker (formerly of Coles Myer), Amanda Sinclair (University of Melbourne Business School), J. Sainsbury plc and the Sainsbury's Archives, Tesco plc, Argyll Group plc, ASDA Stores Ltd, Kroger Co., Safeway Inc. and Jon Brenneis Photography, Woolworths Limited, Ladybird Books Limited and the Shop, Distribu-tive and Allied Employees' Association (Victorian Branch). Many of these people/organisations will not agree with the critique offered here but were nevertheless generous in providing assistance. Various paragraphs in this book appeared in slightly different form in *Meanjin* (Autumn 1994), and *Arena Magazine* (October–November 1995), and I thank the editors of these publications for permission to use these words again. Thanks also to Linda Brainwood (Image Library, State Library of New South Wales) and John Yovanches (Coles Myer Archives) for last minute assistance with the illustrations.

For Nicky Humphery

Introduction

From where I stood, towards the front of the supermarket, I was able to see straight down one of the aisles. I watched them, a young girl and her mother, walk up this aisle, and I followed them at a distance as the girl made her choices. This English supermarket, like many others I have visited in Europe and Australia, offered its younger customers miniature shopping trolleys. These trolleys are a little over two feet high and are the domain of the probationary consumer.

Several choices had already been made by the girl, and her mini-trolley was filling up quickly. The woman with her did not have a trolley of her own and was simply grabbing a few necessities – and a few luxuries as well – while allowing the girl to let her desires wander, obviously curtailing them if her chosen items wandered too far past the budget or the choice she made seemed 'naff', a term I heard the woman apply to one tacky-looking item.

And as I came closer, I lost my status as the observer. I was with this party and these people were my friends, not objects of my detached analysis whose words I need to place in inverted commas. Their words were my words too, as were their everyday pleasures and frustrations. We were doing something we always did when I came to visit them – indulge in a touch of consumer recreation, consumer therapy. For us this was not the weekly essential shopping trip – although there were many frazzled-looking people around us fulfilling that task – but the 'visit'. This was a cheap thrill enforced by limited income and encouraged by the lure of the abundant, the exotic, and the sheer carnival of supermarket shopping: mangoes, rambutan and starfruit from the other side of the world, cheeses from the continent and 'in-house' delicacies, efficient and stressed women with feral children, fumbling male shoppers and crushingly bored checkout people, and, of course, the recreationists like ourselves.

Now, on a very different continent in the city of Darwin, I am watching again in a similar setting. Outside, there is a monsoonal trough that will never dampen Britain and crocodiles that feed a tourist trade along with the mythology of frontier. Here, there are mangoes on the trees as well as on the supermarket shelves. But inside those supermarkets, differences in environment and culture are seemingly minimised. I have not managed to find a mini-trolley as yet, but the frazzled people are here in Darwin's supermarkets, as are the efficient women and fumbling men, the feral children, the exotic fruits (which strangely retain an exotic air even though they are local), the necessities and delicacies, the endless checkout queues, and at least one recreationist-cum-observer.

Between them, Sainsbury's, Tesco and ASDA – the three largest commercial supermarket chains in Britain, where this study began – sell their products to well over 20 million customers a week and account for around 36 per cent of the retail sales of grocery items in the United Kingdom.[1] In Australia, where this study took shape, the three largest corporate supermarket chains, Woolworths, Coles Myer and Franklins, between them control almost 76 per cent of the national retail market in packaged groceries.[2] These basic statistics confirm that the supermarket is a major economic and social institution of highly industrialised nations.

Not so long ago these retail institutions represented new worlds. Now, for most people in the industrialised world, they are familiar places. This study takes the reader inside the supermarket, historically and culturally, in order to follow this transition from the new to the familiar. In doing so it offers an exploration of the supermarket as a retail form and as an arena for everyday consumption. It attempts to situate historically and critically explore the everyday food products we buy, the retail environments in which we buy these products, the attitudes of the retailers who constructed such environments, and the diverse ways in which all of us undertake and think about supermarket shopping.

Although this study outlines briefly the rise of the supermarket in the United States and Britain, it focuses in particular on the emergence of the large corporately owned supermarket in Australia. By looking in detail at the development of the Australian supermarket, we are able to grasp some of the complexities involved in supermarket shopping, reflect on the global nature of retail forms, and trace some of the connections between the supermarket and other aspects of late twentieth-century everyday life. We are also, very importantly, able to explore contemporary social and cultural criticism in relation to what has been called 'consumer culture', to question whether such critique has, to date, been particularly useful in grasping what it means to consume and to be a consumer.

Retail Cultures, Consumer Cultures

According to most retailing histories, the supermarket emerged as a particular retail form in the United States of America during the 1930s. The worldwide spread of this retail form, however, has not simply been a process of transference; it has also been one of permutation. The supermarket emerged within countries outside the United States at different times and, in doing so, took on local as well as global characteristics. There is undoubtedly a similarity to supermarkets around the world, as the above observations make plain, but underneath that similarity, differences are still there.[3]

The supermarket did not fully arrive in Australia until the beginning of the 1960s. While the concept of 'self-service' had long been a facet of grocery and other forms of retailing before this time – and a number of supermarkets were already in operation by the early 1950s – it was only during the early 1960s that large retail companies such as Coles and Woolworths developed chains of purpose-built, free-standing 'one-stop-shops'.

When the big corporate supermarket finally emerged in Australia, it was heralded by retailers as 'tomorrow's shop today', as the symbol *par excellence* of Australia's transition to a high modernity. Drawing heavily on American retailing know-how, Australian retailers nevertheless attempted to localise the new shopping environments and to make the supermarket Australia's own.

Commercially, they were highly successful. From the late 1950s onwards, the supermarket quickly became the dominant form of food distribution in Australia, which now has one of the most highly concentrated retail food markets in the Western world, controlled as it is by only a handful of companies.[4] But the emergence of the supermarket in Australia is not examined here as a story of commercial success or corporate monopoly. It is, more importantly, discussed in terms of its social and cultural significance. Culturally, and economically, the emergence of the supermarket was part of the transformation of post-war Australia into a 'modern consumer society'. Like the large suburban shopping centres that were developed also in the 1960s, the supermarket transformed the culture of retailing, and with it, the way people shop. The transformation also had social importance in that the supermarket encouraged a change in people's relationship to food and other everyday goods; not only how they bought them, but what they ate and used, and the skills they needed or didn't need in order to utilise supermarket products.

These changes have been even more remarkable because of the speed with which they have transformed our relationship to the everyday products we buy, to what is available, to how it is sold, and to how it is produced, packaged and marketed. Indeed, few Australians below 30 or 40 years of age have first-hand knowledge of shopping prior to the emergence of the one-stop-shop.

Launching modernity: opening day at the Coles-Dickins New World supermarket, Dandenong, Victoria, November 1963 (Coles Myer Archives)

While these changes were to affect all Australians, it was women who were and remain the principal users of the supermarket – and the main source of labour in the retail and food manufacturing industries. As Gail Reekie has pointed out, historians of the retail trades and of consumer society have, until recently, failed to sufficiently explore the fact that women have always been the vast majority of shoppers within retail spaces.[5] On the other hand, retailers, at least at management level, have generally been male and, while readily acknowledging women as their 'market', they have done so in ways that have constructed highly gendered images of the 'lady' shopper, the housewife and 'Mrs Consumer'. These gendered aspects of supermarket retailing and everyday shopping are explored throughout the following study.

Although women, along with the children who often accompany them, still remain the principal supermarket shoppers, the 'profile' of those who use the supermarket has changed, particularly over the last decade, to include more solitary male shoppers, and men accompanying women.[6] As the supermarket has become the dominant form of food distribution in Australia, the distinctions between shoppers on the basis of class, age, race and ethnicity have become blurred, giving rise to an apparently 'undifferentiated market' in food retailing. The contemporary Australian supermarket, it seems, is open to almost all, regardless of social demarcations, and many of the goods on sale are affordable to a wide range of people.

This is not to suggest that all supermarkets are the same or are egalitarian spaces deserving of celebration. There are significant differences between particular supermarket chains and individual stores, depending on the ownership, size, stock and location of the store, and the perceived social make-up, and therefore tastes and budgets, of its customers. Moreover, there are very definite class, gender, race and ethnic demarcations between those who work within the supermarketing and food manufacturing industries.

While the supermarket industry has always liked to project an image of itself as the champion of choice and egalitarianism, retailers are well aware of the different buying behaviours, tastes, preferences and financial capabilities of particular groups of people. There is no such thing as homogeneous mass markets. Markets are always subject to demarcation, fragmentation and complexity, however great the number of people who visit a particular retail environment or buy a particular product.

As this study insists, retailers develop *retail forms* and construct *retail cultures*; they do not create smoothly functioning mass consumer cultures, however hard they may try. *Consumer cultures* arise only in the interaction between those who have something to sell and those who look, listen, watch, wander, feel and sometimes buy. These cultures, too, always reflect social difference. In other words, retail environments have no power to make consumer cultures until those environments are peopled, and until those socially and culturally differentiated people begin to identify as possible consumers. Thus consumer cultures, unlike retail spaces, are not planned, they are negotiated.

Of course, for most people in the West, consumption is an important part of our lives. In the apparent choice, independence and power it offers, it is – as we shall see throughout this study – bound up with values of freedom and self-determination. Consumption spaces and cultures can be seductive; they can and do frame the very ways in which we experience the world. But this is not the whole story. The cultures of consumption are fragile and need constant reinforcement. Even when we do enter an environment like the supermarket, we think about and respond to this particular type of retail space in diverse ways. At times the supermarket may be viewed in purely utilitarian terms – a place to buy food. At other times it may present itself as a cheap thrill – a place for a touch of consumer recreation. On the other hand, wandering the supermarket may become a heavy chore. In our wanderings we may become frustrated and even enraged with the crowds, the impersonal service, the oppressive lighting and falsity of choice between products, the prices, the packaging, the hard-sell marketing techniques, and shopping trolleys that seem to move in every direction but the one in which we want to head.

Supermarkets are not simple places. On the contrary, in all their everyday mundanity they embody some of the enormous complexities of living and consuming in a society such as late twentieth-century Australia. It is the task of this study to explore some of this complexity and to draw out some of the connections between the rise of the supermarket and broader social and cultural transformations in post-war Australia. The aim of this study is to give the 'one-stop-shop' a past and a cultural context. Its aim is to leave the reader with a slightly altered sense of what it means to wander the super-market, gaze at its products and take home its goods.

Theoretical Positions

As we explore the supermarket, historically and culturally, we begin also to trace the rise of consumer society within industrialised countries and to examine some of the intellectual debates surrounding this development.

Up to this point we have been using the terms 'consumer society' and 'consumer culture', the definitions of which have been assumed.[7] For many social theorists and cultural critics, the term 'consumer society' has, until recently, carried a rather negative connotation. It has come to refer largely to the (destructive) impact of 'mass consumption' on daily life within industrial and post-industrial societies. As the realm of consumption has expanded to involve increasing numbers of people (i.e. 'the masses'), it has seemingly led to the organisation of many social activities around the practices of con-suming. It has led also to the involvement of people in buying an increasing range of goods and services. At the same time the apparent 'consumerisation' of social life has been accompanied, critics have argued, by the rise of consumer cultures. That is, consumption has not only become an apparently ubiquitous part of our daily life, but has become entangled with and productive of meanings, of the way we view and represent the social world, think about ourselves and communicate with others. These social and cultural aspects of consumption are inseparable.

There is, however, ongoing debate in relation to historicising this process. While some writers have traced the beginnings of a consumer society to the early modern period in the West, most have focused on the emergence of mass-produced goods in the nineteenth century as signalling the beginnings of a fully developed consumer society. More specifically, some writers have suggested that it is only in the post–World War II period that Western societies have become fully characterised by the proliferation of consumer goods and experiences.[8]

Whatever the time-frame offered, the emergence of consumption as a key economic and social activity has given rise to an extensive body of theoretical work. Consumption has been one of the central categories through which theorists and cultural commentators have attempted to interpret modernity and postmodernity, and to critique and explore the nature of everyday life under conditions of industrial and post-industrial capitalism. The 1980s, in particular, witnessed a renewed interest in consumption as a social phenomenon, especially within my own disciplinary areas of history and cultural studies, and it is within this intellectual context that the supermarket presented itself as a potential subject of serious study.[9]

As I entered the supermarkets that were to become part of this book, I did so not only as a shopper but also as a cultural analyst, an ugly term though it is. This latter role became increasingly the reason for my constant wanderings up and down the aisles of my local supermarket and many others I visited in Europe and Australia. Yet as I wandered I struck a problem. The more I experienced the supermarket, the more I began to feel a stranger among contemporary analyses of consumption practices and the more frustrated I became with the apparent one-dimensionality of recent debates on consumer culture.

My remaining task is to explain this estrangement and foreshadow some of the ways in which the following study attempts to step outside this one-dimensionality.

By the early to mid-1980s the consumption of goods and services in contemporary Western societies had been embraced by many writers within cultural studies and other disciplinary areas as a potential arena of personal empowerment, cultural subversion, and even political resistance.[10] Within this analytical framework the 'consumer' was positioned as active, rather than passive, as the 'producer' of *usages* and *meanings* that the marketplace may not have assigned to a particular commodity or consumer space, and which potentially undermined or evaded consumerist ideologies. The mass market of consumer goods, services and experiences, then, was no longer viewed as promoting a mindless, empty materialism. Instead, cultural analysts turned to a recognition of human agency, emphasising the manner in which people 'make do' in transformative and oppositional ways with what is offered to them under conditions of consumer capitalism.[11] In short, the person who consumes was no longer thought of, within cultural studies at least, as being simply manipulated – by wearing make-up, or enjoying shopping, or watching and listening – but also as manipulating back, by often ignoring and sometimes subverting dominant meanings, implied messages and hidden persuaders.[12]

This analytical turn to the active, subversive, resistant consumer – and I am generalising here about a broad body of work – was explicitly formulated in opposition to a perceived critical orthodoxy.[13] This orthodoxy was one involving a rejection, or at least a suspicion, of mass consumer culture, a position shared by many twentieth-century theorists and critics – conservative, liberal, feminist, Marxist, anarchist and postmodernist alike. As a number of writers have argued, many, though certainly not all, twentieth-century social theorists have tended to interpret consumption as embodying the materialism, social fragmentation and destructive individualism seemingly embedded within the rise of Western modernity and, more recently, postmodernity. As a global consumer culture, geared to rampant mass production and endless self-gratification, has become an apparently ubiquitous part of modern and postmodern life, it has been taken as emblematic of all that is negative and bland within twentieth-century Western society.[14]

This study does not explore theories of modernity and postmodernity in detail, a relief perhaps to those readers not keen on 'high theory'. It does, however, draw on these concepts in the process of historicising the supermarket. It also examines the apparent gulf between the cynics and the celebrants of consumer practices, questioning the extent to which there exists a sharp dichotomy between supposedly innovative and orthodox theoretical and critical frameworks. That very 'gulf' is embedded to some extent within the difference between social theory and other forms of contemporary cultural analysis.

Broadly speaking, social theorists have been concerned primarily with social structure and cultural framework. In grappling with the tension between structure and agency, they have tended to emphasise the workings of large, impersonal forces which shape history, social formations and self-identity, and which *act on* individuals, moulding them in the image of dominant ideological frameworks. Alongside this, cultural studies has emerged as an alternative intellectual field, one which certainly engages with social theory and is influenced by it, but which explores the actual practices of daily life under conditions of modernity and postmodernity.[15] In relation to consumption, writers within cultural studies have attempted to shift the ground of cultural analysis, building on theoretical traditions which emphasise the importance of the popular and of a sympathetic exploration of the manner in which everyday actions and thought evade 'containment'.[16]

Clearly, within such a framework a language of resistance remains important. Consumer culture is not accepted or celebrated in its entirety within the recent cultural studies of consumption; rather a structural analysis is suspended in favour of a discussion of specific consumption practices. This approach can be easily grasped by reference to any one of a number of 'sites' or areas of Western consumer culture. The use of the shopping mall, for example, has been explored in these terms. While the shopping mall has been, and continues to be, interpreted as a falsely carnivalesque, bland and alienating space of conspicuous consumption, recent cultural analysis has sought to explore the popular use of these consumer environments as recreational spaces and as arenas within which notions of community and forms of self-identity are expressed.[17]

Such an approach potentially deepens the interpretation of consumer cultures. Once cultural commentators move towards a local, semiotic analysis of products and their purchasers, and away from a predominantly structural analysis of the social, economic and cultural systems in which consumption is embedded, easy assumptions about what the consumer is doing, thinking and feeling become a lot more difficult. As one recent discussion of cultural studies insisted, a social institution such as the shopping mall:

> offers no quintessential insight into the organisation of an epoch or a culture (it is not an emblem or an essence of the postmodern condition or of consumer capitalism); it is a place where many different things happen, and where many different kinds of social relations are played out.[18]

The supermarket also illustrates this complexity. In one sense the corporate supermarket – with its abundance of packaged products, its crowds of nameless shoppers, its overbright lighting and its interminable muzak – seems a culturally barren environment, an empty, unreal space where the person/consumer becomes confused, seduced, compliant, anything but resistant. In another sense, however, this doesn't seem to be what is going on at all. It is not very useful to assume that people are merely compliant consumers when wandering through a retail space such as the supermarket, or that these environments and the use people make of them are culturally bereft. This rests on a further assumption that the meaning of shopping and consumer wandering is 'fixed', or functional to and entrapped by the retail environments and marketing discourses in which consumption takes place. As this study attempts to show, the supermarket's carnivalesque and often unreal qualities do not necessarily mask the retailers' motives or capture the shoppers' imagination – let alone their spending power.

Participation and Refusal

The Australian writer Meaghan Morris has argued, some time ago now, that one of the problems to have emerged in connection with the burgeoning of social theory and cultural studies as academic disciplines is that 'new' frameworks of analysis become very quickly dated and rapidly overused.[19] This 'quick-as-a-flash' adoption of the new tends to make certain frameworks of interpretation appear tired and even obsolete before very much has been said, but not before a whole swag of books have hit the shelves.

The point still stands, and the past decade and a half of interest in the cultural analysis of consumer practices is a good example. By the early to mid-1990s, the focus on the active consumer and on the complex reality of watching, listening and shopping had begun to look like last year's model. The more that was being published on the subject, the less, it seemed, was being said. With each new title on consumer culture I got the unmistakable feeling that I was buying the same text, a text in which the concept of consumption as an active and potentially subversive project had become as much of an assumed truth as earlier theorists' assumptions about a life-world wholly dominated by the shop and the ideologies that went with it.[20]

One of the most positive aspects of the recent attention given to consumer practices is that it has entailed an acceptance of the market as an essential element of everyday life in late twentieth-century Western societies. Moreover, it has promoted the consumer marketplace as a site to be dealt with, not dismissed – as a site of human agency, personal fulfilment and potentially of politics. Yet by the mid-1990s explorations of the active consumer had reached a political dead-end, unwilling or unable to move far beyond simply 'mapping' the various ways in which we as individual consumers are supposedly able to resist and subvert.[21] This perhaps explains why, in the late 1990s, academic interest in the subversive consumer has now all but vanished, although, as I shall argue below, a resistance/containment dichotomy continues to frame discussion.

I am certainly not the first to express frustration with the attention given to consumer practices within recent cultural studies (and I would hope that my own obvious frustration will be seen as critique rather than dismissiveness). Some writers, including many working within the field of cultural studies itself, have long been critical of the manner in which the resistant consumer has been theorised, preferring instead to remain slightly more ambivalent about the political possibilities embedded within consumer cultures.[22] Even those who embraced the notion of the active consumer have differed substantially over how to conceptualise this. More particularly, by the early to mid-1990s some writers were reappraising their previous engagement with the so-called 'resistance school' of cultural analysis.[23]

Overall, the notion of consumer resistance has come in for quite a serve over the last few years. Critics have drawn attention to the naivety with which some writers turned to consumer practices and pleasures, pointing to the adoption of an uncritical 'cultural populism'.[24] What is more, this very eagerness to focus on everyday consumption practices has tended to eclipse the continued importance of exploring the wider social, cultural and economic contexts in which consumption takes place.[25] This was the great strength of earlier 'structural' analyses, which did not seek to completely disentangle the practices of consumption from the ideologies of capitalist production.[26]

But there is another perhaps related criticism that can be levelled at the tendency to focus on resistant consumer practices, one which, to my knowledge, has gone unremarked and is central to the analysis offered in the following pages. It is that talk of the resistant or active consumer has largely failed to preserve or explore an *outside*. In concentrating on people's critical participation in consumption cultures, such work has tended to ignore or downplay an equally important aspect of everyday life in which people stand back from the market, feel anger at its presence, refuse to participate or, at the very least, question its relevance to other aspects of their lives. This process of standing back is not a process of 'making do' but of 'thinking through', of imagining an 'outsidedness' and an oppositionality which is embedded in a process of 'distancing' rather than participation. It is this outsidedness, and people's attempts to actively delimit the areas of their lives that are commodified, which has been almost completely ignored by the celebrants of the resistant consumer. It is almost as if people have been understood as being unable to imagine or to live any aspect of their lives other than through participation in the commodity experience, as if their imagination is wholly defined by (critically) participating in and making do with the products and experiences of the market.[27]

This tendency to view and to speak of everyday experience through the category of consumer culture is not, however, characteristic of the recent cultural studies of consumption alone. As we have noted already, a view of consumer culture as definitive of late twentieth-century Western society and consciousness dominates social and cultural theory of this century, and particularly of the last few decades. It is one of those deep and seemingly inescapable operating assumptions that is embedded within contemporary theory of almost any of the recent brands, from critical theory, to post-industrialism, to neo-Marxism, to postmodernism.

The recent upsurge – and now demise – of interest in the active consumer did *not* fully challenge this position. It did not abandon the notion that consumption redefines and indeed frames everyday life. Rather it took commodity culture as definitive of the contemporary popular, and sought to explore ways in which this commodification of everyday life contains positive elements – contains the seeds of opposition. But as Rachel Bowlby has argued, in the context of recognising that consumption is crucial to self-identity, it may be 'that there is nothing outside the shop – but this is something which, in all its everyday mundanity, we should perhaps not just take or leave as a given'.[28]

This study certainly does not take consumer culture and the ubiquity of its presence as a given, nor does it understand that culture as easily over-turned. Consumption is understood here as powerfully framing, though not wholly defining, our lives. Those lives are understood as expressed through both everyday *participation in* and a *distancing from* commodity cultures. People operate in active and passive, resigned and belligerent ways *within* consumer cultures while attempting also to keep separate other aspects of their lives and to retain an *imagined outside*, an imagined other world or worlds. Thus critiques of popular consumer practices and spaces are not somehow by definition elitist, negativistic or part of a dead theoretical ortho-doxy but are often contained within the practices and thoughts of everyday life itself.

And if, as this argument suggests, people sometimes refuse commodity culture, then they perhaps do so because participation is always circum-scribed; it always offers them far less personal and political empowerment than some cultural analysts have supposed. Participation and the accom-panying notion of empowerment – or the engendering of a sense of place in and control over one's society and life – have been important concepts within the cultural studies of consumption, and more widely within radical political theory since the 1970s. But the notion of empowerment through participa-tion has long remained vaguely defined within radical cultural analysis and has often been invoked without sufficiently exploring the dimensions and limitations of the political power and personal agency being identified. As a consequence, the concept of empowerment has sometimes been rather wildly applied to various consumer practices in what amounts to a patron-ising over-interpretation of the political meaning of everyday social activities.

To return, then, to my estrangement. I feel somewhat disaffected with the past decade or so of analytical moves around consumption. Despite a minor avalanche of work on consumer cultures during the 1980s and 1990s, those cultures threaten to remain a confusing and somewhat lost ground for social and cultural critics, including this one. In terms of current responses to consumer culture from within radical cultural critique, it seems that we are still presently offered a rather one-dimensional choice in which consumer culture continues to be seen as largely undermining and definitionally hostile to a critical and emancipatory politics, or as the popular terrain on which some form of radical politics now takes place and from which any 'critical distance' becomes suspect. Social and cultural analysis, it seems, is good at thinking but not all that good at thinking differently, or moving beyond well-worn frameworks and solidified dichotomies. As Lesley Johnson has argued, consumption practices within this debate remain categorised *a priori* as either resistant and subversive or contained and restrained, with little effort to construct a dialogue between these positions.[29]

That dialogue is perhaps now emerging, while a diversity of disciplinary approaches towards consumption are challenging and eclipsing the assumptions of recent work. Nevertheless, the resistance/containment dichotomy remains a powerful one within both intellectual and popular approaches to consumer cultures, while few alternatives are available for those who wish to reject the dichotomy. As a result, consumption, at least for this 'consumer', is simply not very well understood, or understandable, by way of the available theorisations I can walk into a supermarket armed to the teeth with high theory and contemporary cultural analysis and learn that I am the victim of commodity fetishism (but I don't quite feel it) or alternatively that I am the site of political struggle, with empowerment at my fingertips (but I don't quite feel that either).

Consumption is undoubtedly a terrain of politics, the politics of exploitation, manipulation, pleasure, resistance and so on. Yet the question we need to ask is how can we both participate in consumer cultures and radically oppose them; confirm our role as consumers and undo it? When I first set out on this project, I was particularly struck by the lack of interest in seriously exploring this crucial and somewhat obvious question within discussions of consumer practices. One writer simply told me that consumption practices undermine the hegemony of the systems with which they interact, but without offering any real exploration of this assertion; another writer insisted that mass consumption and the apparatuses of mass distribution are 'technologies with an enormous capacity for mobilising new political communities', but offered little to show how.[30]

To draw attention to this is not to ask for a return to a dismissiveness towards consumer culture and people's participation in it. It is to recognise that a *critical* analysis of consumption cannot be content with an endless mapping of what people do within the consumer present, but must continue also to explore the wider effects and limitations of those cultures, and to suggest what else is possible and how those possibilities may be made real. As the demise of interest in the subversive consumer undoubtedly illustrates, this is a political mode that critical social and cultural analysis cannot abandon in favour of an exclusive emphasis on specific sites and individual usages. On its own, usage is a pretty thin concept, however 'thick' or detailed the description of particular consumer practices may be.

And yet a mode of abandonment is precisely what has seemed to characterise much of the cultural studies of consumption until at least the early 1990s. The focus on the active consumer did not testify simply to an increasing 'respect for the popular' within cultural studies, but also to the left's fear of being *unpopular*. In this context cultural critics sought to reformulate a radical politics by clumsily trying to fit that politics into popular confines. At the same time the popular was redefined in almost purely participatory terms, while the concept of use eclipsed alternative modes of interpretation, particularly ones attempting to abandon the resistance/containment dichotomy.

The result was – and perhaps still is – a loss within radical cultural analysis of a sense of anger about the way the world is and a certain timidity of response, involving a muting and even fear of writing *critical* analysis and of entering the terrain of 'political value'. Even those who have sought to retain an ambivalence towards consumption cultures, refusing to either condemn or to celebrate (a position with which I have great sympathy), have been left with little ground on which to construct a political critique of the present, forced instead to restating the obvious; things are complex, no judgement can be made.

These comments are pointed, but they are not meant as polemic. This book does not rest on an easy dismissal of recent theoretical and critical work on consumption. It does not seek to critique straw arguments and claim for itself an entirely untrodden ground; to pronounce past intellectual strategies utterly dead and parade the new. Rather, this study necessarily works within, and is informed by, much of the recent scholarship discussed in this introductory chapter. Yet it also attempts to move on, to question the intellectual parameters of the current debate on consumption cultures, and to connect with a politically engaged analysis of contemporary retailing. In this, it is a study that will no doubt connect with the work of others. With the dissolution of interest in the subversive consumer, perhaps there is a return now to a less blandly populist, less ambivalent and more critically engaged form of exploring consumption. If so, this book is part of that return. The supermarket, the shopping mall and other retail environments are certainly structures-in-use; they never simply reflect a static culture bereft of everyday agency and human vitality. But it seems just a little *too* cautious and ultimately banal simply to see these as places where 'many different things happen'. It seems also rather absurd to deny that such retail forms can have an 'emblematic moment', that they can have something more general to say about the kind of society in which we live and the social relationships within which we are, at times, embedded. For cultural critics and historians, then, it remains important to explore not simply what people do *within* consumption cultures, but to ask of ourselves and others, are they what we want and do they actually embody the way we want to live?

The New and the Familiar

Two distinctions have been made throughout this introduction, one between *retail cultures* and *consumer cultures*, the other between *popular participation* and an *everyday outsidedness*. These distinctions form the basis of the following study. What is offered here is a detailed exploration of the public construction of post-war retail cultures on the one hand, and a cultural analysis of changing attitudes towards supermarket shopping on the other. As such the focus of this study is limited. It is not, for example, a work of labour history or a contribution to the political economy of global food distribution, nor does it offer a history of retailing in general or, more locally, a discussion of the impact of consumption on indigenous Australians.[31] Historical interpretation is, however, crucial to the study as a whole, not least because it enables the introduction of a third related distinction upon which the work is based, namely, that between the *new* and the *familiar*.

In a thought-provoking article on history and cultural studies, Carolyn Steedman argued that history was indispensable to the cultural studies project but that writers needed to ask of themselves how and why history was to be used.[32] Similarly, Ann Curthoys has suggested that history needs cultural studies as a means of enriching historical scholarship.[33] Not all historians are this open to combining historical and cultural analysis. Arguably, many historians view the use of history within contemporary cultural studies as rather shallow, informed by little understanding of the subtleties of historical methodology. This is not the place to enter into the sometimes heated debate over the relationship between history and contemporary social and cultural theory. Nevertheless, I would agree that history is often ignored within cultural studies and, where it is used, lacks depth or serves as a kind of addendum to theory rather than as a means to problematise and reframe theory itself. It is in this more reflexive vein that the history of the supermarket is explored here. I share with Steedman and Curthoys an interest in combining historical and cultural forms of analysis. In the context of the present study, historical interpretation offers a way into the 'complexity' of which many writers, including myself, now tirelessly speak when invoking the notion of consumer culture. Historical work enables us to trace the changes over time and the subtleties within particular historical moments connected with a retail environment like the supermarket, and with the cultures of consumption.

This approach has theoretical implications as well as descriptive interest. It is only through historical interpretation that one can flesh out the manner in which retail environments like the supermarket progressively lose a sense of their newness and become familiar places. Embedded within this historical process is one of the keys to understanding the manner in which people are able to escape capture by the supposedly dream-like qualities of consumer cultures and to imagine and construct aspects of that 'outsidedness' of which we spoke above.

If newness is defined by that which is unfamiliar, then familiarity is the motion of undoing the new. Familiarity is the process of making things no longer novel. Implicit in this is a contradiction that social and cultural theorists have tended to overlook. As retail environments like the supermarket and the shopping mall have become more numerous, the consumer cultures of which they are a part have been understood by many theorists as increasingly 'colonising' or taking over everyday life. It may be, however, that any such colonisation is undermined by an accompanying process whereby, as retail environments and consumer cultures become more widespread, they also become less 'magical' and more ordinary; they both gain a social presence but begin to lose a certain power of attraction, and their aura of modernity (understood in progressivist terms). In this situation everyday life may indeed be somewhat colonised by the spaces and ideologies of consumerism, but we also more readily begin to become bored with what is offered, to become suspicious of the promises of consumer abundance; we begin to 'see through' consumer cultures and to look for something different, or at the very least, for ways of preserving aspects of everyday life that are not dependent for their articulation and their felt reality on the consumer present.

This does not make the environments and ideologies of consumption easy to refuse or to remake. It does suggest, however, that colonisation is not a teleological process; it is not a process by which slowly, sometimes quickly, everyday life is simply gobbled up by the ideologies of consumer capitalism. On the contrary, those ideologies sometimes lose their grasp. This is precisely why retailers – as this history illustrates – are constantly in search of new retail forms, not only to maximise profit, but to regain a cultural presence and power as older retail forms atrophy in terms of their ability to capture the imagination and desires of the consumer. If the spaces, practices and ideologies of consumer capitalism do have a power to reshape everyday life in their own image, and I would not dismiss this, it is a power which constantly has to be worked at, reframed and reconceptualised; it is a power constantly undermined both by its own logic and by the people it attempts to subject.

The supermarkets explored here, then, are not cathedrals of a manipulative and unproblematically domineering consumer capitalism, but nor are they carnivalesque arenas of playful consumers. They are not simply palaces of commodity fetishisation and the site where the richness of the life-world is hollowed out, but nor are they sites of endless permutation, personal empowerment and everyday pleasures. The supermarkets explored here, and the people who move within them, are understood to be embedded within certain social and cultural settings, to be subject to certain locational frustrations, and to be the creators of certain personal pleasures and strategies for survival. The social settings are ever present but not inescapable, the frustrations are constant but usually endured, and the pleasures and evasions are real, but of poor quality, and are understood as such.

Part I

Emergent Cultures

Chapter 1

The Discovery of the Consumer

'History begins', wrote Professor Elizabeth Levett, 'with discontent, with the development, slow or sudden, of new desires'.[1] The desires Levett was referring to, in an essay entitled 'The Consumer in History', were those aroused by commodities. Levett was contributing to a large two-volume edition ponderously entitled *Self and Society: Social and Economic Problems from the Hitherto Neglected Point of View of the Consumer*. This British collection, published in 1930, was one of the first attempts in England to bring together social critics and historians on the subject of consumption.

Those contributing to *Self and Society* were concerned to explore the connection between commodity culture, self-identity, and political action in the world's first industrial nation. This was a nation to which Commonwealth countries such as Australia looked for political and commercial guidance. Some contributors spoke of the link between consumption and personal enjoyment, while others sought to explore the potential power of the consumer to influence the economy and society, and to remake notions of citizenship and political participation. Yet the collection was not highly theoretical. It was populist in tone and journalistic in style, consisting of a set of pamphlets written by Fabian socialists, social democrats and co-operativists all in celebration of the 'co-op', the English phenomenon that had arisen in the mid-1800s as a working-class, collectivist response to the commercial distribution of foodstuffs and other household goods.

For these writers, consumption in itself was no evil but its pleasures needed to be harnessed to worthy social ends, to the goal of socially just distribution. Consumption was taken seriously as a key social activity, rather than simply the 'completion' of the production process, and as involving a potential power to influence what was produced and distributed. This 'power', however, came from collectively organising consumption and cultivating a kind of disciplined pleasure. As the editor, Percy Redfern, insisted, the consuming pleasures promoted by industry encouraged a social irresponsibility and an apparent individualism that was altogether false, since it masked the chaotic, mob-like behaviour of shoppers all too easily 'disciplined' by retailers and manufacturers.[2]

This expressed a concern about the ends, purpose and organisation of consumption, and about the need to develop a 'consumerist ethic' that envisaged a balance and communicative dynamic between production, consumption and society. As Professor Harold J. Laski wrote in his contribution to the Redfern collection:

> because our process of consumption is highly individualistic, because, that is to say, we make no organised effort to supply ascertained demand from the angle of social benefit, there is nothing in the satisfaction of wants that has spiritual principle inherent therein.[3]

This spiritual principle was to come from people recognising that they were *citizen-consumers*, and that, as Beatrice Webb insisted, a more co-operative form of consumption was both more rational and embodied the essence of a democratic social order.[4]

Self and Society was published, however, at precisely the time when commercial retailers were themselves moving towards giving the consumer greater 'power'. This was a power that did not originate from collective organisation and self-discipline, but from a notion of the consumer as *autonomous*, as an individual faced with a plethora of choices and increasingly free to make the choices she or he desired. It was a notion of power that centred on the person rather than the collective, and on a conceptualisation of consumption as servicing the individual rather than provisioning the community. This was to constitute a major challenge to co-operativism.

The early twentieth century thus witnessed the problematic resolution of a long moment of struggle between two different ways of consuming, and two different definitions of what it was to be a consumer; one centred on the collective, the other on the autonomous self. Neither of these conceptualisations rejected consumption, or even capitalism, but the former preserved a notion of a collective otherness in opposition to the individualistic directions in which capitalism was pushing the social organisation and culture of shopping. In 1930 Beatrice Webb had insisted that the discovery of the consumer had been a long historical process.[5] If this was true, then by the early twentieth century discovery was no longer the issue. Rather, what was at stake was the way in which retailing and consumption were to be understood by the seller and by the shopper.

Autonomy was to win out. Although notions of informed, co-operative and socially responsible consumption did not disappear – and nor, importantly, did co-operative retailing – notions of the consumer as autonomous were to slowly push co-operativism out of the picture. The individual consumer as the locus of power became, from the early twentieth century, part of the very definition of Western consumer culture, and the possibilities of a collective response in relation to retailing and consumption would become increasingly closed off, culturally as well as economically. Even the 'consumer movements' that arose in the United States, Britain, Australia and elsewhere following World War II only partially challenged this notion of consumer autonomy. Although they sought from the outset to develop a 'consumer consciousness', they did so in a way that confirmed the notion that consumer power lay with the individual and at the point of purchase, not distribution.[6]

Co-operativists and social critics continued to see the anti-collectivist 'power' of the new consumerism as false, as a means by which consumers could effectively be manipulated by retailers. In reality, retailers were to become involved in a rather more complex and ironic situation, particularly with the development of techniques such as self-service. By gradually abandoning personalised service and letting go of a highly interventionary power over what people consumed, retailers could effectively sell more goods. By allowing more autonomy – in the shape of the wandering shopper gazing at a plethora of products on open display – they sold more things. This individually based consumer power, then, was not a ruse nor pure manipulation; consumers were to be given more room to look, to feel, to try and to buy. As a result a more fluid relationship between the seller and the shopper developed. But given such 'freedom', the desires of consumers were multiplied, and so were the profits of retailing. With the rise of the autonomous consumer, retailers began to concentrate on the space between the offer and the choice by relinquishing a tight hold over the products bought and concentrating instead on the minds of the people who bought them and the retail space in which they did so.

In this chapter we begin to explore some of the dimensions of this consumer autonomy by briefly examining the rise of 'modern retail systems' and of a consumer culture in Britain and North America. We explore also related transformations in food manufacturing and grocery retailing within these two countries and begin to trace the imitative adoption of modern retailing cultures in colonial and early twentieth-century Australia.

Retailing Revolutions, Retail Spectacles

Talk of revolution abounds within retailing history. For a field that is, apart from its co-operative tradition, so intensely pro-capitalist, there is more often than not a celebration of revolutions – as long as they are in retailing and not in society. This is particularly the case within business history, which has tended to dominate the field. Each new development in retailing – the emergence of the 'fixed' or permanent shop, the department store, the retail chain, self-service and the supermarket – is seen in revolutionary terms and the retail pioneers hailed as the architects of social progress.

Nevertheless, some of the more scholarly work on retailing has been less dominated by celebratory account even if the metaphor of revolution remains. In the British context, on which a great deal of work has been done, the rise of modern retailing, or 'distributive systems', has been skilfully traced, often in minute empirical detail. As most studies have insisted, retailing entered its 'era of modernity' within industrialising countries during the second half of the nineteenth century. It was at this time that a number of dramatic changes took place in the forms of retail distribution, the range of merchandise available, and in the market for retail goods.

In his 1954 study of retailing in Britain, James Jefferys argued that transformations which took place in the distributive trades between 1850 and 1914 were comparable to the revolutionary changes taking place in industry.[7] For Jefferys, and for writers who followed, these changes revolved around the displacement of fairs, markets, itinerant traders and specialist producer-retailers (such as shoemakers, tailors and dairymen) as the dominant form of retail distribution. By 1850 this dominance was being challenged by a rapid growth in the number of 'fixed' shops including grocery stores, the establishment of department and variety stores, the development of retail co-operatives, and the emergence of chain store firms, or 'multiples' as they came to be known. Part and parcel of these developments was the rise of manufactured and nationally distributed products, the increasing use of advertising and marketing methods, the packaging, branding and price-marking of goods, and the gradual de-skilling of the shopkeeper – the traditional producer-retailer was giving way to an increasing division of functions between producer, wholesaler and seller.[8]

The timing of this supposed revolution, however, has been challenged by writers attempting to bridge the gap between a narrowly focused history of retailing and a broader history of consumption. As both David Alexander and Gareth Shaw have illustrated, changes in the pattern of retail trading and consumption practices in Britain were well underway before 1850.[9] This was particularly the case with the development of the fixed shop. Carol Sharmas and Hoh-Cheung and Lorna Mui have argued that by the mid-eighteenth century, there was in fact a large, firmly established network of shops in Britain, including the small, 'lower-class' backstreet store.[10]

Clearly, long-term transformations in the British retail trades were not simply congruent with industrialisation, just as the rise of consumer cultures was no simple product of the industrial revolution. Talk of nineteenth-century retailing revolutions is thus somewhat overblown, and retailing is perhaps more usefully conceived as undergoing constant permutation. In this sense, retailing in Britain of the mid- to late nineteenth century was not simply disconnected from a pre-industrial past. It was, however, substantially different in part because of the changed usage of shops, their size and organisation, and the range of goods available within them.

If the notion of revolution has dominated the field of retailing history, it is the concept of spectacle that has informed much of the more recent cultural history of consumption. Besides debating the 'birth' of consumer society, cultural historians, concentrating on Western consumer cultures of the late nineteenth and early twentieth centuries, have explored the spectacular and dream-like aspects of consumerism and its role in the making of Western modernity. This work has sought to analyse the rise of advertising and the popularisation of mass consumer goods and practices. In particular, it has focused on one retail environment that has come to represent, for many writers, the very embodiment of the abundant, spectacular and transfixing qualities of modern consumer cultures; the department store.

It was in the second half of the nineteenth century, argues Rachel Bowlby, that the concerns of industrialism shifted from production to selling, from the satisfaction of stable needs to the 'invention' of new desires.[11] It was within the department store that this new concern for selling took on a life of its own and in which shopping finally became completely detached from necessity, while the merchandise was transformed into a spectacle. Rosalind Williams earlier described this process as giving rise in late nineteenth-century France to *dreamworlds* – a changed pattern of personal and social consciousness in which life was given meaning through consumable things, and the meanings offered were ones that drew on the inner fantasies and desires of the consumer.[12] Williams, in tracing the rise of the world's first department stores in France, argues that it was in this period – centred on the opening of Paris's Bon Marché in 1869 – that a modern European consumer culture was cemented. Similarly, Michael B. Miller has suggested that while the department store did not, alone, lead to the appearance of consumer society, it did stand at the centre of the phenomenon.[13] According to Miller, the rise of the department store was both a reflection of an encroaching bourgeois culture and a vehicle for the construction of a modern culture of mass consumption which would increasingly affect all social classes.[14]

This point has been put even more forcefully by Thomas Richards in his analysis of commodity culture in Victorian England.[15] For Richards, between the Great Exhibition of 1851 and the consolidation of English retailing up until 1914, the commodity became 'the one subject of mass culture, the centrepiece of everyday life, the focal point of all representation, the dead centre of the modern world'.[16] This apparently overwhelming dominance was achieved through the fashioning of a new kind of being – the consumer – and new kind of ideology – consumerism – the creation of which was facilitated by the growth of advertising. North American writers have written of a similar process underway in the United States in the late nineteenth and early twentieth centuries. For North American historians of consumption, as for those in Europe, the period from 1850 to 1930 in Western industrialised societies is seen as the era in which consumer culture was consolidated, and in which it came to define in some important sense the very nature of modern life and of modern 'subjectivity' or self-identity.[17]

Much of this work has provided a fascinating and informative exploration of the rise of Western consumer cultures. Yet just as there are problems with an overblown use of the metaphor of retail revolutions, the concept of spectacle has its limitations. The analysis offered throughout this book emphasises the importance of the *mundane* and the *everyday*, rather than the spectacular, in the construction of retail and consumer cultures. Consumption not only transforms life through spectacle, but through far less exciting processes such as routine and the physical reconstruction of everyday public space. In concentrating on the spectacular aspects of modern consumer cultures, historians have tended to ignore these more mundane processes through which consumerism becomes entrenched and to confirm the notion that consumption is connected to fantasy, excitement and pleasure – to dreamworlds, and moreover, dreamworlds that hold enormous power over their dreamers.

Consumption *is* undoubtedly connected to these fantastic worlds. But it may be that pleasure and excitement are overly 'written in' when it comes to the cultural analysis of consumer society. An equally important aspect of that society is the manner in which everyday life is altered in deep but quite unspectacular ways. This is a process nowhere more evident than within the development of modern food manufacturing and retailing. For the bulk of the population in industrialising countries such as nineteenth-century Britain, it was not so much the rise of the department store that was of importance in the transformation of daily consumption patterns, but the emergence of new grocery outlets and manufactured foodstuffs. Even within this more mundane and far less 'dream-like' shopping arena, a new culture of consumption – and of eating – developed, and it developed on an everyday level.[18]

Packaging Time

The expansion of the grocery trade in late nineteenth-century Britain was centred primarily on meeting and creating a rising demand for foodstuffs, especially among the British working classes. As incomes rose in the second half of the nineteenth century in Britain, the priority for the working classes was the consumption of better quality and easily available everyday goods.

As a consequence there was a rise in per capita expenditure on food, particularly canned and frozen meat and fish, milk and dairy products, fruit, such as bananas, and tea and sugar.[19] Many of these products were imported from countries such as Australia, New Zealand, Canada and the West Indies. In nineteenth-century Britain, food was in fact a major part of the working-class budget. Carol Sharmas has estimated that the proportion of income spent by the British working classes on food was about 50 per cent between 1850 and 1914, a figure which fell to 30 per cent by the 1950s.[20]

This is not to suggest that the expansion in the British grocery trade and the transformation in the foodstuffs consumed were solely generated by 'working-class demand'. While retail transformations in nineteenth-century Britain were very much framed by class stratification, reference to the development of a 'mass' consumer society tends to elide a recognition of the quite different ways in which people engaged with and used the new retail forms and consumer goods on offer.

The growth in the manufacture and importation of foodstuffs brought with it a mixed emphasis on the exotic, the luxurious, the convenient and the economical, all of which were emphasised in the manufacturers' efforts to promote their products. The middle classes took eagerly to factory-prepared foods such as soups, sauces, tinned and frozen meats, jams, and packet jellies.[21] Indeed, Hamish Fraser notes that for the British middle classes certain 'new' foods took on definite status, while the lower middle classes used such status foods to disguise their real income. The English breakfast of bacon and eggs had, for example, only just become 'traditional' by the 1860s, while the 'tradition' of afternoon tea emerged at much the same time and brought with it an increased consumption of manufactured biscuits, jams and factory-produced cakes.[22]

Biscuit production, in particular, was quickly monopolised by large British firms such as Carrs, Peek Freans and Jacobs, and is illustrative of the manner in which the manufacturing realm began, by the late nineteenth century, to colonise the provision of everyday goods. Peek Freans introduced the first 'cream cracker' in the 1880s with enormous market success. Other firms emerged also, such as McVities which introduced the 'digestive' in the 1890s and the first British chocolate biscuit in 1911.[23] Similarly, manufactured jams became increasingly popular in the late 1800s, as did factory-produced relishes and pickles, the production of which was quickly dominated by large firms such as Crosse & Blackwell and Chivers. Even tea, which had long been imported and consumed on a wide scale, was given an increased market through both the reduction of tariffs and the introduction of the small 'packet' by the Brooke Bond company in the 1860s and later by Lipton.

Similar transformations took place in the United States. As Susan Strasser has illustrated, the American food manufacturing industries were markedly transformed between 1880 and 1920. Utilising new production techniques and marketing methods American manufacturers launched a whole economy of branded, nationally distributed, standardised and packaged products that were heavily promoted through newspaper and billboard advertising.[24]

By the 1880s new manufacturing technology, along with developments in transport, made it possible to produce standardised products in large volume and in small packages through the use of continuous process machinery. This allowed the branded production of everything from cigarettes, matches, chewing gum, toothpaste and photographic film, to flour, breakfast cereals, soups and other canned products. As in Britain, this involved the emergence of large manufacturers such as Campbell's, Heinz, Quaker Oats, Carnation, Kellogg, Procter & Gamble and many other firms that would eventually come to dominate food manufacturing on a global scale.[25]

Rosalind Williams has noted how technological innovations in late nineteenth-century industrialising societies altered the social universe of consumption. Mass production and the employment of key technologies, such as electricity, not only provided new products and new techniques of producing them, but new ways of materially realising people's dreams and desires through investing life with a fantastic, fairyland quality.[26] The same could be said for the new and seemingly far more mundane 'democratised luxury' of processed food. Dianne Barthel has explored the manner in which commodities such as mass-produced chocolate quickly took on the feminised symbolism of luxury and transgression.[27] Tinned food also took on the symbolism of affordable luxury and convenience, while the food production processes themselves were thought of in almost metaphysical terms. As Professor Simon Patten of the University of Pennsylvania declared in the early 1900s:

> the preservation of food by canning is to time what transporta-
> tion is to space. One opens up an indefinite territory and the
> other secures an indefinite time in which to consume what has
> been quickly perishable.[28]

The supposed cleanliness and uniformity of manufactured goods were also sources of celebration. As Glenna Matthews has illustrated, home economics experts in early twentieth-century America envisioned the new packaged goods as emanating from the minds of commercial poets and dreamers, and as allowing the *scientific* production of food rather than reliance on the laborious and supposedly hit-and-miss practices of the 'traditional' housewife.[29]

Quite apart from its seemingly futuristic qualities, its ability to deceive time and transcend human imperfection, the emergence of modern food production and packaging, with its ability to break down a commodity into standardised units, facilitated a more systematic means of producing *and* selling the goods. Both the production and the distribution process became embedded within an ideology of efficiency.[30] In addition, packaging and food manufacturing facilitated an increased – though limited – blurring of class distinctions within food consumption. As mass food markets were constructed, an alternative range of foods were brought within the economic reach of a wider array of people.

Given these dramatic transformations, the full emergence of the food manufacturing sector in industrialising countries such as the United States and Britain signalled a major cultural shift involving both the cultural construction of new needs and attitudes and a transformation in the work of the household.[31] This transformation affected women in particular. While food shopping had long been the task of women, its construction as convenience and increasingly as pleasure, beside that of housewifely duty, was quite new.

Up until the late nineteenth century there was, as Dorothy Davis points out, a sharp distinction between 'marketing', which was a chore for working-class women, and 'shopping', which was a leisure activity for the well-off involving mostly non-food items.[32] Increasingly, however, the acquisition of food and household goods became a definitive part of the activity of shopping. As the use of domestic servants declined, and the family became a more privatised unit within early twentieth-century Western societies, everyday shopping became a central activity of both the working- and middle-class housewife. As a result, argues Glenna Matthews, housewifery was transformed from a skilled craft into trivialised domesticity, an activity embedded within the functioning of consumer capitalism.[33] Other writers have talked of similar transformations taking place in Australia and of the manner in which the domestication of consumption became embroiled in the construction of sexual identity.[34] Thus, shopping of all kinds, even the everyday purchase of food and household goods, became both a woman's 'duty' *and* a medium through which women were supposedly able to assert who they were and gain pleasure.

The Transformation of Retail Space

In terms of the distribution of manufactured and imported foodstuffs, the initial impetus for the creation of a mass grocery market serviced from large 'chain stores' came, at least in nineteenth-century Britain, from within the co-operative rather than commercial retail sector. Co-operatives were set up, particularly in the north of England, in response to the working-class demand for reasonable quality, low-priced food and household goods. They enabled any profits to be shared among co-operative members, through lower prices and dividends on purchases, and through the extension of credit to those in need.

It was not, however, until the mid-nineteenth century that co-operatives, in pursuit of both political aims and commercial viability, began to develop large-scale retailing techniques involving the opening of branch shops within the one co-operative society. Co-operatives embarked also on what would later become known as 'vertical integration' – or taking control of the wholesaling as well as retailing functions. Multiple shops within the one society increased turnover and thus overall profits, while taking on the function of the wholesaler allowed the various societies to group together and negotiate directly with producers, importers and manufacturers, placing large-scale orders and gaining favourable terms.[35]

Although this development of 'economies of scale' is now the principal logic behind the contemporary commercial retail industries, in the mid-nineteenth century such practices were novel. The co-operative societies proved enormously successful and rapidly increased in number, membership and turnover throughout the second half of the nineteenth century. By 1900 co-operative societies had over one million members and accounted for about 16 per cent of the retail sales of food and household goods in Britain, increasing to 19 per cent in 1915 and 24 per cent in 1939.[36]

Yet the growth of large-scale co-operative retailing in Britain was soon matched and, in terms of the speed of growth, overtaken by similar developments within commercial retailing. Although commercial retail firms were, as early as the 1850s, involved in operating branch shops, it was not until the 1870s that chain store firms emerged in the grocery trade.[37] With the emergence of these commercial 'multiples', specialism was to increasingly give way to the all-embracing grocery and provision store, the forerunner of the later one-stop shopping environments.

The new commercial firms concentrated on selling imported foodstuffs within working-class districts, and on a handful of basic foods such as butter, bacon, ham, eggs, tea and margarine. These products were sold cheaply and for cash in small shops, all with the same stock and the same standard appearance. While counter service remained, and was to do so for at least another half-century, the staff in the new branch shops had little to do but sell as the new firms undertook the wholesaling and traditional grocers' function of blending the teas, grinding and bagging the sugar, and weighing up the goods in the small, packaged, affordable quantities demanded by the working-class 'consumer'. These firms began also to advertise and to introduce 'bargain' lines, while progressively expanding into a wider range of products such as factory-produced jams, sauces, jellies, custards, mineral water, confectionery, tinned milk and other foodstuffs.[38]

Here lay the mythological beginnings of the 'great' British grocery firms. From a single grocery shop in Glasgow opened in 1872, Thomas Lipton,

A British grocery store: Sainsbury's, Guildford, 1906 (Sainsbury's Archives)

concentrating on tea and dairy products, had over 70 branches operating in London alone by 1890.[39] Likewise, the Home and Colonial Stores, concentrating on tea, butter and margarine, and first established in Newcastle, had more than 200 branches throughout England by the late 1890s.[40] Many other firms such as John Sainsbury and Maypole Dairy Company followed the same pattern, and in doing so placed themselves at the centre of the transformation of Britain into a consumer society. Sainsbury's, for example, had 123 branches by 1919 and 244 by 1938.[41] Other retailers followed suit. By 1900 there were 80 different grocery firms with ten or more branches in Britain, and of this number there were seven firms with 100 or more separate shops. By 1939, 26 firms had 100 or more outlets.[42]

These statistics only become meaningful when viewed in relation to the development of a 'mass' consumer culture in late nineteenth-century Britain. The rise of the 'multiples' within the grocery trade was not a development separate from the rise of the more spectacular phenomenon of the department store but was linked, as Gareth Shaw has argued, through the pursuit of economies of scale; one centred on larger 'emporiums', the other on a greater number of shops and an abundance of key everyday commodities.[43] Both were based on the creation of retail empires and on the development of new consumer markets. In these terms the commercial grocery chains, like department stores, were to prove phenomenally successful. The large commercial firms accounted for 14 per cent of grocery sales in Britain by 1914, rising to 25 per cent by 1939.[44] Consequently, the food 'multiples' were crucial to the development of a modern retail and consumer culture. As Hamish Fraser has written, 'The multiples were the shops of the mass market . . . their style of presentation, their deliberate courting of mass consumers, inevitably forced changes on all retailers'.[45]

By the early twentieth century there were multiple store retailers in almost all retail trades in Britain, though they were to dominate the grocery trade in particular. Although the number of grocery firms, and the number of shops operated by them, grew during the first half of the twentieth century, such growth disguised the increasing concentration of commercial food retailing in fewer hands. Between 1924 and 1931 most of the major commercial grocery firms in England embarked on programs of acquisition and merger, and by 1930 three firms controlled well over half the number of grocery chain stores in Britain. By 1950 only five firms controlled most of the commercial grocery sector.[46]

The emergence of large, powerful firms within the grocery trade was even more pronounced in the United States of America. This was evident in the establishment of giant firms such as the Great Atlantic and Pacific Tea Company (A&P) in 1859 and Kroger in 1883. These and other retail firms grew to an enormous size in the early decades of the twentieth century and were unchallenged by any significant co-operative movement. A&P operated 200 grocery stores by 1900, rocketing to a peak of 15 700 outlets 30 years later. Similarly, Kroger operated 5575 stores by 1930.[47]

Part of these companies' commercial success in North America was the speed with which they experimented with new retail forms, particularly, as we shall see, with the idea of self-service. As early as 1912, A&P introduced a 'new' type of store, the 'economy store', which sold cheap groceries on a cash and carry basis. These stores were small, opened in low-rent areas, and operated by a single worker. They were also highly popular and were largely responsible for the rapid expansion of the firm.[48]

Even before the birth of self-service, these transformations were seen as heralding new 'distributive systems' and new 'company identities'. The grocery chains in the United States were quick to adopt a 'science of selling', centred on the development of marketing and management skills, and drawing on the burgeoning social sciences. It was in early twentieth-century North America, as Rachel Bowlby has argued, that the linkage between consumption and the fledgling discipline of psychology was forged and in which a distinction was drawn between the 'classical' consumer, interested in utility, and the romantic, modern consumer motivated by desire.[49] The modern shopper was open to suggestion, and the shop became increasingly important as one of the spaces where the suggestion was made. As part of these developments, retail companies began to introduce staff training schemes in which retailing was lifted out of the intuitive and placed within the realm of the 'scientific'.

Such developments cannot be read simply as leading to a further de-skilling of the retailer, as most historians of the retail trade have contended. The early development of 'scientific selling' – however clumsy and analytically shallow the science was – put in motion an elevation of the 'top-end' of the retail labour force to the professional realm. New skills were required for a transformed culture of retailing and consumption, and the knowledge developed concentrated not on the *nature* of commodities but on the *selling* of them, and on the space in which this selling took place. The marketing systems that were to be created within the grocery trade from the early twentieth century onwards thus facilitated a loss, or at least a fragmentation, of a knowledge of commodities *as commodities*. As Arjun Appadurai has noted in his study of the social life of things, 'as commodities travel greater distances (institutional, spatial, temporal), knowledge about them tends to become partial, contradictory and differentiated'.[50]

In this situation, then, goods become singular; they become – as they are produced, packaged and placed on a shelf – free-standing and individualised. Products begin to exist in and of themselves, independent of the processes that make them and of the other products surrounding them. In this new guise they are given an additional and very particular sensuality. Tea, instead of being dug from a chest by the grocer, is contained in exact proportion and weight on a shelf; biscuits, instead of being part of a visible batch, are clothed in individual packets. To these packets can be added colours, company logos, promotional spiels, and images. The identity of the product as a material thing becomes increasingly drawn into the cultural realm until even the most everyday of products seems to lose some of its materiality and becomes bound up with ideas and emotions to do with cleanliness, uniformity, convenience, progress, modernity, class status, gender roles and identities, luxury, sensuality and so on. In this climate the selling of the non-material, of the meanings attached to a product rather than simply the product itself, becomes *the* central part of retailing. This is mirrored in the transformation of what it means to be a consumer – the transformation from consumption as chiefly tied to material and social needs and goals to consumption as a process of personal pleasure and autonomous self-expression.

This is a process of permutation rather than birth. Commodities and the selling of them may have long been embroiled in meaning rather than pure utility, may have long been acquired through desire as much as necessity and bought within retail environments designed to make products appealing. However, the emergence of industrial manufacturing techniques, of new products connected to this development, and of reorganised and enlarged retail environments in which such products were sold, meant that by the late

nineteenth to early twentieth century the conditions were set for the emergence of a transformed culture of consumption in the West.

Living at Woolworths

During the colonial and early post-colonial period, Australia joined the rest
of the industrialising world in transforming the nature of retailing and
remaking the cultures of shopping. Unfortunately, however, there are no
scholarly accounts of Australian retailing equivalent in scope to those
available on Britain and the United States. Moreover, it is only recently that
social and cultural historians have written in detail about the development
of an Australian shopping and consumer culture, despite the fact that
suburbanism, shopping and consumption have been central themes within
post-war intellectual and literary responses to Australian society.[51]

During the nineteenth and early twentieth centuries Australian retailing
followed a roughly similar path of development to that of Britain. There is
an important sense in which England – and later the United States – represented a model of civilisation not simply as a social structure, but as a *retail
and consumer space*. As elsewhere in the industrialising world, retail and
consumer cultures emerged in nineteenth-century Australia, giving rise to
new retail forms and perhaps also to dreamworlds of consumption. But there
was a specificity to the forms of retail and consumer culture which were to
arise in Australia, connected to its history as a colonial and post-colonial
society, its geographic location and its demographic structure. In particular,
the rise of retail and consumer cultures in Australia was influenced from the
outset by notions of empire, nationhood and economic liberalism.

In 1848, one contemporary observer boasted that George Street, Sydney,
had a 'range of well built edifices . . . presenting an external appearance
which London might well be proud of . . . private residences, sale rooms,
respectable shops'.[52] By 1879, the street had developed into a full-scale,
pseudo-European promenade and anyone 'doing the block at 4 o'clock' could
see 'veritable swells of both sexes dressed in the latest fashions, all before the
fashionable shops'.[53] Melbourne matched this 'progress'. 'Collins Street',
wrote Clara Aspinall in 1862, 'is to Melbourne what Regent Street is to
London. Here all things are conducted calmly, quietly and harmoniously'.[54]

Here, too, in these vignettes of colonial bourgeois street life, were many
of the images of a European modernity: appearance, fashion, respectability
and commercial dynamism. From the outset in white Australia 'consumer
culture' was about buying nationhood as much as a changed relationship to
objects – about buying a place in the Western world, or at least on the crimson
map of British Empire. This was to be achieved by making what that world had
to offer *purchasable* in Australia, and by rivalling those goods, and the retail
spaces in which they were bought, with products and shops of its own.

As Graeme Davison has argued, the Sydney and Melbourne 'Exhibitions' of the late 1800s were the ultimate claim to this commercial nationhood. These exhibitions spoke of a desire to be known, to be seen, a visibility that was itself blind to all but the presence of a white, and largely male, commercial culture.[55] In a colonial society without national history – or at least without much of it – what it manufactured, exchanged and purchased became and remained of crucial importance in representing the nation.

This commodity nationalism was further complicated in the Australian context, from the late nineteenth century onwards, by the problem of whose 'consumer modernity' to choose. While Britain represented the obvious immediate model of solid industrial and commercial progress, the United States appealed also as a model of a more dynamic and competitive modernity. Thus Australia was to look to *both* countries for instructions on how to operate the shop, as well as run the country.

This was a cultural rather than economic phenomenon. Throughout the nineteenth century Britain had been the principal source of investment capital and Australia's main trading partner, a relationship which continued until the 1960s.[56] But culture doesn't simply follow capital. American commercialism was to be an early influence on the construction of retail cultures, and many of the retail forms that were in place by the mid-twentieth century were to be taken directly from the United States.[57]

For the retailer, Australia was an ideal place for this mix of British progress and American dynamism. Australia in the nineteenth and early twentieth centuries was a rapidly expanding, highly urbanised society, clearly eager to be part of a world of which, geographically, it wasn't. The non-Aboriginal Australian population had increased to about 3.8 million by 1901 and it increased by another million between 1901 and 1914.[58] These populations, and thus potential consumers, were highly concentrated geographically, despite the enormity of the Australian land mass.

By 1901 Sydney and Melbourne each had a population of about half a million, placing them among the 30 largest cities in the world.[59] Suburban growth of these two main cities had begun as early as the 1860s and the inner suburbs were already densely populated by the 1880s.[60] Although the population of these inner suburbs fell between 1880 and 1920, it was to the newer 'outer' suburbs, serviced by the growing public transport system, that people moved.[61] Suburbanisation was accompanied by high rates of home ownership. By the beginning of the 1920s home ownership rates had risen to 46 per cent in Melbourne and 41 per cent in Sydney.[62] Finally, throughout the late nineteenth and early twentieth centuries, there was a general rise in the standard of living in Australia, and in levels of expendable income, despite the setback of the 1890s depression.

In these circumstances, Australian retailers could hardly have gone wrong. As in Europe, the department store, with its vast display of goods, was to be instrumental in the development of an Australian shopping culture and, as Gail Reekie has argued, in the definition of shopping as a female realm.[63] The rise of 'universal providers', such as the Sydney-based Anthony Hordern & Sons, was mirrored by the rise of other 'great' firms such as David Jones, Farmer's, Marcus Clarke, Mark Foy's, and Grace Brothers, all of which began as small shops and grew to large departmentalised emporia by the early twentieth century. Large emporia emerged also in Melbourne such as Buckley and Nunn, Mutual Stores, London Stores, Craig Williamson, Foy and Gibson, George and George, and Myer.[64]

Yet the department store, as a 'fixed' retail environment, did not stand alone. Besides existing alongside the small city retailer, the corner shop, the rural 'general store', the produce markets, and the street trader, it competed in the mid- to late nineteenth century with the 'shopping arcade' which offered a cosmopolitan, bazaar-like collection of shops.[65] Both the arcade and the department store were pre-eminently European institutions, representing a solid colonial commercialism. Indeed, in colonial societies such as Australia, the arcades and the 'big stores' were of crucial importance in the imaginary eradication of a physical and social distance from Europe.

It was, then, the emergence of the 'chain' variety store, particularly Woolworths and Coles, that signalled the cultural shift in retailing towards a North American commercialism. These stores began to cater exclusively to a working-class market and, given the potential size of this market, the variety chains expanded quickly into Australia's largest retail companies.

G.J. Coles opened his first Melbourne store in Smith Street, Collingwood, in 1914, basing the business on the North American 'five and ten cent stores' which he had experienced first hand during his visit to the United States a year earlier.[66] The 'novel' quality of these stores was their lack of class exclusivity, their cheapness through the adoption of economies of scale, their efficient and open-plan use of sales space, and their vast display of goods. The novelty proved successful. By 1933 Coles had developed an Australia-wide chain of 29 stores, a pace of development matched only by its major rival, the Sydney-based Woolworths company. The 'Woolworths Stupendous Bargain Basement' opened in Sydney in 1924, promising its shoppers:

> Practically it's a self-help store. You just wander round and gather bargains – we wrap them and take the money . . . Cash and carry – that's it . . . Come and see. Come and buy. You'll want to live at Woolworths.[67]

Woolworths in fact had no connection to the North American F.W. Woolworth company – it simply copied the name as well as the concept. By 1933 it had 23 stores Australia-wide and eight stores in New Zealand.[68]

Woolworths 'Bargain Basement' store, Sydney, 1920s (Woolworths Limited)

The speed with which the variety store took hold in Australia necessitated the rapid adoption of new, 'scientific' retail systems. These systems, as in Europe and the United States, signalled the beginnings of a slow shift from retailing as 'intuitive', the product of maverick retailing minds and family dynasties, towards a formalisation of retailing skills and the full imposition of masculine notions of technological progress and competitive commercialism.[69] Nevertheless, this process should not be exaggerated. The traditional and the modern existed alongside each other in the context of Australian retailing until well beyond the mid-twentieth century, just as old and new retail forms continued (and continue) to exist alongside each other.

If the discourse of scientific management and marketing was, at least partially, to win out, this was because of a much wider and problematic transition towards a consumer culture in Australia. The 1920s, in particular, were significant, as Greg Whitwell has argued, in the further creation of a mass market for consumer goods and experiences. This was exemplified in the speed with which the new 'consumer durables' such as automobiles and electrical appliances were to find ready markets.[70] This, in turn, was facilitated by the development of an Australian advertising and market research industry.[71] At the same time a further wave of suburban expansion took hold of Australian cities during the 1920s, bringing with it a growth in the number of outer-urban shopping 'strips', often situated along the new suburban 'high' streets. These 'strips' usually included a draper, a mercer, bootmaker, butcher, fruiterer, grocer, tobacconist, cake shop, chemist, newsagent, confectioner, estate agent and hairdresser.[72] Suburban retailing began to rival that of the central business district, a fact reflected in efforts by larger retailers to establish suburban branches during the 1920s.

For retailers suburban development and economic growth were a source of business optimism; for others they were a source of concern. The apparent commodification of everyday life quickly became the subject of cultural critique. When the authors of *Tomorrow and Tomorrow* described Friday night shopping in 1920s Sydney, comparisons with the best streets of London had given way to a bitter dismissiveness towards:

> Bright shop windows, endless wish fulfilment, emblems of para-
> disiacal, unattainable living . . . trade far beyond commodities,
> selling hope and love and faith . . . humanity feeding on this
> display as on a new pasture, satisfying eye and imagination for
> nothing, taking the bait and leaving the hook . . .[73]

This trade beyond commodities was to be interrupted by the depression of the 1930s and by World War II. Nevertheless, the Australian economy doubled in size and living standards rose by about 10 per cent in the 30 years between 1909 and 1939, establishing the conditions for a further trans-formation of Australian consumer culture.[74] As in Britain and North America, however, these conditions were set through both the 'stupendous' and the far less spectacular transformation of shopping environments. It is, then, to those unspectacular changes and the seemingly mundane realm of everyday shopping in colonial and early twentieth-century Australia that we now turn.

Chapter 2
Really Modern Retailing

In the 1920s the Australian novelist Hal Porter looked around his familial home and noted how traditional and how seemingly comfortable its contents were:

> It contains many indications of Empire: small silk Union Jacks, a red-blotched map of the world, Pears' Soap, Epps's Cocoa, Lea and Perrin's Sauce . . . Beecham's Pills . . . The house contains also many indications of a lower middle-class lavishness Australians regard as bare necessities. In the meat-safe are a sirloin, pounds of rump steak and cutlets. In the pantry are a case of apples, pineapple, peaches, oranges and bananas. The shelves are lined with bottles of jam, with sauces, pickles, chutneys and jars of Rose's Marmalade.[1]

Although tinged with an anti-suburban disdain for these items of everyday lower middle-class life, Porter's description draws our attention to the Britishness of everyday consumption in early twentieth-century Australia, a Britishness complemented by a very Australian penchant for red meat. Porter was not alone in these observations. Mr Edward Cadbury, of the Cadbury confectionery company, had noticed the same thing during his visit to Australia in 1901. Full of praise for the apparent dynamism of Australian retailing, Cadbury was nevertheless 'struck', as he put it, 'by the similarity of brands to those seen in the shops at home'.[2]

It was not just the goods that were British; the shops themselves were largely 'imitations'. Of all the retail trades in early twentieth-century

A 'traditional' Australian grocery store, Cootamundra, New South Wales, 1940s
(Image Library, State Library of New South Wales)

Australia, the grocery trade had remained one of the most British in outlook, both in terms of the arrangement of the shop and the role of the grocer. This Empire orientation continued to define the industry until mid-century, even though an increasing number of food retailers began to look towards American commercialism as a model for future industry growth.

Until well into the 1950s in Australia, women, and occasionally men, purchased most food and household goods from the other side of a counter or ordered them through the weekly visit of the 'grocery boy' and had the goods home delivered. Groceries and other household provisions were all available from the local grocer who, through apprenticeship and increasingly through training at night school, became a skilled 'master' of 'his' profession. Although cash and carry, and the related concept of self-service, were becoming more common by the 1950s, many women preferred the service of the traditional grocer trading through the local 'mixed business corner store' or in larger, well-stocked and professionally staffed grocery shops.[3] Not only did the grocer deliver, but in many instances offered credit, with accounts settled at the end of the month. Importantly too, the grocer was a familiar face and knew each customer by name.

The grocery existed alongside other retail outlets selling food and house-hold goods; butchers, green-grocers, fishmongers, bakers and confectioners;

produce markets selling fish, meat, game, and fruit and vegetables; street traders and hawkers; and, in rural areas, the general store. The grocery store, as in Britain, traded initially in specific goods such as butter, cheese, tea, flour and sugar, and began to expand its range of items from the late nineteenth century onwards as more manufactured goods became available. As it did so the grocery shop, at least for urban populations, came to occupy a central place in food shopping, particularly as the larger cities developed suburban centres. The larger grocery retailing grew, the more also it became embroiled, albeit unconsciously, in much wider cultural concerns involving notions of industrial and technological progress, the rhetoric of modernity and consumer choice, and transformations in the meanings of masculinity and femininity. It is these themes, in relation to early twentieth-century food retailing in Australia, that are explored throughout this chapter.

The Product of the Nation

As in most industrialising economies, the increased availability of manufactured foods, packaged in small quantities, was crucial to the emergence of the grocery shop as the principal site of food distribution within urban Australia. Anne Gollan has noted that by the mid-nineteenth century, the food available in white Australia began to improve in quality and to be more varied, a result of the increased importation of foodstuffs from Britain and of the establishment of market gardens by Chinese and other 'gold-rush' immigrants.[4] More significantly in terms of food retailing, foodstuffs began to be manufactured locally from the 1850s. In Victoria – the main manufacturing centre during the second half of the nineteenth century – the number of factories jumped from 68 in 1850 to nearly 2000 in 1872.[5] Many of these factories were involved in the production of foods such as jams, bread, biscuits, butter, margarine, condensed milk and cheese and, in particular, preserved (and later frozen) meat on which a major export industry would be built.

By the late nineteenth century large food manufacturing concerns had become an important part of Australia's industrial landscape. Their products were also becoming household names. Jam makers such as Henry Jones and Company, which began operating in Hobart in 1861, eventually grew to supply both a home market and other British colonies.[6] The Rosella Preserving Company, established in Melbourne in the 1880s, was producing an extensive range of sauces, pickles and soups by the turn of the century. And in Sydney in the late 1890s, the Sanitarium company began manufacturing a range of 'health food' products.[7] By federation, Australian manufacturers – or rather their workers – were producing a wide array of tinned, bottled and packaged foods marketed in much the same manner as British and North American products, with an emphasis on nationally available 'brands' of uniform quality.

Companies producing other household goods such as cleaning products emerged also. The British Lever Brothers company opened a Sydney branch in 1889, manufacturing items such as 'Sunlight Soap', 'Rinso', and 'Vim'. Similarly, the Australian company J. Kitchen & Sons, first established in Melbourne in 1856, was by the end of the century producing 'Velvet Soap' and 'Persil' laundry detergent.[8]

Biscuit, cake and pudding manufacturing also developed during the late nineteenth century and was quick to mechanise its production techniques and, in the process, Taylorise its work practices. In 1870 William Arnott expanded his biscuit shop into a factory in Newcastle, eventually equipping it with twelve 'rotary ovens' turned by steam engine and fired by coke.[9] In Melbourne the firm of Swallow & Ariell, established in 1854, had fully mechanised its production of biscuits and puddings by 1885.[10] Large confectionery companies such as Mac.Robertson's, which opened in Melbourne in the 1880s, expanded just as rapidly, particularly through the mechanisation of production. By the turn of the century Mac.Robertson's was producing hundreds of different varieties of chocolates and sweets, and the company and its owner quickly became an Australian commercial icon.

Many of these firms expanded even more rapidly in the period after federation. Mac.Robertson's, for example, situated in the inner-Melbourne suburb of Fitzroy, became a manufacturing empire by the 1930s, employing a staff of 2600, controlling a 30-acre block of 19 factories, and with sub-sidiary interests in milk, maize and cardboard production.[11] Similarly, by the 1930s the Swallow & Ariell company, which had operated one of Victoria's largest factories since the 1890s, was producing over 200 different varieties of biscuits, cakes and puddings, all of which were produced, the company insisted, without 'human handling' until the final process of packaging.[12]

With the expansion and mechanisation of the Australian food industry, an increasing number of women, men and children found employment in food processing. By as early as 1901 food production, according to Jenny Lee, had come to represent the new face of industrial capitalism, and the industry 'pioneered' the adoption of modern assembly-line techniques reliant on a mass, largely female and juvenile workforce undertaking highly routinised tasks.[13] Between 1901 and 1930 the number of people employed in food manufacturing in Australia rose from about 35 000 to 67 000.[14]

The Australian food manufacturing industry was not only quickly mech-anised but soon internationalised as well. From the early twentieth century, British, American and other overseas food manufacturers were quick to move into the Australian market in their efforts to globalise their operations. By the 1920s 'international' food products were thus being manufactured in Australia, confusing the boundaries between the local and the global, 'Australian made' and world products. The Swiss Nestlé company, for example, had begun manufacturing condensed milk in Australia as early as 1908 and eventually opened a chocolate factory in Sydney in 1918.[15] Their rival, the British Cadbury empire, began the Australian-based Cadbury-Fry-Pascall company in Hobart in 1922, expanding into chocolate products by 1928.[16] The American breakfast cereal company Kellogg opened a Sydney-based factory in 1924.[17] Likewise, H.J. Heinz, another North American company with a long history of distribution in Australia, opened a manufacturing plant in the Melbourne suburb of Richmond in 1935, producing foodstuffs such as canned baked beans and spaghetti, and bottled tomato sauce.[18]

These and other overseas corporations were closely involved in the internationalisation of food manufacturing and consumption. As such, they brought to Australia new production and management techniques and a culture of aggressive marketing through advertising. At the same time overseas manufacturers joined with Australian companies in developing many of the goods that would become everyday symbols of Australian national production. Indeed, Australia's continuing adherence to a 'product nationalism' throughout the twentieth century would often be pinned on products and expertise developed elsewhere. In 1926, for example, the KraftWalker Cheese company was formed in Melbourne, through an amalgamation of American and Australian firms. By the 1930s, KraftWalker had become the largest manufacturer of processed cheese in the southern hemisphere, a food technology derived from its American parent company.[19]

This importation of overseas, and particularly North American, food technology was put on a more official footing during World War II when American advisers were sent out to Australia to supervise the provisioning of United States forces in the Pacific. Their influence was significant. As one self-effacing manufacturer wrote in 1945; 'almost every phase of Australia's food industry has been profoundly affected by the activities of the remarkable team of specialists brought out from the US to guide and advise us'.[20]

This influence was cultural, not just technological. A whole gamut of products developed by either Australian or overseas companies, or a combination of both, would become identifiable objects of everyday life in early twentieth-century Australia, just as products such as Lipton's tea, McVities digestive biscuits, or Lea and Perrin's sauce, had become symbols of British food manufacturing. Manufactured and packaged products were attractive to people since, as elsewhere in the industrialising world, they came to represent a complex network of uses and desires: Heinz offered abundance and choice with its '57 Varieties', Rosella soups went 'unrivalled', Gravox was 'The Housewife's Friend in Need', Sunlight Soap meant 'Less Labour More Comfort', and Rinso, so the slogan went, 'Works While You Sleep'.[21]

As food manufacturers familiarised themselves with modern, largely American, advertising and marketing techniques, they sought to play on an array of sometimes contradictory desires connected to changing definitions of housewifery, the imperative to 'buy Australian' (or 'buy Empire goods') and the willingness to partake in a wider world of modern manufactured household products. Indeed, Richard White has argued that as manufacturing became a more important part of the Australian economy, from the 1930s on manufacturers encouraged a view of Australia, and a culture of consumption, which linked industrial and commercial progress with cultural maturity and urban sophistication.[22]

This identification between commerce and the very life of the nation was nowhere more evident than in *The National Handbook of Australia's Industries*. Quite simply, claimed the editor, Ambrose Pratt, this handbook 'will thus enable every reader to see and to know Australia precisely as Australia lives and functions to-day'.[23] Here, industry and commerce became the mirror of the nation, just as the great Melbourne and Sydney exhibitions of the nineteenth century had been designed to make Australia known. Ideologically, however, Australian commerce remained firmly wedded to Empire and committed above all, as Pratt put it, to 'Imperial economic development'.[24]

Advertising was crucial to this linkage between commerce and nation. Nationally available products required heavy advertising, and manufacturers made extensive use of newspapers, billboards, cinema advertising and, after 1923, radio. This was facilitated by the establishment of the Australian advertising industry during the 1920s. In this climate, manufacturers not only sold more goods but products quickly came to reflect something of the 'Australian way of life'. The Melbourne-based Hoadley company launched the 'Violet Crumble' in 1923, and in the same year the Peters ice-cream company began marketing its 'Eskimo Pie'.[25] The yeast extract, Vegemite was developed by the Kraft company's chief food scientist Cyril Callister in 1924, and a decade later Nestlé launched 'Milo Tonic Food'.[26] For generations of Australians these and many other food and household products became symbols of everyday life in Australia, and the slogans and advertising images attached to them became part of a subconscious recollection of childhood, a medium through which history could be relived.

The critics of the commercialisation of Australian everyday life were not slow to ridicule this. When David Meredith, the central character of George Johnston's *Clean Straw For Nothing*, was offered afternoon tea in a dank war-time Melbourne, his companion drew a biting comparison between the Australian 'way of life' and its everyday products:

> Sugar there. No milk, I'm afraid. Biscuits in that tin if you want.
> Uneeda or Milk Arrowroot. Would have had Iced Baws Baws if I

knew you were coming. Do ourselves well though, don't we? Bloody Australia! Land of rich resources. Home of the bon vivant, eh?[27]

Not everyone shared this cynicism. People were not just ruled by the desires which the new products promised to satisfy. There were material advantages as well as cultural imperatives to the new consumerism. Manufactured products were often more convenient in meal preparation, and offered a wider selection of tastes at increasingly cheap prices. As such they became standard items on the weekly 'order' at the local grocery store. By the 1930s the typical order of those on a moderate income included sugar, tea, jam, tinned fruit, tinned salmon, Velvet Soap, Rinso, rice, oatmeal, matches, jelly crystals, tinned sardines and various other dry goods.[28] During 1939, the weekly order book of Mrs J.C. Robinson, a Melbourne housewife, showed regular orders of cornflakes, Kraft cheese, Persil, Weetbix, Lux Soap, jelly crystals, jams, tinned salmon, and paper serviettes along with the staples such as sugar and tea.[29]

In 1901 about 38 per cent of earnings were spent by Australians on food and non-alcoholic drinks and although, as in all industrialised countries, this percentage rate gradually fell throughout the twentieth century, expenditure on food remained high in monetary terms as incomes increased.[30] In this situation people turned, through complex motivations, to purchasing more manufactured foodstuffs – canned and packaged goods and, eventually, refrigerated and frozen food products. By the late 1940s about 27 per cent of personal consumption expenditure went on food, but this decline disguised the transformation in the type of foods purchased.[31] Between 1938 and 1948 alone, the per capita consumption of milk and cheese, manufactured sugar products, ready-to-eat breakfast foods, tinned meat and fruits, coffee, and other manufactured products rose significantly. At the same time the consumption of more traditional foodstuffs, often requiring lengthy preparation, such as rice, tapioca, and barley, decreased, suggesting a transformation in the nature of domestic food production.[32] This trend continued, and by the mid-1950s the transition towards manufactured products had become so entrenched that it led R.C. Hutchinson in his detailed study of the Australian diet to declare that; 'The purchase of grocery items from bulk supplies has been almost entirely supplanted by the purchase of nationally advertised packaged goods.'[33] For Hutchinson, it was the guaranteed uniform quality, and the fact that a nutritionally adequate diet could be had with a minimum of effort, that constituted the appeal of manufactured products. Increasingly, however, this appeal lay also – at least according to the retailer – in the activity of purchasing the goods themselves. As everyday goods in Australia became more wrapped in meanings, ranging from convenience to luxury, so too did the shop become more embedded within notions of leisure, pleasure and selling.

The Confines of the Shop

By the early twentieth century the grocery store was rapidly becoming an important part of urban Australian shopping culture. This was facilitated by a growth in the number of 'independent' grocery shops and by the establishment of grocery chains. The emergence of the grocer was heralded also by the establishment of professional grocers' organisations. Such organisations were designed both to lift the status of operating a grocery shop to that of a respectable profession and to assist the organisation of the industry by providing information on shop management, professional standards and the regulation of apprenticeship and training.[34]

In 1892 the journal of the then recently formed Grocers' Association of Victoria lamented the poor state of the grocery trade in the colony, arguing that the trade was unremunerative because of overcompetition and 'price-cutting', poor professional standards, and high levels of customer debt due to the prevalence of 'credit'. The grocery trade needed to be lifted out of this situation, the journal insisted, by the establishment of a few 'strong firms', and it was only then, it intoned, that 'we may hope that a new era will dawn for the Australian grocery trade'.[35]

Evidently, after the depression of the 1890s, the new era came. By the turn of the century many grocers had tightened up on the administration of customer credit. The chain stores, in particular, instituted a cash and carry system and moved from an over-dependency on English supplies to stocking an increasing amount of 'home-manufactures'.[36] By the 1920s the trade had 'progressed' on a national scale. At the beginning of the decade *The Australasian Grocer* published a series of 'impressions' of the grocery trade around the country in which it reported on the growth in the number of well-stocked grocery shops and an increasing shift towards 'cash and carry' trading, particularly in Queensland.[37] Although there are no reliable overall figures for the number of grocery stores in early twentieth-century Australia, by the 1920s the larger cities of Melbourne and Sydney had an extensive network of both independent and chain grocery shops. In Melbourne, for example, the number of grocery stores had reached an all-time peak of 2168 by 1923.[38] In fact the trade had progressed so rapidly that by the end of World War I, Melbourne was considered by the Interstate Commission to be positively oversupplied with grocers, with a grocer or general store for every eighty families.[39]

Increasingly, the grocery shop was the place in which household income was spent by all social classes. Even in 1913 the New South Wales 'Inquiry into the Living Wage' found that while much food was bought by working-class housewives from street traders doing daily rounds, food shopping in grocery stores, particularly on a Friday evening, had become important as a means by which to obtain products at competitive prices and as a social outing, often with husbands.[40]

The rise of the professional grocer was thus connected with efforts to restructure the retailing of food and household goods around the 'fixed' shop; to take food retailing off the streets and away from large public markets and enclose it within the boundaries of the store. This restructuring was as much social as it was economic. The increasing enclosure of food consumption within the bounds of a store mirrored, in many respects, the increasing privatisation of family and domestic life that accompanied the suburban expansion of the early twentieth century, and the redefinition of housewifery through the growth of the domestic science movement.[41]

As we noted in the previous chapter, feminist scholars, both in Australia and overseas, have suggested that the rise of a pseudo-scientific domesticity in early twentieth-century Western societies was embedded in a shift from production to consumption within the home. Gabriella Turnaturi, for example, has argued that consumption was newly constructed as a 'socially useful' female task and as an essential aspect of managing the household in early twentieth-century America.[42] This implied a decrease in domestic production, although not necessarily any relief in the workload of the housewife. There is ample evidence to suggest that a similar process took place in Australia, although there is a need for caution in exaggerating the extent to which women in industrialising countries abandoned domestic production in favour of mass consumption. Kerreen Reiger has noted how the size of kitchen pantries in Australia grew smaller during the 1920s and 1930s, disappearing altogether as a part of kitchen design by the 1940s. Kitchens became more compact, able to accommodate domestic appliances such as refrigerators, and designed for a rapid turnover of groceries rather than bulk storage.[43] Likewise, Gail Reekie has traced the manner in which women's role as domestic consumers was reconfirmed by the establishment of women's consumer groups and Housewives Associations during the 1920s. These groups both validated women as consumers, and carved out a politics of consumption based on a critique of retailers and manufacturers.[44]

Transformations in the nature of 'home' mirrored the metamorphosis of shopping. As the pantry got smaller, shops got larger and more numerous. In this situation the spatial aspects of the grocery store itself, as well as the public role of the grocer, quickly became crucial to the professional image and the expansion of the grocery trade. This image was promoted by employee unions as well as professional organisations. *The Grocers' Assistant*, the official organ of the Federated Grocers Employees' Union of Australia, carried numerous articles throughout the early twentieth century on the need for the (usually teenage) assistant to take a knowledgeable attitude towards 'his' work. Part of this knowledge was an understanding of the shop as a specialised space, rather than just a place to sell goods. Unions were just as eager as employer organisations to place the grocery trade on a professional footing. *The Grocers' Assistant* complained in 1915:

> Notwithstanding the fact that the Grocer is an absolutely
> indispensable factor to the community at large, few, if any, of the
> purchasing public are inclined to give adequate consideration to
> the position he holds in the commercial world . . . In the main
> they fail utterly to realise that efficiency in this respect demands
> business aptitude of the highest order; intelligent discrimination
> in the keenest commercial sense, and such a knowledge of food
> products generally, and their domestic values, as vouchsafed to
> few outside the domain occupied by medical experts.[45]

Undoubtedly, this comment showed a talent for pomposity. Yet a knowledge
of grocery commodities *as commodities* rather than simply consumer items
was part of the grocer's skill, a skill that was undermined and transformed as
the nature of food production, packaging and distribution became more
industrially fragmented, and retailing turned to the realm of business and
management skills.

By the early twentieth century the grocery shop in Australia was, ideally,
divided into two 'departments', one specialising in groceries, the other in
provisions. The shop itself was dominated by extensive counter-space,
equipped with cash register, weighing equipment, cutting and wrapping
surfaces, implements, and floor to ceiling shelves, lined with tinned and
packaged products. Very few goods were available for the customer to touch.
Smaller stores were run and operated by the owner; larger ones, either
independently owned or part of a chain, were run by a master grocer and
assistants.[46]

The grocery department generally included most 'dry' goods usually
shelved behind the counter. Here were such things as large tins of biscuits,
spices, cream of tartar, bicarbonate of soda, flour, sugar, salt, rice, oatmeal
and so on, all of which were either weighed out in front of the customer or
were already 'weighed up' in paper bags. Manufactured products, such as
bottled sauces, pickles and jams were also part of the dry goods display.
Provisions, on the other hand, included perishable staple commodities such
as bacon, butter, cheese, lard and so on. These products were weighed up in
front of the customer, with commodities such as butter and cheese cut from
large blocks which rested on marble cutting surfaces. An increasing array of
provisions, however, came ready packaged, such as processed cheese or tubs
of margarine.[47]

Although business skills were an obvious necessity, the training of a grocer
emphasised personal habits and practical skills far more. Punctuality, proper
handling of the goods, efficient preparation of 'the orders', courtesy to the
customer, cleanliness in appearance – all of these attributes were seen as
necessary to the grocer. So too was the development of the skill of weighing
and packing loose commodities such as tea, sugar, rice, sago and tapioca, a

skill for which the proper use of 'the scoop' and a feel for correct weight had to be internalised. Parcel wrapping and ticket-writing, or the making-up of price labels, were necessary skills as well.[48] Above all, the grocer needed to develop an intimate knowledge of the origin and use of the commodities sold, and to sell them with 'tact, discretion and courtesy' along with due regard to the customer's temperament.[49] Combined, these attitudes and skills were the stuff of the professional grocer, a profession that seemingly had its own particular romance. As *The Grocers' Assistant* put it in 1916:

> There is a fascination about counter work which never palls
> ... Men who know and understand the commodities passing
> their hands and are conversant with trade development find in
> each something to interest. The world's products pass hourly
> under review. One article conjures up visions of the frozen North;
> the next the golden glamour of the Tropic seas. Nothing is
> prosaic, much palpitates with romance.[50]

In reality things were not quite so romantic. Tom Cairns, in his vivid account of a Melbourne grocery store during the 1930s, noted that shops were usually cramped and poorly equipped, while the goods on sale were often of poor quality. There was a considerable gap between the rhetoric of modern shop design and management, and daily reality. Despite the fact that Cairns worked for the relatively wealthy Crofts chain of grocery stores, grocers' assistants at this time were provided with little concerted training and were expected to provide their own uniforms and ticket-writing equipment.[51] One became a master grocer through hard work, and through the sheer luck of being kept on as an 'improver' rather than laid off at the expiry of an apprenticeship.[52] While the grocery trade presented an image of professional-ism and quality, this hid a far less organisationally smooth and commercially respectable practice. 'There was nobody tougher or meaner', Cairns insisted, 'than the old-time grocers'. Most grocers, according to Cairns, would sell virtually anything, regardless of quality.[53]

Hours within the trade were long and arduous. Tom Cairns worked a 48-hour week with no holidays, no sick pay, and no morning or afternoon tea. The shop opened at 8.45 a.m. and closed at 6 p.m. on Monday to Thursday, 9 p.m. on a Friday and 1 p.m. on Saturday. This was considerably better than the hours expected of shop workers in the late nineteenth century. Some reports spoke of food shops trading for up to 70 hours a week during the 1890s.[54] By the turn of the century, however, shorter hours were won through the introduction of Early Closing legislation in the various colonies. Working conditions also began to improve with the introduction of related legislation regulating the operation of factories and shops, and with the increased unionisation of the workforce.

As with manufacturing, employment in shops, particularly female employment, expanded rapidly from the late nineteenth century on. Work as a shop assistant became a viable, and much favoured, alternative to domestic or factory work for young women. Yet as women moved into retailing as employees rather than shoppers, retail work became gradually de-skilled through the increased segmentation of the retail workforce into assistants and management, the latter dominated by men. Further, certain areas of retailing were deemed inappropriate for women workers, either because of the potentially 'heavy' physical activity involved, such as in ironmongery, or because moral sensitivities forbade the presence of women, such as in men's clothing.[55]

Unions were more active in confirming these demarcations than employers. Given the cheaper cost of female labour, employers were eager to take on female workers in as many areas of retailing as possible. During the first half of the twentieth century, employee unions agitated for better wages and conditions for both male and female retail workers. Yet at the same time they resisted efforts to widen female employment in retailing in an effort to protect male jobs.

Throughout this chapter the grocer and the grocery assistant have been referred to as male. This has been deliberate. While corner shops were often run by a husband-and-wife team, and occasionally by a woman, grocery retailing was culturally constructed as a male profession, and women were excluded from training as a master grocer. Of all the retail trades grocery retailing was one of the most male dominated until the mid-twentieth century. Both professional organisations and employee unions colluded in the exclusion of female labour, not only to protect male jobs but to preserve the trade as a source of male identity.

In 1916 *The Grocers' Assistant* commented on the introduction of female labour in the grocery trade, insisting that there was no need for the formulation of a female rate of pay by the Victorian Retail Wages Board because there was no shortage of suitable men ready to take on employment.[56] Indeed, the Grocers' Union insisted that if women were introduced to the trade they should be paid at the same rate as men. On the face of it, this was an egalitarian resolution, in reality it was designed to discourage employers from taking women on.

The grocery chains were the first to move towards the employment of women as assistants and managers, attracted by the lower wages. But even here it was not until the 1940s, with the shortage of men during World War II, that women found employment within the grocery trade. By the mid-1940s Crofts, for example, employed 'manageresses' in about a third of its stores and one 'Branch Letter' patronisingly noted that women had performed 'most creditably' in the sales competitions run by the company, for which it offered 'bonus' cheques to winning branches.[57]

Even the vexed issue of trading hours had contradictory effects in regards to women. While restrictions on trading hours were important for retail workers, the nine-to-five, five-and-a-half-day week – which had become the general pattern of retail opening hours by the 1950s – was fundamentally based on a notion of shopping as women's work.[58] Restricted trading hours assumed that shopping could be done during working hours by the housewife, thus largely excluding men from the responsibility of shopping and increasing the burden on many women as more of them entered the workforce in the post-war period.

The Grocer in Chains

Many grocery stores in early twentieth-century Australia were independent, single branch concerns. Shop assistants, for example, were employed only in 1000 of the 2168 stores in Victoria in 1923, the remainder being run by the owner or a husband-and-wife team. Nevertheless, an increasing share of the trade was taken by the grocery chains, and cash trading was the key to expansion.

In 1939, the New South Wales parliamentary inquiry into the operation of chain stores reported that there were about 22 grocery chains in the state, with some, such as S.R. Buttle, Derrin Bros. and the Victorian-based Moran & Cato, operating upwards of 50 to over 100 stores.[59] Between 1931 and 1936 the number of independent grocers had in fact fallen in metropolitan Sydney from 3098 to 2311. At the same time the number of chain stores had increased from 157 to 415. These stores represented only 15 per cent of grocery shops in the state but accounted for 27 per cent of the business.[60] This growth of the chains in Sydney was matched in other cities such as Melbourne and Brisbane.

The establishment of chains had long been an issue within all of the retail trades. Within the grocery trade in particular, some had argued that large-scale retailing was the only means by which to develop the fledgling Australian industry. Others disagreed. During his visit to Australia in 1901, Edward Cadbury was impressed by the small-business nature of Australian retailing, and by the absence of big trading companies 'with branches everywhere'. He approvingly noted the lack of co-operative stores as well, observing that 'the field of colonial grocer's activities had not yet been invaded by the co-operative movement so firmly established in England'.[61] Although a limited consumer co-operative movement certainly existed in Australia, Cadbury was right in observing that it held little threat of 'invasion' for the independent grocer.[62]

Such was not the case with the growth of larger retail firms. Their growth within all the retail trades was seemingly so rapid that pressure from independent retailers, at least in New South Wales, eventually led to the

'Chain Store Inquiry'. Independent retailers, garnering the support of the opposition Labor Party, looked to the position of their counterparts in the United States, where federal legislation had been introduced during the 1930s in order to prevent the demise of the independent retailer.[63]

Representatives of various retail chains appeared before the inquiry to dispute the charges of the New South Wales Labor Party that chains concentrated on selling cheaply produced imported goods, held unfair advantage over the independent retailer, and paid low wages. The chains' defence was vocal. In March 1938 the pro-chain journal *Retail Merchandiser and Chain Store Review* argued that far from being exploitative of workers:

> The working classes have found that the chain stores supply goods of high quality at reasonable prices. . . . Chain store organisations have shown the consumer what can be expected from really modern retailing.[64]

The inquiry largely accepted this argument, the final report recommending that no action be taken against the chains.[65] While some criticism was made of the grocery chains for their use of juvenile labour and price-cutting policies, the report, once again, stopped short of recommending any specific measures to curtail the decline of the independent grocer.[66]

Even if government had intervened to control the growth of the chains, it is unlikely that sufficiently strong measures would have been taken to prevent the restructuring of the retail industry, which by then was well underway. In any case the essential cultural importance of the rise of the chains lay not in some internecine brawl between big and small business, but in their aggressive pursuit of a retailing logic based on economies of scale and their enthusiastic embrace of 'really modern retailing', as characterised by the Bureau of Modern Merchandising. The grocery chains were simply one part of this process of retail modernisation.

One of the oldest and largest of the Australian grocery chains was the Melbourne-based Moran & Cato company. First established in North Melbourne in 1876, Moran & Cato expanded rapidly during the 1880s, opening stores in all the major inner suburbs of Melbourne.[67] Like other chains around Australia, the firm was able to take advantage of economies of scale, working on lower profit margins and a high turnover of goods. Moran & Cato's slogan was 'Food for the Millions' and, by 1906, it had 60 stores in metropolitan and country Victoria. By 1909 the company had opened seven stores in Sydney, thus expanding beyond state borders. Other large grocery chains emerged also in the late nineteenth and early twentieth century. In 1906, for example, the Melbourne-based firm Crofts Stores opened its first shop and within 30 years had grown to a chain of 103 suburban and country outlets.[68]

Like their British and North American counterparts, the chain grocery stores in Australia sought to extend their operations by embarking on 'vertical' as well as 'lateral' expansion. Moran & Cato established its own food manufacturing and packaging plant in the late nineteenth century in the Melbourne suburb of Brunswick, where a workforce of 500 white-uniformed 'girls' packed Moran & Cato labelled butter, tea, baking powder, self-raising flour, jelly crystals, salt and other foodstuffs. By the 1920s Moran & Cato packet tea came in three different grades, and the company claimed that one in every five people in Victoria and New South Wales drank the M&C brand.[69]

Spatially, and in terms of service, chain stores were little different from the independent grocer. Although often slightly larger in size, they served from the counter. Nevertheless, the chains were highly conscious of a corporate image, and many chain stores were, as far as possible, uniform in appearance. The headquarters of Crofts, for example, sent out a weekly 'Branch Letter' that gave detailed instructions to each store on the display of goods, the handling of merchandise, commodity prices, and tips on sales-manship.[70] The company further provided each branch with a standard set of window display plans that were rotated at six-weekly intervals.[71]

In comparison to the independent grocer, the chains offered a larger range of goods as well as lower prices, and thus attracted customers in much the same way as the new variety stores such as Coles and Woolworths. Like the variety stores, they could embark also on a more systematic approach to retail management. By the 1940s the chains were beginning to introduce staff-training schemes, albeit ad hoc in nature. Crofts Stores introduced a ten-week, on-the-job training scheme in 1943 conducted as a correspondence course. The young shop assistants were given lessons on appearance, salesmanship, company loyalty, and customer relations.[72] The term 'training scheme', however, was rather grandiose since it was little more than a chance to instil corporate loyalty into the young employees and offered them no recognised certificate.

Such schemes mirrored wider efforts within the retail trade to institu-tionalise retail training. In 1936 the Retail Traders Training Institute of New South Wales was established to provide evening classes for junior and adult retail employees, the first institute of its kind in the country. The Institute provided training in parcel wrapping, docket writing, stockkeeping, handling of goods and the principles of salesmanship, and awarded a diploma. At a more advanced level, it even offered executive training in the 'psychology of buying and selling'.[73]

The Measure of the Man

In embarking on such management techniques, and on the construction of large retail companies, the chains were, as the *Retail Merchandiser* insisted, instrumental in moving grocers towards modernity, however ill-defined that concept remained. In this effort to modernise their profession, grocers moved also, often quite unknowingly, towards a dissolution of traditional skills, not quite sensing the incompatibility between what would effectively become different notions of the shop and of the shopper – one based on practical expertise, the other on more abstract managerial knowledge.

In practice, modernity for the retailer essentially meant the methods and categorisations of science and the labour savings of technology. As early as the 1920s grocers, like other retailers, had seized onto the notion of 'scientific retailing' in a further effort to formalise and aggrandise their profession. Given the size of their operations, the chains took immediate advantage of this knowledge. Retail 'systems' theory and the psychology of selling had by then become subjects of interest in Australia, particularly with the growth of the advertising industry.[74] The influential business magazine, *Rydges*, was replete throughout the 1930s and 1940s with 'How To' articles on business management, staff training, marketing and advertising. Indeed, this was the period in which the Australian market research industry came of age.

Although originally used to bolster the social standing of the traditional grocer, this discourse of scientific retailing quickly became instrumental in transforming that 'tradition' itself. In 1916 *The Grocers' Assistant* carried an article by Max Mack entitled 'What is Salesmanship', which began as it meant to go on:

> 'What we call learning a business', said Herbert Spencer, 'really implies learning the science involved in it'. How often do you hear men speak of the science of advertising, of the science of insurance, and of many others which are prominent factors of business. It is easily apparent to those engaged that the organ-isation of the principles involved brings greater efficiency and success.[75]

This organisation of principles was a pretty thin affair. There was very little intellectual rigour in the new science of efficiency and success or in the numerous other tracts on modern retailing that began to appear in Australian trade journals by the 1920s. Initially the epithet 'science' was little more than a grand way of referring to formalisations of traditional retailing knowledge. The management systems dreamt up, and the typologies created of the shoppers who frequented retail stores, were for the most part simplistic and intellectually vacuous. Although an instrumental rationalism had become part of retailing, and of the self-image of the retailer, this did not simply displace pre-modern retailing practices and knowledges. Science became the rhetoric of retailing rather than its rationale, and the hold over the retail industry by managerial systems theory and consumer psychology would remain partial for decades until Australia entered fully into a post-industrial culture.

The turn to science, at least within grocery retailing, was interconnected with retailers' concerns about their masculinity. Australian grocers were at pains throughout the early to mid-twentieth century to preserve for the industry not simply a class status but a sense of masculine enterprise and masculine knowledge. The most obvious way in which this was ensured was through the exclusion, or at least partial exclusion, of female labour. Less obvious, but equally important, was the control over the culture of the shop.

Of all the retail trades the grocery industry was perhaps the most closely bound up within a framework of social interaction between men and women. The grocery shop, along with the butcher, the green-grocer and other such stores, was one of the few social spaces in which men needed an intimate knowledge of the female 'sphere' of domestic production. Professional grocers thus became almost obsessively concerned to deny a commonality of knowledge between men and women and to differentiate their 'abstract' controlling knowledge from the everyday, 'immersed' knowledge of the housewife.

As Marilyn Lake has argued there was, in late nineteenth and early twentieth-century Australia, a vigorous contest between different conceptualisations of masculinity. The conception of an Australian national character was largely based, argues Lake, on 'masculinist' notions of the unrestrained, anti-domestic, lone male. By the 1920s this particular version of the masculine would be eclipsed by a more domesticated notion of the man as responsible breadwinner.[76] Nevertheless, even 'Domestic Man' was impelled to preserve for himself a certain distance from the 'home'.

This distancing was, for the grocer, presumably even more imperative. To deal in groceries was to potentially undercut one's masculinity by undertaking the 'menial' task of serving at the counter rather than the physical creativity of producing. It was to deal directly in the domestic sphere, in femininity. Everything about the grocery shop trod a fine line between the feminine and the masculine, the private and the public. For a start, when the shop was full, men were always in a minority. What is more, much of the conversation within the shop was likely to have involved 'female' tasks and knowledge.

Grocers thus constructed a discourse of the trade which emphasised both service *and* control. This was nowhere more evident than in the grocer's love/hate relationship with his female customer, and in retailers' efforts to 'type' the shopper and sell her the goods.

In 1916 *The Grocers' Assistant* ran a series of articles outlining the seductive art-cum-science of salesmanship which, the journal insisted, was fundamentally based on a careful 'character study' of the customer.[77] Of the types identified there was, first, 'The easy going customer with no particular

The Official Organ of the Federated Grocers Employees' Union of Australia.
Registered at G.P.O., Melbourne, for transmission by post as a Newspaper.

Vol. 6, No. 4.   MELBOURNE, DECEMBER 20, 1916.   Price, 1/6 Per Annum, Post Free.

☞ The Grocers' Assistant. ☞

A Monthly Journal published by THE FEDER-
ATED GROCERS EMPLOYEES' UNION OF
AUSTRALIA at 226 Little Collins Street, Mel-
bourne.

Telephone Central 8080.
All Communications to be addressed to the Secretary.

Correspondents forwarding letters to "The Grocers' Assistant"
are requested to forward their name and address, not necessarily
for publication but as a guarantee of good faith.

> Remember, man, the "Universal Cause
> Acts not by partial, but by general laws,"
> And makes what happiness we justly call
> Subsist not in the good of one, BUT ALL!
> —Pope.

The Art of Salesmanship.

I.

We have often heard it said that any fool can sell
a customer the article which he or she comes to
the shop expressly for, but that it takes a "salesman"
to sell them something that they do not come for.
While that is true in a limited sense, it does not express the whole qualification of a good salesman by
any means. In fact, it may at times give an erron-
eous idea altogether, for it is bad business to push
on to a customer an article they not only not asked
for, but that gives nothing but dissatisfaction when
purchased. The art of salesmanship may rather be

said to be that combination of pushfulness and tact
which gives the greatest amount of satisfaction to
the purchaser with the greatest amount of profit to
the vendor. It is obvious then that no hard and fast
rules can be laid down on this subject, but we can
point out general principles to be observed and mis-
takes to be avoided.

The whole art of salesmanship resolves itself in
a large degree into a character study of the customer. We shall deal with some of the types out
of the many that present themselves at the grocer's
counter daily and see how the salesman should deal
with each. First there is:

The easy-going customer with no particular mind
of her own. She likes to be advised and led. She
wants tea, but appears indifferent as to whether it
is eighteenpence or two shillings per pound, and is
equally pleased with "Brightlight" or "Venus," and
her reply to the query: "What kind of cheese will
you have?" is merely, "Oh, send me some nice!"
Now there are assistants, and masters too, who take
advantage of a customer of this description, trot out
all the old stock, send her the stale butter, let her
have the highest-priced tea, all under the cover of the
excuse: "She's not particular; let her have it."
That's not salesmanship. The good lady may be indifferent in the shop, and may seem easily satisfied, but the groceries are going to be tried by the
tribunal of the home, and if they are not up to the
standard demanded by that tribunal our easy-going
friend, instead of returning them and "making a
stir" about them, quietly drops the shop and goes
elsewhere. Rather should such a customer be
handled with extra care, for don't you see, that if
she leaves it pretty much to you what to send her,
the whole of the blame, if the goods are not satisfactory, comes on to you? Take into consideration
her station in life, and don't sell her two-shilling tea
if you know that fifteenpenny is used by nine-tenths

Studying character: *The Grocers' Assistant* offers some advice on customer types,
1916 (State Library of Victoria)

mind of her own. She likes to be advised and led.' Not quite so accommo-
dating was the 'faddy and particular customer'. This customer liked to be
'made a fuss of'. Even worse was 'the suspicious customer whose especial
dread is that the shopman will somehow cheat her'. Finally, there was 'the
bargain hunter and cutter . . . She studies all the price lists and advertise-

ments, and with more or less (generally less) correct recollection of them goes to the shop fully intending not to pay a halfpenny more than necessary'.[78] The overall advice to the student of this typology was basically one of commercial chivalry. The grocer was not to take advantage of the easy going, to treat the faddy with delicacy and to appeal to her vanity, exhibit an openness towards the suspicious, and to gently deceive the bargain hunter into thinking she'd bought things cheap. Similar typologies were to appear in trade journals in the following decades, and were to become more elaborate as the science of market research developed.

Gail Reekie has suggested that such typologies underwrote the nature of the relationship between male retailer and female shopper, a relationship predominantly based on metaphors of seduction. Certainly, grocery shopping was embedded within sexualised cultures; the grocer, like other retailers, attempted to seduce. Nevertheless, grocery shopping was, as I have begun to argue here, equally involved in a contest over domestic knowledge and its ownership. Grocers not only wanted to seduce women into the shop but also needed to position themselves in relation to other working men and to retain an area of skill beyond that apparently available to women. In operation here, therefore, was a dynamic *between men*, as much as between the sexes. As Moran & Cato's *Hints on Better Salesmanship* insisted in the 1920s:

> Be Manly.
> While being courteous and anxious to please, we do not wish our
> boys to be in any way obsequious. We abhor servility. All we ask
> is that they should grow up manly and be gentlemen, with a keen
> moral perception of DUTY.[79]

Likewise, the booklet argued that 'We do not want our men to be bazaar salesmen . . . We want our men to be real salesmen, not merely "order takers".'[80] Grocers, however, were clearly confused about how to achieve these masculine roles within the shop, and about how to express a servility and courteousness while clinging, at the same time, to a 'superiority' over the female customer. As *Hints on Better Salesmanship* advised:

> An important point is to clinch the sale immediately it is decided
> upon. Do not discuss its merits or talk about it, as many a sale
> has been lost by giving a customer a chance to change her mind.
> At the same time remember that a customer has a perfect right
> to change her mind.[81]

This was flat contradiction. It expressed perfectly the gap between service and salesmanship, and the struggle across the counter between the interests of the retailer and the customer, the man and the woman.

This confusion over the status of retailing knowledge, and the relationship between service and salesmanship, was one reason why male retailers were drawn towards scientific retailing. Its attraction lay not simply in its supposed economic advantages but in its very ability to make knowledge abstract and formal. As recent feminist critiques have suggested, the discourse of science and technology is deeply implicated in expressing and consolidating relations among men.[82] The more 'formal' retailing became, the more 'rational' its organising schemas, the more distance could be put between those who ran the shop and those who bought the goods, as well as between retail workers of different status. This demarcation between abstract and immersed knowledge, between service and salesmanship, and between control and desire, became even more evident when men began to withdraw from the shop altogether, and to set the shopper 'free'. That supposed 'freedom' was to come with the rise of self-service.

Part II

New Worlds

Chapter 3

Engineering the Shop

In 1958 a new 'Ladybird Learning to Read Book' appeared entitled *Shopping With Mother*.[1] At the time, Ladybird books were popular in both Britain and Australia, at least with adults, as they provided 'wholesome' educational entertainment for young middle-class readers. In *Shopping with Mother* Susan and John, the young protagonists, experience the excitement of shopping. Leaving Tibby, the cat, and Mike, the dog, at home, the children visit, under the careful guidance of 'Mother', the grocer's shop for jam and sugar, the baker's for cakes, the fish shop, the butcher, the green-grocer's and, finally, the ironmonger to buy a hammer for Dad. After a couple of hours this odyssey is brought to an end and Susan, John and Mother return home to unpack the goods – an event which excites even the animals.

Clearly, the young readers of *Shopping with Mother* were doing an awful lot more than learning to read. They were learning to consume, learning about what one could buy, about who usually did the buying, and about the pleasures of it all. But there is another far less obvious aspect to the book that is also of interest – as a representation of shopping, the book came perilously close to being out-of-date.

By 1958 shopping, particularly for food and household items, was undergoing further change. Already, in the birthplace of the supermarket, the representation of children and shopping was dramatically different from the Ladybird vision. In 1954 young North American readers could consult *The First Book of Supermarkets*.[2] This little book provided an introduction to 'modern' shopping, complete with illustrations of the obligatory boy and girl couplet revelling in the one-stop shopping experience. This was a narrative that emphasised the pleasures of shopping even more than did its English counterpart:

The pleasures of shopping – over the counter (*Shopping with Mother*, 1958, illustrator J.H. Wingfield, Ladybird Books Ltd)

The pleasures of shopping – off the shelf (*The First Book of Supermarkets*, 1954, illustrator J. Bendick)

Can you go into the supermarket and do the week's marketing? You have to get a very big basket, because a family uses a lot of things in a week! Some supermarkets have big baskets for grown-ups, and smaller ones for children so they can choose *their* favourite things.[3]

This image of North American shopping as both convenience and pleasure was confirmed a year later. In 1955 *Life* magazine published a special issue on food in the United States. Its cover showed a young child seated comfortably in a supermarket trolley, being pushed by 'Mother', and surrounded by some very attractive packaged goods, or to use the phrase *Life* used, 'mass luxury' items.[4]

These different images of shopping for everyday items illustrate a transitional stage in the retailing of food and household goods in the West during the second half of the twentieth century. While the pace of this transition differed between countries, by the late 1950s the trend towards self-service and supermarket shopping had taken hold, not only in the United States, but also in England, Australia and elsewhere. With this emergence of the one-stop shopping environment, Susan and John were thus being introduced, as they roamed from one little shop to another, to a world that was on the way out.

In this chapter we explore the eclipse of this older retailing world in North America and Britain. By briefly documenting the emergence of the supermarket in the United States and England we are able to further contextualise the rise of the supermarket in Australia and to trace the beginnings of a process by which supermarket retailing became an increasingly global phenomenon. This process of globalisation was, as we shall see, sometimes startling in the speed with which supermarket environments took on a uniformity of appearance and internal organisation across national boundaries.[5] However, this process of globalisation was not one of simple transference of the supermarket concept from one country to the next. The notion of global culture is as empirically suspect as that of mass culture. Both concepts tend to elide a recognition of those elements of everyday life, and of national cultures, which disturb, unsettle and reconstruct channels of influence and communication between people and between nations. In this chapter, and even more so in those that follow, we explore some of the ways in which the global and the local interact in the construction of national retail cultures.

Embracing the Impersonal

In 1964 the British retail expert W.G. McClelland observed that the development of the supermarket 'alters radically the type of social contact that most shopping has up to now involved'.[6] In his essay entitled 'The Supermarket and Society', McClelland explored some of the dimensions of this alteration, the chief one being that in the self-service store 'there needs to be, and often is, hardly any human contact'.[7]

This was a common concern of retailers in face of the emergence of self-service. It was equally the concern of many of the critics of a mass consumer society, a society which it was argued gave rise to social fragmentation, alienation and rampant but ultimately unsatisfying consumerism. Indeed, by the 1950s there was a sizeable body of critical literature on Western consumer cultures.

Within European Marxism, in particular, theorists such as Georg Lukacs, Walter Benjamin, and Max Horkheimer and Theodor W. Adorno had, from the 1920s, turned towards a cultural analysis of 'the age of mechanical reproduction'.[8] This work further developed Marx's analysis of the manner in which, within capitalist societies, the 'immense collection of commodities' gave rise to a situation in which working people were forced into satisfying their needs through an impersonal market.[9] Lukacs, exploring this process in more detail, argued that culturally as well as economically capitalism 'requires that a society should learn to satisfy all its needs in terms of commodity exchange'.[10] By the late 1930s, Adorno and Horkheimer were speaking in disparaging terms about the rise of consumer culture in societies such as the United States. Mass culture and consumerism, they argued, undermined the possibility of preserving an 'authentic', non-commercial culture and stymied revolutionary social change.[11] Arguably, only Walter Benjamin really went beyond the condemnation of mass culture – and into everyday shopping environments – to analyse the manner in which people were drawn into a different mode of participation under conditions of consumer modernity. For Benjamin, consumer cultures certainly involved a possible manipulation of the masses, but equally, these cultures gave rise to a popular creativity and a new democratic aesthetics.[12]

Non-Marxist sociologists of modernity looked also to an emerging consumerism with some suspicion. The American sociologist Thorstein Veblen, who coined the term 'conspicuous consumption', wrote in the early twentieth century of the development of an American leisure class that derived its social status in part through the meanings attached to the goods it consumed. These goods were often conspicuous through their very lack of necessity or function.[13] At much the same time, the German sociologist Georg Simmel wrote of the manner in which, under conditions of modernity, the commodity became a potentially positive medium of self-expression and economic freedom but within a form of metropolitan life and a money economy that made human relations increasingly impersonal, fragmented and emotionally empty.[14]

The critique of consumer society was not, however, confined to Marxist theory or academic sociology. By the 1950s more 'popular' texts by writers of various political persuasions, such as Vance Packard and John Kenneth Galbraith in the United States, and F.R. Leavis and Richard Hoggart in England, offered biting critiques of the supposedly manipulative and debasing aspects of consumerism and mass culture.[15]

McClelland, the retailer, was no high theorist, nor even a popular critic. When he spoke of self-service he was talking of the shop, not of contemporary culture. Yet he observed a similar thing. He noticed, much like the theorists of consumer culture, the transition from a more personalised counter service in which customer and shop worker were in a face-to-face relationship, to an 'impersonal' environment in which interaction between customers and staff was greatly reduced. In the large, anonymous environment of the supermarket, McClelland wrote, 'the typical transaction represents as little real human contact as there is with a vending machine'.[16]

Instead of seeing this as part of a degenerate culture of consumer capitalism, however, McClelland insisted with the faith of a commercial zealot on the need to restore, in altered form, the social function of the shop. In fact, he argued that the supermarket already provided some of the conditions for remaking the social nature of the old retailing order. The supermarket provided a new means of family solidarity through the shopping excursion, offered women a greater sense of self-reliance and efficient housewifery, provided extensive product choice, and broke down inter-class differences in food consumption.[17] As for the loss of social contact, this too could be remedied. Citing the American 'motivation research' consultant, Dr Ernest Dichter, McClelland suggested that packaged products, the physical characteristics of the shop, company logos and advertising images were now all the more important as a means of linking the shopper to the shop; they replaced the traditional grocer as channels of communication. As Dr Dichter had intoned, 'The package is an extremely important substitute for the personal relationship that people desire'.[18]

This notion of inanimate objects and physical spaces as the means by which to preserve, albeit in altered form, the communicative, social aspects of the shop was central to the development of the supermarket. For the critics of consumer society, the concept of a sociability based on people relating to things and commercial spaces was yet more evidence of the manner in which the quality of human relationships was being robbed of any real content by commodity culture. Even for retailers, the problem of how to ensure that people, particularly women, would feel emotionally satisfied within the supermarket would remain a concern evident within the industry literature. Yet within this literature such concerns were made secondary to an enthusiastic adoption of a 'post-traditional' view of selling as involving the careful engineering of the shop, as well as the attempted engineering of human desires. In the self-service store the shopper was to be left entirely alone, to be fully individualised and left to interact with almost nothing but the shop. The self-service store, and eventually the supermarket, was no longer a place where the good grocer should know his (and occasionally her) customers and affably interact with them, but rather an arena in which the shopper must come to know the shop, to feel familiar in its surroundings, comforted by its layout, and drawn in by its products and the clean, bright atmosphere within which they seemingly floated.

The Shopping Self: Confirmation and Forgetting

Supermarkets have not attracted a great deal of scholarly attention. Most histories of the supermarket have been provided by its 'pioneers' or people within the food retailing industry and offer a rather perfunctory and highly celebratory account within the context of tracing the rise to dominance of large retail chains. These texts themselves actively contribute to positioning the supermarket as a key point of advancement within modern, industrialised societies.

The supermarket grew out of the development of self-service stores, the origin of which is traced back, in many of the North American studies of the supermarket, to around 1916.[19] Godfrey Lebhar argues that the 'revolutionary' idea of the self-service grocery store was 'invented' by Clarence Saunders of Memphis, Tennessee, who opened the first of such stores under the name of Piggly Wiggly.[20] The saccharine name was reflected in the novel design. The stores were so named because the internal layout required the customer to enter through a turnstile and follow a set path moving past the various goods displayed on the shelves, not unlike, Saunders obviously realised, a pig run. The customers were provided with handbaskets in order to carry the items chosen to a checkout counter, and the goods were paid for in cash and taken home by the customers themselves.[21]

This change from the counter to the open shelf was, for the time, a relatively novel form of retailing. It was also highly successful. The Piggly Wiggly concept was quickly franchised with thousands of such grocery stores operating under the Piggly Wiggly logo by the 1920s.

Self-service was not, however, simply 'invented' in 1916. A number of very large grocery stores already existed in the United States by the end of the nineteenth century, some of which experimented with self-service.[22] The search for definitive origins within the retailing literature serves as a means by which to construct an ideology of progress and a canon of inventive genius. Self-service in fact emerged unevenly and as a consequence of the changing nature of food products and packaging, the emergence of other retail environments such as the variety store, the growth of large retailing firms intent on high turnover, and shifts in the pattern of consumer demand and urban demographics.

The development of self-service in the United States obviously relied heavily on the accompanying development of food manufacturing and packaging. Self-service, as well as the trend towards larger stores, not only made for cheaper overall labour costs – through greater turnover and reduced staff numbers per shop – but was an ideal way to sell the new packaged products, allowing a greater selection of goods. By 1915 the average grocery store in the United States carried 750 to 1000 different items, with larger stores carrying up to 5000 different products.[23] Swamped with such a plethora of goods, the new self-service stores confirmed Thomas Edison's view in 1910 that selling and distribution should be ideally 'machines for getting products to consumers'.[24]

The development of self-service did indeed imply a certain mechanisation of distribution, bringing with it a dramatic change in the social relationship between retailer and shopper, as well as the functions and skills of each. Besides undermining the face-to-face relationship between retailer and shopper, self-service was to complete the de-skilling of the shopkeeper, or rather the transition from one set of traditional retailing skills to a new set that emphasised managerial and marketing techniques and the training of male retail executives. The customer, too, was to take on a new role; the woman shopper was, under the guise of choice, economy and self-direction, to take on even more of the work of the retailer and to confirm the relationship between shopping, housewifely duty and feminine pleasure.

This confirmation of the links between retail management and masculinity, on the one hand, and shopping and femininity, on the other, contrasts with issues of class. Self-service was equally a process involving class stratification, but a process where the notion of difference became inverted.

While self-service may have *confirmed* sexual demarcations, in terms of class it drew the customer into a process of partial *forgetting*. Self-service stores had originally been working-class institutions. As self-service spread, however, the concept became increasingly *déclassé*, at least in terms of the people who frequented self-service environments. Class demarcations remained evident, of course, particularly in terms of the nature of the products purchased and the locality of the shop. Packages and tins, for example, came in a range of sizes with smaller quantities aimed at those on a low income. Yet as self-service spaces became larger and more numerous, class divisions between customers came to be seemingly irrelevant, mirroring the increasing separation of the product from its conditions of production, and the increasing separation of people within the self-service store. As people became 'unknown' consumers within ever larger self-service environments, they were potentially 'lifted out' of class cultures, at least momentarily, since anyone, apart from the destitute, could walk into a self-service store and purchase a range of the products within it.

This dual process of confirmation and forgetting was very much a global phenomenon as the supermarket emerged first in the United States, then in Europe and Australasia. However, in tracing even a small part of this global emergence one can sense also the manner in which the supermarket was to take on subtly different forms as it toured the world.

The Supermarket Emergent

In 1946, the retailing specialist Carl W. Dipman rather belatedly observed that, 'Self-service food store operation is no longer on trial. It is rapidly becoming the dominant form of food retailing.'[25] Dipman urged all small independent retailers – for whom he wrote – to convert to self-service in the interests of efficiency and profitability, citing evidence that up to 85 per cent of American women preferred self-service and a 'pleasant, harmonious store in which the merchandise is well displayed'.[26] Part of what made self-service essential to the small retailer, as Dipman insisted, was the transition during the 1930s to an even bigger and 'better' form of self-service, the supermarket proper.

The term 'supermarket' was, perhaps rather suitably, coined in Hollywood. Rom Markin has argued that during the 1930s two types of supermarket appeared; one prototype emerged in Los Angeles with an emphasis on 'style', and another emerged in the urban areas of the eastern states with an emphasis on price and volume.[27] Indeed, what distinguished the supermarket from the self-service store was essentially the greater amount of floor space devoted to merchandise and the wider range of food and household goods on offer. Supermarkets were to be further differentiated from self-service stores through the adoption and promotion of an image of spacious, abundant, efficient, hygienic and convenient modernity.

The first supermarkets in the United States were not set up by the large retail chains but by independent retailers in an effort to challenge the dominant position of the chains in the food retailing process. The first of such stores were the King Kullen stores established in New York in 1930 by Michael J. Cullen who, with the characteristic modesty of the retailer, promoted himself as the 'World's Greatest Price Wrecker'.[28]

The King Kullen stores were warehouse-size shops, situated in the working-class, suburban outskirts of New York. The stores were set up in abandoned factories and warehouses with minimal expense on interior design. Cullen made all sales in cash, provided no delivery service and filled the shop with nationally branded, and nationally advertised, merchandise. By 1936 Cullen was running 15 such supermarkets based on the new 'retail culture' of volume, cheapness and national uniformity.[29] These early stores were hardly the tidy retailing machines that Edison had envisaged, but they did introduce a type of 'production line' culture into food distribution. Along with the rise of the retail chains, they positively transformed everyday shopping. So much so that one 'retailing expert' declared in 1931 that 'the major scene of the industrial revolution has definitely shifted from production to distribution'.[30]

He might have been right. By 1935 there were about 300 supermarkets in operation in the United States, a figure that rocketed to 6175 by 1940.[31] Profit margins were very low compared to the traditional grocery store, although so were total labour and running expenses, and thus net profits were higher. Volume and absolutely minimal service became the key to increased retail profits.

The novelty and cheapness of this approach, retailers believed, struck a chord with low-income 'consumers'.[32] This attraction was based both on price and, as contemporary observers believed, on the new *culture* of grocery shopping, a culture that emphasised choice, independence, convenience and pleasure. As one contemporary observer wrote, invoking the new psychoanalytic theories of repressed desire:

> Depression weary housewives enjoyed visiting the [super] markets, for the circusy, bizarre atmosphere that prevailed provided release for the suppressed emotions piled up within many women by the dreary monotony of depression days.[33]

The nationwide spread of these 'circuses' was due largely to the entry of the big retail firms into supermarketing. Of the large retail firms in the United States, it was A&P that first converted to supermarkets, in part because of the threat to the profitability of its conventional grocery stores by the fast-growing number of 'food colosseums'. In 1936 A&P opened 20 supermarkets, and by 1941 had opened 1594 supermarkets. This was accompanied by a drop in the overall number of A&P stores from around 15 000 in the mid-1930s to about 6000 by the early 1940s.[34]

Other major retail companies, such as Kroger and Safeway, eventually followed suit. Safeway, for example, which traded under the almost governmental slogan 'Distribution Without Waste', began converting its stores to self-service during the 1940s and at the same time bought out the Piggly Wiggly company.[35]

By this time, too, supermarketing was becoming a 'science' in the unmistakable style of the period. In 1937 the Super Market Institute was formed in order to further the interests of the fledgling industry.[36] Retailers became increasingly interested in theories of shelf arrangement, store design, display techniques, 'traffic' flow, and the phenomenon of the 'impulse buy'. In the carefully designed self-service store, retailers came to believe, the customer literally 'sold herself' the goods.[37]

Energy was put also into solving the 'problems' of the new retail form. Eventually, the wicker or wire, hand-held, carry baskets were replaced by the

American style: a 1950s Safeway supermarket, USA (Safeway Inc./Jon Brenneis)

'revolutionary' trolley. According to Richard Tedlow, the trolley, or at least a prototype of the one with which we are now familiar, was invented by Sylvan N. Goldman of Oklahoma, who introduced his 'No Basket Carrying Plan' in the late 1930s. Initially, customers didn't take to it, compelling Goldman to hire people of all ages and both sexes to push carts filled with goods outside the entrance to his store, thus 'training' the shopper in the new art of supermarket wandering.[38]

People learned. After World War II, supermarketing in the United States experienced a renewed and rapid growth in line with the development of new suburbs, changing income distribution, greater use of automobiles and domestic refrigerators, and technological developments in the canning, freezing and food packaging industries.[39] In 1950 the supermarket accounted for 35 per cent of food sales in the United States, and by the end of the decade supermarkets sold 70 per cent of North America's food for home consumption.[40] Post-war stores were characterised by even more carefully designed interiors and exteriors, greater floor space and parking facilities, as well as such 'luxuries' as air-conditioning and in-store music.[41] Furthermore, they were staffed increasingly, at a non-management level, by women. The outbreak of war had brought an influx of women workers into the trade, and by 1945 over half of those working in the food industry were female, a percentage that was to rise in the post-war decades.[42]

In tandem with this 'market growth' the 'science of supermarketing' became ever more sophisticated. By the 1960s there was a considerable literature on supermarket operations and business practice. In 1963, for example, Edward A. Brand published his *Modern Supermarket Operation*, which became one of the standard industry textbooks.[43] Noting that most modern supermarkets were now designed by specialists, he emphasised the importance of intricately planned and stylish layout in order to increase customer circulation, allow 'logical' shopping, and encourage efficient space utilisation. Careful planning led to 'balanced profits' by the integrated display of high-demand and convenience goods, and high-margin impulse merchandise.[44] Each of the departments – groceries, meat, produce, dairy, frozen foods and non-foods – was to be carefully placed, as was the merchandise within them. Brand insisted that the meat, for example, should always be positioned at the back of the store since this would draw the customer through the supermarket and thus increase 'full store shopping'.[45] Similarly, he advocated the use of long gondolas – or free-standing shelves – running from the front to the back of the shop with no 'breakthroughs' so that; 'the customer is forced to move to the back of the store before being able to shop the next aisle'.[46] In terms of product placement on the shelves, Brand argued that 'eye-level' goods sold the most readily while high-margin impulse items were best placed at the checkout and the ends of aisles.[47]

This new 'science' was partially triumphant. One study by the *Progressive Grocer*, entitled 'Consumer Dynamics in the Supermarket', found that by the 1960s grocery shopping had become a 'family activity', and that people were visiting the supermarket more often and spending more time there. This and other such studies established the high incidence of impulse buying and found that few people – only about 25 per cent according to the *Progressive Grocer* – used written shopping lists.[48]

Given this level of 'consumer acceptance', the number of supermarkets and the range of items they carried increased dramatically in the post-war period. By the 1960s Safeway was operating over 2000 supermarkets and A&P 4400.[49] Similarly, between 1948 and 1958 about 50 000 new products sought supermarket shelf-space, most of which were not so much 'new' as variations on a theme.[50]

An increasing number of these products made it onto the shelves. The number of items carried by the average American supermarket rose from 5900 in 1960 to 7800 items in 1970.[51] Indeed, by the late 1960s this plethora of goods had reached a point where supermarkets offered an apparently absurd, almost surreal field of 'choice', encouraging one commentator to coin the term 'stupormarket'.[52] Another industry professional patronisingly, and with comic exactitude, estimated that; 'Mrs Housewife passes 3800 items in 12 minutes. This means she passes 317 items per minute'.[53]

By the 1960s, then, everyday time in the United States was being measured by the packet. The supermarket may have emerged as a cheap and efficient alternative to the traditional grocery store, but within two decades it had become much more than this. By the 1960s the supermarket had become a symbol of all that was American. In 1958, *Life* magazine labelled it an American institution, and during the late 1950s both the Queen of England and Soviet Premier Krushchev toured model examples of this 'new' and, as yet, largely North American retail form.[54] The supermarket simply *was* America according to celebrants of consumption such as Daniel J. Boorstin. For Boorstin what distinguished post-war American society was 'our very notion of a standard of living and our New World way of thinking about and consuming material goods'.[55] Boorstin wrote in high praise of the fact that 'all experience tends to be treated more and more like the experience of consuming'.[56]

For the critics of the consumer society, it was precisely this transformation of experience that was so alarming. In one of the most influential critiques of the 1960s, Herbert Marcuse, writing in the tradition of Adorno and Horkheimer, understood everyday life under conditions of capitalist modernity within the United States as having become one-dimensional or locked-in to patterns of thought and behaviour that could not look beyond consumer culture and imagine happiness and pleasure elsewhere.[57] Although Marcuse spoke of the culture of consumption as giving rise to social forces that could transform it, he placed much more emphasis on the dominating and manipulative aspect of consumer capitalism.[58] Feminist critics of the 1960s, particularly Betty Friedan, also condemned consumer culture, identifying it as having contributed to the subordination of women and the devaluation of their skills and intelligence.[59] The optimism of Boorstin was thus matched by the increasing distress of radical critics, and as the supermarket moved beyond the United States the debate over consumer culture as a more general Western phenomenon intensified.

The Supermarket Transported

Retail forms, and the cultures attached to them, have been crucial in the globalisation of a Western consumer culture. The department store, the supermarket, the shopping mall are all keen travellers, adapting to different social environments but retaining their particular form. This introduces a hybridity within a uniformity on an international scale. One can now visit a supermarket almost anywhere in the world and feel a familiarity but recognise also a particularity relating to the layout, the goods available, the people within it and the national and local cultures outside it.

In England, the supermarket did not emerge until the mid-1950s. Its eventual English debut was closely bound to developments in the United States, but its history is a separate one. English social conditions were not so conducive to the rise of the autonomous shopper and, economically, large retail food stores were initially less viable than in the United States.

As in the United States, however, self-service stores preceded the emergence of the supermarket in England. According to David Powell the 'first' English self-service grocery store was opened by Harold Wicker of the London Co-operative Society in 1942.[60] Although other grocers experimented with self-service, post-war rationing worked against such retailing and it was not until after 1954 that self-service took hold in England with the relaxation of war-time controls.[61]

In her 1964 study of British retailing, Christina Fulop noted that there were no more than ten self-service shops in England in 1947, but nearly 12 000 by 1963, including about 1000 supermarkets with an average stock of 5000 items.[62] In Europe as a whole, self-service shops increased in number from about 1200 in 1950 to over 45 000 in 1960, the bulk of them situated in England and West Germany.[63]

Developments in the United States were a crucial influence on these British and European transformations. In addressing a conference of North American retailers in 1961, W.G. McClelland exclaimed with humility:

> I am here, therefore, not to teach you the business of retailing but to give to his teachers an interim report about the progress of a pupil who may perhaps be regarded as "not without promise, but a late starter".[64]

Others shared this humility in the face of American retailing ingenuity. During the 1930s and 1940s Jack Cohen, the founder of Tesco, visited the United States several times in order to study developments in self-service, declaring after one trip that, 'The improvements since my last visit were beyond belief . . . there were gleaming palaces, well lit, roomy and clean'.[65] Sainsbury's executives were equally entranced. When Alan Sainsbury and other executives of the company visited the United States in 1949, they enthusiastically reported that they literally 'lived' in supermarkets, every day contemplating the means by which to introduce the new concept in Britain with a due regard for the 'traditional' in grocery retailing.[66]

In England, however, self-service was not only strategically difficult because of war-time rationing but was subject also to class exigencies. In 1947 Cohen converted one of his London stores to self-service, only to have to convert back to counter service in part because middle-class customers disliked the idea of 'serving' themselves.[67] Nevertheless, by 1955, Tesco stores were almost all self-service, a concept which appealed in particular to working-class customers attracted by the savings, and probably also by the lack of formality and pressure to buy.[68] For the British retailer, self-service was equally 'attractive' in terms of reduced labour costs and increased retail turnover.[69]

Like Tesco, Sainsbury's experimented quickly with self-service as war rationing was scaled down. The company opened its first self-service store in

Croydon in 1950, and was particularly concerned to educate consumers in the new art of buying. As one company publication put it:

> The customers came in a little bewildered and in need of guidance. They were helped to find their way around, shown where to find what they wanted and told where to pay. The method was accepted immediately by Croydon's housewives.[70]

The 'method' was to be accepted by others as well, whether they liked it or not. By the mid-1950s Sainsbury's, like Tesco, was converting all of its stores to self-service and claimed to open the first British supermarket proper in the London outer suburb of Lewisham in 1955. This, the official company history insists, was the biggest supermarket in Europe at the time.[71] More importantly, it signalled the full abandonment of traditional forms of grocery retailing since the 'logic' of self-service meant that Sainsbury's ceased the delivery of goods and closed down its credit facilities.[72] Tesco soon followed suit with the opening of its first supermarket in 1956 in Essex.[73] The transformation to supermarketing had thus begun, so much so that at the end of the 1950s the Sainsbury's house journal declared with Churchillian dramatics:

> There can be few decades in the history of the firm, or for that matter in the whole history of food production and distribution, which have brought greater changes and greater development than the past ten years.[74]

As in North America, shop-floor size and the range of goods on offer essentially distinguished the British supermarket from the self-service store. Similarly, a supermarket culture very quickly took hold of Britain as supermarkets offered an increasing range of goods and services to their customers in purpose-built and carefully planned retail environments. 'We design our stores', said John Sainsbury in 1967,

> . . . so that our goods may be displayed in an ordered, logical and tidy way making it as easy as possible for the customer to see what she is getting and to compare alternatives before making her choice . . . We think our design will have failed if our customers have to read the name of the shop they are entering.[75]

Distinguishing a Sainsbury's from another supermarket therefore became as automatic as consumption itself. This was a product, as in the United States, of a 'transition to what might be called the engineering approach', as W.G. McClelland put it.[76] This 'approach' required training, and steps to initiate formal education in retailing were taken in post-war Britain at both a company and a governmental level.[77]

The rise of the engineered shop was part and parcel of broader social transformations involving increased urbanisation and mobility, a growing proportion of women in the labour force, increased leisure time, and what Christina Fulop rather vaguely identified as a change in the conceptualisation of 'convenience'.[78] But it was more than this. It was a change also in the notion of what was exciting, a change embedded in concepts of post-war modernity and the new consumer products and experiences to which it gave rise.

That very modernity, supermarket retailers believed, appealed in particular to 'Beginners . . . growing up into a faster, brighter, smaller world where trips to the moon are no longer a nursery fable . . . and shopping has turned every day into Christmas time'.[79] Women were apparently equally excited by this 'carnivalisation' of shopping since it was they who were at the 'frontier' of the new developments in retailing. As if to confirm this, one 'feature page' in the *J.S. Journal* of November 1959 showed yet another new suburban supermarket in an equally new suburban setting. Its caption read: 'Having babies, going shopping, keeping a dog, buying a new motor car, wondering if it's worthwhile waiting in the queues at Sainsbury's and finding out that it is; that's how people on this frontier live'.[80] Clearly, there was no notion here, in the bright, abundant, surgically clean space of the supermarket, of living differently. All retail environments, all forms of consumption, even the most seemingly mundane, became sites of pleasure and fulfilment – at least according to the retailer.

British retailers didn't just learn from the United States, they eventually began competing with it. The expanding British supermarket industry was attractive to multi-national retailers, and the North American firm Safeway was quick to move in during the early 1960s. For the Safeway company this move represented 'the coming together of the latest American supermarket concepts and an essentially traditional but still innovative form of British retailing'.[81]

Safeway moved into England, as the company was to do in Australia, by acquiring small existing grocery chains, and by 1963 Safeway had launched its first purpose-built British supermarket. At the opening of this Bedford store, the company proudly reported, police assistance was needed in order to control the crowds who were apparently 'queuing to experience the "American" style of shopping'.[82]

Safeway stores attempted to attract customers by a whole range of modern 'American' convenience concepts. Early stores had snack bars, extensive bakeries, pram parks and post offices, and one even had a laundrette so that women could 'shop while you wash'.[83] Few of these concepts worked. But Safeway was quick to introduce pre-packed meat and vegetables and imported fruit on refrigerated stands, which was in part a key to its market success. Like all the major chains, the company also developed central warehousing and fleet transport.

Companies such as Safeway did not, however, seriously rival the dominance of firms such as Sainsbury's and Tesco. Expansion and progress were apparently unstoppable for these local firms and it seemed, at least according to the company literature, that each new store that opened during the 1950s and 1960s was the biggest in Europe. In 1966 alone Tesco opened 51 new supermarkets, and two years later the company opened the first Tesco 'superstore' in Sussex, involving 40 000 square feet of food and non-food items.[84] During the 1960s Tesco, along with the other large supermarket chains, began to move beyond London and the home counties into the north of England, Wales and Scotland, through both the acquisition of smaller rival firms and by participating in the development of new shopping centres. Urban decentralisation was a particularly important aspect of this transition. From 1961 to 1970, 52 metropolitan centres in England and Wales had population increases of over 25 per cent in their outer-metropolitan zones.[85] Companies such as Sainsbury's, Tesco and ASDA were in a position to take full advantage of these demographic shifts and embarked on the building of large, free-standing, 'edge-of-town' supermarkets, which were to become a feature of British retailing.[86]

As these British supermarket empires grew throughout the 1950s and 1960s, it was not only the shops that changed but also, as in the United States, the composition of the retail workforce. Women soon became a dominant proportion of the supermarket labour force as the need for unskilled labour at the checkout and in shelf-filling increased. By the mid-1950s women made up nearly 60 per cent of the retail labour force in Britain.[87]

As a result, the face-to-face relationships within British food stores shifted from being mainly between men and women to being predominantly between women only. The supermarket was to be a feminised space in terms of both workers and customers. Ironically, however, the culture of the supermarket remained mediated and extensively controlled by a less visible and almost exclusively male management, often placed outside the supermarket in company head offices, or behind the shop walls. Just as the withdrawal of over-the-counter contact in the self-service store meant no relinquishing of attempted influence over the consumer, the absence of the male grocer would bring about no diminution of a male 'presence' within the supermarket.

Towards Hyperrealities

As supermarkets around the world grew in size and number during the 1950s and 60s, grocery retailing intervened extensively in the relationship between people and the communities in which they lived. Although based on the notion of abundance and choice, the growth of the supermarket in fact stemmed from a logic that increasingly narrowed the range and number of retail environments the consumer could visit.

Historically, the emergence of self-service and the supermarket has meant a dramatic drop in the number of food outlets within industrialised countries, along with a massive increase in the size of those remaining.[88] While customers became autonomous within the self-service store, this autonomy was based on a commercial logic that gave people fewer and fewer environments in which to express their supposed individuality.

Although the small independent shopkeeper was certainly not to disappear in the face of the rise of the supermarket, large commercial retailers have gained an increasing share of the domestic food market within Western economies from the mid-twentieth century on. This has also been at the expense of co-operative retailing.[89] Similarly, the size of these self-service stores has grown exponentially. The average British supermarket by 1960 was, for example, already 12 times the size of the 'traditional' grocery store.[90] This trend continued, particularly with the development of the superstore, and eventually, the hypermarket. These larger stores were originally developed, not in the United States, but in France, the first 'hypermarché' opening in St Genevieve-de-Bois near Paris in 1963.[91] This was a retail form, as we shall see in a later chapter, that was to partially remake the supermarket concept.

The market dominance of commercial grocery firms, the size of the supermarkets they operated, and the increasingly sophisticated marketing methods they utilised had implications well beyond the concerns of small versus big business, and co-operative versus commercial retailing. The concerns were social and cultural. As food retailing in countries such as the United States and England became concentrated in fewer hands, and in ever larger retail environments, supermarketing changed the environment *outside* as well as inside the shop. As supermarkets grew in size, shopping became a less localised activity increasingly dependent on the use of the motor car. Food shopping became less of an everyday function, and more of an event. Although not offering the commercial variety of the shopping mall, the large supermarket increasingly became the site of a consumer expedition. One-stop shopping meant what it said; people frequented the one, large store surrounded by anonymous others.

Many social critics in Europe, as in North America, saw these developments as furthering the breakdown of local communities, resulting in 'soulless' suburban shopping strips or village centres, or even eradicating them completely. By the late 1960s it was not just the United States that was apparently one-dimensional. Europe too, according to radical theorists such as Guy Debord, had become a society of the spectacle in which, through the seemingly unstoppable expansion of consumer culture, everyday life had become literally unreal, dominated by the images of consumer happiness.[92] Henri Lefebvre shared this left pessimism, though perhaps with more sympathy than Debord for the oppositional qualities of everyday life. For Lefebvre contemporary society was the 'bureaucratic society of controlled consumption'.[93] Consumer goods and the meanings attached to them had become a means by which everyday life could be governed. By the 1960s, then, consumption both in Europe and the United States seemed to many of its theorists to be something of an iron cage of social control. There seemed to be little space left for the shopper who did not conform.

In this chapter we have begun to explore the emergence and globalisation of the supermarket as a retail space. We have discussed also some of the commercial ideologies that lay behind the supermarket, and briefly contrasted these ideas with the work of cultural critics. What is so striking about the discourse of supermarket retailers, and many retail historians, is their unshakeable belief in both commercial progress and in the ability of retailing to reshape consumer cultures and capture consumer markets. On the other hand, one of the most notable aspects of theoretical work on consumption is that theorists have rarely seemed to enter into the consumer cultures and shopping environments of which they speak, preferring instead to maintain a very intellectual distance. Yet, ironically, both those who championed the culture of supermarketing and those who have criticised it saw in the rise of modern retailing an enormous power to engineer the social, to remake the culture of everyday life. As we will see in the remaining chapters, the situation, at least in Australia, has been perhaps a little more complex than either the celebrants or critics allowed. Both the logic of modern retailing itself and the activities and thoughts of those who shopped within retail environments were to undermine the supposed power of the retailer.

Chapter 4

She Likes to Look

Jack Mayhew stood back, waiting for the women to be served
. . . There were only about six housewives, but it was the kind of
corner grocer's shop that seemed crowded whenever there were
more than two people in it. There were so many things that there
wasn't much room for people.

The shelves behind the counter reached to the roof, and they
were packed with everything under the sun, and the pattern of
cans and cartons and colours changed day by day, as the grocer
added new stock wherever there was space for it . . . Only the
grocer knew how to reach out, unerringly, and get what he
wanted . . . There was only enough space, on a couple of square
feet of the counter, for the grocer to carry on business with the
women one at a time.[1]

When the Australian novelist Gavin Casey opened his *Amid the Plenty* with
this 1950s scene of a local grocer, it was pervaded with a nostalgia for a world
only just disappearing. Jack Mayhew, the male interloper in a predominantly
female environment, had through unemployment and impending starvation
come, cap in hand, to the local grocer to get a few things 'on tick'. The grocer
objected; '"You mob! All you mob around here, you go to the supermarket
when you got cash, don't you?"'[2] But the grocer eventually gave in. He was,
after all, not simply a businessman, he did not run one of 'them flash places',
but had a keen sense of social responsibility towards a man down on his luck.
Here was an environment that spoke of a cluttered, paternalistic and almost
amateur form of retailing, as well as the security of a local community,

anchored in part around the highly gendered activity of everyday shopping. Neither this form of retailing, nor of local community, was to last unaltered.

In the period following World War II, Australian retailers connected a very particular notion of modernity with a new conception of the shop, and of the shopper. During the 1950s food retailers, in particular, looked not simply to the science of retail management but to a new spatial arrangement of the store as a means by which to move with the times. While some grocers clung to counter service as a mark of tradition, many others turned to open shelves as a mark of progress and commercial good sense. Although seemingly banal in the face of major political and social events, these transformations in food retailing, and thus in the way people shopped and what they ate, were of crucial importance in the shaping of everyday life in post-war Australia. As self-service emerged, it intensified earlier concerns about the influence in Australia of American commercialism, the de-skilling of the grocer and, more generally, the growth of a consumer society. Self-service also encouraged the articulation of fears about the very autonomy to which a modern consumer society apparently gave rise. Ultimately, however, these concerns and fears were largely displaced by the full embrace of the self-service store and, with it, of the autonomous shopper.

Modern Stores

Self-service came slowly to the Australian food retailing industry. Unlike the situation in the United States, its appearance did not quickly transform the shopping experience but rested alongside more traditional forms of food retailing for several decades. If modernity, chiefly in the form of a vaguely defined process of Americanisation, was a hallmark of Australian society in the post-war period, then that process of modernisation – at least in terms of everyday shopping – was a problematic and uneven one.

In the first 'Census of Retail Establishments' undertaken by the Commonwealth Government in 1948/49, 21 594 shops were identified as grocery stores but no distinction was drawn between counter and self-service establishments.[3] Such a distinction was not made until the census of 1961/62 in which the number of grocery shops was estimated at 22 225, with 4867 or 22 per cent of these shops operating as self-service.[4] These self-service stores accounted for over half of the national sales of grocery items.[5] A concerted shift towards self-service thus took place during the 1950s, with the pace of 'conversion' gaining real momentum by the end of the decade. As one editorial in *The Australasian Grocer* heralded in August 1958, 'never in the history of the trade have we seen such dramatic changes taking place with such startling rapidity as we have in the past six months'.[6]

By the late 1950s self-service seemed virtually unstoppable: it made commercial sense, it provided a better retail medium through which to sell the ever-increasing range of packaged products, and it was popular with the public, or so retailers believed. Market research appeared to back this up. In 1958 the Federal Marketing and Consumer Research company surveyed 9000 Melbourne 'housewives' and found that 61 per cent preferred self-service, 19 per cent preferred delivery service and only 16 per cent favoured counter service. The stated reasons for preferring self-service were: cheaper prices, greater product choice, the ability to compare products, quicker service, and the fact that displayed goods acted as 'reminders'.[7]

Apparently this sort of 'evidence' was enough for many Australian food retailers. Bolstered by trade reports concerning the rapid transition to self-service in Europe, and by evidence which suggested that packaged good were now far outselling their so-called 'naked' rivals, grocers altered their shops.[8] By 1957 the *Australian Financial Review* reported that food retailers were converting to self-service at the rate of 40 stores a month.[9]

There were, however, much earlier 'experiments', suggesting that the process of modernisation within food retailing was not quite so rapid. The origin of self-service food stores in Australia is often traced back, within the limited retailing literature, to the establishment of the Brisbane Cash and Carry (BCC) stores in Queensland in the early 1920s. These stores were founded by one of the doyens of the Australian food retailing industry, Claude Fraser, who has been credited – somewhat inaccurately – with introducing to Australia the concepts of self-service, turnstiles, checkouts, shopping trolleys and fridge displays. BCC was directly modelled on the American Piggly Wiggly stores and ran under the slogan 'Live Better for Less'.[10] By 1958, the year in which the BCC group was taken over by Woolworths, the company had developed into a small chain of 32 outlets.

There were other, similar attempts at modernity. In 1921 a Victorian master grocer described his visit to the new, 'experimental' food hall of the Grace Brothers department store in Sydney, a visit that was to give rise to several later official delegations from master grocers interested in the 'cash and carry' concept. The 1921 observer meticulously noted the details of the visit as if describing the everyday intricacies of an entirely different culture:

> The floor devoted to the sale of groceries was trellised off, with a turnstile entrance at one end. Small tables, upon which were piled stacks of groceries, were placed all around the room. A large card in front of each pile of goods indicated the price of the commodity. The customer went from one table to the other placing whatever article she required in a basket. When she secured all the articles required she proceeded to the other end of the room, where a young lady was seated near another turnstile, and the goods were counted and the account handed to her. Then the customer went on a little further to another turnstile,

where a cashier was seated in front of each cash register, and paid her account . . . There is only one entrance to the grocery section, but four or five exits, and during the busy periods, such as Friday afternoon and evening and Saturday morning, a cashier is placed at each exit, so that customers may get away quickly . . .[11]

This was, clearly, an early supermarket, and one that mirrored the most recent American 'innovations' that coupled cash and carry with the additional concept of self-service.

The reaction of grocers, however, was a mixture of dismissiveness and attraction towards the new circus-like retail space. One observer wrote of the new store that:

The general impression formed by the visit was that the department was decidedly out of the way, that it caused purchasers considerable waste of time to find and obtain what they desired, and that the results achieved did not merit competitive tactics by grocers who concentrated their energies on family trade.[12]

In contrast, others were drawn towards the concept and even had trouble suppressing a certain excitement. Yet another master grocer, visiting the Grace Brothers 'experiment' in 1924, noted that the tables – by now numbering 400 – were stacked two feet high with goods, the walls lined with shelves of merchandise and the atmosphere enlivened by slogans such as; 'It Pays You to Wait on Yourself'. Far from encountering dissatisfied customers, this commentator found; 'a very large number of bargain hunters busily engaged in inspecting the enormous range of goods on the tables . . . and it is obvious', he added, 'that any possible scruples their patrons may have had to carrying their own shopping have been overcome'.[13]

The concept was indeed popular with some patrons, and the company boasted that it served 7000 customers on a Friday, one of the busiest shopping days. Other department stores, such as Anthony Hordern & Sons and David Jones, were also eventually to open self-service food halls.[14] However, self-service did not become a general phenomenon in Australia until well after the 'Sydney Experiment'. Although self-service stores continued trading throughout the 1930s and late 1940s, the culture of retailing and shopping worked against their expansion. When the new Brunswick Market opened in Melbourne in 1930, incorporating a Dickins grocery store, the Dickins chain experimented for the first time with self-service. Yet the new retail space failed to appeal to shoppers, who presumably disliked having to serve themselves as well as the absence of credit facilities. As a consequence, the store closed in 1935.[15]

If self-service was of mixed appeal to 'consumers', it was anathema to independent grocers. For the independent grocer, self-service signalled price-cutting and lower profit margins, de-skilling, and the development of retail conditions that would altogether favour the chains. As a result, conversion to self-service, and even the much more accepted concept of cash and carry, was resisted by many grocers until the mid-1950s. Even the chains themselves were slow to 'convert'.

This was in part due to economic and social conditions. As in Britain, war-time controls had hindered the development of self-service and restricted food manufacturing. Rationing and price-control of an extensive list of commodities such as butter, sugar, meat and tea were not lifted until the late 1940s.[16] Retail trading hours were also curtailed during the war with the abandonment of Friday night shopping.[17] Finally, the Australian economy remained largely stagnant during the depression and war years until it entered its second long 'boom' in the post-war period.

This boom facilitated the further restructuring of the Australian retail industry. Between 1939 and 1974 consumption expenditure per person in Australia increased by 126 per cent, rising by about 3.4 per cent a year during the 1950s.[18] The bulk of this increase went on consumer durables such as cars and electrical goods.[19] Expenditure on food continued to decline as a proportion of total expenditure, and by 1962/63 had fallen to 24 per cent of personal consumption expenditure.[20] Nevertheless, in monetary terms expenditure on food rose from about £380 million in 1948/49 to £1.2 billion by 1962/63.[21] At the same time the number of retail food outlets shrank, while the size of those stores remaining became much larger. From a post-war peak of 24 178 grocery stores in 1957, the number of stores fell to 22 225 in 1962.[22]

The decrease in the number of food outlets was accompanied by the continuing increase in the purchase of manufactured products and in the introduction of 'domestic' frozen foods.[23] In 1953, the Australian Edgell company joined with the American Birds Eye corporation to introduce frozen vegetables to the Australian domestic food market. By the early 1960s a wide range of frozen foods were available to the shopper including fish fingers, chickens, and 'TV dinners'.[24] Self-service stores were to prove far better than traditional grocery shops at 'shifting' these sorts of products and in encouraging people to buy more of them.[25] Advertising pushed this further. Expenditure on advertising rose dramatically from £30 million in 1949/50 to £123 million by 1960/61.[26]

All these transformations spelt potential success for the food retailer prepared to experiment with modernity. In June 1958, 348 men and two women attending a conference of the National Packaging Association of Australia heard claims that 94 per cent of women who entered self-service stores bought more than they intended, and that in Victoria alone, four out

of five 'housewives' visited a self-service store once a week.[27] A full transformation of Australian shopping habits, it seemed, had begun to take place.

Between the Old and the New

The transition to self-service can be seen as mirroring one of the major
characteristic features of modernity identified by social theorists – the breakdown of traditional social arrangements and the increasing concentration on
the autonomy of the self, on the need for people to continually reflect on their
relationships with others, on how they present themselves to the world, and
on 'who they are'.[28] Although not considered in these abstract terms, arguments over the introduction of self-service touched constantly on these issues
suggesting that the modernisation of Australian shopping was for retailers a
problematic process for cultural as well as commercial reasons.

Even by the mid-1950s grocers were still, at best, tentative about the move
to self-service, not least because of a lack of first-hand knowledge of its operation and because of the social changes it wrought within the shop. Commercially 'progressive' grocers saw it as their task to hasten the acquisition of
new skills and to quieten any concerns. One English observer – with the
wonderfully apt name, Mr Ford Kitchen – while touring the grocery hotspots
of Australia in 1949 suggested that the Australian grocery industry had stood
still during the war; it needed modernising and semi-self-service was the
answer. In words reminiscent of a Movietone newsreel and with the sound of
triumphal music no doubt thudding in his ears, Mr Kitchen added that 'The
Australian grocery store is on the move! After a war-caused lag of nearly ten
years, the ember of progress is glowing'.[29]

As Kitchen admitted, however, self-service proper involved a regrettable
loss of the personal touch of the family grocer. He therefore saw semi-self-
service as a good compromise – a bit of tradition and a dose of modernity.
Semi-self-service allowed a customer to wander the shop and to choose
products from open shelves while waiting to be personally served for other
items by the grocer. This avoided annoying queues and increased the
retailer's turnover through impulse buys.

A number of grocers took Kitchen's advice. Mr W. McKay, for example,
converted his Melbourne stores in Beaumaris, Sandringham, Hampton and
Highett to semi-self-service in 1954.[30] In doing so McKay noted that while
about 40 per cent of his customers used self-service, most opted for a mixture
of self-service, counter service, and goods delivery, thus somewhat under-
cutting the industry belief that housewives preferred self-service above
all else.

Clearly women, particularly those reliant on public transport, while
making use of self-service, did not necessarily desire the subsequent
abandonment of counter and delivery services. In the race to convert to self-

service its popularity was in fact exaggerated by the industry as a means by which to construct retail developments as 'customer driven'. As one woman journalist in the Sydney *Sun-Herald* complained in 1958:

> The basic trouble with most of the present self-service stores seems to be that the shopkeeper converting from the old-style shop, has taken the easy way out all along the line. He's dumped his goods on open shelves, without worrying much if the customer can easily identify the various sections and find what she is looking for. He's sold his home delivery van and cut down his staff so drastically that there is no one visible, excepting the assistants poised over the cash register.[31]

This writer drew a direct contrast between the corporate desires of male retailers and the daily needs of female consumers. She noted that at one retail convention, which displayed a model supermarket, 'All the male delegates . . . were completely sold on it. They admired all the shining rows of goods, they wheeled the empty trolleys . . . about. The supermarket, they agreed, is a wonderful idea'.[32] In opposition to this male fascination with retailing ingenuity, the writer disputed that self-service was more convenient or that it was cheaper. She argued instead that it signalled the 'end of intelligent shopping' and the dissolution of housewives' skills. These criticisms reflected a long and ongoing struggle between retailers, manufacturers and 'housewives', evident in the cost-of-living demonstrations and the formation of housewives' associations in the early 1900s and in the growth of a 'consumer movement' during the 1950s, formalised by the establishment of the Australian Consumers' Association in 1959.[33] Such complaints had, at times, attracted some prominent allies. In February 1951 the Premier of Victoria, Mr McDonald, noting that service was becoming a novelty rather than the basis of retail trading, declared that 'Women are fast becoming the packhorses of the home, and are taking the place of beasts of burden'.[34]

Of course, not all grocers were so quick to abandon 'service'. Given the potential de-skilling of the master grocer involved in the process, the perceived danger of increased theft, and the likelihood of cost-cutting through increased competition, many grocers remained sceptical of the move towards the self, towards the shopper as autonomous. The traditional grocer was not yet ready to relinquish a role in food retailing.

Nevertheless, what seemed novel in the 1920s was by the 1950s increasingly common, as we have seen. Throughout the 1950s, trade journals tirelessly tutored shopkeepers in converting to self-service, and in doing it 'scientifically'. As one editorial in *The Australasian Grocer* put it, 'Self-service operation is not something that can be done haphazardly; it must definitely be scientific in its approach . . .'[35] The development of this approach was facilitated by trade journals and manufacturers offering extensive advice on store design, shop layout, promotional techniques, and technological developments in refrigeration, storage, accounting and other equipment. This advice was often directly 'borrowed' from trade literature in the United States and bore all the marks of commercial evangelism.

As self-service became more entrenched, so too did retail theories concerning the spatial management of the shop and the temporal habits of the shopper. Within trade journals, article after article emphasised the need for careful arrangement of the gondolas, and of the goods they displayed, in order to ensure customer flow. The concept of 'flow' – the movement of the shopper throughout the whole store – was central to self-service, and later to supermarketing. As Ford Kitchen put it in 1949, 'Fundamentally the aim of the careful stocking of shelves is this: to lead the customer right through the store, jog her memory and make her buy . . . To do this you must first entice the customer deep into the store'.[36] One way to effect this 'deep retailing' was to work on the idea of product association, such as stacking the tea with the biscuits. Another was to encourage an anti-clockwise movement through the store so that the customer could hold her basket in her left hand and select goods with her right.[37] The most common advice of all was to place high-demand items at the back of the store – thus enticing the customer in – and situating impulse buys at the end of gondolas and at the checkouts – thus taking the last of the customers' money as they left.

A concern for the spatial management of the shop was coupled with a more abstract concern for the ease and pleasure of the shopping experience and therefore the time spent in the store. One way to increase wandering – and more wandering usually meant more purchases – was to give the store, as one trade article put it, 'a unity in design which carried the theme [of the shop] beyond the limits of the shopfront'. This 'unity' was to give the shop a feel, a mood, and to present an image which fostered an immediate 'knowledge' of the shop even before the shopper entered.[38]

This concern with image connected with wider social transformations, particularly the introduction of television to Australia in 1956. There is a whole history of the rising importance of 'the visual' within Australian modernity still to be written. The 1950s witnessed a cultural shift from the aural to the visual; television replaced radio as the favoured medium of news and entertainment while, within the shop, *display* – even of the most mundane of items – became of central importance. The notion of spectacle, long part of retailing, now filtered right down to everyday products.

Many food retailers recognised and embraced this shift towards sensual selling. As one article in *Rydges* insisted, display was the major drawcard of the retailer since, as psychologists had established, 87 per cent of shoppers were predominantly attracted to goods through sight.[39] Bolstered by such evidence, package designers were quick to emphasise the importance of a professional approach towards the look of a product. One packaging expert proclaimed in the mid-1950s, 'Gone are the days when the shopkeeper did the selling. Now the package must do its own selling job, and for that reason a great deal more interest must be taken in the proper packaging of merchandise'.[40] Retailers and manufacturers needed to ask, urged yet another expert, 'Does the package have display value?', does it have a 'power idea' that ensured the product stood out?[41] As D.A. Cruickschank argued, the package must 'get attention, arouse interest, create desire, get action'.[42] Technological developments within the packaging industry facilitated this emphasis on visibility. The 1950s witnessed the increasing use of polythene, pliofilm, cellophane, cellulose acetate, and foil in which to clothe the products.

Whether independent grocers were receptive or not to the advice of management and marketing experts, the adoption of self-service was eventually forced on them once they realised that, in face of the chains, the old traditional family grocer was losing market share, and rapidly so. The grocery chains had continued to expand in the post-war period, and as in Britain they moved into self-service more quickly than the independent grocers. Chains such as Dickins, Franklins, Crofts and Moran & Cato all began converting to self-service in the 1950s.

In Melbourne, Crofts Stores claimed to be the first major Victorian chain to convert. In March 1951, store number 53 in the Melbourne suburb of Northcote began this conversion process and by the mid-1950s about half of Croft's 130 outlets were operating along self-service lines.[43] Despite this, the company attempted to tread a fine line between the excitement of self-service and the tradition of service. As one advertisement for a new 'Crofts Superette' put it:

> Crofts Stores, Australia's greatest name in groceries, proudly . . . present the new Crofts Superette which, with its modern money saving self-service methods of marketing, has already been acclaimed by thousands of housewives in Northcote, Port Melbourne, St Kilda, etc. A visit to the Superette will be the most exciting event of the week. Special Note – Our popular store at No. 260 Carlisle Street will be retained to provide [for] those customers who prefer the intimate atmosphere of the service branch, with its specialised counter service, deliveries, and other features . . .[44]

In the face of such cautious 'innovation', the independent grocers retaliated. By the 1950s an increasing number of independent grocers were banding together into retailer-owned 'buying groups', embarking on the collective purchasing of goods, which were bought in bulk and distributed

Opening day crush under the imperious surveillance of the manager (bottom right), Crofts Stores branch no. 53, High Street, Northcote, Melbourne, 1951 (Crofts Stores papers, University of Melbourne Archives)

among the groups' member stores. This was particularly the case in Victoria, which was home to only 19.2 per cent of chain stores in Australia but 52.3 per cent of 'group stores' by the early 1960s.[45] The concept of the 'buying group' was not new. As early as 1935 the Master Grocers Association of Victoria had formed 'Composite Buyers' to act as a wholesaler of groceries to member stores.[46] Other buying groups were formed during the 1950s, including Amalgamated Wholesalers in New South Wales, SSW and Foodland in Victoria, and Queensland Independent Wholesalers. These groups supplied goods to stores operating and advertising under various 'banners', which allowed the construction of a unified retail identity while retaining a less corporate, more local feel. In some instances the growth of buying groups was rapid. By mid-1958, barely three months after its establishment, Foodland in Victoria had over 500 member stores, 71 per cent of which had converted to self-service.[47]

There was a concerted commercial evangelism connected with the forma-tion of such groups, and the competitive rhetoric of independent retailers was often bitter in face of what they saw as unfair chain competition. This competitiveness expressed also a more general unease and confusion about the economic forces apparently unleashed by advanced consumer capitalism. Independent grocers found themselves, quite unknowingly, at the divide between industrial and post-industrial modernity; wanting to cash-in on the economic boom, but to reject the corporate and rationalising logic in which commerce was by then embedded. In this sense, the divide between the independent grocer and the corporate chain was connected to much more than the mundane and self-interested commercial battles of Australian food retailers.

The restructuring of the grocery trade during the late 1950s, which was reshaping the whole of the Australian food industry and, more importantly, what people purchased and the retail environments in which they did so, also had an impact on the transformation of the retail workforce. While self-service reduced the demand for sales assistants within each store, as well as the number of outlets, the growth of the retail industry as a whole brought about an increase in the number of retail workers in Australia from 234 900 in June 1953 to 276 000 in June 1962.[48] There were accompanying changes in the composition of this workforce centred around the growth of female and part-time and casual employment, as well as a gradual decline in the wages and status of retail work, and a growing proportion of unskilled jobs within the industry compared with other parts of the services sector.[49]

These changes in grocery retailing during the 1950s were understood as nothing short of revolutionary. The *Australian Financial Review* ran a major article on the Australian retail trade in July 1957 in which it identified the coming 'revolution in food distribution through self-service supermarkets and superettes'. This was apparently an integral part of the accompanying shift to suburban shopping and the emergence of the regional shopping centre. Indeed, the article went on to argue that it was highly probable that Australia would come to reflect North American retailing, given that Australian social and economic developments provided the conditions which were now favouring large-scale retailing and 'vigorous and progressive management'.[50] Buying patterns in self-service stores seemed to support this. The BCC group reported that in the late 1950s, 50 per cent of its trading in suburban areas took place on Friday and Saturday, 60 per cent of its suburban customers used cars for shopping, and the average purchase in suburban stores was double that of stores in the inner city.[51]

By far the major and most important element of this 'revolutionary' restructuring was the move by the variety chain store firms into food retailing. This was seen by almost all grocers, and even the smaller chains, as the major threat; the threat of supermarkets proper. In this situation the traditional grocer was fast becoming, argued Alex Paton in the liberal weekly, *Nation*, the proletarian of retailing, merely a corporate employee. Paton noted that profit margins were now so low, about 12–13 per cent, that 'The grocer you knew in your youth belongs to a race that is rapidly becoming extinct'.[52] Even the title of 'grocer' was now passé, Paton lamented, having been replaced with 'supermarket, superette, markette, self-service store, food market, foodland, foodlane, food corner or foodarama'.[53] In fact, the traditional grocery store was not to become entirely 'extinct' in suburban Australia, as Paton so feared. Many such stores would eventually be 're-born' as milk bars and corner shops, trading in a limited range of packaged products, fruit and vegetables, and delicatessen items.

Accompanying Paton's critique of corporate retailing was an additional lamentation for that masculinity connected with the skill, knowledge and authority of the traditional grocer. As Michael Roper has argued, within capitalist societies there is a strong link between the social construction of certain types of manhood and the emotional fulfilments of production; any erosion of that fulfilment strikes at the very root of that masculine identity.[54] Some sense of this threat could be gleaned in the little vignette that concluded Paton's defence of the grocer. Here the grocer's anger was directed at the perceived (female) devaluation of his skills, as much as the growth of the corporate chains:

> In a shop in a middle-class suburb – a shop that had obvious signs of departed prosperity – an interesting tableau was enacted. While I was talking to the elderly proprietor a customer came in . . . She ordered eight pounds of potatoes, four pounds of onions and a dozen bottles of lemonade.
>
> As she passed through the door the shopkeeper lost all control. He flung his pencil furiously on the counter and turned to me: "You see what happens. She comes in here and orders all the heavy things she's too damn' lazy to carry. She expects me to deliver them this afternoon and she won't pay me for a month.
>
> "And now she's off to the self-service store to get their cut-price specials!"[55]

Despite this potential loss of status and emasculation of the grocer, trade magazines continued to express optimism about the continued coexistence of service and self-service, of the independent grocer and the supermarket, of tradition and modernity. In an effort to outline the pros and cons, in both economic and cultural terms, one article talked of self-service as labour saving (at least for the grocer), as reducing the need for specialty skills in food retailing, as encouraging impulse buying and thus greater turnover, and as providing a new 'leisure shopping' experience for the customer. Service, on the other hand, the article noted, allowed less pilfering, preserved the traditional skills of the grocer and, above all, was intimate; it rejected the 'soulless and impersonal' nature of the self-service environment.[56]

But really all this was a last gasp. By the late 1950s the argument had been well and truly lost. Semi-self-service was based not only on a mis-

'Leisure shopping' on a small scale: a Crofts Superette, Port Melbourne, c.1954
(Crofts Stores papers, University of Melbourne Archives)

understanding of the economics of large-scale retailing but of post-industrial
modernity itself. To launch into self-service was to play with the culture
of the shop and to connect retailing with wider social and cultural transformations way beyond the shopfront. It was to begin to speak to customers
as consuming selves, to play with personal consumer choice, and to participate in a reframing of attitudes towards shopping and consumption more
generally, which could not be contained by half measures.

Mrs Consumer: Autonomy Embraced

Transformations in the retailer's conception of the shopper, and of the
activity of consumption, were part and parcel of transformations in the
nature of the shop. While shopping has historically been defined as a female
activity, the conceptualisation and management of retail environments have
almost always been the province of men. As such, beliefs about who the
shopper was, and about how she might act in any given retail environment,
have had a great deal to do with the conjunction between commercialism,
masculinity, and the 'knowledges of modernity'.

Customer typologies, as we noted in a previous chapter, became a
favourite tool of retailers from the early twentieth century on. During the

1950s typologies became ostensibly more sophisticated in conjunction with 'advances' in market research techniques. This drew on the 'scientisation' of sociological knowledge and the growth of sociology and psychology as academic disciplines. The classification of social types, or 'social morphology' as Emile Durkheim had called it, was increasingly based on the rules of sociological method, rather than on the impressionistic accounts of retailers.[57]

Utilising such 'knowledges', market research organisations became prominent in Australia in the post-war period.[58] As Gail Reekie has argued, post-war market research attempted to 'know' the female consumer through both statistical and psychological frameworks. Such research, argues Reekie, both perpetuated conventional (male) views of the housewife as an irrational, duplicitous consumer, while exploring in detail the private world of consumption. In the process, market research facilitated a recognition of the changing roles of the housewife, helped reformulate beliefs about femininity, and provided a partial channel through which women could actively make known their views about the products of the consumer society and their role as consumers.[59]

Despite this, market research still operated within narrow ideological boundaries, its knowledge framed by the 'sexed' interests and preoccupations of manufacturers and retailers. There is a striking continuity between pre- and post-war 'customer typologies' which suggests that, far from registering shifts in consumer types, retailers often continued to cling to a fairly restricted view of the shopper. In general, the consumer remained difficult, fickle, and female.

Within trade journals such as *The Australasian Grocer*, customer typologies changed little between 1920 and 1960. By 1960 the journal was still promoting a narrow 'three types' view of the customer. In an article entitled 'Handling Women Customers', shoppers were classified as dependent, independent or individualistic, echoing much earlier, but less 'scientific' distinctions between customer types.[60]

Typologies, and the advice given to retailers on how to 'sell' to various women, were still often based on the assumption of face-to-face interaction between the retailer and the consumer. Yet self-service retailing required different forms of 'market knowledge'. This was one of the principal reasons why food retailers proved receptive to psychoanalytic theories of the shopper, as well as to sociological and psychometric measurement of shopper behaviour. In seeking to 'understand' the housewife-consumer, retailers looked to North American models, particularly the work of Dr Ernest Dichter, the founder of the psychoanalytically based 'motivation research'.[61] Dichter undertook a lecture tour of Australia in 1958, spreading the new merchandising ideas.[62] These ideas gave new 'scientific depth' to very old theories of the irrational shopper. As the 'self' came to be seen as being more important in the practices of shopping and the spatial arrangement of retail environments, retailers became more interested in theories of self-identity. Indeed, in terms of the development of self-service, retailers, advertisers and psychoanalysts shared an interest. All of them looked to the 'self' and promoted the unconscious as the subject of scientific study, retail strategies, and psychological/ commercial intervention. For the retailer, self-service meant that Mrs Consumer became someone to know but not to meet; to sell to, but not to see.

This was increasingly articulated within trade literature. During the 1940s psychology and selling were incorporated in Australian advice literature such as in J.C. Timms' *Greater Retail Turnover*.[63] By the 1950s *The Australasian Grocer* and other retail trade journals began to combine a typologies approach with more general, and less measurement-based, psychoanalytic theories of consumer desire. Durkheimian research into social types sat alongside Freudian theories of the pleasure-seeking, irrationally driven individual. As *Rydges* insisted in an article entitled 'Emotional Selling', 'Modern psychologists say that the majority of people are governed by their emotions rather than reason'.[64]

Retailers took such pop psychology seriously. In one article entitled 'Mrs Customer and Your Store', *The Australasian Grocer* informed retailers of the four essential things they now needed to know about shopping habits:

> She knows what she wants.
> She doesn't like to search – but she likes to look.
> She wants things within easy reach.
> She likes to shop in comfort.[65]

Here the shopper was spoken of in general but still rigidly gendered terms, and above all as an emotionally driven being. This was not the language of types but of a universalised female desire. Here was the language of wants, of looking and of comfort. Where the traditional grocer had tried to compete with and 'control' the woman in terms of a knowledge of commodities and their use, the self-service store turned to the terrain of dreams, aspirations and tastes as a new means by which to 'manage' the shopper. As the Australian market analyst David Bottomley insisted, drawing directly on American research, 'we associate a whole field of meaning around the objects we use, which sometimes is far removed from the intrinsic characteristics of the products themselves'.[66]

The lesson to the retailer in all this was that he was now compelled to construct retail environments that would attempt to caress the shopper, treat her right, and satisfy her wants. Embodied within the above adages was the contradiction of modern shopping. She knew what she wanted, but she still liked to look. What she wanted thus only became 'known' at the moment it was sighted. In this situation it was the job of the retailer to place things within her view and to leave her alone.

But solitude is a relative concept. In many respects the phrase 'noisy autonomy' could be used to describe the nature of the shopping experience within self-service stores. Retailers both embraced the concept of autonomy but delimited its meaning. The shopper was encircled within the mechanics of the shop: directed around its perimeter and through its aisles, cajoled by its colourful and abundant products, and befriended by its public address system. The shopper's aloneness was thus always constantly interrupted by the retailer's commercial imperative, reminding her that autonomy was conditional – that it came at a price.

Here too, within the new self-service store, was another of the central contradictions of modernity. As people became more individualised within spaces such as the shop, the knowledges of modernity – psychology, sociology, market research – attempted, at one and the same time, to 'know' the individual *and* to 're-group' people; to make sense of the fragmentation of society into a 'multiplicity of individuals' by delimiting that multiplicity intellectually, and even by constituting an overarching unity through giving everyone a gendered unconscious.

But to what extent *was* twentieth-century consumption gendered in the period leading up to, and including, the 1960s? Was it just 'she' who liked to look or also 'he'? Earlier we spoke of the manner in which social theorists have interpreted the rise of the autonomous self as a central feature of Western modernity. Within such accounts, particularly those which concentrate on the transformation of urban space and the separation of people from a stable sense of place and time, the experience of modernity has been assumed to be the same for everyone. As Jenny Ryan has argued, theorists of modernity have tended to ignore the possible differences based on gender, age, race and ethnicity with which people experience modern societies.[67]

In pursuing this point, Lesley Johnson has noted that much feminist scholarship has suggested that women have a very particular relationship to the modern cultural ideal of the self-determining, autonomous individual.[68] Consumption is important in this respect. As Johnson argues, during the 1950s and 1960s the consumer industries in Australia set out to create a form of agency for women that was embedded within a subjective fulfilment through narcissistic consumption.[69]

This is illustrated in the beliefs of Australian food retailers. They made it quite clear – as they moved towards shops for the self and traded on theories of desire – that it was consumption, or the acquisition of things and meanings beyond the self, through which women could express an independence and a personal identity. Clearly, this is not necessarily reflected in the lived experience of women. To assume so would be to treat women as the objects of retailing strategies rather than active social beings and, as I shall argue in later chapters, to ignore the manner in which women sometimes distanced themselves from consumption as an avenue of self-expression. Nor should a recognition of the link between consumption and the feminine eclipse the importance of contradictory cultural imperatives in the post-war period which continued to link female identity with certain forms of production, such as cooking and sewing, and with reproduction.

Yet in terms of broad cultural beliefs about gender identity, the strategies of retailers in the two decades after World War II do suggest that women were seen as attaining a sense of selfhood in ways quite different from those of men. Women were clearly thought to have less stable ego boundaries and less self-control than men, and were thus supposedly more susceptible to the pleasures of rampant consumption. Men were drawn into the terrain of consumption as well. But their source of identity was allowed to remain more anchored within themselves – through what they *did*, particularly in relation to paid work – rather than being dependent for its expression on bought objects and their display. Men too could be drawn into consumption as a process of abandonment and pleasure, such as in the purchase of a house, a car or a lawnmower. Yet even here the activity of consumption was closely linked to production and/or the rational notion of practicality, since the consumer object was a machine or structure that was functional and that could be 'maintained', not just admired, shown-off, cleaned and cared for.

This demarcation between men as largely rational, 'disinterested' consumers and women as 'irrational' shoppers explains in part why retailers focused almost exclusively on women. This strategy was further justified by the fact that marketing experts in the post-war period estimated that women were responsible for up to 90 per cent of consumption decisions.[70] But that, surely, is only part of the explanation. Why, after all, virtually ignore men as potential consumers; why not make a more concerted attempt to draw them into the market and thus potentially increase the profits of retailing? Perhaps part of the reason for this lay within post-war masculinity itself. To suggest that men were seducible would be to undermine a certain notion of masculinity by challenging the entrenched dichotomy between male reason and female abandon. Perhaps, too, there was in this apparent non-recognition of the pleasure-seeking male shopper an underlying homophobia since to talk of seducing desirous men on the shop floor was to enter dangerous sexual territory.

If many men, or at least many Anglo-Australian men, tended to eschew the activity of everyday shopping in the post-war period, then they did so because of both limited shopping hours and because shopping, by design, provided little ground on which to express a socially acceptable male identity. Eventually retailers would attempt to confront this partial non-recognition of the male consumer in an effort to broaden consumer markets. By the

1970s retailers would begin searching out ways in which to make shopping a ground on which masculinities could be expressed and confirmed, while not necessarily challenging gender demarcations and sexual identities.

It is outside the scope of this study to explore the gendered nature of post-war shopping beyond that of food retailing. In discussing everyday consumption in these terms, however, it is not my intention to suggest that men's and women's experience of modernity was entirely unrelated, nor that expressions of femininity and masculinity could not take place in the same social environments or through the same everyday activities. A number of writers have usefully explored the manner in which modern mass culture, like suburbia, has been constructed as 'female'.[71] Yet we need to remain cautious about assuming that the lived experience of men and women has simply mirrored culturally powerful dichotomies between the masculine and the feminine. In the context of the present study, it would seem that notions of *both* femininity and masculinity became bound up with consumerism. Australian retailers certainly participated in the construction of shopping as a female activity, but their own gender identity was just as bound up with the development of modern suburban shopping. They saw themselves as part of this modernity, part of consumer culture, just as much as they constructed that culture as an irrational female 'other'. Likewise, some men willingly took part in shopping and in other supposedly female activities such as home-making, thus confusing the gendered boundaries between the public and the private, and production and consumption.[72] In this sense there is little use in speaking of mass consumption, the shop, or the suburb as a strictly female realm within which men gained little identity or sense of self-fulfilment.

Booster Bloomers: Autonomy Feared

As theorists of modernity have insisted, autonomy is full of risk. As a social being one must, under conditions of modernity, increasingly make short- and long-term choices about life, and, as a consumer, about what to buy. If this is the case then self-service both mirrored and reinforced these cultural processes. The trouble for retailers was that some people chose not to buy, but to take, and take the risk of being caught. Retailers thus feared autonomy as well as embraced it, and in doing so they articulated a more general social unease about the contradictory effects of modernity. As traditions seemingly broke down and contemporary life became more embedded within a culture of personal (consumer) choice, such 'freedom' gave rise, it was believed, to excess and irresponsibility.

Retailers were well aware that self-service created a new 'problem', or at least exaggerated an old one; the 'shoplifting problem'. It was, however, to the familiar bugbears of individual moral depravity – female psychology, lack of self-control, and poor parental guidance – that retailers turned in pursuit of explanations. While retailers wished to believe that retail systems and strategies successfully encouraged people to buy, they took very little blame for encouraging people to steal. Rather than seeing retailing as being deeply implicated in the very processes that unleashed consumer desires, and that overvalued the possession of consumer products, retailers simply blamed human nature. Impulse shopping certainly took people to the edge of their desires, but it was their own fault if they stepped over. As one article in *National Retailing* warned:

> 'Opportunity makes the thief', says the proverb. And in today's shopping centres opportunities for theft are greater than ever. Even a moderate size self-service store carries hundreds of items temptingly arrayed for impulse shopping. Unfortunately, one-stop impulse shopping too often becomes one-stop impulse shoplifting. It behoves every retailer to offset the very fundamental human urge to 'get something for nothing' by using every device and technique which can be adopted to reduce the shoplifting problem.[73]

Retailers constructed typologies of the thief just as they had done for the shopper. Although shoplifting had long been a problem for other self-service environments such as department stores and variety stores, food retailers only began to fully engage with theories of theft as they abandoned their counters and replaced them with open shelves.[74] By the 1950s food trade journals were offering detailed advice on shoplifting types and on how to combat pilfering. Four types were usually identified: the amateur unduly tempted by open-shelved merchandise, the professional, the derelict and the juvenile.[75] Shoplifting techniques were identified also. Retailers were warned to be alert for large shopping bags, kiddies either unattended by adults or used to 'shield' nefarious activities, and more elaborate devices such as secret compartments within bags, or 'booster belts' and 'booster panties'. Booster belts were belts worn by the shoplifter with dangling hooks so that merchandise could be attached and hidden under a coat. Booster panties or bloomers were pants worn by women under their skirt or dress, securely fastened around the legs so that products could be hidden there without falling through.

Much of this was mythology rampant. Stories about such tactics were already a century old.[76] Retailers presented very little evidence to suggest that shoplifters in Australia were going to such elaborate lengths, relying instead on information borrowed from North American trade journals. The evidence that was presented was largely anecdotal. When Detective O.D. Denton of the Adelaide CIB addressed one grocers' convention in the mid-1960s, his talk was littered with off-the-cuff examples; 'One large woman had a zip connected to a pillow-case under her skirt . . . Then there was the mother who had taught her children to steal . . . they were experts. Unseen, they took a whole side of lamb from a store'.[77] Clever kids!

There were loud echoes here of nineteenth-century fears of kleptomaniac women and uncontrollable youth. Indeed, women and young people were the main targets of anti-shoplifting advice since they were the ones that featured most regularly in police statistics. Given that women and young people were by far the majority of shoppers in food stores, this was unsurprising. Nevertheless, mythology coloured the statistical evidence; women and children were construed as a danger because of themselves, not because of their proportionate numbers within the store. In 1958 the Sydney *Sun-Herald* conducted a 'test' involving four shopkeepers, and 'established' that men were generally more 'honest' than women when given the wrong change.[78] Similarly, the *Food Store Operator's Manual* of the National Association of Retail Grocers' Associations quoted security company evidence that suggested that 36 per cent of thefts were committed by lone women, 24 per cent by lone men and 23 per cent by lone children.[79] The manual failed, however, to compare these statistics with demographic studies of shop populations which suggested that well over two-thirds of shoppers were women and children. In this context adult men would have appeared no more 'honest' than women or young people.

Retailers were additionally frustrated by the fact that most shoplifters were 'one-timers' or had no apparent need to steal. Detective Denton recounted another vignette in which one young man had been arrested for stealing $1.26 worth of goods but had $2600 in his pockets.[80] Throughout the 1950s and 60s retailers complained bitterly that the community failed to take shoplifting seriously enough as a 'social evil', and that it was 'soft' on offenders. Trade journals provided endless advice on how to 'discipline' the potential thief. There were numerous means by which retailers could compromise the autonomy of the shopper without them knowing it. Retail literature advocated the use of hidden peep holes, convex and two-way mirrors, and raised offices to overlook the shop. Retailers were advised also to post signs warning against pilferage and to encourage staff to greet customers so that shoppers felt 'identified'; a pleasantry to the honest shopper but unnerving for the thief.

The call for a tougher stance on shoplifting was eventually heeded. Under pressure from retailers, police tightened up on prosecuting shoplifters and on directing their attention to women and young people as the principal offenders. Between 1960 and 1965 the number of reported shoplifting offences in Victoria, for example, rose from 2763 to 3642, rising further to 5656 by 1970. Correspondingly, the number of shoplifters proceeded against in the Victorian courts rose from 1396 in 1961 to 3569 in 1970. There was an accompanying rise in the number of women and children proceeded against.

In 1961, 38 per cent of shoplifters proceeded against were women and 28 per cent were juveniles. By 1965, 53 per cent of those proceeded against were female and 39 per cent were young people. The former figure reached 60 per cent by 1970.[81]

Predictably, retailers read police statistics as indicating a steady increase in shoplifting rather than an increase in its reportage. They continued also to argue that as a social evil it was much more widespread than police statistics indicated. This inability to talk of shoplifting as anything but a commercial liability and demonic act was still evident as the 1960s came to an end. Yet there was a grudging recognition, in some quarters, of the connection between shoplifting and cultural change. Dennis Challinger, writing under the auspices of the Australian Crime Prevention Council, rehashed the theft as social evil line. But he also noted that shoplifting was a product of 'modern society' and of modern retail environments. He even tentatively suggested that retailers should take on more staff as a means to increase shopper surveillance, and reinstitute a form of direct customer service.[82] This was an improvement on moral indignation. It was also astoundingly naive. Given the rapid growth of supermarket shopping throughout the 1960s, the enormous expansion in the size of the shop, and the development of electronic surveillance techniques, any return to service was highly unlikely.

Autonomy mooted, autonomy embraced and autonomy feared. These three 'stages' within the rise of self-service retailing during the 1950s and on into the 1960s connected, as I have argued here, with much broader post-war social and cultural transformations. These transformations included rising consumer expenditure, suburbanisation, the further expansion of food manufacturing, the growth of the advertising and market research industries, and the increasing dominance of chains and corporate giants within retailing. Above all, the post-war decades witnessed the very deliberate creation of a culture of personal consumer choice and self-fulfilment. These processes of transformation gained a momentum in the 1950s, and the rapid shift to self-service was representative of the pace with which social and cultural change was taking place. But change did not end there. Self-service retailing was not to reach its apogee until Australia entered its next decade. By then, as *The Australasian Grocer* triumphantly put it, the 'self-service 50s' had given way to the 'supermarket 60s'.[83]

Chapter 5

Tomorrow's Shop Today

In February 1957, Max Zimmerman, America's 'genius of the supermarket', opened a Sydney retail trade convention complete with two walk-through 'model' self-service stores. In his address to a dozen women and over 800 men, and with these stores as his backdrop, Zimmerman insisted that 'Mrs Consumer should be left alone. She will sell herself more than the smoothest salesmen could hope for'.[1]

The Australian food retailing industry was, as we have seen in the previous chapter, all too willing to accept his advice. Already, by this time, self-service had transformed the traditional counter-service grocery shop. Throughout the 1950s 'Mrs Housewife', and the increasing number of male shoppers as well, were left to their own devices.

The Australian supermarket was not, however, to emerge in its complete, corporate form until 1960, the year in which both Coles and Woolworths – Australia's two largest retail companies – opened their first purpose-built, free-standing 'one-stop-shops'. In doing so, these companies put in train yet another major transformation of Australian retail culture, a transformation linked with the concurrent emergence of the suburban regional shopping centre as a retail form.

When it did finally emerge, the corporate supermarket was one of the most obvious symbols of Australia's transition to a high modernity, and it was understood and promoted as such by corporate retailers. It was a quite deliberate and rather deft move, for example, to link one-stop shopping with technological and social 'advancement' by placing a large model space rocket on the outside of the new Coles supermarkets along with a piece of the earth's surface protruding from the roof. These rockets were almost the real thing,

The Dandenong New World, 1963, with the flags of nation and empire, the space-age technology of a superpower and the scenes of local history (front windows) (Coles Myer Archives)

modelled as they were on the American 'Nike Zeus' spacecraft.[2] If Australia couldn't quite compete in the space race proper, it was at least going to have the retail environments that went along with it.

The logo on which to hang the new Coles image was at first somewhat confused. Coles originally chose the altogether mundane 'Coles Food Market', but soon ditched this in favour of emblazoning across its larger stores the far more visionary slogan, 'New World of Shopping'.[3]

It was an expansive claim, but not, as this chapter suggests, inaccurate.

Other Modernities

Americanisation, symbolised by the rise of self-service, was not the only means by which Australian shopping culture was being unevenly transformed during the 1950s and 1960s. Post-war Australian retailing was certainly stamped with an American twang. But there was, additionally, an emergent, alternative definition of consumer modernity reliant on the cosmopolitan pleasures of an older European-style retailing.

By 1963 about two million post-war immigrants had arrived in Australia. Many of these immigrants were British, but over half came from other European countries such as Italy, Greece, Holland, Yugoslavia, Germany and Poland.[4] For Anglo-Australians one of the most confronting ways in which these migrant communities became visible was through the transformation of public space. By the late 1940s the arrival of European immigrants was already being recognised as transforming Australian everyday life through the introduction of a more 'cosmopolitan' form of retailing and new products for consumption. Eventually, the role of post-war migrants in changing Australian food culture would become one of the standard and increasingly patronising means by which to acknowledge their presence. While certain commercial forms, such as the delicatessen or the cafe, were to provide migrant communities with a way of resisting cultural assimilation, within the dominant culture these commercial activities were constructed as a means of gaining citizenship. Post-war novelists, such as the authors of *Tomorrow and Tomorrow*, were among the first to draw attention to the impact of immigration on Australian retailing:

> The Cross, people said, was more like Montparnasse than ever with the foreigners about. The refugees . . . This was a new infiltration, a medley of people from Central Europe, from Germany, Poland, Spain . . . They congregated at the Cross . . . Their shops began to appear, little shops with an air, chic. Delicatessen with sharp flavoured new goods, patisserie with elaborate torte and gateaux, fatal lure to the obese, dress shops that were different, gloves and handbags with a continental flair.[5]

Far from being assimilated into Australian shopping culture, migrant communities seemed, to the horror of some and the delight of others, to be remaking that culture, albeit on a local level. In the process, these communities partially revived small-scale retailing in the face of the chains. This was, at least initially, a mainly inner-urban phenomenon and one that brought a perceived increase in the cosmopolitan dangers of city life. Dymphna Cusack and Florence James in their novel *Come In Spinner*, set in war-time Sydney, captured well the mixture of fear and attraction with which suburban Anglo-Australia approached such change. When the seventeen-year-old Monnie Malone comes into Darlinghurst from the suburbs, the city seems entirely foreign:

> She had never seen such a gay crowd doing their Saturday-morning shopping; women in slacks and sandals and brief beach dresses; men in bright shirts and shorts, choosing their meat and vegetables and groceries with as much care as the women. And there was so much chatter and laughter – it was more like a picnic than a week-end shopping rush. The striped awnings shading the little shops made it different too, like something you'd see in a technicolour film. And the windows glowing with colour; the greengrocers where strange fruits were piled among the familiar ones . . .[6]

For Monnie, the city contains both the pleasure and danger of cosmopolitan difference and even of gender role confusion. This cosmopolitanism was modern but it was not the neatly gendered and increasingly rationalised modernity of the suburb and the self-service store. Instead, the modernities of the inner-urban and suburban clashed, a clash that was expressed, in part, through the shop and intensified by the ongoing arrival of post-war immigrants, many of whom were drawn to the inner-urban areas of Australian cities.

Despite this clash of modernities, an Anglo-suburban way of life would certainly prove triumphant during the 1950s and 1960s, and any substantial challenge from immigrant cultures would have to wait. Alternative modernities were present but they were to be pushed into the background while in the foreground and in every available public space, the supermarket was emerging.

One-Stop Shopping

In 1959, in an article entitled 'Supermarkets are Coming', Sir Edgar Coles spoke of the need to tread carefully in applying what he called 'revolutionary ideas' to Australian retailing. He insisted, nevertheless, that the time was now ripe for a full-scale move by the Coles company into one-stop shopping. 'The Australian public', he wrote, 'are food conscious. They now accept self-service and supermarkets as part of their daily living'.[7]

The Coles organisation was going to bring to the Australian public the 'real thing'. While it seemed that every grocer had now put in a checkout and utilised the word supermarket, Coles was to go all-American. As Sir Edgar pointed out, a supermarket proper was 'a very large self-service store, stocking a complete range of groceries, fruit and vegetables, frozen foods, pre-packed meat and delicatessen'.[8]

The coming of these 'real' supermarkets was, it seemed, an inevitable part of the maturing of Australia as an economic entity. Thus Sir Edgar concluded, 'the outlook for future retailing in Australia appears to be good, and our company must continue its present policy of expanding to new areas . . . in order to keep abreast with the natural growth of the nation'.[9] This nationalistic optimism was part of a general feeling within the retail trade that the 1960s was going to be a special decade. With the emergence of the large corporate supermarket and the even larger regional shopping centre, Australian shopping culture would be transformed beyond all recognition, or so retailers believed.

As in the United States and Britain, the independent food store did not simply disappear with the arrival of the large corporate supermarket. Rather, many one-time grocery stores were eventually transformed into milk bars, corner shops and small, family-run supermarkets. Yet the independents' share of the national grocery market declined dramatically throughout the 1960s. By contrast, the variety store chains, dominated in Australia by Coles and Woolworths, rapidly increased their share of the retail food market, and by the end of the decade they effectively dictated where and by what means most Australians purchased food and household items.

By the late 1950s large supermarkets had begun opening all over Australia. In November 1958 *The Australasian Grocer* reported on the opening of a 'Giant Supermarket in Melbourne' of 20 000 square feet.[10] With a selling space of 10 000 square feet and parking space for 300 cars, this was, at the time, one of Australia's biggest supermarkets. Situated in the newly suburbanised outer-metropolitan region of Mentone, it was packed with crowd-pulling features which reconfirmed the increasing attentiveness to images of efficiency and modernity within food retailing. 'Shoppers at Mentone', *The Australasian Grocer* noted, 'would be able to watch the preparation and packing of foods through large plate glass windows that had been placed to give a full view of the meat preparation room and bakery'.[11] By now even the packers and food workers were to become part of an image of modern shopping, though this was only a sanitised representation of actual working conditions within food manufacturing. This was work turned advertising. It was an indication also that as 'service' became less of a feature of retailing, much more needed to be made of the *image* of service itself.

But there were other supermarket giants long before the Mentone edifice. The business magazine *Rydges* reported on the establishment in 1947 of a 'beautifully equipped and well-stocked supermarket' of 16 000 square feet in Sydney. This store had all the latest American features – with meat, fruit and vegetable, grocery and bakery departments – and was, one observer proclaimed, Australia's first complete food store.[12] A similar 'American' supermarket opened in Sydney in 1951 complete with pre-packed meat displays and even a playroom for children.[13]

It was retailers such as Norman Tieck, a former employee of Woolworths, who did most to promote supermarketing in Australia. Embarking on a tour of the United States and Europe in 1950, he gathered detailed information on supermarket operation and, on his return to Australia, wasted no time in promoting full self-service as 'the answer to the grocery retailing problems in this country'.[14] Tieck was clearly excited by what he saw as the 'streamlined cleanliness and gleaming efficiency' of the American supermarket, a phenomenon that had arisen there for two simple reasons: the emergence of the automobile and 'the apparent inherent American desire for speedy, efficient service, thus giving rise to the only possible solution: self-service'.[15]

Like Sir Edgar Coles, Tieck insisted that the 'American supermarket principle' needed to be adapted to Australian conditions, not least because of Australia's restricted retail trading hours, its lower level of motor car ownership and its comparatively limited supply and variety of pre-packed merchandise. For Tieck no time was to be wasted in beginning this trans-formation to a new kind of shopping. 'The sooner this is realised', he wrote, 'the quicker the Australian food industry as a whole will reduce the gap of progress estimated at twenty-five years between the two great "A's" – Australia and America.'[16]

By the 1960s this 'closing of the gap' had become an imperative of Australian retailing. Borrowing an American modernity was not simply a way to reap higher profits, it was a way of defining and taking hold of an Australian future. In this climate retail developments became emblematic of the Australian way of life. As one *Rydges* editorial, entitled 'Selling Our Way of Life', sermonised in 1964:

> We live today in an era that people are trying continually to classify with appropriate labels. This second half of the twentieth century has been called the age of science, the nuclear age, the space age, the age of acceleration. It has been described as the age of leisure, the age of self-determination, and as the greatest period of change the world has ever known. It is all of these and more; but perhaps even more importantly it is the age of mass communication and mass marketing.[17]

Here commerce claimed for itself an emblematic status, a status that many cultural critics were equally prepared to give the ever larger and spectacular retail centres that modern commerce created. If cultural critics understood such retail environments as representative of an emergent culture of conspicuous consumption, so too did retailers, though in wholly celebratory terms. As the *Rydges* editorial intoned, while taking a swipe at communism for good measure, 'If we, as a free enterprise country expect to survive we must do more than just sell the products of our free enterprise system, we must sell the system itself.'[18]

This was jingoistic stuff. But it was powerful within the discourses of retailing. The emergence of new retail environments like the supermarket was deeply embedded in a heightened historical consciousness about the possibilities and dangers of the age, a consciousness that went way beyond a concern with profit margins and economies of scale.

These possibilities were wrapped up in notions of masculinity as well as capitalist modernity. The use of the space rocket to symbolise the new retailing spoke both of an ethos of accelerated progress and of boy's-own adventure. In January 1959, not long after the launch of Sputnik had begun the space race, a large rocket dominated the cover of *Rydges* magazine. This cover symbolised, the magazine insisted, forthcoming commercial develop-ments and technological advances.[19] Within supermarketing, in particular, there was, by the late 1950s, a renewed fascination with retail and management systems that expressed an intensely masculine delight with things systematic, rational, technological. Retailers at a management level seemed to sense a new, almost macho power to build corporate empires and to become social engineers. As such, formal executive training was being referred to as a means of consciously 'making men', not simply better managers. As one *Rydges* article put it in 1956, 'The development of men has always taken place in many enterprises, but not as a formal, conscious activity of management'.[20]

This was no slip of the pen. Being a man and being a manager were closely intertwined in retailing and other commercial activities in the post-war period. In one article entitled 'The Place of Women in Business and the Professions', the journalist (and later Liberal Senator) Michael Baume concluded that, regardless of women's skills, there was basically no place for them at all.[21] Given this mentality, retail management became even more intensely male-defined with the advent of the corporate supermarket.

By contrast, this was precisely the time when retailing was becoming dominated by female labour at a shop-floor level. Between 1961 and 1974 the proportion of women in the retail workforce – a major area of women's paid employment – rose from 53 per cent to 60 per cent.[22] Within food retailing, most of these women were employed as 'checkers' and in other semi-skilled positions. Retail work became also increasingly casual and part-time in nature. Between 1960 and 1980 the proportion of women employed on a full-time basis within the retail industry fell from about 75 per cent to 50 per cent.[23] Male employment was the target of much less 'casualisation'. Over the same period the proportion of men employed on a full-time basis within retailing fell from 86 per cent to 75 per cent.[24]

By the late 1960s, then, men were increasingly withdrawing from any form of direct service within food retailing. Indeed, as low-paid retail workers they had become a minority. As I argued earlier, however, men only began to physically withdraw from the shop or from certain areas of retail work once they had designed corporate structures which they believed would ensure for them a retention and even increase of control over the food store as a commercial and social space. In this situation, the less important and potentially emasculating activity of serving could now finally be left almost entirely to women, or to the 'little man' who continued to run an independent shop.

This colonisation of the top-end of retail employment by men was reflected just as firmly in the leadership of the Shop, Distributive and Allied Employees' Association (SDA), the major trade union representing retail workers around the nation.[25] By the mid-1970s women comprised over 80 per cent of shop union membership in Australia.[26] Despite this, the SDA leadership was overwhelmingly male in the post-war decades. This leadership was a conservative one, connected as it was with the National Civic

Council. Stuart Rosewarne has argued that as a result the SDA did little throughout the 1960s and 1970s to contest the process of casualisation or represent the interests of most retail workers.[27] In fact the SDA espoused a traditional belief in the nuclear family, thus supporting the employers' understanding of retail work not as a potential career for women, but as providing 'pin money' for housewives, and pre-marriage employment for younger female workers.[28]

Spaces of Consumption

It was in the outer-metropolitan suburbs of Australian cities that super-market retailers first attempted to sell their new way of life. The rapid suburbanisation of these areas meant that retailers had a growing and captive market of highly mobile and increasingly wealthy 'consumers'.

The major indicator of this mobility was car ownership. From an owner-ship rate of one vehicle for every 8.7 people in 1945, car ownership soared to a rate of one vehicle for every 2.8 people in 1968.[29] Increases were evident also in consumer expenditure. Throughout the 1960s private consumption expenditure rose by about 4.9 per cent per year.[30] At the same time, house ownership rose to an all-time high. In 1947, 53 per cent of private dwellings were owned or being purchased by their occupiers. By 1961 this figure had risen to 70 per cent and was to remain at that level for decades to come.[31] This brought a concomitant rise in housing construction. Between 1948/49 and 1962/63 the number of houses and flats constructed increased by 3.7 per cent a year.[32] Finally, Australia's population boomed in the post-war period through both immigration and births, increasing from 7.43 million at the end of World War II to just over 11 million by 1963.[33]

In this social and economic climate, the new suburbs were the ideal places to experiment with new retail forms. As housing construction moved further into the outlying regions of Australian cities, there was little existing retail infrastructure with which supermarket operators had to compete. For the large retailer, working on tight profit margins, this was just as well, since food consumption as a percentage of overall consumer expenditure continued to decrease throughout the 1960s. In 1960/61, 23.2 per cent of personal con-sumption expenditure went on food. This had declined by 1969/70 to 19.2 per cent making the retail food market increasingly competitive.[34]

The move to the suburbs enabled retailers to express their status as social engineers as well as compete for profits. Here were new spaces over which retailers, along with governments, town planners, architects and developers, could have a directing hand.[35] Space, understood as the material site of political and social relationships, has become an important area of research within contemporary social theory and critical human geography.[36] In the work of David Harvey, for example, the manner in which urban spaces and everyday time is organised and divided up within capitalist societies is seen to both articulate dominant cultural beliefs and to structure everyday social action. People thus experience modernity through a certain spatial and temporal reorganisation of inner-urban and suburban life. In this sense, following the work of Henri Lefebvre, the planning of public and private space is seen as a pervasive source of social power, a means through which to control the material settings of everyday social existence.[37]

Australian corporate retailers certainly took hold of this power. Yet it is important to avoid universalising the experiences on offer in the post-war suburb. As noted in the previous chapter, the lived reality of urban space and time under conditions of modernity or postmodernity may be quite different depending on the class, race, ethnicity, gender, sexuality or age of those living that reality.[38] Furthermore, modern space as envisaged by the social planner, developer or retailer does not simply translate into a power over everyday life but is made into *place* – or lived space – by those who people it. Thus planned spaces such as the supermarket or shopping centre are only partially able to mould everyday experience.

As the new supermarkets became an integral part of urban Australia during the 1960s, the experiences they did have to offer also became a part of suburban entertainment. The new retailing was quick to make links with the equally new television culture. Food manufacturers were one of the biggest television advertisers, and supermarkets themselves became a part of small-screen show biz. In 1960 the Coles company launched the television quiz program 'Coles £3000 Question', which by 1964 had become Australia's most popular quiz show.[39] Better still, television sometimes extended beyond the screen and into the supermarket proper. Fanfare openings of new supermarkets became regular events. In December 1962, for example, the new SSW supermarket in the Melbourne suburb of Beaumaris was opened by television's 'singalong team', Evie Hayes and Bill McCormack.[40] Similarly, Graham Kennedy, the 'King' of Melbourne television, opened the first Safeway supermarket in the Melbourne suburb of Forest Hill in June 1964.[41]

On very special occasions a link could be made with political authority. In Canberra, in March 1963, Coles procured the services of the long-serving conservative Prime Minister Robert Menzies in opening a New World. Menzies, who had probably never seen the inside of a supermarket in his life, was obviously somewhat lost for words and perfunctorily insisted that 'Canberra people are entitled to have the last word in shopping facilities. Here, believe me, they have it'.[42] The conservative Victorian Premier, Henry Bolte, was more effusive when opening yet another New World in the industrial suburb of Dandenong. In his opening speech Bolte praised the 'hygienic' new giant and proclaimed that supermarkets were representative of a country 'dedicated to the idea of progress and development'.[43]

This popularisation of the supermarket went some way to answering shopper complaints about the 'blandness' of suburban retailing. In one article on 'The Pleasures of Shopping', Nan Hutton contended that shopping had lost its 'glamour' with the move from the city to the suburbs. 'We need glamour there too', she pleaded.[44] With ever larger supermarkets, and with expansive shopping centres, retailers tried to meet such requests. But they did not do so by providing the old glamour of inner-city shopping that Hutton so missed. Instead they opted for the new attractiveness of the 'three C's': convenience, cleanliness and consumer choice.

The facilities provided by the new supermarkets seemed ever expanding, yet as retail environments they were carefully designed to increase turnover rather than universally provide better shopping facilities. Supermarkets only 'gave' certain things while taking away others. Service, including the delivery of goods, was the most obvious casualty. Depite this, some retailers clung doggedly to the notion that service remained the hallmark of food retailing. When Norman Tieck spoke of the supermarket, he insisted that service remained the watchword of the business since customer services such as 'Kiddies Corners', telephones, and store directories were provided.[45] This was self-justifying nonsense. Supermarket shoppers and commentators knew full well that as food retailers abandoned counter service, delivery services and customer credit facilities, the shopper was compelled to take on more of the work of the retailer; to visit the shop, select and fetch the goods, and, more often than not, transport them home.

Some retailers, recognising that shopping had indeed become more of a chore with the rise of the supermarket, sought ways in which to convince the shopper otherwise, to overcome shopper fatigue and, as one retail analyst put it, to more thoughtfully design 'self-help outlets'.[46] The euphemism of self-help to describe self-service was a telling one. It implied a certain empowerment of the shopper. Somehow taking things off the shelves was now a socially positive exercise in providing for oneself, a sort of act of assertiveness and of consumer citizenship.

In foisting this version of shopping on a 'consuming public', the 1960s saw the further development of market research techniques, particularly in the area of 'motivation research' and 'consumer depth-probing'. Motivation research, which became the principal target of cultural critics such as Vance Packard, had by now become the science of mapping the consumer unconscious through the 'depth interview' – literally putting the consumer on the couch. It dealt, as one proponent claimed, with 'the deep, subconscious meanings of commodities . . . with the symbolic power of objects, their auras or "souls" so to speak'.[47]

This 'depth-probing' was not something of which 'consumers' were unaware. By the early 1960s *The Australian Women's Weekly* was offering advice to its readers on how to resist the new marketing methods. As one article on tips for the housewife warned, 'Be conscious of your emotional mood when you shop. In periods of stress, crisis, loneliness you are much more likely to reach out and buy something you don't need.'[48]

Retailers' attempts to capture the unconscious, however inadequate, were one means by which 'consumer choice' could be reined in. Another was to give the impression of choice where none actually existed. When the new Dickins supermarket was opened in the Victorian rural city of Ballarat in August 1961, one trade journal noted with admiration that there were 100 shopping trolleys provided, but only 12 baskets.[49] This now familiar super-marketing strategy encouraged high levels of consumption. It also favoured those with personal transport. Indeed, most shoppers needed and used a car to visit the new supermarkets. As such, the bargains of the one-stop-shop were, as the authors of *Retailing in Melbourne* found in the late 1960s, essentially available only to car owners. Those without personal transport were still reliant on local shops and on making several shopping trips a week.[50]

The local shop itself, however, was in an increasingly precarious position. The number of grocery outlets continued to decline with the appearance of large supermarkets, despite the increase in population and outer-urban living. The trade journal *Retail World* reported in 1968 that the number of grocery stores in Australia had fallen by 2421 since 1952, but that the turnover of those remaining, given their increased size, had soared.[51]

Likewise, the number of items available to the shopper, despite the plethora of new manufactured goods, did not necessarily increase with the appearance of the supermarket. Rather, the nature and origin of products changed. Within much of the retailing literature there was a belief that the advent of the supermarket increased the number and range of products available to the shopper. During the 1960s elaborate product displays within supermarkets were popular as a means of emphasising the abundance of goods available.[52] By the early 1960s the average smaller supermarket in Australia carried about 2700 different products. By the end of the decade middle-sized supermarkets, such as Franklins, each carried about 4500 items, while the large Coles New World supermarkets each stocked about 5000 different products.[53] This was certainly a large number of items. However, there is evidence to suggest that this did not differ all that markedly from the number of items stocked within more traditional stores. One article in *Rydges* in 1928, for example, noted that there were about 18 000 items in the average 'grocery and hardware store'.[54] This figure was probably inflated but it does undercut the claim that the 'supermarket 60s' was a decade of unrivalled abundance.

Such criticisms hardly reached the ears of retailers. What did was the ring of cash registers. Sir Edgar Coles had been right in arguing that the slow introduction of supermarkets to Australia would pay off, at least for retailers.

Supermarket retailers and commercial architects were able to design purpose-built and highly profitable stores using American know-how rather than simply converting large existing buildings in an ad hoc manner.[55] This enabled them to compete with smaller retailers even more effectively.

The Big Boys

The Melbourne-based Coles company entered food retailing in the late 1950s, a decade which an official company history later defined as the 'take-over period'.[56] In 1958, Coles acquired John Connell Dickins and Company, which operated a chain of 54 grocery stores in Victoria, mostly along self-service lines. Even before this Coles had been 'experimenting' within its larger variety stores, having set up small 'food departments'. The experiment, the company believed, had proved popular with shoppers as it allowed each customer to choose 'exactly what she desires'.[57]

By the early 1960s Coles had acquired further smaller grocery chains in South Australia and New South Wales and, being 'past the stage of experimenting' as Sir Edgar Coles put it, embarked on a program of opening large, purpose-built, free-standing supermarkets in suburban areas.[58] In an auspicious beginning to a new commercial decade, the first of these super- markets opened in the Melbourne suburb of Balwyn in March 1960. This one-stop-shop included a full range of merchandise, pre-packed meat, fruit and vegetables, and cakes cooked daily on the premises. Extensive parking facilities were provided as well, an essential element of supermarketing in Australia as in North America.[59]

Conceptually, Coles supermarkets were, as we have already noted, based on a knowledge of and unrestrained fascination with American retailing. The Coles company regularly sent its executives on overseas fact-finding missions. Just as Norman Tieck had toured American supermarkets a decade earlier, returning with wonderment in his eyes, Mr Arthur Staggart, of the Coles Food Division, undertook a similarly invigorating tour in 1960. 'The supermarkets are big, beautiful and very profitable', he wrote on his return, 'and are very exciting places to shop. The range of groceries in the super- market is staggering and difficult to describe'.[60]

This was the stuff of fantasy. In many respects companies such as Coles embarked not simply on the rationalisation of the retail industry but on the realisation of commercial dreams. Fantasy as well as the profit motive was an important aspect of Australian retailing during the 1960s. Retailers undoubtedly set out to capture markets, but equally they set out to realise futures, to remould the social as well as the commercial world. This 'remoulding' was not understood in the Brave New World terms of its critics but as a creative expression of business acumen and civic vision. In this spirit Coles had already opened eight large purpose-built supermarkets by 1962, all gleaming and modern in design. As *Colesanco* described one such super-market, 'everything about it has an air of "tomorrow's shop today" '.[61]

By 1963 'New Worlds' had been opened in New South Wales, Queensland, and the Australian Capital Territory as well as in Victoria. This program was accelerated in 1964, and by the end of the year the company had 29 New World supermarkets in operation and 11 more planned. These comple-mented its existing 264 'Food Markets', 248 variety stores and 11 country department stores.[62] Coles supermarkets generally had upwards of 12 000 square feet of selling space, as many as 14 checkouts, some of which were motorised, extensive refrigerated displays, and added features such as 'magic carpet' automatic doors, cafes, and play corners for children.

The move into supermarkets clearly paid off. By the mid-1960s, the company was convinced, mainly by its bulging profits, that the New World concept had begun to transform Australian shopping culture. 'The large space rocket decor', the 1964 *Annual Report* claimed, 'has now become a familiar symbol of these modern and attractive supermarkets which offer the housewife everything in the way of food needs'.[63]

Others shared this vision, and in the profits. The Sydney-based Wool-worths company followed a similar path of expansion to Coles and began its move into food retailing with the acquisition of the Brisbane Cash and Carry Stores in 1958.[64] By 1960, a year which the official company history described as nothing short of 'momentous', further acquisitions had been made in Western Australia and New South Wales.[65] This was also the year in which Woolworths opened its first free-standing supermarket in Warrawong, New South Wales with further supermarkets opening in Queensland and South Australia.[66] Like Coles, Woolworths emphasised the gleaming newness of its one-stop-shops and made good its commercial gamble by rapidly increasing company profits. Woolworths' executives were equally convinced that supermarketing was what the shoppers wanted, and by 1967 the company was operating over 200 supermarkets, far outnumbering the rival New Worlds.[67]

As in Britain, the North American company, Safeway, was quick to move into an expanding Australian consumer market. Safeway originally forged a partnership with the small independent firm of Pratts Supermarkets in 1963. Pratts had converted to self-service in 1950 and opened an 'American-style' supermarket in the Melbourne suburb of Frankston in 1961, complete with roof-top carpark.[68] By 1964, however, Pratts had been effectively taken over by the American company and the new 'Australian Safeway Stores' were launched with the opening of the first purpose-built Safeway Supermarket in the Melbourne suburb of Forest Hill.[69]

With the rise of Australian Safeway, North American concepts were now to be directly imported, rather than simply borrowed. When Safeway opened its Croydon store in November 1964, the building's design, with its arched

Shopping panorama: New World interior, Maidstone, Victoria, 1964 (Coles Myer Archives)

roof, was directly based on that of its North American counterparts.[70] This global architectural vision was embodied in all Safeway's Victorian stores, taking the insistence on a 'unity of design' to new Australian heights. By 1969 Safeway had 21 supermarkets operating in Victoria.[71]

The movement into supermarketing by these and other large retail firms – or the 'big boys' as they were tellingly known within the trade – was 'successful' in two respects. Firstly, the corporate chains 'captured' a substantial, and by the end of the 1960s, a majority share of the national grocery market. By 1968 the chains' share of the market had reached 50.2 per cent while the independents' share had decreased to 13 per cent. The other large share of the market, 36.8 per cent, was held by the 'buying groups'.[72]

As in Britain and the United States, this market dominance was achieved with a comparatively small number of stores. By the end of the 1960s Australia had 657 large supermarkets.[73] This was only a fraction of the 23 000 grocery establishments then in operation, yet these 650-odd supermarkets accounted for over 30 per cent of the retail sales of food items.[74] Many of these large stores were controlled by the two major companies. By 1967 Woolworths had 471 grocery stores, 206 of which were classified as supermarkets. Coles, on the other hand, had 230 grocery stores of which 91 were supermarkets.[75]

Even given these basic statistics, it is evident how quickly the supermarket took hold of Australian retail culture. This was the second sense in which the emergence of the supermarket was a retail success. Despite the relatively small number of supermarkets in relation to the thousands of other grocery outlets, Sir Edgar Coles was at least half right in asserting in 1964 that

'Supermarkets have captured the imagination of the public and are rapidly taking their place as an important segment of Australia's shopping life'.[76]

Not only were corporate empires being built but the framework of everyday suburban life was indeed being changed. It was, as we noted above, an open question as to how all-encompassing, how much of a 'capture' this change was, and how shoppers themselves were reacting to these retail transformations. Nevertheless, retailers felt that their wildest commercial dreams were now being realised. On one level, they were reaping the profits. On another, they were contributing, they believed, to the modernisation of Australian social life, and particularly to the pleasure of the consumer experience. When, in 1968, Coles opened its 100th New World supermarket in the Melbourne suburb of Tooronga, the company journal had no hesitation in asserting that 'the impact of the supermarket, with its modern amenities and pleasant surroundings, was such that the housewife's buying of her weekly food requirements was no longer a chore but an experience to look forward to'.[77]

This claim was significant. Shopping, even for everyday items, had now almost entirely lost its status as an activity and become simply an *experience*. It had lost a materiality and become a cultural event. Apparently, there was now virtually no terrain of consumption that lay outside the field of leisure and pleasure. Retail innovations that supposedly made the housewife's duties less onerous attempted to dissolve any notion of everyday shopping as unpaid work, and as potentially boring, repetitive and tedious. The increased time spent on 'modern' everyday shopping was not considered work at all. In a very real sense the emergence of the supermarket, precisely because it dealt in the most ordinary and seemingly least exciting of consumer items, was the final move in constructing a modern retail culture in which there was an unbreakable identification between consumption and pleasure, shopping and the self.

One Great Commercial Centre

This study is quite deliberately focused almost exclusively on food retailing and the rise and corporatisation of self-service. The large corporate supermarket is a very particular retail form, and shopping within it is a very particular consumer activity the history of which has gone largely unexplored. Nevertheless, the supermarket has always existed alongside other shops. In fact, by the early 1960s supermarket retailers in Australia believed they had discovered an even more sure-fire way to cement the relationship between the one-stop-shop and the leisure experience: offer the consumer not simply a variety of products but a variety of stores.

In Australia, the large regional shopping centre, like the supermarket, was a phenomenon born in the 1960s. The supermarket in Australia, as elsewhere, emerged independently of the regional shopping centre and stood alone, often literally, as a particular retail environment. Yet the supermarket was to become an integral part of the shopping mall, or 'centre' – as it was called in Australia – a retail form once again borrowed from North America. Just as the 1960s had been described as the decade of the supermarket, so too was it dubbed 'the decade of shopping centre development'.[78] If the suburbs had become Australia's new mass market, as *Rydges* magazine insisted, then retailers required expansive new retail environments through which to promote mass consumption. The 'scientifically planned' shopping centre was envisaged as the answer; as a 'selling machine' and as 'capable of changing the shopping habits of people'.[79]

Urban Australia had long had local 'high street' shopping centres in which shops were grouped around train stations and tram stops. This 'ribbon' or 'strip' arrangement of shops was, until the 1960s, the most common form of retailing. In 1961 R.J. Johnston and P.J. Rimmer, in their detailed study of retailing in Melbourne, identified 718 separate retail 'centres' comprising three shops or more in the Melbourne metropolitan area.[80] By the 1960s, however, the term 'shopping centre' was taking on a more complex meaning. Borrowing terminology from the United States, Australian retailers began distinguishing between planned and unplanned shopping areas. The shopping centre was now envisaged not simply as a group of shops but as 'an integrated retailing development, planned as a unit, owned by one individual or corporation, housed in one or more related structures, with enough stores so that it offers . . . complete shopping facilities'.[81] Retailers also distinguished between three different types of shopping centre: the neighbourhood, the community, and the regional centre. This distinction was roughly based on the size of the area, the number and variety of stores within the centre, and the shopping population it served. All three types of shopping centre were developed in Australia, but it was the large regional shopping centre that seemed to capture the imagination of retailers and media commentators.

The regional shopping centre was the only one that qualified, retailers believed, for the term 'one-stop shopping', since it was built around a major department store and included one or more supermarkets, a variety store and many smaller shops. Extensive parking facilities were an additional key feature. The first of such centres in Australia were the Chermside Centre in Brisbane and the Top Ryde Centre in Sydney, both opened in 1957. Chermside included a department store, a supermarket and 30 smaller shops, while the Top Ryde Centre included a department store and a variety store, a supermarket, 47 smaller shops and parking space for 400 cars.[82]

These were quickly bettered by the development of still larger centres. By 1960 the Myer company had opened Australia's largest shopping centre in the Melbourne suburb of Chadstone. Chadstone had parking space for 2500

cars, contained a large branch of the Myer department store, a Coles supermarket, and 80 smaller shops.[83] This was the beginning of a Myer plan to
surround Melbourne, quite literally, with regional shopping centres. By the
late 1960s the Myer group had cornered the market in more ways than one.
By then 'Chaddy' had been joined by Eastland, Northland and Southland.
Melbourne could not boast the highest number of shopping centres – that
honour was left to Sydney – but it could claim the biggest, and, it seemed,
the most legendary. 'The triumphant success of Chadstone', the Myer
corporation insisted in 1964, 'is now merchandising history'.[84] In the same
year the company kept the legend alive with the opening of Northland, a
centre that included no less than four separate department stores, a complete
'ultra-modern' supermarket and a 'unique English fruit and vegetable
market'.[85] By 1968 Northland had 112 separate shops that served an average
of 30 000 customers a day.[86]

Given Australia's urban sprawl, regional shopping centres multiplied
rapidly. In 1960 Australia had 14 large shopping centres; by 1966 this number
had increased to 86 with another 50 in the planning stage.[87] This was way
below the 9500 shopping malls that were said to operate in the United States
and Canada, but nevertheless Australia was believed to be second only to
these two countries in the extent and pace of shopping centre development.[88]

Supermarket retailers made sure they were part of this expansion,
particularly since the supermarket was one of the central 'anchors' around
which all shopping centres, large and small, were designed. The Coles
company, for example, was operating four of its own shopping centres in
South Australia and Queensland by 1966. These centres, although not as
large as the big Melbourne projects, contained a supermarket, a Coles variety
store and various other shops.[89] Usually, however, both Coles and Woolworths, as well as smaller companies such as Franklins, simply leased space
within the larger centres developed by companies such as Myer or investment corporations such as Lend Lease.

All this was too much for some. In August 1968, after Southland was
opened, an article in the Melbourne daily *The Age* asked if shopping could
ever be the same again, and expressed apprehension about what the new
'Mega-Emporiums' were doing to us all, or at least to the housewife:

> Southland, where a suburban housewife can become a voyeur of
> luxury in an air conditioned, neon lit, "through the looking glass"
> world where literally millions of dollars worth of goods lie spread
> before her – the princely smorgasbord of the consumer society.[90]

The article continued in this tone, ending with the apocalyptic comment: 'It
is only one step to a science fiction world where people will be born and die
in one great commercial centre'. In one respect, at least, the authors were

absolutely right; shopping had changed, though perhaps not quite as dramatically as they assumed. Like the supermarket, the development of the shopping centre was clearly embroiled in cultural as well as commercial transformations.

Commercially, the growth of the shopping centre facilitated a further shift in retailing from the city centres to the suburbs. In metropolitan Melbourne the central business district's share of retail expenditure fell from 49 per cent in 1948 to 27 per cent in 1961 and continued to fall throughout the 1960s.[91] In Sydney the drop was just as dramatic. In 1948 suburban retailers held about 48 per cent of the retail trade, by the early 1960s this figure had risen to 60 per cent.[92] In light of this, as well as the rapid establishment of shopping centres, commentators such as Yvonne Preston were suggesting that Australia was becoming 'over-shopped', with too many shops in Australia per head of population and retail profits spread too thinly. [93] In fact, by the mid-1960s Australia had more shops per head of population than Britain, yet increases in consumer expenditure were slowing down. As a result, many smaller shopping centres, which had been badly planned and too quickly erected, were to prove commercial failures.[94]

This would suggest that the race for a greater share of a shrinking market was not the only reason retailers turned to the development of great commercial centres. The establishment of shopping centres, as with supermarkets, was about profit. It was expressive also of a fascination with new retail designs, systems and futures. The shopping centre, like the supermarket, captured the imagination of retailers as much if not more so than its shoppers. With the rise of the regional shopping centre retailers consciously and enthusiastically embarked on the construction of 'little cities'; they consciously sought, as one architectural critic put it in 1969, 'to give identity to life in the suburbs'.[95] The rhetoric of leisure, pleasure and excitement, so much a hallmark of supermarket retailing, would thus reach new heights with the establishment of the regional shopping centre. When the new Roselands centre opened in Sydney in 1965, one promotional leaflet claimed that, 'For a woman the Roselands story is simply this: never again will shopping be a chore. From the moment Roselands opens, shopping will become an outing with a touch of adventure, a day out rather than a tedious task'.[96]

In one sense this further effort to deny the materiality of shopping was pure advertising drivel, and it is in this sense that cultural critics have tended to interpret such texts. However, retailers themselves were drawn to the apparent pleasures of the new shopping environments and did not totally disbelieve their own promotional rhetoric. This rhetoric, however hyperbolical, conveyed something of the manner in which the gleaming, integrated and complete modernity of the shopping centre and the supermarket embodied the masculine ideal of what *was* pleasurable. Retailers were not

The 'Mega-Emporium': Miranda Fair Shopping Centre, Sydney, 1964 (Image Library, State Library of New South Wales)

completely detached, commercially rational individuals motivated purely by the promise of wealth. They were men with a (masculine) desire to partake in the reframing of Australian social life. The institutions they constructed expressed this eagerness to give suburbia an identity and to, quite literally, make concrete commercial dreams.

Modernity Triumphant?

Between 1945 and 1970 Australian retail cultures, and the physical environments in which people shopped, were substantially remade. In less than three decades everyday shopping and shopping spaces had been transformed not beyond recognition but way beyond the traditional. Where there had been a counter, there was now a shelf. Where there had been a solicitous grocer, there was now a carefully designed package. Where there had been a grouping of local shops, there was now a little city beyond which the shopper never needed to tread. Above all, retailing had moved from being a trade to becoming a hybrid of the commercial and human sciences. The corporate retailer was not a shopkeeper; he was the maker of social institutions, the part-creator of suburban cultures, and, for some, the source of national pride.

Not everyone, of course, saw something to celebrate in post-war retail cultures, and not everyone accepted that retailing was as powerful in framing post-war social life as it believed itself to be. Even corporate retailers themselves increasingly recognised that the conveniences and pleasures modern shopping promised were not unproblematic.

In 1970 the *Sydney Morning Herald* columnist Sandra Jobson wrote a series of articles expressing concern about the past decade of retail change. In doing so, Jobson trod a fine line between dismissiveness and critique. In one article, Jobson talked of a mass-produced individualism in the suburbs and, in another, spoke of Roselands as 'a science fiction, air-conditioned city' and as the 'palace of modern Australian consumerism and peppermint dreams'.[97] But these criticisms were not one-dimensional, or simply elitist dismissals of the modern shopper. Jobson also expressed a much less abstract, and more popularly shared discontent with the corporatisation of retailing and the increasingly impersonal nature of shopping. Some media commentators and critics, particularly women, refused to take the rhetoric of convenience and pleasure at face value and attempted to articulate a popular critique of the new shopping, rather than simply critique 'the popular' as social theorists and cultural critics were apt to do. As the author of one lengthy study of Australian shopping centres argued in 1967:

> Shopping is not and never has been a glamorous occupation, but the centres are concerned to create an aura of glamour around their operation to make the suburban housewife feel like a V.I.P. This is particularly the function of the big centres, aiming to sell the housewife happiness along with her weekly groceries.[98]

Comments such as this were aimed at the shallow understandings of social life exhibited by the corporate retailer, not solely at the supposed gullibility of the shopper. They sought to delineate the limits of what the new retail environments actually offered women and the increasing number of male shoppers as well.

Architects and town planners joined in this critique of the new carnival of shopping. In 1969 the retail architect G.W. Smith rejected a nostalgia for traditional retailing but nevertheless lamented the 'artificiality' of the new shopping centres and the loss of a social consciousness within urban planning. 'It seems to me', Smith wrote, 'that we must think less in terms of maximising profits (or minimising costs) and more of satisfying the variety of social needs in the creation of our future market places'.[99]

Some retailers took such criticism seriously. Underlying retailers' expressions of satisfaction with the commercial centres they constructed was a contradictory and often suppressed awareness that not all was running quite so smoothly. Sandra Jobson cited Roger Layton, the Professor of Marketing at Sydney University, who claimed in 1970 that shoppers would increasingly demand more personal attention in the future.[100] Other retailers and marketing experts agreed, echoing long-held concerns about the loss of a 'personal touch' with the move to larger, self-service shopping environments. There was a further concern as well. By the end of the 1960s, some retailers were expressing a renewed apprehension about the autonomy of the shopper. Perhaps, some retailers complained, shoppers had been given too much and, in the process, had become *too* independent.

This was most clearly expressed in yet another article on 'What Makes Women Buy'.[101] This article noted that women had become increasingly powerful in the selection and purchase of consumer goods throughout the 1960s. But where earlier articles on the commercial seduction of women expressed a confidence about the techniques available to the retailer in 'capturing' the housewife-consumer, this 1968 article exhibited a frustration and loss of nerve. Under the influence of the emerging feminist movement and a general trend towards individualism, the article lamented, the woman shopper had become 'masculinised'. The notion of good housewifery was increasingly losing its power as a selling point. Instead, women, like men, were now attracted to images of efficiency, individualism and style rather than price and the fulfilment of social roles. In short, the article almost tearfully bemoaned, the woman shopper now needed to be regarded as independent and intelligent.

This was an extraordinary and rampantly misogynist admission of frustration and confusion in face of the rise of a supposedly new type of 'militant' female shopper. This was retailing with its pants round its ankles, inspecting its virility, and finding, accurately or not, that it had shrunk. Throughout the post-war years the discourse of Australian retailing had developed a complex self-image which interpreted the retailer as powerful and the shopper as only occasionally assertive. Post-war retailers, with all the resources of marketing science behind them, believed that they literally created shopping cultures and the modern consumer. As retailing became more corporatised it did indeed take on significant power to reframe the institutions of everyday consumption. However, in making shopping more self-directed, in giving the shopper that limited autonomy, retailers ran the risk of losing control, of having to face the fact that any power they possessed had always been tenuous. In the following chapter we explore this tenuousness.

Chapter 6
Living the Transformation

It seems that almost everyone has a story about and an opinion of the super-market. Time and again when casually talking to people about this study they would offer me a memory of or a reaction to supermarket shopping. When I first set out on this project I was reticent in telling people that I was writing a history of the supermarket. I was expecting their response to be at best bemused, at worst derisive. I was wrong. Some eyes did glaze over, but most people responded with real interest. And then there were the stories; all kinds of stories concerning supermarkets in the past or now, about what was wrong with them and how they compared to other shopping environments such as the counter-service grocery store or open-air market. Some people simply told me 'supermarket jokes'. Others told secrets of the tantalising underside of the one-stop-shop; of the supermarket as a gay beat or a heterosexual 'perving zone'.

One of the best and I think most telling stories, in terms of the present chapter, came from a man in his late-40s and was told to me across a noisy dinner table. He had a vivid memory of his first visit to a supermarket at the age of nine or ten. As he wandered the aisles and his mother selected the goods he became increasingly worried that his mother, in a fit of pique, was stealing the items. Suppressing panic, he furtively began looking around for watchful eyes and attempted to replace each item as it went in to the basket, thus forcing his mother to stop in her tracks and slowly explain to him the new protocols of modern shopping.

This is a sweet story, but it is not just that. It captures very well the sense of newness surrounding the emergence of the supermarket in Australia and how quickly that newness disappeared into memory. It offers, too, a sense of how a knowledge of shopping is transferred between generations and particularly between women and children.

Hearing other people's stories encouraged me to remember my own. While as a child and teenager I would regularly accompany my mother shopping – and occasionally the whole family would shop together – more often than not I would fetch a few things after school from the supermarket five minutes up the road. I remember this supermarket vividly because I visited it so regularly and disliked it so much, at least physically. It was a small independent supermarket, much more like an early superette than a modern New World. In fact it was the SSW opened in 1962, which I referred to in the previous chapter. By the time I got to wander its aisles, it was decidedly unglamorous. It was dark and cold and poorly laid out. It had chipped wooden checkouts and narrow shopping trolleys that moved sluggishly and refused to turn corners, or at least when you wanted them to. But for all this, I did like going there to look at the products and to shop. Alongside this supermarket was the cake shop, and then the butcher and the delicatessen, with the toy shop and post office situated between them. Across the road was the green-grocer and the hardware (then still referred to in my family as the ironmonger). Here, then, in this small suburban shopping strip, were really two historically overlapping retail cultures: the superette and the counter-service shop, both of which seemed to me in the late 1960s to be in a state of decline. Even as a child I can remember thinking that the SSW, in comparison to the big supermarket at the new regional shopping centre three or four miles away, was decidedly unmodern. As for the other little shops surrounding the SSW, they seemed positively quaint, even to an eight or nine year old.

In this chapter I shall explore stories like these in more detail. Drawing on a set of lengthy interviews with a group of elderly and not so elderly people with strong ties to the outer-Melbourne suburb of Dandenong, this chapter offers a glimpse at some of the many personal narratives surrounding the demise of the traditional grocery store, the emergence of the supermarket, and the nature of everyday shopping in post-war Australia.[1]

Throughout the previous chapters we have concentrated on the retailer rather than the consumer. We have explored the rise of a modern retail culture in post-war Australia, particularly in relation to the corporate supermarket. We have traced also the manner in which retailers attempted to bring a certain consumer culture into existence through utilising the motifs of modernity, leisure, excitement, autonomy and so on. In this chapter we shift the ground of analysis and begin to question how successful those attempts were in terms of shaping the thoughts and actions of the shopper.

In the introduction to this book I argued that consumer cultures need to be understood as arising at that moment where retail cultures, as constructed by retailers themselves, intermingle with the everyday actions and beliefs of the people who wander retail spaces and gaze at, buy, interpret – and occasionally steal – the goods on display. In other words, consumer cultures are always in flux and are brought into being not simply by manufacturers, retailers and advertisers but by 'consumers' themselves. Different consumer cultures thus lie alongside each other; the retailer and the shopper may have quite disparate though sometimes overlapping understandings of what consumer culture is and their place within it.

In exploring some of these understandings in relation to the 'shopper', it is not my intention to suggest that the oral history employed in this chapter provides a more legitimate or authentic knowledge of consumer cultures in comparison to other forms of historical and cultural analysis. As is now well recognised by oral historians, everyday memory does not provide a firm or unmediated grasp on the 'realities' of everyday life. Indeed, the articulation of historical memory – as much recent scholarship has insisted – is a complex act of invoking and creating a (collective) past, taking up particular subject positions, and presenting a personal narrative through structured genres of social interaction such as the interview. Equally, it is a process through which those who are 'recording' people's stories are involved in a highly mediated and mediating process of defining the historical and the role of the historian.[2] These factors, however, should not be viewed simply as constraints on documenting the past, but rather as themselves facets of how history is made. Conversing with people is useful in the construction of historical interpretation if only because, at the very least, it promises to take the historian out of her or himself (and away from the logic of historical scholarship); to take them beyond what they themselves can read about or imagine. Used dynamically, the information gained and metaphors unleashed by talking with others both extend and lend texture to historical analysis, while positioning memory itself as a means of questioning how history is constructed.

This is particularly important when applied to everyday activities such as shopping. It is relatively easy to trace the construction of retail cultures since an abundance of written records exist. When it comes to the analysis of shopping, to exploring the lived experience of retail forms such as the supermarket, things are not so easy. Yet it is the largely unrecorded aspects of everyday consumption practices that speak of a human depth to those activities, a depth not evident in the celebratory rhetoric of retailers, or indeed in the surface analysis of some social critics. In this sense, the orthodox claim for oral history as giving access to the 'silenced' aspects of everyday life is quite apposite here, even given the difficulties of this sometimes wildly romanticised supposition.[3]

What I want to suggest in this chapter, and also in chapter nine, is that consumption has been 'popularly' as well as intellectually understood as bound up within a framework of attraction/resistance, choice/manipulation, self-expression/conformity, and pleasure/guilt. As such, the act of remembering shopping experiences is an act also of grappling with an ambivalence towards consumption that is born of negotiating (either in the past or the present) these perceived dichotomies. It is an act of reliving and/or inventing that very movement between *participation* and *outsidedness* of which I spoke in the introduction to this book. In the following pages, some aspects of this movement are traced in straightforward, narrative terms – terms in which people's memories are understood as both momentarily grasping the actualities of the past and as working also on an imaginary level. In other words, the interviews detailed here speak of past shopping *practices* while at the same time offering contemporary frameworks of *representing* consumption.[4]

Shopping Dandenong

> For a long time I still went back to my green-grocer, who stayed there, and the butcher for a long, long time before I started getting meat and fruit and vegetables at the supermarket . . . I liked to go to this place where you got personal attention. I was used to it. People called you by name. And when I came back to Dandenong in 1988 I found that I was just one of the busy shoppers. Nobody knew who I was. I miss that, I really miss that.

This is Anetta Barr talking about her experience during the 1960s of the transition to supermarket retailing and how shopping in that decade compares with everyday shopping in the 1990s. By the time the first big supermarket – a New World – arrived in Noble Park (the newly suburbanised outer-Melbourne town where Anetta lived), the old counter-service grocery store had almost entirely disappeared. For people like Anetta, and for younger people as well, everyday shopping has a history which can be grasped through these transitions from one type of shop to another.

In one sense Anetta Barr's commentary can be read as nostalgia; and a great deal of remembering, after all, has an element of this. To treat such remembrances as merely sentimentality, however, robs such observations and statements of their content as cultural critique. Many other people spoken to as part of this study felt a similar sense of loss, although this was not necessarily connected with any sense of looking backwards or of a complete rejection of the 'consumer' present. Indeed, many people expressed a sense of both gain and loss in relation to the changed nature of everyday shopping, and they themselves recognised the difficulties in handling this apparent contradiction. Everyday thought is not neat; contradictions are not simply allowable but are an integral part of this form of observation and critique – and perhaps its strength.

Anetta Barr moved to Dandenong with her parents in 1930 and, after she married, to nearby Noble Park in the late 1940s. In the inter-war years Dandenong, although feeling the effects of the depression, was a thriving rural market town servicing both the surrounding farming areas and its own small population. After World War II, however, and by the time Anetta Barr was in her teens, Dandenong was already being transformed into one of Melbourne's major industrial outer suburbs. By the mid-1950s Dandenong was the new Australian 'home' of International Harvester, H.J. Heinz and General Motors Holden, and was the destination for a large number of post-war migrants.[5] As one of Australia's fastest growing metropolitan areas, Dandenong was of interest also to major retailers. The grocery chains, such as Moran & Cato, Crooks National Stores and Crofts, opened branches in Dandenong in the inter-war years. But it was in the post-war period that retailing in Dandenong was fully transformed in line with the growth of large-scale retailing Australia-wide. Part of this transformation was the arrival of the supermarket.

As Kevin Synott, another long-time Dandenong resident, has commented: 'One of the things we were taught at school was that you should know the name of every business in the main street. As a result you were able to name every shop'.[6] For the school child this parochial lesson in local commerce was probably rather tedious. But for the historian it is invaluable. Many images of the 'traditional' grocery store and of the framework of everyday shopping in the past surfaced while talking with or listening to people in Dandenong, all of whom were in their sixties or older and whose memories were often vivid. Evelyn Mitchell, whose father and mother ran a grocery shop in Dandenong in the inter-war years, described in wonderful detail the store's interior and its products:

> It was a large general store and everything was very solid, massive shelves. And the biscuits for instance, there'd be a whole wall of shelves of biscuits in the biscuit tins, all with their nice labels. And all the cream biscuits were kept on the top rows . . . tremendous variety of biscuits in those days. And they'd be weighed out by the pound . . . There were tins of boiled lollies, fair-sized tins, and they had to be very well sealed every time you used them so they wouldn't get sticky. There was not much packaged in those days . . . And I can remember that you used to buy the butter in big square boxes, a big piece of butter would come from the butter factory. And the customers, they all had their favourite. I think Dad got butter from four different factories. And someone giving their order would want a pound of Korumburra butter, someone else would want a pound of

Western District butter, or Dandenong butter . . . They were all in this big glass case and they would be cut off and then patted nicely, wrapped in grease-proof paper . . . All the things like spices, they all came in boxes or something because I used to love weighing them up, little paper bags, an ounce or whatever it was. And the dates, I remember the dates always came in a great big square the size of the butter. And there was a dipper of water, you had to dampen your hands otherwise you couldn't handle the dates, they'd be so sticky. And I know the men in the shop, they never liked weighing up the pepper because it made them sneeze . . . The honey used to come in a great big tin . . . it would hold about four gallons . . . A big square tin, the honey used to come in that, and it'd be weighed into jars.[7]

For those without such memories of everyday shopping, this description is striking for the sheer proximity between the raw product and the shopkeeper/shopper. Although brands, or at least origins, were clearly already an important consideration in the choice of butter, for example, this grocery shop traded very definitely in unpackaged commodities rather than nationally available packaged products. In fact Evelyn Mitchell only mentions the big manufacturer 'brands' by implication when she refers to 'nice labels'. Similarly, when long-time Dandenong residents Edna and Albert Bramley remembered grocery shopping in the inter-war years, they mentioned Arnott's and Swallow & Ariel biscuits, but concentrated mainly on the layout of the grocery store, its 'raw' products and the friendly interactions across the counter.[8]

This suggests that while manufactured food products were becoming increasingly available in the inter-war period, everyday shopping in the past is not necessarily recalled through a procession of 'much-loved' brands but through more tangible aspects of the shopping experience. Australian manufacturers of food and household goods might have attempted, right throughout the twentieth century, to instil in us all a 'product loyalty', but one of the most notable aspects of the interviews drawn on here was that brand names were rarely used to remember a shopping past. It was not brands that people recalled but specific food products, the interior arrangement of shops, and most of all, the social experience of shopping.

As a much younger person than Anetta Barr, Evelyn Mitchell or Edna and Albert Bramley, one of the ways in which I tried to imagine their past was through existing shops that preserved some aspects of the stores they remembered. The delicatessen is the most obvious example, and 'delis' perhaps offer us now the closest sense of an older style of shopping for everyday goods. In cities such as Melbourne, large open-air markets also preserve something of an older retail culture. In these shopping environments there are still a few stores where butter and cheese cut from the 'block' and biscuits by the bag can be bought. The many small stalls within these markets now provide a sort of historical diorama of an older shopping world. But these markets, thankfully, are not yet simply heritage centres; they are living retail and shopping environments that attest to the manner in which historically different retail and consumer cultures overlay each other. In this sense, the market and the delicatessen are both history and not history. Melbourne's markets, in particular, are certainly illustrative of a past – or a 'tradition' as the television commercials for the Victoria Market insist – but as retail spaces they are not in need of this historical consciousness for their everyday dynamism.[9]

Besides the shop interior and its products, some people had memories of the 'behind the counter' life of the grocery store as well. As we noted previously, grocers had a reputation for selling virtually anything that would reap a profit, no matter how old the stock. Sometimes this was mean-spirited dishonesty. In his written account of life as a 'grocery boy' during the 1930s, Tom Cairns noted how butter and bacon in particular were often sold close to rancidity.[10] But many customers were wise to the quality of the products sold, and in a market town like Dandenong, with a large number of grocers trading, there was little restriction on taking one's custom elsewhere. In this situation less saleable products were shifted through a type of gentle deception rather than outright dishonesty. Albert Bramley commented with good humour on one grocer who mastered the art of massaging consumer perceptions, not just the grocery trade:

> He used to sell plenty of butter and all this kind of thing. So people would come, he was selling Dandenong butter also from the Dandenong butter factory, and they would come in and say 'Oh no, I don't like Dandenong butter, I'll have Western Star'. And they'd name all the different butters that they'd like. So he said 'I'll fix them'. So he thought, 'Now, I'll give it a name'. So he circulated all his customers and he said that he was getting some special butter done called 'Paradise butter'. And it was Dandenong butter. But nobody wanted Dandenong butter, so for this Paradise butter people kept coming in and saying; 'Mr ——, that butter is beautiful, where do you get it from?' He said; 'Manufactured for me especially'. [laughter] And they all loved it . . . beautiful butter.

Evelyn Mitchell recounted a similar tale about her father:

> And I can remember one batch of honey that Dad bought and he tasted it and it was terrible and my mother said 'Oh, no one will

ever buy that'. So he got a bottle of almond essence from the shop. The honey was warmed in the tin in a copper full of hot water and when it was softened a bit Dad added the bottle of almond essence to it. And my mother said that for months after everybody was wanting that special honey which Dad just couldn't get again.

This was a very gentle form of deception in comparison to mass advertising but, to invoke Gail Reekie's argument, it underscores the element of seduction involved in over-the-counter retailing at this time.[11] Clearly, grocers took the 'art of salesmanship' seriously and sought to massage the consumer consciousness, to charm the (predominantly female) shopper. This was equally a game over knowledge. It illustrated in action the invocation to 'give the customer what she wants', and the fact that what she wanted may not always have been what she actually got.

Perhaps what precluded deception from too often turning to outright dishonesty was that the relationship between grocer and customer was characterised by one of give and take and even a certain intimacy. Many people in Dandenong emphasised the social aspects of the 'traditional' store in a way that sometimes smacked of nostalgia but at other times seemed to articulate an acute awareness of shopping as an important social activity. Firstly, there were the remembrances of commercial niceties. Evelyn Mitchell once again:

And I do remember when people paid their account at the end of every month, Dad would always get a great big brown paper bag and he'd give them a bag of beautiful biscuits, not broken biscuits, beautiful biscuits, they always got that when they paid their account.

But there were more substantial ties of friendship between retailer and customer as well. Anetta Barr:

Our grocer was our friend. They knew your family, because they came into the home. Monday morning the grocer came and sat at the table. If it was a very cold morning and he wasn't in a terrible hurry he would even have a cup of tea.

This 'friendship' was still a commercially framed one. It was no doubt imbued with contradictory power relations in terms of the interaction between male grocer and female customer, and the 'servility' which the grocer would be expected to show towards the shopper. But Anetta Barr's comment does illustrate that there was sometimes a depth to that relationship that was dependent on a localised and sustained knowledge of the everyday details of people's lives.

In periods of economic depression or personal hardship, the line between commerce and friendship could become even more blurred. In chapter four we noted how the grocer, even by the late 1950s, was still portrayed as a sort of informal local welfare agency as much as a commercial enterprise. There were historical reasons for this. Grocers had, at times, acted as an arm of a fledgling welfare state. During the depression those unemployed and on 'susso' – sustenance payments from the Commonwealth government – were compelled to register with a grocer and a butcher where an allotted sum of money was to be spent on food. Once again, Anetta Barr offered an evocative reminder of this practice, and a reminder, too, that delivery services were not simply for the well-off but for all those who shopped at the grocer:

> My Dad was many months without work and had to go on what they then called sustenance. No money, just – we were able to put in a list for food to the grocer's, go to the butcher's and buy meat, to a certain value . . . You always had to go to the same one. They had to keep everything down below a certain amount of money. I think meat was about 3s 6d a week, which was around 35 cents. The groceries were, I think, 7s 6d, but that I'm not sure about. But for a family of nine that's not very much, even on costs in those days. My mother used to write out a shopping list. The grocer would come to the house one day and pick it up and bring the order back the next day. If there was too much on order, well something had to be crossed off.[12]

The provision of customer credit further contributed to the welfare status of the grocer. While the practice of credit within grocery retailing was tightened up during the 1930s – and the chains in particular encouraged a more general abandonment of credit within the industry – many independent grocers retained account customers until well into the 1950s. Offering credit, particularly in hard economic times, was risky for the retailer but served to reconfirm a form of commercial practice that looked beyond profit and expressed a certain 'community consciousness'. Maurie Jarvis, another long-time Dandenong resident, illustrated this well when speaking of the depression years:

> A lot of shopkeepers went broke, went insolvent during those days. Anybody that gave credit, you'd see the shops boarded up after some considerable time. It was almost impossible to get credit. The old time grocer like Crumps, and those type of people down the main street, where McEwan's are now, those old people

> that had been the local family grocers for a hundred years, if they
> knew you well enough you'd get a little bit of credit. But most
> people of course would, as soon as they got their sustenance
> money, be in to pay it. But people like the chain stores, Crofts,
> Moran & Cato etc. – cash only, if you didn't have money you
> didn't eat.[13]

Maurie Jarvis's clear bitterness towards the chains is illustrative of the
manner in which chain stores very quickly came to be treated with some
suspicion. In many ways, the chains represented the denial of that 'community consciousness' on which independent grocery retailing had prided
itself during the early twentieth century and to which it continued to cling
until the 1960s. The arrival of the chain store grocer was a first taste for many
people of a different kind of commercial logic; a first taste of the overly
calculating and impersonal in retailing.

This is not to suggest that the chain grocery store was entirely commercially
oriented. Ongoing social relationships were forged between customer and
grocer within chain stores, as in the independent shop. Jack Lightfoot, who
started working for Crofts Stores at 17 years of age, opened the Dandenong
branch of Crofts as manager in 1932. Although Jack acknowledged that there
was always some tension between the chains and the independents, he
suggested that how well the store was received by customers – and by other
grocers – came down to the individual characteristics of the grocer.

Not all memories of 'traditional' grocery shopping, of course, are fond ones.
Fay Hussey, who married during the war and moved to Dandenong at the
beginning of the 1950s, found no reason to miss 'pre-modern' shopping at all.
The years before 1950 were 'tough days' for Fay, and the food available, she
insisted, was often of poor quality and of a very limited variety. Even those
who did feel a sense of loss in regard to the social aspects of everyday shopping in the past drew attention to what they saw as the very limited nature of
the commodities available in pre-1950s Australia. Despite the rapid growth in
the availability of manufactured and packaged foods in the first half of the
twentieth century, such products remained comparatively expensive, and
items like cream biscuits were bought as a treat – at least by many people in
Dandenong – rather than as a standard weekly item. Most people's diet was
largely made up of unchanging staples.

If limited variety was a problem for Anglo-Celtic Australians, the situation
was even worse for post-war immigrants. The food available to the 'New
Australian' in a city such as Dandenong was monocultural. Figuratively
starved of culturally relevant everyday products, Kitty Rynsent recalled the
excitement that surrounded the opening of Dandenong's first continental
delicatessen in the early 1950s:

There was huge excitement because a continental shop was opening up in Lonsdale Street [Dandenong]. And so everybody spread the word, 'Hey guess what, I mean they're going to have some dropjes'. Dropjes are like a licorice. Well we couldn't believe our luck, dropjes. And so up early, shop opens at nine. Well, we were lined up already at eight o'clock. And then there was I don't know how many people in front of us already. Oh this excitement about 'I wonder what they're going to sell?'. I can't even remember whether they had German or Polish. All I was interested in was the Dutch taste, and that's all my parents were interested in and they bought everything they could see. Anyway it was a huge success because they had nothing left on the shelf by the end of the day.[14]

Post-war immigrants in Dandenong not only found Australian food products rather limited, but its shops difficult to negotiate. Where Anglo-Celtic Australians found the personal service of the grocery shop a social experience, some migrants found it utterly frustrating and humiliating. Lily Midro, a Polish (and multilingual) migrant who arrived from Germany in the early 1950s, offered a vivid account of this experience:

Because when it came to the shop, and I want something, and I couldn't express myself what I want. Because these days you've got supermarket. You can only walk in and pick up and put in your basket what you want. But when we came there was no supermarket. There was only shop. We come, we join the queue and we wait till our turn come. And she says, 'What can I do for you?'. So I have to say I want a pound of sugar, I want a pound of flour or whatever. And before I went to the shop, that's why I went to the lady and explained to them, I show her. Flour, like that, and she didn't know what it meant. And then I went to my cupboard and I brought the packet, and I said that's what I want. And she told me that the plain. So I write it down, 'Plain Flour', I want two pounds, say for instance . . . So then, slowly, slowly I would learn . . . So I start to do it, and I start to learn the names what I want. And was hard. And many Australian would stand beside me and they were laughing because they didn't know what I was talking about. And they couldn't help me either, that was funny for them . . .[15]

In light of such difficulties some migrants were offered an amateur but well-meaning assistance in the art of Australian shopping. Edna Bramley recalled:

> I joined the Migration Committee [in Dandenong] which was really a Church group and that was fascinating because I could speak a little French, schoolgirl French, and so there were lots of lasses from Lebanon and they spoke French, and so I thought I was very privileged to take them shopping and take them to the doctor.

But such 'assistance' was limited and many migrants were left to their own devices. In any case, there was a question here of just who was doing the learning. As Lily Midro taught herself to communicate, Anglo-Celtic Australians did much to educate their taste buds. In Dandenong at least, a modernity of sorts initially came in the form of new, cosmopolitan products rather than American-style retailing. Fay Hussey remarked that this was one of the big changes that post-war shopping underwent:

> Then of course all the other people from overseas were coming out here and then gradually a lot more interesting foods crept onto the shelves here too, so it made a difference.
>   Eventually, bit by bit, there were much more interesting things available. Because they were asking for this, that and the shops eventually got them in. I think it made a big difference to the food in Australia, probably the whole of Australia.

Although Fay noted that some people 'went crook' about such change, she personally found it exciting. As a demonstrator of Sunbeam electrical appliances at McEwan's during the 1950s, Fay remembered with some humour the store's rather clumsy attempt to attract Dutch customers by stocking up on wooden clogs.

Soon, however, the shopping cosmopolitanism brought to Dandenong by immigration was joined with a different modernity, a different newness – the rise of American-style retailing.

New Suburbs, New Shops

Many people I talked with or listened to as part of this study did not simply remember shopping in the past, they noted its absence. By far one of the most remembered features of shopping in Dandenong prior to the emergence of the supermarket was that you didn't need to do it. As Jean Cusson put it, 'I think we always went to the market. But you see, people called; the butcher, and the baker, and the grocer, they all called for your orders. So you didn't shop quite as much'.[16] Dorothy Hart reinforced the point, 'Of course those days, too, all the tradespeople came to the door, you didn't have to ever go out and do any shopping if you didn't want to'.[17] In this situation it was, as both Anetta Barr and Fay Hussey pointed out, only the 'bits and pieces' that you would pick up by hand. Often one went into the grocer merely to pay the bill.

Until well into the 1950s, then, shopping was usually undertaken for a specific purpose. Although frequent shopping trips were made by many women, Muriel Norris remembered having very seldom to go into the grocery store at all, since the grocer always picked up her order and delivered it the next day, 'I found it very good because you got what you really needed. You weren't tempted with things that you really couldn't afford [laughter], and it was a very satisfactory life and I missed it'.

As these women and many other people were to find out, supermarket retailing relied precisely on drawing people into the shop in order to get to them to buy more goods. It required also, as we noted earlier, that the shopper do more of the work of the retailer; visit the shop, select and fetch the goods, and even transport them home. Jack Lightfoot, as a past employee of the Crofts company, readily acknowledged this transfer of labour and its contradictory implications for both the grocer and the housewife. As a worker he liked the conversion of Crofts to self-service, though as a skilled grocer he also seemed to speak of the rise of self-service with a certain sense of resignation:

> It had a lot of good points. For argument's sake, you knew when you finished work and all this . . . [it] was more hygienic. I'm not against that part of it. Well, I've got no say, but what I meant is that it was a lot cleaner and all that type of thing . . . It's a coming thing and you got to go with it, that's what it amounts to. I had to adapt meself to it, that's all it amounted to.

Eventually, Jack and the shoppers of Dandenong had to adapt themselves to something much bigger than a Crofts Superette. The Coles company, as we noted before, opened what was then the largest free-standing super-market in Dandenong in November 1963. At the time this was Australia's biggest supermarket with 14 checkouts and over 160 feet of refrigerated cabinets.[18] The Dandenong New World included also, to paraphrase one *Colesanco* article: a 'large meat shop', a 'fresh fruit and vegetable department', a 'modern bakehouse' and a 'luncheonette with seating for 34 people'.[19] The historically significant nature of the arrival of Dandenong's New World was emphasised by the inclusion of 'Four feature windows depicting early land-marks of Dandenong nearly 100 years ago'.[20] Later, in 1965, another equally glamorous New World was opened in the nearby suburb of Noble Park.

The emergence of supermarket retailing in Dandenong gave rise to mixed feelings. The self-service shop had already come to Dandenong in the early 1950s when the McEwan's company converted its large homewares store,

Announcing . .

THE GRAND OPENING OF

McEWAN'S

210 LONSDALE STREET - DANDENONG

SELF-SERVICE GROCERY

DEPARTMENT

THURSDAY, JULY 10

HOW TO SHOP

1. You will find here all types of Grocery, Hardware, etc. neatly arranged on shelves, where all prices are indicated in a clear and easily readable manner;

2. At the entry of the store, you leave your own basket and other purchases with the cashier;

3. You will take a "McEWAN" shopping basket;

4. Move freely in the store, completely at your ease;

5. If you need advice, just apply to the staff;

6. "Serve yourself" — if you see something you like, just "take" it and put it in your "McEWAN'S" basket;

7. **Serve yourself** just means quick service, and **lower prices**, thus saving you time and money;

8. For delivery, follow directions as above, and attach an address label to a McEWAN'S basket and when your shopping is complete, leave with the cashier.

FIRST GRADE TEA 3/7 lb. You Save 5d.	**KIA ORA Tomato Sauce 1/8½** You Save 4½d.	**CORN FLAKES – Large** 2/6½ per pkt. You save 2½d.
HEINZ VARIETY SOUPS – Onion Pea Vegetable Celery Asparagus 3 FOR 5/3 You Save 1/1½d.	**KRAFT CHEESE 1/9 pkt.** Velveeta or Cheddar You Save 2d.	**CUSTARD POWDER –** Dainty Maid. 1/8½ per pkt. You save 4½d.
	CANNED FRUIT – Pears Apricots 2/4½ per tin Peaches. You save 3d.	**COTTEES STRAWBERRY JAM** 1/6. You save 2½d.
TOM PIPER PLUM PUDDINGS 3 FOR 5/- You Save 1/7½	**JOHN BULL OATS 2/- pkt.** You Save 2½d.	**AND A FREE GIFT FOR EVERY CUSTOMER**

DON'T FORGET, LOW PRICES EVERY DAY, AND WE DELIVER FREE, ORDERS 25/- OR OVER

JAMES McEWAN & CO   210 LONSDALE STREET   DANDENONG

Learning to serve yourself: a McEwan's handbill instructs the shoppers of Dandenong on self-service, 1953 (Heritage Hill, Dandenong)

including a grocery section, to self-service in 1953. Similarly, the Dandenong branch of Crooks National Stores and of Crofts Stores converted to semi-self-service in the mid-1950s. Jack Lightfoot recalled the details of this rather half-hearted 'conversion':

> After those rounds [delivery service] they brought in a stunt which was semi [self-service]. They use to call it self-service grocery. But, it was on the style of a supermarket, but only carried about a tenth of the lines. In other words there was no fruit there, there was no meat there, and all this business. Well that went on for about 10 years I s'pose.

At McEwan's the conversion to self-service was rather more comprehensive and American in style. Fay Hussey remembered the opening of the new McEwan's self-service grocery and the way in which people were quickly drawn to this different type of shopping. As a worker at McEwan's she would notice the area outside the turnstiles filled with prams, and the store itself packed with shoppers. Fay, too, was drawn towards the new type of shopping; 'Well, I thought it was a bit exciting in one way because you could actually pick up and handle the stuff and that appealed to me'.

It appealed to some male shoppers as well. With the rise of self-service, some men participated more readily in everyday shopping activities. After the McEwan's self-service store opened, John Crichton, for example, would visit the store regularly while his wife stayed home to look after their children. As John commented: 'I used to do it on a weekly basis with a list after work . . . there used to be quite a few men that'd be in there.'

In contrast, many people insisted that the presence of male shoppers was a rarity within the counter-service grocery store, at least in Dandenong. This was in part because of limited opening hours, which made it difficult for the 'working man' to undertake the weekly shopping. It was reflective also of the very definite status attached to shopping as 'women's work'. As Anetta Barr commented:

> My husband never went shopping, he never went, not food shopping. He used to go Christmas shopping and occasionally clothing . . . Well, he worked long hours. I was home. I never went to work. I just naturally accepted it was my job to keep the home going, do the shopping, and have everything done for him.

Within the traditional grocery store although women sometimes served behind the counter, it was, according to Muriel Norris, always a man who came to get the order. Conversely, apart from the odd male interloper it was mostly women who shopped in the grocery store itself. Fay Hussey agreed.

She noted that you simply didn't see men shopping as much as you do now since they would be 'embarrassed if they met one of their mates'. Fay's husband, however, never minded going to the supermarket – as opposed to the grocery store – and regularly went shopping with a list that she provided for him. Yet having a husband prepared to shop in the supermarket was not always such a convenience. As Fay Hussey noted, 'Of course that was another complaint a lot of wives had, that if their husbands got loose in the supermarket they spent about three weeks' pay picking up things they fancied'. This image of the feral husband is a particularly poignant reminder that while retailers believed it was female shoppers who were driven by uncontrolled desire, men were often far more unrestrained as shoppers, a fact that retailers were rather slow to realise, as we have already noted.

Where men still refused to shop alone, the self-service store sometimes provided the ground on which to shop as a couple. By the 1960s, for example, Anetta Barr's husband was accompanying her shopping. By then for the Barrs shopping had become more of a family outing, something to be done together. 'You would meet other people with their children. The kids used to go off and run up and down the aisles and come back with something interesting and saying, "Mum, can we have this?".'

If, as these memories of everyday shopping suggest, self-service began to provide the ground on which to attract men into the shop, either alone or in the company of women, then perhaps this was due to the sense of independence self-service shopping encouraged. For complex reasons supermarket shopping, although still very much defined as women's work, seemed to be just slightly less feminised than everyday shopping in its pre-self-service form. This is a phenomenon we will explore in more detail in chapter nine.

While Fay Hussey personally liked self-service she recognised that it meant a significant loss of convenience in terms of being able to order everyday goods. For others this factor was, at least initially, simply too much to bear. When Anetta Barr visited the new Crofts Superette in Dandenong in the mid-1950s, she reacted very differently to the absence of a counter:

> I thought it was terrible, I went back to Noble Park because our grocer was still serving from behind the counter . . . I didn't like it, no, I didn't like it. I liked, yes, I liked my little grocer. But once he left Noble Park, well, of course, there was nobody else.

By the time the New World supermarket arrived, however, even Anetta Barr – and others who were uneasy about retail change – felt somewhat excited to have a large, modern store close by. Drawn in by the promise of a more pleasurable place to shop, though without a car to get there, Anetta Barr attempted, with her baby in her arms, to visit the Noble Park New World on opening day, only to have to abandon the trip because of illness.

Despite this setback she eventually experienced the new store, began to shop there regularly and even found some of the social pleasures of old:

> Well it was very exciting to think that Noble Park had their own self-service, New World, you know. We were proud of our little town, it was a growing township that had stood still for a long time. But because I grew up in Dandenong, I remember Noble Park as a very quiet place with, you know, just the one row of shops, and not very exciting place at all. It [the New World] developed it [Noble Park]. It made things more exciting, you met people when you went shopping. I guess we accepted it all. We found that we could go in there and buy everything: fruit, vegetables, meat and our groceries, and milk.

These remembrances give a vivid sense of how real the excitement and modernity of the supermarket were to some people, even given a consciousness of the manner in which the supermarket was extinguishing a shopping past. They give a sense of how people could feel, at one and the same time, both a resistance *and* attraction towards the new retailing. The modernity of which retailers spoke was not false; it had a material presence in the shape of gleaming new shops, unfamiliar products, new shopping experiences. This was a magic that was even more present in areas such as Dandenong and Noble Park where the contrast between the rural old and the urban new was made stark by the rise of the one-stop-shop.

Others recalled also an atmosphere of anticipation surrounding the rise of the supermarket. Muriel Norris, for example, noted that there was great excitement about the opening of the Dandenong New World in 1963. Nevertheless, Muriel as well as Fay Hussey did not visit the new attraction for a long time after it opened simply because, as with Anetta Barr, they lacked the private transport on which supermarket shopping largely depended. For them the taste of modernity had to be postponed. John Crichton, on the other hand, visited the New World not long after it opened and was not only impressed by its size and the range of stock but the historical photos along the side windows; by the effort to give the new store a Dandenong identity.

Once the doors were opened, however, and people began to 'visit', the modernity of the supermarket was no longer purely in the hands of the retailer and the marketing expert. Retailers could construct massive new shops, talk endlessly of a new age and put rockets on the front of their stores to prove it, but the modernity of which they spoke would come to be *interpreted* by those who walked the aisles. If the Australian supermarket had an initial magic, it also had its problems. Some Dandenong residents remained resolutely unimpressed by the big new stores. Muriel Norris put her disappointment in clear terms, a disappointment articulated by others as well:

Through the doors: the opening moments of the Dandenong New World with male managerial staff presiding, 1963 (Coles Myer Archives)

> Went down, went in there and I thought, 'Oh this is a step back in time, you've got to hunt around and find everything yourself' . . . When I first went in there I, no, I disliked it greatly. Because, well all our lives we'd been used to going into a store and asking for what we got, and getting it. There [at the New World] you went in and COLD TURKEY, you had to find it . . . where I would've spent five minutes perhaps getting me few groceries at the grocery store, I was spending quarter of an hour looking for things [laughter] and thinking, they call this PROGRESS! [laughter]

While not everyone so readily questioned the mythology of progress connected with the rise of the supermarket, many people I talked with recognised that the modernity of the one-stop-shop came at a cost, even given its potential excitement. While John Crichton liked the ability to wander the aisles and pop things in the basket that were not on his list, he knew full well that self-service was designed to encourage you to do just this. For non-Anglo-Celtic Australians the effects of the new supermarkets were equally ambiguous in terms of their claim to progress. As Lily Midro pointed out, giving the loss of personal service a new twist:

There was self-service [eventually] and we were very happy. Because we don't have to worry. When we saw something we always grab it and put in the basket . . . But in one way it's alright when it's self-service. But, on the other hand, it's not, because you not learn English . . . Because I see there are times I want and I grab it right. And I don't know what name is. Just grab it and put it in the basket. But if you don't see it, then you learn . . . Then you learn because you speak to the people. But if you don't you never learn.

As these comments and others cited throughout this chapter illustrate, people have reacted to the rise of the supermarket in complex ways. The supermarket was certainly understood by many of the people cited here as emblematic of a post-war Australian modernity, and its emergence was seen to be accompanied by a sense of excitement, progress and convenience. But the notion of progress was also questioned, and the magic and excitement of supermarket retailing was thought through in the context of a known but disappearing past and of the perceived economic and social costs of a retailing present. This thinking through was not necessarily embedded in an unwillingness to change, but rather involved an effort to grasp the various dimensions of the changes that people had experienced.

In this chapter we have explored some of the meanings surrounding the transition between service and self-service within food retailing, particularly as they were seen to take effect in the newly industrialised and suburbanised city of Dandenong. We have only touched on these meanings and the ambiguity of feelings surrounding the rise of the supermarket. Likewise, those very feelings, as now articulated and retold in the 1990s, are mediated through a whole series of factors connected with the act of retelling itself, and with the perceived need to occupy certain critical positions and enact certain aspects of one's self-identity (connected in particular, here, with class, gender and ethnicity). But the opinions and remembrances expressed by the people cited throughout this chapter are not simply to be understood as the murmurings of everyday life, or simply as narrative constructions, as texts. They are more than that. They are an indication of the ways in which retail cultures are taken into possession by the people they are directed towards (both in the concrete and imaginary realms) and are subjected to an everyday critical analysis. It is in a very real sense through this process of *taking hold of* and *thinking about* everyday shopping environments and activities that people contribute to the making of consumer cultures. In the following and final section of this book we thus shift the focus of analysis from the rise of the post-war supermarket to its more recent development and the manner in which, in contemporary Australia, this process of taking hold and thinking through continues.

Part III

Familiar Places

Chapter 7
Magic Futures

The magic of the new doesn't last. The supermarket, like the department store or the shopping mall, can be a bizarre, circus-like place that transfixes the consumer with abundance and choice. When it first emerged in post-war Australia, any such power of the modern corporate supermarket to transfix in this way was at its height. However, the supermarket is a rather more shadowy environment than the department store or the mall since it can more readily present as mundane, as part of the everyday activity of living and thus as potentially boring and routine, particularly as people get used to it. As such, the magic of the big corporate supermarket is hard to maintain.

Supermarkets straddle the divide between consumption as fantasy and consumption as necessity. Historically they have been central to the construction of consumer cultures in the West, if only because the supermarket is one of the most regularly visited retail environments, and because it deals in food and everyday goods. The supermarket, as we noted in the introduction, is a particularly useful retail space to study because it embodies, perhaps more than any other, the ambivalent, indefinite nature of consumption. In wandering the supermarket one enters into a continuum between enjoyment and tedium, contentment and anger.

As the Australian supermarket came of age throughout the 1960s, retailers were forced to confront this transition from the new to the familiar, from the magic of modern retailing to the mundanity of a no longer new world. In this chapter we discuss developments within supermarket retailing from the 1970s to the present, tracing the manner in which retailers dealt – and continue to deal – with shifts in the nature of the 'consumer marketplace'. We begin also to explore the manner in which the very logic of large-scale supermarket retailing both facilitates and undermines the power of the retailer to construct and control consumer cultures.

Modernity Undermined, Postmodernity Emergent?

As the 1960s came to an end, the emphasis on pleasure within supermarketing was gradually fading, partly in the face of new economic imperatives. By the 1970s the talk of glamour, excitement and newness was giving way to a more mundane emphasis on cheapness as the supermarket became a more familiar aspect of everyday life, and as retailers pursued economies of scale in the context of an increasingly competitive retail market.

The supermarket as a retail form remained largely unchanged throughout the 1970s and 1980s. There were, however, significant changes to the commercial context in which it operated. During the 1970s the number and the size of supermarkets continued to grow, while the corporate chains increased their overall share of grocery sales nationally. These companies also sought to further diversify their operations by introducing to Australia the discount department store, a sort of glorified, self-service variety store, the first of which was K Mart. At the same time retailing in Australia was further restructured by the emergence of the hypermarket, the discount grocery store and the convenience store.

The first of the K Mart stores was opened by Coles, in partnership with the North American Kresge corporation, in the Melbourne suburb of Balwyn in 1969.[1] By 1974 Coles had opened sixteen K Marts, all of which incorporated a groceries section. This complemented its 197 New World Supermarkets, 116 smaller Food Markets, and 240 variety stores.[2]

Woolworths matched and bettered this expansion with the opening of its first, saccharinely named 'Woolworths Family Centres' in Brisbane in 1969. Family could not exactly be bought here, but it could be consolidated by way of the family outing, and the company promoted these centres as the place to do so. By 1973 Woolworths was operating 24 centres, renamed in the late 1970s as Big W Discount Stores.[3] Like Coles, Woolworths continued to focus on increasing its overall number of retail outlets. By 1977 Woolworths operated 238 large supermarkets, 207 smaller food stores and 132 variety stores.[4]

The Safeway and Franklins chains were equally bent on increasing store numbers. By 1977 Safeway operated 60 supermarkets while Franklins ran 75.[5] In the same year, Australia's four major supermarket chains secured between them a 47 per cent share of the national groceries market. Woolworths led the way with a sizeable 18.3 per cent share, while Coles followed just behind with 18.1 per cent.[6]

This consolidation and growth of the major supermarket chains occurred despite the economic recession of the 1970s. In 1975 inflation, as measured by the consumer price index, had rocketed to over 16 per cent a year and unemployment had risen to 4.5 per cent of the workforce.[7] Although company reports complained bitterly about government economic mismanagement, interventionary measures such as the establishment by the Whitlam government in 1973 of the Prices Justification Tribunal, and the so-called 'wages spiral', all this seemed to do corporate supermarketing little harm. Both Coles and Woolworths recorded record profits in the late 1970s, a result made possible by rising consumer expenditure, merger and acquisition, and a further shift in the supermarket workforce towards part-time and casual employment. Of importance also in the maintenance of company profits was increased 'shop-floor' efficiency facilitated by the computerisation of stock control, and eventually of sales at the checkout.[8]

The 1970s in Australia witnessed the end of the 'long boom' and, as elsewhere in the Western world, the beginnings of a redistribution of income and wealth that would have important implications for the nature of retail markets. Accompanying this was a shift in employment practices throughout the whole of the Australian labour market, as in other industrialised countries. The term post-Fordism has been used by neo-Marxist theorists to describe these recent transitions within Western economies.[9] Theorists have suggested that capitalist economies, faced with economic crisis in the mid-1970s, shifted rapidly from a Fordist emphasis on mass production and mass consumption to a new framework of industrial and commercial practices emphasising *flexibility* in the processes of production, the organisation of work and the marketing of consumer goods and services.

The aim of this has been to allow a swifter response by capitalist enterprise to changing economic circumstances. An emphasis on casual and contract employment, for example, means that a workforce can be 'shed' more easily in tough economic times, while the emphasis on a multi-skilled workforce ensures that labour can be transferred between different tasks more efficiently. Accompanying this has been a continuing shift to a post-industrial and more feminised workforce; that is, a decline in blue-collar work and a dramatic rise in the number of people employed in the services sector.[10] An equally important part of this growth of service employment has been the shift to new information technologies and the rise of computer-based industries.

In this climate, theorists have suggested, the old emphasis on the production of standardised, uniform commodities has been increasingly replaced, or at least joined, with smaller-batch production and high levels of product differentiation. The mass market for consumer goods and services is therefore seen as having become fragmented into segments of consumer taste, lifestyle and economic power, and these increasingly differentiated consumer markets are in part a very product of shifts in the nature of the workforce and of resulting income distribution.

Transformations within Australian retailing during the 1970s and on into the 1980s can be seen as mirroring some of these broad changes in the nature and culture of capitalist economies. Nevertheless, concepts such as post-Fordism remain problematic, not least because of the tendency of some writers to exaggerate the extent of recent transitions, and to ignore the enormous unevenness with which different people, different world regions, and individual countries experience structural economic change.[11]

Within Australian retailing it was the emergence of yet more 'new' retail forms that signalled the unevenness of this transition towards post-Fordist patterns of distribution and consumption. By the late 1970s, in pursuit of even greater economies of scale, the larger retailers in Australia began experimenting with the European concept of hypermarkets. The identifying features of a hypermarket were basically size, along with a proportion of sales devoted to 'non-food items'.[12] Safeway opened the first Australian hypermarket in the Melbourne suburb of Endeavour Hills in 1979. With a selling space of 60 000 square feet this was at the time the biggest Safeway supermarket in the world, eclipsing even its North American siblings.[13]

The larger companies were slow to follow suit. Although Coles combined some New World Supermarkets and K Marts into the 'Super K' in 1982 as a gesture towards the hypermarket, supermarkets in Australia generally remained well below hypermarket size. In fact, Coles abandoned the Super K concept in 1988. Even the slightly lesser 'giant', the superstore, was not to take as firm a hold in Australia as it did in other countries such as Britain.[14]

Hypermarkets were contradictory retail forms. On the one hand they seemed to reconfirm a belief in mass markets and highly organised and centralised forms of distribution, a point that does not sit easily with a post-Fordist view of their emergence. Yet, culturally, they seemed to be the pre-eminent marker of certain aspects of postmodernity, transforming the supermarket into a 'hyperspace'.[15] This mirrored the transformation of the shopping mall into what some social commentators saw as a self-contained consumer theme-park in which all sense of reality could be suspended as malls became larger and more carnival-like.

It is for this reason that the shopping mall, and other retail environments such as the hypermarket, have been understood by some recent critics of consumer culture as emblematic of the emergence of postmodernity itself. By the mid-1980s, the North American critic Fredric Jameson was speaking of the postmodern shopping space as a 'hyperspatial' environment in which social reality was transformed into a series of fleeting images and disconnected locales, an environment in which we become lost in a seemingly timeless and disorienting commercial space of countless levels and endless aisles.[16] Jameson's analysis drew on the concept of 'hyperreality', a term utilised by the French theorist of postmodernity, Jean Baudrillard, to describe the manner in which under the dominating influence of media and consumer cultures people lose an ability to distinguish between the real and the simulated. Within Baudrillard's increasingly negativistic interpretation and nihilistic embracement of the consumer present, the real eventually becomes lost to us; the experience of postmodernity becomes lived through media and commercially generated 'virtual realities' in which what is actually real can no longer be grasped.[17]

Jameson's negative assessment of postmodern retail forms as expressive of a socially destructive hyperreality, as well as the even more influential work of Baudrillard, intersected with the rise of postmodernism as an intellectual field.[18] A fuller exploration of this is beyond the scope of this study. It should be noted, however, that this analysis has itself been the subject of substantial critique, not least because of the manner in which it speaks of postmodernity as a generalised experience and seemingly fails to recognise the manner in which retail environments are made into sociable places by those who *use* them. Within much of the recent cultural studies of consumption, for example, the consumer present has also been understood through the concept of an emerging postmodernity, but both the dismissiveness of Jameson and the negativism of Baudrillard have been rejected in favour of a less totalising and more active conception of consumer practices and environments. Moreover, theoretical speculation about the cultural effects of postmodern retail environments is not necessarily applicable to Australian conditions; Jameson's American consumer hyperspace is not simply the Australian shopping centre or hypermarket with a different accent. While shopping centres and supermarkets in Australia grew in size and number during the 1970s and 1980s, these retail forms have remained considerably smaller and less 'virtual' in comparison to those in the United States, Canada, Japan and elsewhere.[19]

If the Australian supermarket – and the mall – differed from some of their overseas counterparts in the extent to which supermarkets had gone postmodern, those supermarkets were, on a more mundane level, further differentiated by the slowness with which they developed 'house brands'.[20] Coles launched its own 'Farmland' label in the early 1970s, and Woolworths launched a house brand at much the same time. These brands comprised a narrow range of high-turnover food and household items, but never really challenged manufacturers' brands in terms of sales. It was the so-called 'generics', first introduced by Franklins in 1978, that proved popular as low-price products. Generics were no-name or plain-label products.

Low price was in fact the key to supermarketing by the late 1970s and into the 1980s. This emphasis on cheapness was decidedly ordinary rather than wrapped up in the consumer excitement of postmodern retailing. Although Safeway insisted that its supermarkets were 'Everything you want from a Store, and a Little Bit More', this was really the tail-end of promoting supermarkets as somehow bigger than life itself. The trend towards 'price consciousness', as retailers called it, was reflected in the emergence of the discount grocery stores set up in opposition to the chains. With almost war-like names such as Jack the Slasher and Tom the Cheap, this was a return to an older, 'original' form of supermarketing, one which was a decidedly unglamorous, price-oriented form of self-service reliant on a high turnover of nationally branded goods.

But there were contradictory trends as well, indicating a differentiation in the wants of consumers – or as retailers liked to call it, a market segmenta-tion – and yet further signs of an emerging postmodernity. By the late 1970s retailers began talking of the consumer driven by 'time consciousness' rather than 'price consciousness'. The result was the arrival of the convenience store, the first of which, a 7 Eleven, was opened in the Melbourne suburb of Oakleigh in 1977.[21] Here was another return, this time to the smaller self-service superette. But it was a return embedded in a radically altered cultural context. The convenience store offered a limited array of goods, though far more than the local milk bar with which it mainly competed, at markedly higher prices than the supermarket. Its drawcard was that it made retailing 'timeless' and gave even the 'local shop' a global form; it opened day and night and it made an internationally recognisable image out of this very convenience and the overbright, carefully designed sales space in which the products could be bought. By 1987, 124 7 Eleven stores were operating Australia-wide and were competing with 78 Food Plus stores and 47 Majik Market stores.[22]

The rise of the convenience store was also linked to changes in the gendered nature of everyday shopping. If a majority of shoppers in the supermarket were women, in the convenience store the opposite was the case. One study reported that in the mid-1980s, 60 per cent of convenience store shoppers were male, 60 per cent were aged between 18 and 34, and the average visit lasted three minutes.[23]

The high use of convenience stores by men seemed to confirm a belief that men were somehow less organised than women in their food purchases, less economical in their spending and – contrary to the image of the rational male consumer – more ready to buy on impulse. Supermarket retailers had long recognised this but were slow in their attempts to dismantle the highly gendered nature of everyday shopping and to challenge the stereotype of the impulsive woman. Cultural historians in both Britain and Australia have suggested, however, that by the 1980s men were being purposefully drawn in to the terrain of consumption, and that shopping spaces such as the mall and department store were becoming more sexually ambiguous in line with a postmodern emphasis on diversity and the fragmentation of sexual and social boundaries.[24] As Gail Reekie has argued, within some areas of leisure retailing during the 1980s space and gender were becoming uncoupled.[25]

Yet the rise of the 'genderless' consumer – and I think we have to remain cautious about the use of this concept – has not simply affected leisure retailing. It is not simply the case that the supermarket has been left untouched and remains simply a functional and purely female shopping space. The separation between functionality and leisure within retailing – between what retailers call convenience and comparison shopping – has never been clear-cut. Convenience shopping is usually defined as shopping within regularly visited and conveniently located stores for the 'essentials'; that is, groceries, household items and basic clothing. Comparison shopping, on the other hand, is less functional, and less likely to be perceived as a chore and more as an outing, in which various goods – often to adorn the self or the household – are compared and a choice is made. In practice, of course, everyday convenience shopping does not lie entirely outside the realm of leisure and comparison shopping completely within it. Rather, shopping as I have argued throughout this book is subject to a continuum between pleasure and frustration, need and desire; a continuum that is applicable to all forms of consumption. Over the last three decades men have increasingly been drawn into the supermarket as well as the mall, and they have entered because of both need and attraction, and due to a gradual weakening of the cultural meanings attached to everyday shopping as an unskilled female task.

By the early 1980s supermarket shopping was clearly becoming a less feminised activity. One study of supermarket shopping in Melbourne suggested that nearly 35 per cent of shoppers were male and 86 per cent of those men took either a complete or partial responsibility for the household shopping.[26] Men, however, were more likely to be seen in inner-urban rather than suburban supermarkets, suggesting that the cosmopolitan space of the city continued to provide more ground on which to 'gender-bend' consumption.[27] More recently, one market study has suggested that there was a 110 per cent increase in the number of men buying groceries throughout the 1980s.[28] This study tellingly dubbed these male shoppers 'Mrs Men', thus still doggedly clinging to a notion of everyday shopping as essentially feminine even though it urged grocery retailers to target the male consumer.

Although indicating a degree of change, these statistics hide a certain complexity attached to the rise of the male supermarket shopper. At the end of the 1980s women still retained the main responsibility for everyday shopping, and were still the majority of supermarket shoppers. What is more, men and women do not necessarily think about and experience supermarket shopping in the same way. One British consumer study – which talked of the dramatic increase in male supermarket shoppers in England during the 1980s – suggested that men are much more likely to buy on impulse because of an ignorance of, or lack of interest in, everyday necessities.[29] Moreover, this study further argued that in assuming shopping duties, many men were simply opting for the least onerous way of taking on some responsibility for housework.[30] It may well be, then, that during the 1980s everyday shopping within countries such as Australia and England became a relatively new and somewhat easy means through which changing family and household arrangements and even a certain 'new age' masculinity could be expressed, a proposition that is explored more fully in chapter nine.

The apparent trend towards an increasingly 'convenience-oriented' and sexually and socially fragmented retail market in Australia posed a potential threat to the large supermarket chains. So much so, that the 1980s were described by one industry observer as signalling the decline of the conventional, mass-oriented supermarket.[31] This was overstatement. The supermarket chains were in a position to compete effectively with new retail ventures such as the convenience store, and by the mid-1980s the three big chains, Coles, Woolworths and Franklins, accounted for almost 65 per cent of grocery sales nationally.[32] The two main voluntary chains, Associated Australian Warehouses and Composite Buyers, accounted for an additional 34 per cent of sales.[33] This made the Australian groceries market one of the most highly concentrated retail markets in the world in terms of ownership.[34] The further growth in the market share of the chains occurred throughout a decade in which the Australian economy dipped in and out of recession, consumer expenditure increased at an annual average rate of 2.5 per cent, and the proportion of consumer expenditure accounted for by food dropped from 16.8 per cent in 1981/82 to 16.1 in 1986/87.[35]

Yet there *was* a sense in which the supermarket was in decline. During the 1980s retailers increasingly believed that the supermarket was losing its mass appeal as an emblem of convenience and modernity, in part because the notion of the mass market itself was coming undone. Now, even leading retailers, rather than just a few prescient retail experts, began to speak of the supermarket as having become too depersonalised and as unable to satisfy the desires of an increasingly discriminating and differentiated consumer market. Thus, in 1987 Bevan Bradbury (former chairman of Coles Myer) expressed anger at the highly impersonal nature of shopping in an almost wistful longing for the face-to-face relations of the traditional store. 'What we have not computerised or automated', Bradbury warned, 'is the customer's need to be recognised or the means of satisfying that'.[36]

Excitement and the promise of tomorrow had in fact given way to confusion in the minds of retailers as to just what had been created. Other industry observers, such as Michael Collins of the Australian Centre for Retail Studies, now chastised the retail industry for having become too 'systems or operations driven rather than customer driven'.[37] Likewise, Linden Brown argued that the concentration on price and on systematically run 'mass' stores had led to the neglect of 'less tangible consumer needs'. 'As the stores get larger', Brown wrote:

. . . operations become depersonalised and routine. Research shows that very few people enjoy the prospect or the experience of grocery shopping. What was once considered to be a pleasurable experience has become a chore to be completed as quickly and as painlessly as possible. It is not clear whether present attitudes can be reversed.[38]

The predicament was stated even more forcefully, and patronisingly, by Philip Luker, the long-time editor of the industry magazine *Foodweek*:

Supermarket customers are bored, and who can blame them? There is little to get excited about in boring supermarkets full of boring products and staffed by bored employees. Homemakers have more interesting things to do than their mothers, who in the 1950s and 60s escaped from their boring homes to go super-market shopping.[39]

Luker could hardly have fitted more boredom in here. Complaints such as this indicated that somehow things had gone wrong, not economically but in terms of the retail cultures constructed throughout the previous three decades. The promise of tomorrow had not been delivered. Autonomy had yielded anchorless shoppers who had no feeling of identity with the massive stores they shopped in. Abundance had yielded boredom. In short, the retail rockets of the 1960s had fallen back to earth and modernity was failing.

In the late 1980s it was estimated that 18 000 shoppers passed through the average supermarket each week, 41 per cent of them making a purchase and each spending, on average, 21.5 minutes in the store.[40] The number of products stocked in the supermarket had also reached new heights. Franklins stocked up to 10 000 items, Coles and Woolworths, 6000 to 7000, and the warehouse supermarkets about 11 000 items.[41] Most of these products went through the checkout by way of optical scanning of their bar codes, first introduced to Australia in 1982. Similarly, EFTPOS – Electronic Funds Transfer at Point of Sale – was soon to become a standard feature of many stores. By this time, too, Australia had become well and truly 'over-shopped' and observers were speaking of a saturated market. Franklins operated 177 supermarkets, Coles 446 and Woolworths 466.[42]

But just as the supermarket reached its pre-eminent position as an institution of everyday life, social and cultural conditions seemed to undercut the achievement. The corporate supermarket, as we noted in the intro-duction to this chapter, has always been that retail space where the mythology of shopping as the ultimate leisure experience has been most difficult to maintain. By the late 1980s Australian retailers were acknowl-edging this and talking of the need to build new forms of identity between the shop and the shopper, ones that recognised consumer differentiation and remade the social understanding of everyday shopping as embedded in convenience, choice, comfort and sociability. Retailers no longer thought it adequate to leave the shopper alone and offer them ever more abundance. They were preparing, yet again, to take hold of a future and to remake the notion of supermarketing as pleasure. In doing so, retailers were looking to construct a different type of supermarketing and were even beginning to speak of the eventual end of the supermarket itself as a way of fulfilling these goals. Here was a loss of faith in modernity, or at least one version of it, as progress through uniformity and an inflexible systems theory. Here, too, was an emerging view of the social world as becoming increasingly fragmented rather than homogeneous, along with a belief that pluralistic and local marketing strategies, rather than mass-oriented ones, were now necessary. This was not to displace the construction of large-scale retail cultures, nor was it simply to make shopping into a universalised postmodern experience. Nevertheless changes in retailing were underway and were to be further cemented as Australia entered the 1990s.

Revolution Renewed

By mid-1992 there were 9486 retail outlets in Australia officially described as supermarkets or grocery stores.[43] This represented a 10 per cent drop in the number of these stores since 1986.[44] In terms of turnover, however, supermarket sales increased by 16 per cent over the same period.[45] These 9486 stores employed over 180 000 people – or 17 per cent of the retail workforce – and represented the largest single area of retailing in terms of employees and turnover.[46] About 60 per cent of those who worked in supermarkets were employed part-time and most, about 63 per cent, were female.[47] The historically entrenched demarcation between men and women within retailing continued unabated. Senior management positions within supermarketing remained overwhelmingly dominated by men. Within Coles Myer, for example, by 1992 there were no female senior managers employed within the supermarketing division and no women on the Board of Directors.[48]

As the 1980s came to a close the national groceries market remained even more firmly dominated by the corporate giants, Woolworths and Coles Myer, followed by Franklins and the independent wholesalers supplying 'banner group' stores.[49] By 1992 Coles operated 383 large supermarkets (as well as over 120 Bi-Lo discount food stores) with 8000 to 10 000 items stocked in its smaller stores and about 15 000 items in its larger ones.[50] By this time, too, Coles had abandoned its New World slogan. Supermarketing was not new anymore, it was an integral part of Australian everyday life. Woolworths by the end of 1992 operated 415 supermarkets and nearly 100 other discount food stores. At the same time the company was embarking on an expansion plan to build 10 large supermarkets a year during the 1990s.[51]

Five years later, Woolworths had met and was bettering this prediction. With 548 supermarkets trading in 1997, serving nine million customers a week and taking 35.1 per cent of supermarket sales nationally, the company was geared to opening 15 new supermarkets annually until the year 2000.[52] Coles also had grabbed more of the market by 1997. With 510 stores in operation and serving four and a half million customers a week, Coles supermarkets accounted for 27.9 per cent of supermarket sales.[53]

The increasing market share of the large retailer and the continuing struggle between big and small business framed much of the public debate about retailing as Australia entered the 1990s. This debate was brought to a head in late 1994 when the then Labor Prime Minister Paul Keating addressed an audience at the 'Supermarket Show' in Sydney, organised by the Australian Supermarket Institute. Keating insisted that the government would be forced to intervene if the large retail firms continued to increase market share by taking over smaller retailers.[54] This comment came not long after the Trade Practices Commission had blocked the Coles Myer takeover of Foodland, the grocery wholesaler supplying numerous independent supermarkets, on the grounds that it would involve an unacceptable restriction on competition.[55] But such intervention has been rare, and Paul Keating's comments came at a time when the large retailers had long secured market dominance, making a nonsense of the threat of concerted government intervention.

Other Australian governments were actively encouraging an expansion in large-scale retailing rather than any curtailing of it. In 1993 the Kennett Liberal government in Victoria approved a massive expansion of Melbourne's regional shopping centres, dismissing claims that such development would further decimate suburban shopping strips and centralise shopping in large, dispersed centres.[56] The way was now left open for the construction of the 'mega-mall', sibling of the old and now tired regional centre. The Shopping Towns of Melbourne and the Penrith Plazas of Sydney have now been overhauled and some doubled in size to appeal to the 45 per cent of shoppers who, marketing experts insist, do not go to malls primarily to shop but to be entertained. The new emphasis is thus on ambience, 'themed' precincts, and on recreating the old, intimate atmosphere of the very shops that the mall puts out of business. The aim is to get people to stay longer in these environments and thus, of course, increase the chance that they will spend more money.[57] This renewed and seemingly unstoppable push towards larger shopping centres has signalled an accompanying return to a view of Australia as drastically 'over-shopped', with independent retailers calling for a stop to further development.[58]

Most feared of all by small retailers, and even the large department stores, has been the emergence of 'niche marketing' through specialty independent or chain retailers offering a boutique shopping experience and through the 'category killers' – as they have become known – specialising in just one line of products, such as toys or white goods, and selling them at highly competitive prices in hypermarket-size stores. Of equal concern to small retailers has been the more recent emergence of 'co-branding' in which major retail companies join forces by having a 'co-presence' in the one site. Thus Hungry Jacks can be frequented at the same time as buying Shell petrol, or the Commonwealth Bank can be accessed while shopping in Franklins Big Fresh.[59]

But the industry talk surrounding retailing in the 1990s has been about social and cultural issues as well as commercial and economic restructuring. This has been coupled with a sense of retailing in 'crisis', born of a highly competitive, corporately dominated market, the race for new retailing concepts, ever larger shopping malls, competition from 'global' retailers, and pressure from the so-called discerning consumer looking for new shopping experiences as well as products. As we noted earlier, the supermarket has remained largely unchanged since its emergence in the 1960s despite its partial transformation into a large retail store operated through information technologies. This partial stasis is now being challenged. Talk of a modernity and of a postmodernity in relation to supermarkets has re-emerged despite, or perhaps because of, the perceived loss of customer satisfaction and of a 'magic' within supermarketing.

Quite apart from a comparatively rapid shift to part-time employment during the 1980s – and therefore to an even more flexible retail workforce – recent developments in information technologies are now seen as potentially transforming the nature of everyday shopping once again. The futurists of retailing now talk and produce prototypes of electronic price labels, mobile electronic checkouts, and 'smart' shopping trolleys with video displays of in-store specials. Above all, retailers speak now of the rise (or rather re-emergence) of home shopping, where items are ordered through a home computer terminal and delivered without the need to visit a supermarket at all.[60] As one television program on the future of shopping proclaimed in 1994, all this pointed to, not the end of the supermarket, but the end of the shopping we hate to do, leaving only the shopping we love.[61] The supermarket is to become, according to this scenario, an exotic food mall full of quality products enjoyable to touch, smell and select.

There is industry talk, then, of yet another retailing revolution, of the final death of old-style strip shopping and the small store, and the emergence of something different. The language of change no longer involves images of outer space, but it remains the language of the masculine frontier. One retail expert, Phil Ruthven, who pops up regularly in the media as a market futurologist, speaks of the next decade in retailing as involving the 'final shoot-out at the OK Corral' between big and small retailers.[62] Once again, spurred on by the discontent that many people now feel towards the supermarket, retailers are propagating the belief that all the future holds is the virtual end of necessity shopping and a realm of pleasure sought out in 24-hour mega-malls with gourmet grazing, specialty boutiques and vast entertainment facilities.

This re-emergence of a futurism within retailing is fascinating for the manner in which it signals a return to, rather than any great departure from, an older discourse of retail change. During a 1994 edition of *Lateline* on ABC television which covered the future of retailing, various 'experts' spoke with almost enuretic enthusiasm of the rise of 'new' malls which recreated the shopping pleasures of old, served as community centres and made shopping into leisure.[63] These retail prophets were seemingly oblivious to the fact that promises of modernity and magic futures had a *history*; that the talk of the end of necessity shopping and of consumption as the ultimate pleasure was not new at all.

What is new, of course, is the technologies available to the retailer, and the social and cultural terrain on which they are to be utilised. Home shopping, for example, although often conceived by the retailer as simply a return to home delivery and pushed as a convenience concept, is not that at all. The technologies of ordering goods have now changed – the computer is the primary tool, as opposed to the phone or face-to-face contact. The social networks in which people operate have also altered radically over the last 50 years, suggesting that the rise of home shopping might be putting a system in place that could further encourage impulse buying in the interest of retail profits and add to levels of social isolation. Scanning technology and the increasing use of credit cards allow the collection of specific data on individual shoppers relating to spending patterns, food choice, frequency of shopping trips and so on. This is a potentially powerful 'marketing tool' now being vigorously explored by the major retailers. Yet it also raises questions of privacy and of the cultural meaning of 'profiling' people as consumers.

These issues are ignored by retailers, industry futurologists and financial journalists in favour of the same kind of wide-eyed marvelling at retail progress that accompanied the rise of the supermarket. One gob-smacking headline in *The Australian* announced in December 1993 that 'Shopping is becoming a Leisure Experience', seemingly without any realisation that this announcement might be just a touch late – at least a century or so.[64] Retailing has little historical consciousness. It has a present and a future, and the past is always a fading memory that often goes without recognition at all other than as a nostalgic backdrop to corporate expansion. Retailers therefore continue unselfconsciously to draw on the language of the 1950s and 60s to promote their commercial endeavours. As one mall manager in Sydney argued, in words that mirrored those of an unacknowledged past, 'If there is any level of success it is because they [malls] become places where people have a level of participation and ownership'.[65]

Yet for all this, the talk of retailing in the 1990s is also much altered and still somewhat confused. As the market is seen to fragment, so does the style of shopping that is focused upon. In the early 1990s Michael Collins of the Australian Centre for Retail Studies usefully identified a number of emergent trends in Australian retailing including a further concentration of ownership, a proliferation of different kinds of retail formats, a new 'consumer orienta- tion' (or an emphasis on customer satisfaction), a further move into informa- tion technologies, and a growing internationalisation of retail ownership. Collins also emphasised the importance of differentiation and positioning within retailing, that is, on retail companies targeting particular 'market segments' or 'micro-markets' and seeking to differentiate themselves from competitors by appealing to these different consumer niches.[66] Above all, then, the 1990s has, it appears, signalled the end of the mass market. It is no longer possible, retailers insist, to talk of targeting the middle 80 per cent. Ironically, retailers and cultural analysts now agree on one thing; there is no 'middle' or 'mass' anymore, there is just diversity and continual change.

For this very reason, the corporate supermarket chains are now seeking to continually refurbish their stores and to experiment with new retail formats and products in order to keep pace with this perceived volatility in consumption patterns. The current patterns are seen to have involved, as one commentator put it, a 'convulsive change' in the nature of food shopping away from the big weekly or fortnightly shop towards more regular and highly selective purchasing.[67] On average people now visit the supermarket three times per week. In line with this, corporate supermarketing has, throughout the 1990s, placed increasing emphasis on the provision of fresh produce 'freed' from seasonal fluctuations in supply, on the expansion and development of 'quality' house-branded products, and on 'ready-to-eat' foods. Thus emphasis is also placed on the tropes of food shopping as lifestyle choice, consumer discernment and culinary cultural diversity.[68] As Mr Reg Clairs, Managing Director of Woolworths, declared in January 1997:

> There will be a constant shift now in terms of requirements from the consumers towards a greater convenience aspect and a greater move towards a more casual lifestyle. It's a whole new global phenomenon as we move towards the new millennium and the babies of the baby boomers mature into consumers . . . and I don't think we will ever revert back again to what we may have described as conventional shopping.[69]

Despite this lifestyling of the market and the death of convention, the consumer is nevertheless still sometimes spoken of in general terms, and still conceived of as a knowable entity. One industry survey conducted in 1996 sought to breathe life back into an old retailing favourite by classifying the supermarket shopper into four types. The survey identified 35 per cent of shoppers as 'supermarket lovers', 22 per cent as 'elitists', another 22 per cent as 'price-conscious shoppers', and 21 per cent as 'ready-to-eaters'.[70] The 'elitists' were the ones who disliked supermarket shopping, hence the use of negative terminology to describe them.

If shopper typologies have been revived, so too has the notion of consumer sovereignty, and of consumer citizenship. Indeed, the 1990s are variously spoken of as the age of the discerning, demanding, time-conscious, convenience-oriented consumer, and as the decade of the 'promiscuous shopper' shunning store loyalty and, in economic terms, literally putting it about.[71] The 1990s consumer, then, is being characterised (and sexualised yet again) as a sort of shopper dominatrix, shaping rather than being shaped by retail change, asserting consumer rights and economic citizenship. This coincides with a more general political shift within Western countries towards a reconceptualisation of individual rights, civic responsibility and even collective identity as expressible through consumption practices. Although 'Thatcherite' inspired, this impetus towards consumer citizenship is evident also in potentially 'oppositional' practices such as 'green' or 'pink' consumerism.[72]

Issues of citizenship aside, Hugh Mackay, taking a slightly different tack, has spoken of the consumer of the 1990s as 'talking about ways of escape'.[73] What they want to escape from, asserts Mackay, are the anxiety and in-security resulting from the enormous social change of the past few decades. People now realise, so the Mackay narrative goes, that the 'me generation' of the 1960s resulted in a 'value shedding', leaving people with a sense of emptiness. As a consequence, consumers (by which Mackay means people) want to regain a sense of shared morality and stable community identity.

Retailers have always taken such overblown social commentary seriously and they continue to do so. Hence the renewed talk within retailing of community of customer orientation and personal choice. This is heralded as a turn towards, to use the wonderful phrase of current retailing discourse, 'relationship marketing'; that is, selling by forging a human rather than simply commercial link between retailer and individual customer. The retail-ing wheel, then, turns full circle. Of course, a sense of community and a sociability is there within modern shopping environments, but this is often in spite of the efforts of retailers rather than because of them. Retailers' images of community are always shallow precisely because their principal interest is not in community per se, but its utility as a means of drawing people into shopping spaces. It is important then, as I have argued throughout this book, to speak of two communities, two sociabilities, two cultures of the shop: one thinly conceptualised by the retailer, the other made complex by the shopper.

Relationship marketing: the promotional smile of Woolworths (Woolworths *Company Profile* 1991, Woolworths Limited)

If retailers have continued to be drawn into the 'romance of retailing', the mainstream media also has proved to be as fascinated with current retail changes as it was in the 'supermarket 60s'. The media has, during the 1990s, given over considerable space to exploring both the future and the cultures of shopping. Just as journalists in the 1960s wrote of retail transformations, commentators now write mirror articles trying to capture the feel of contemporary shopping and speculate on its future. There is often a cursory knowledge within such articles of the latest cultural theories on consumer desire and the pleasures of shopping. At times there is also a real interest in consumption as a cultural phenomenon. As Suzy Freeman-Greene wrote in one *Age* article: '. . . the shopping experience is more than just hunting and gathering. It is about hidden pleasures, family bonding, declaring who you are and what you stand for'.[74] Freeman-Greene drives the point home even further: 'Shopping is a way of bringing people together – even though price tags keep them apart. It can be intimidating yet strangely empowering'. This openness to the contradictions and potential pleasures of the shopping experience is common in the contemporary mainstream media and connects with recent work in the cultural studies of consumption.[75]

Shopping, however, is not always spoken of in the media as empowering. During the 1990s it has been constructed also as a social and particularly a female 'problem'. There has been a fascination with the darker side of shopping as well as with its pleasures, with the 'shopaholic', or consumption as pathology. One feature article in *The Age*, for example, spoke of compulsive shopping as a 'disorder' on the increase and provided a whole list of cues through which to 'diagnose' the shopaholic.[76] This article certainly drew attention to what is, for some people, a real problem. It also, however, blithely pathologised a whole range of shopping behaviours and spoke of compulsive shopping as a purely personal malady while largely ignoring the economic and cultural context in which shopping, compulsive or not, takes place.

Finally, within the mainstream media there has been an ongoing cultural critique of consumption and even a return to a critical orthodoxy. The Aboriginal activist Gary Foley wrote in 1993 of consumerism as damaging to the fundamental Aboriginal values of communality and non-materialism.[77] Similarly, Richard Neville in 1994 revived the notion of 'conspicuous consumption' and wrote of the manner in which its promotion in these economically rationalist times eclipses any possibility of living alternatively, particularly in an environmentally sustainable manner.[78] In a slightly different vein, Kate Legge in 1997 reflected on the so-called 'death' of the kitchen, exploring the social – and culinary – ramifications of the increased popularity of ready-to-eat meals.[79]

It is against this diverse and ever present background of industry and media talk about retail futures, shopping cultures, shopper pathologies and consumerism that people respond to the retail environment of the supermarket and to shopping as a social activity. As we will see in the remaining chapters of this book, this response, in the case of Australian intellectuals, has been rather mixed. As for shoppers, themselves, they have been quite able to tell the difference between the market-forged relationship and the 'real' one, between shopping as leisure and as chore, and between empowerment and ephemeral pleasures.

As this chapter has illustrated, corporate retailers have clearly found it difficult over the last three decades to maintain the mythology of supermarket shopping as pleasurable, self-expressive and self-empowering. Any commercial 'triumph' has been undercut by the very logic of an impersonal, large-scale retailing framed within an intensely capitalist and individualistic world view. Ironically, in the very process of becoming a familiar part of the urban landscape in Australia, the supermarket has moved from being a supposedly exciting shopping arena to being an increasingly mundane and sometimes isolating environment, critiqued by both its analysts and by those who shop there. It is to that formal and more popular critique that we now turn.

Chapter 8

Strangers in Paradise

Like many Australian families, mine has a pile of prints, slides and 8mm home movies through which it has come to know some of its past. Out of the hundreds of different images there is one that now comes to mind. In this image there is a suburban brick house (ours had some 'individuality' in that it was white brick), a carport and car (a Hillman rather than the stereotypical Holden), and a very large backyard (with the obligatory Hills hoist) planted up with mostly European shrubs but a few natives as well. This physical environment is peopled with friends and family – pretend aunts and uncles, siblings and other kids. The men are in short-sleeved shirts and shorts, the women in summer dresses with thick red lips and pointy sunglasses. Smoke from the barbecue wafts into one corner of the image. The light is white and bright. The decade is the 1960s.

This image has a complexity for me that speaks not simply of a past suburban blandness, but of the people in it. The image is not just a text, it is much more than that. There are the physical and 'readable' signs here of white Australian everyday life in the decade that saw the arrival of the supermarket and shopping centre. But there are also traces here of social and emotional relationships which can only be understood historically and by a writer in some way connected with this past. This is not an advertising image – although it could have been used as such – nor is it an illustration accompanying some text on Australian suburbia – although it could be used for that as well. It has a depth, at least for me, way beyond these uses; a depth that speaks to me now of a social and familial group negotiating and wondering about the world in which they lived, not acting in mindless conformity with the ideologies of suburbia.

I begin with this personal image of suburbia as a way of illustrating the gulf between cultural surfaces and social depths, between the image and everyday life. Suburbia has been one of the principal targets of Australian social critics in the post-war period and, as is now well acknowledged, it has largely been the surfaces they have attended to, not the complexities. Many post-war critics have interpreted the framework of everyday life in Australia as if 'sitting in' on suburban existence, having been transported there by mysterious means and feeling no connection with the people around them. The social critic has more often than not been the 'visitor' or the stranger – an estrangement most keenly felt by the critics themselves. Usually Anglo-Celtic, male and middle-class, the critic has been the awkward-looking bloke in the corner of the proverbial suburban loungeroom, the one who refused the Salada biscuits and cheese when the plate came around and who wanted to escape (to Europe) as soon as possible.

Within more recent work on Australian suburbia this dismissiveness of post-war intellectuals towards suburbanism has been reviewed and found wanting.[1] Contemporary writing on suburbia now almost always positions itself – as I have done in the paragraph above – in opposition to a post-war anti-suburbanism. In this chapter, however, I want to explore that post-war commentary on suburbia, not for its interpretation of the brick veneer abode, but for what it has said about that other great facet of Australian everyday life – consumption. In the process, I also want to question the extent to which post-war social and cultural critique in Australia can be seen as embodying a straightforward shift, often understood in largely pro-gressivist terms, from a past dismissiveness and analytical superficiality to a new critical populism attuned to complexity and contradiction. A large chunk of post-war cultural commentary in Australia has certainly been as dismissive of consumerism as it has been of suburbanisation. But the talk of intellectuals has not exclusively been marked by disdain. On the contrary, post-war social and cultural analysis in Australia has, I would argue, hovered around quite different modes of disdain, celebration and ambivalence. It is this 'mixed' critical tradition and the possible connection as well as dis-junction between past and present understandings of consumption that are explored here.[2]

It is not easy to detach the critique of consumption from the critique of suburbia within post-war intellectual work. It is, however, worth the try if only to unravel the way in which consumption as a particular phenomenon has been portrayed by intellectuals, and to unclothe the manner in which critics, like retailers, borrowed ideas from elsewhere as much as responded to the social world around them. If Australia was transformed into a consumer society in the decades after World War II, then this was, at least in part, 'talked' into existence by post-war social and cultural observers.

In taking post-war transformations in suburban retailing and everyday shopping as their point of departure, Australian intellectuals, until well into the 1960s, drew no boundary between retail and marketing cultures, as expressed through retail forms such as the supermarket and the shopping centre, and consumer cultures, as expressed through the use made of these environments by those who peopled them. Whatever the retailer, the advertiser and the marketing expert did, the consumer followed. For many critics, the concept of contradictory *usage* was simply not an issue. In this climate, consumption, according to most post-war commentators, had by the 1960s become definitive of Australian everyday life. Shops and shopping, television and various consumer-oriented leisure pursuits have been seen as the cement of a highly materialistic and conformist social existence, or at least as integral to understanding the development of white Australia as one massive and ever-expanding suburb of democracy. Even Donald Horne – one of the most sympathetic of writers towards suburban and consumer cultures – proclaimed in *The Lucky Country* that: 'Australia was one of the first nations to find part of the meaning of life in the purchase of consumer goods'.[3]

This approach clearly gives consumption enormous social and cultural importance. One of the perplexing characteristics of post-war critique, however, is that there has been surprisingly little detailed analysis of consumption as a social practice. The importance of consumption has been emphasised but its workings largely ignored. For the most part, social and cultural commentary on Australia as a consumer society has remained largely observational, and even here the observation has, more often than not, been rather thin.

In taking the development of particular retail environments and market- ing discourses as reflective of consumer culture itself, 'consumerism' has been roundly condemned. Critics have expressed either a dislike for the aesthetics and cultural mediocrity of (suburban) consumption or a dis- pleasure at the lack of authenticity of consumer cultures and their embed- dedness within a rampantly individualistic and conformist materialism.

This dismissiveness and suspicion abounded until at least the mid-1960s. By then, however, there were signs of an emerging interpretative shift of which the work of Donald Horne was representative. It was liberal critics such as Horne who in the 1960s formulated a less dismissive, more populist response to Australian consumerism and suburbanisation. At the same time, in feminist commentary, while the consumer marketplace was understood as the site of oppression, a certain political ambivalence towards women's participation in consumer activities was emerging in the work of writers such as Julie Rigg. By the 1970s left-wing critics, particularly writers such as John Docker, were also taking a more positive approach towards Australian popular culture, of which consumption was seen to be a major part. But this is to run on too far, too quickly. Before exploring this interpretative shift it is necessary to place its emergence in context.

From Pomposity to Populism?

Robin Boyd looked at the culture of consumption as he looked at everything around him, as something to be read off physical structures. In talking about suburbia it has now become almost compulsory to refer to Boyd's work as one of the principal and most articulate voices of anti-suburbanism. It was not just suburbia, however, that Boyd the architect-cum-cultural critic thought 'ugly', it was shopping as well. In his *The Australian Ugliness*, first published in 1960, Boyd railed against the 'veneer on international western culture' that had made the Australian urban landscape decidedly unaesthetic, even pathetic.[4] He was the critic who coined the term 'Austerica' to describe an Australia in which the 'American flavouring' had become evenly and unimaginatively assimilated.[5]

Boyd understood this process of imitation well. Noting how American style was seen as a little too glamorous for an Australian consuming public, he argued that Austerican imitations were, as a consequence, always two or three years behind the latest American design.[6] As a seemingly bland, unimaginative copy of American retail space, the Austerican supermarket was precisely the kind of depthless, ugly urban architecture at which this scorn was directed.

But Boyd seemed to understand very little about the social uses to which these ugly structures were put. There are very few people in Boyd's social criticism, and very little social practice. When it came to the practices of consumption Boyd simply interpreted this, as did many of his 'fellow' critics, as bland materialism, as mirroring the part of the Australian character that scorned ideas, art, and difference, and which was content to settle for a dull, consumption-defined conformity. As Boyd lamented:

> The busy factories churn out for us all the good things of twentieth century life: pre-cooked foods, air conditioners, every-thing that can be pressure-packed to make life more bearable between cigarettes. And much of the money made by these factories returns to the pockets of Australians to buy more pressure-packed relief.[7]

Boyd, however, was not an anti-modernist (and for this reason he saw himself in opposition to an Australian conservatism), nor was he wholly dismissive of the 'Australian tradition' or the 'Australian way of life'.

Post-war consumerism, like suburbanism, has been interpreted in the context of the long debate within Australian intellectual work over nation-hood and national character. Consumerism has been interpreted as both cultural defeat and a depletion of national identity, a perversion of the national psyche – understood in overwhelmingly white, male and heterosexual terms

– particularly given the link between Australian consumer culture and American modernity. Like critics on the left, Boyd held on to his own version of the 'Australian Legend', a largely masculine tradition of independent-mindedness and self-reliance. The trouble was that Australia was borrowing its modernity rather than forging its own, and in the process chipping away at the Legend itself. 'It dies a little', Boyd wrote, 'with every belatedly copied concept, every adopted movement, every plagiarised product we make'.[8]

Other critics were less 'appreciative' of the Australian character, while sharing the Boydian distaste of Americanised consumerism. Post-war critics were quick to resuscitate a view of the Australian way of life as pre-eminently classless, practical and anti-intellectual. In its nastier guises practical meant materialistic and uncultured.[9] As late as 1965 conservative critics such as the British writer John Douglas Pringle dropped little gems like, 'The standard of taste in all but the very best shops is abysmally low', and warn of a 'terrifying crudity in the manners and pursuits of the masses'.[10] All that statements such as this made plain was that the British gent made the worst kind of pseudo-anthropologist.

The most vociferous conservative attack on contemporary Australian culture (and on the left-wing 'radical nationalist' tradition) was embodied in the collection of essays entitled *Australian Civilisation* edited by Peter Coleman and published in 1962.[11] Many of the contributors took up the theme, long pushed within the pages of *Quadrant*, of suburbia as cultural defeat.[12] They had passing jabs also at consumerism, echoing the work of Vance Packard and J.K. Galbraith. Max Harris, for example, insisted that given the bleak uniformity of Australian suburban culture, the suburbs were 'one of the richest fields for conformist techniques and admass media'.[13] Indeed, the suburb was the ideal site, according to Harris, for promoting consumption since 'suburbia, devoted to the ideal of material security, relies heavily on order, authority and conformism for its working pattern'.[14]

Conservative critics in Australia were to cling doggedly to this analytical framework. When Ronald Conway published his *The Great Australian Stupor* in 1971, his complaints about Australian consumer society, now analysed in Freudian terms, departed little from the old *Quadrant* line.[15] As Conway wrote of the new consumerism:

> This paralysis of primary emotions and natural appetites, this creation of conditioned attachments to fabricated objects instead of people – herein lies the cause of much psychic illness. Some of the admass cultures of the Northern Hemisphere are visibly more organised in producing the brainwashed Consumer-man than we are. But in the absence of any patrist traditions or loyalties which are felt to be stubbornly Antipodean, Australians do not even bother to recognise this advancing threat to their mental

freedom. They scramble after the same indigestible spoils according to the same insane imperatives.[16]

Perhaps if Conway had bothered to visit a supermarket he might have
discovered that these 'spoils' were in fact sometimes eminently digestible,
and that people did not simply buy because they were brainwashed. While
Conway conceded that the 'trend towards a pre-packaged consumer civilisation in Australia is far from complete', he still insisted in glib, patronising and
now laughable prose that, 'In the end, we are confronted with an Orwellian
nightmare of entire societies psychologically debauched by childish oral-
narcissistic, and anal-acquisitive appetites'.[17]

A few years later, conservative critique still seemed to be stuck in the same
groove. By the late 1970s John Carroll was arguing that:

> As a passive consumer, whether buying cashew nuts in the super-
> market, or lying in bed watching football on colour television, the
> modern individual is granted no more responsibility than a child;
> his freedom is restricted to asking for more, or for this rather
> than that.[18]

Carroll suggested that consumerism had been one of three main influences
on Australian culture, along with upper-middle-class Victorian values and
institutions, and a working-class (Irish) egalitarianism.[19] For Carroll this
consumerism, embedded in 'an attitude to life cultivated by the economic
needs of advanced industrial societies', posed a threat to a distinctive Australian culture precisely because 'progressively higher degrees of uniformity
are imposed, both within and between different Western societies'.[20]

But there was a softening of critique here as well. Where Conway had
taken the valorisation of the automobile in Australia as the symbol *par
excellence* of rampant, aimless consumerism, Carroll argued that car ownership gave the person (or rather the man) a real sense of power and an avenue
towards citizenship. Carroll recognised also the increasing importance of
consumption as a complex cultural experience.[21]

Yet the superiority was still there. When Carroll wandered into his local
shopping mall – constituting himself in the process as the rational and
detached male observer of a female environment – consumerism seemed to
him to have passed from a commodity fetishism to a metaphysical realm in
which the shopper sought to 'consume herself'. Here, Carroll returned to a
more dismissive position; shopping in the mall was, for women, a substitute
satisfaction for wishes and hopes unfulfilled 'within the frame of the
monotonous stability and incipient aimlessness of suburban life'.[22]

Of all conservative critics it was Donald Horne who broke most decisively
with the dismissive framework of analysis. Horne had been a contributor to

the Coleman collection, and in his essay on the Australian businessman gave signs of an emerging conservative détente with Australian commercial and popular culture (as well as his own transition towards a more social democratic politics). This was cemented in *The Lucky Country*, a book in which Horne argued that, 'Almost all Australian writers – whatever their politics – are reactionaries whose attitude to the massive diversities of suburban life is to ignore or condemn it rather than discover what it is'.[23]

This was powerful stuff. Horne's type of sociological journalism did not depart from the tradition of an observational reading of Australian culture, but it did take it a little further. Horne at least began to enter into the culture of which he spoke as the sympathetic quasi-ethnographer, although he did not go as far as to identify with it personally. In this respect Horne's work was a little prefigurative of later cultural studies, a point which has now been acknowledged.[24]

Populist he may have been, but Horne was also highly ambivalent about aspects of the culture in which he lived. Horne may have fought against the 'failure to take Australian life seriously' but he also saw that life as puritanical, mediocre and dull.[25] His populism seemed to be more of a benevolent realism; the critic should accept the way Australian everyday life was and look for the good in it.

This tension between acceptance and ambivalence was especially marked when it came to consumption. Despite Horne's insistence that Australia was a consumer nation, he said very little about consumption in *The Lucky Country*. He had rather more to say about consumerism a decade later in *Money Made Us*. In this book, Horne argued that some of the most important dates within Australian social history were the opening of Coles Variety Store in Melbourne in 1914, Woolworths in Sydney in 1924 and Roselands Shopping Centre in the 1960s.[26] These retail forms, for Horne, represented a characteristically Australian tendency to 'democratise' everyday life, in this case the pleasures of shopping. It also underwrote the development of Australia as a 'shopping civilisation'.

At times, Horne seemed to express a strong distaste for the plastic modernity of the shopping centre, the 'industrialisation of fantasy' evident in new retail forms and advertising techniques, and the invention of new categories of the person such as the 'consumer' and the 'shopper'. Yet Horne (who had himself worked in advertising) moved towards a conception of the consumer as active, and he argued against an understanding of this shopping civilisation as culturally empty or simply banal.[27]

Horne's awkward populism seemed to offer a new avenue of analysis, one taken up by Craig McGregor in his left-leaning critique-cum-celebration of Australian popular culture published in 1966 under the title *Profile of Australia*.[28] Once again, however, consumption was given an important place but little actual analysis. For McGregor there was a vitality and dynamism to the everyday use of the shopping centre, but he did not actually venture very far into these commercial and social spaces.

In a much later reflection on his work, written in the late 1970s, McGregor explicitly argued against a left critique of popular culture as mirroring the ideologies of consumer capitalism and criticised what he saw as the old left's denunciation of consumers as 'zombies'.[29] Instead, McGregor, picking up on traditions within British cultural studies, emphasised the richness and diversity of everyday life under conditions of consumer capitalism and talked of the meanings people created within their lives *despite* the system.[30]

In a slightly different vein Hugh Stretton was also, by the early 1970s, rejecting the left-wing intellectual obsession with a 'suburban non-life'. His work offered one of the most concerted attempts to sensitively explore that suburbia.[31] Stretton wrote in defence of the complexity of the suburb and its daily routines while insisting also that there was room for improvement in terms of the 'mentality' of suburban living and Australia's urban infrastructure.

In this critique of the 'old' left McGregor, Stretton and others were on firm ground. Left-wing critics had evinced a definite attitude towards suburbia and consumption throughout the 1950s and 1960s and, as with conservative critics, it was not a happy one. Ian Turner argued in 1959 that:

> The pressures towards conformity are becoming stronger
> . . . Australian workers are tied more closely to their jobs through
> the desire to acquire the money to buy those goods and engage in
> those leisure activities which tend to destroy their traditional
> independence of mind.[32]

There was no mistaking it; consumption was smothering the Australian Legend. Allan Ashbolt was even more high-handed when it came to assessing the mindset of the average suburbanite consumer. In his contribution to the 'Godzone' series in *Meanjin* in 1966, Ashbolt unapologetically portrayed the suburban man as a 'mass-produced', 'mass-manipulated' rump of the real Australian man of independence and enterprise.[33] Likewise Peter Groenewegen, in his analysis of Australian consumer capitalism, spoke of the power of consumer choice and activity as myth; choice was artificial and consumer demand was straightforwardly manipulated through advertising and institutional pressures to conform.[34]

Like conservative critics – and as many writers have now pointed out – left-wing commentators clearly understood consumerism and suburbia as emasculating. By the 1970s, however, there were radical critics of both a left pessimism and the notion of emasculation through consumption. In his *Australian Cultural Elites*, John Docker showed definite signs of an emerging Australian left populism and an acceptance of consumer practices as complex, particularly in relation to cultural consumption.[35] Feminist critics also trod a little more carefully through the terrain of suburban shopping, even though there was a fair bit of dismissiveness here too.

For a start, feminist critics broke the obsession with a masculinity undermined by suburbia and mass consumption. The suburbs and their shopping environments were at last discussed in terms of the sexual division of public and private life and of labour. Julie Rigg in 1969 offered one of the first cultural analyses of the Australian woman as consumer – and for that matter of Australian consumerism per se.[36] Rigg identified shopping as having become a realm of women's power – as well as being embedded in the sexual division of labour – particularly since women made up to 90 per cent of consumption decisions. This was very much a 'transitional text', precariously balanced between an insistence that women had been de-skilled and seduced by the consumerisation of everyday life and a belief that they had been empowered by it or at least given a realm in which they could express an autonomy and experience a pleasure. As Rigg rather ambivalently argued:

> The housewifely skills today are less and less those of creation
> and improvisation, more and more those of selection. Decisions
> about purchases may well provide Australian women a degree of
> autonomy and an affirmation of identity which many men find in
> their work. 'I buy therefore I am'.[37]

Clearly, Rigg did not want to celebrate, but nor did she want to condemn women's participation in consumption. Others were less divided. 'Going to the supermarket', Anne Summers wrote in *Damned Whores and God's Police*, 'might be a change from domestic routines and a superficial relief from the isolation and loneliness of being cooped up in a house with small children but it is hardly a recreation or a challenge'.[38] And of the shopping centre, Summers was even more sceptical, 'These mass circuses may distract women shoppers from their personal problems but they are only momentary escapades, not real alternatives to the isolation of women in the suburbs from each other'.[39]

It is important to recognise that statements such as these were part of a broader text that was highly sympathetic to women's negotiation of everyday life. While shopping and its environments were still suspect, feminist critics nevertheless began to take consumption seriously as a key realm within the cultural construction of sexual difference and gender identity. As Ann Game and Rosemary Pringle argued in 'Sexuality and the Suburban Dream', consumption was not only a central part of the suburban fantasy but commodities and shopping had become firmly embedded in the sexualisation of everyday life.[40]

Here again was an attempt to tread the divide between a critique of consumerism and an understanding of consumption as an active process. Game and Pringle rejected the Marcusean understanding of consumption as 'repressive desublimation', as a co-option of the working class, adding that 'We believe this approach exaggerates homogeneity and passivity and oversimplifies the links between sexuality, consumption and consensus'.[41] But the scepticism remained and consumption continued to be characterised as being subordinate to the more 'creative' process of production. As Game and Pringle wrote: 'While shopping does involve skills and responsibilities it does not provide the same sense of personal worth as does production of use values in the home' (that is, through what the authors referred to as 'creative housewifery skills').[42]

A few years later, however, the ground of analysis had shifted a little further. By the early 1980s Rosemary Pringle was arguing much more forcefully that the workings of consumption remained obscure and now needed concerted exploration. In a crucial essay on 'Women and Consumer Capitalism', Pringle argued that consumption had been ignored by male critics precisely because it was a largely female domain and was thus seen as trivial and subordinate to production.[43] Drawing on the work of Jean Baudrillard and Mary Douglas, Pringle explicitly argued against a view of consumption as passive, insisting that it had an economic, symbolic, emotional and sexual complexity. For Pringle, consumption was to be divided into three phases; buying or purchasing, transforming or servicing, and destroying, appropriating or using-up.[44] Each of these phases had its own dynamic; a dynamic that suggested that consumption was not necessarily tied in to a process of co-option and materialism.[45]

Pringle's essay connected with an emerging trend, particularly in Britain, towards exploring the cultural politics of consumption and its relationship to the formation of (gendered) self-identity, a trend already discussed in the introduction to this book. It was this emphasis on consumption as complex text – as imbued with myriad symbolic meanings – that was to be taken up by cultural studies. Yet Pringle was not emphasising solely these aspects of the consumer experience. She clearly wished to retain a conception of consumption as women's work, rather than purely symbolic practice, and to promote the need for a collectivist response – such as consumer boycotts and consumer strikes – rather than simply immersing analysis in an exploration of the production of personal meanings.

Male critics also began to see consumption by the late 1970s as a realm to be dealt with, not dismissed. Gerry Gill in *Arena* wrote of the manner in which consumption, under conditions of modernity, was one means through which people were 'compelled into active self-formation', a means through which everyday life presented itself as a series of choices, possibilities and opportunities.[46] For Gill, the consumer's sense of self-authorship or autonomy was not an illusion. Self-formation, however, was carried out, Gill quite rightly insisted, in a society where certain fundamental choices were blocked off.

If there was still a slight ring of suspicion here, such was not the case in the work of John Docker. By the early 1980s he was getting well and truly stuck into the Marxist critics of popular consumer culture. Influenced by the work of Stuart Hall and British cultural studies (though not exclusively these sources), Docker argued for a conception of popular (consumer) culture as complex and active.[47]

There were, however, the stalwart defenders of the old left. Anthony Ashbolt replying to Docker in the pages of *Arena* accused him of having effectively abandoned Marxism. In opposition to Docker, Ashbolt simply restated the old distinction between (authentic) working-class culture and mass consumerism.[48] A far better reply was offered by Ingrid Hagstrom who pointed out that Docker too easily defined popular culture as working class, drew too simple a distinction between high and low culture, and under-estimated the contradictory nature of people's participation in consumption.[49] Docker eventually offered a counter-reply, accusing Marxist critics of having refused popular culture the dignity of textual analysis; 'it has been treated', he wrote, 'as mere effects of other practices'.[50] For Docker the notion of mass culture and of social control through consumption was a myth, one that failed to come to terms with the complexity of working-class participation in the consumer present.[51]

There were some within the 'old left', however, who had already recognised this, suggesting that Docker's typification of Marxist anti-populism was a bit over-generalised. Ian Turner, for example, by the late 1970s was arguing for an abandonment of the notion that the mode of production determined culture and for a recognition of the vitality and potential oppositionality of popular arts and entertainments.[52] Docker's claim that a textual analysis of the popular was somehow absent within Australian social criticism also seems rather odd. Popular culture as text, as something to be observed and read, has, it seems to me, been a dominant framework of cultural analysis in Australia since the 1960s. Docker was surely asking for a deeper and more sympathetic reading of the everyday aspects of Australian social life, and an attention to social practice, rather than any particularly new recognition of culture as text.

The same criticism can be directed at *Myths of Oz* published in 1987, a study that brought the critical analysis of Australian post-war consumer culture full circle, and which pursued a 'textual' approach.[53] Drawing on the 'subversion thesis' of consumer cultures, then at its height within British cultural studies, John Fiske, Bob Hodge and Graeme Turner took different aspects of Australian everyday life – the pub, the beach, the shopping centre – and attempted to illustrate the complexity of meanings these terrains had for those who used them. In many respects, the attempt is a good one. Yet in its celebratory tendency to define popular (and often intensely masculine) activities as emblematic of a cultural vibrancy and political oppositionality,

Myths of Oz did not seem to move very far beyond the earlier work of Horne or McGregor.

While *Myths of Oz* was expressly written in opposition to Australian critics of suburbia, the authors were rather sloppy in identifying exactly who these critics were. The sloppiness continued when it came to theorising and documenting the supposedly pleasurable and oppositional aspects of everyday activities such as shopping. The authors spoke of leisure shopping as an escape from the drudgery of work and 'as situated at the crucial interface between individual desire and social control'. Yet this 'interface' remained only vaguely explored.[54] Nor did *Myths of Oz* actually break as decisively as the authors claimed from a particular tradition of textual analysis within Australian social criticism. Certainly, the authors provided a far more detailed and self-reflexive discussion of environments such as the shopping centre than had earlier critics. They also utilised a quite different theoretical language. But what *Myths of Oz* offered was still an observational *reading* in which 'the people' – now theorised as resistant – remained a posited entity about which the analyst could speak in a knowing if slightly more tentative voice.

Ambivalence Regained, Complexity Pursued

Myths of Oz marks a convenient break in this discussion of the post-war critique of Australian consumer cultures. By the late 1980s complexity and contradiction, rather than uniformity and blandness, had become the central motifs through which critics interpreted Australian consumer (and suburban) realities. In part this was bound-up with the rise of cultural studies as an academic discipline, a development that began to transform the nature of cultural critique in Australia in ways that have only recently been explored.[55]

But this transition itself has at times come close to a 'progressivist' disavowal of the poverty, vanguardism or elitism of past cultural criticism. The authors of *Myths of Oz*, for example, tended to write of their interest in the vitality and oppositionality of Australian popular culture as an 'advance'.[56] I'm not as hostile to this book as it might appear, yet such a position provides a too-easy means of delineating the theoretical and methodological differences between past and present intellectual work. At its worst, a progressivist framework valorises the theoretically 'new', and in the process ignores the possible connection between past and present forms of social and cultural analysis. A progressivist view of cultural critique is also radically ahistorical. Critics from one decade to the next do not theorise about the same cultures, and for this reason cultural analysis does not necessarily *progress*, does not simply get better; rather, it transforms itself in its attempts to interpret its own historical context. Past critical frameworks may indeed warrant abandonment, and may even be found useless in interpreting the present, but it surely remains important and informative to ask why past critics responded in the way they did and whether elements of that response may still relate to and inform our own.

In this more historical sense it might be that cultural critics of the 1980s could begin to talk more readily of complexity and contradiction in part because the cultures of consumption, as the foregoing historical analysis suggests, were fragmenting. Post-war critics in Australia may have been obsessed with a suburban consumer blandness, a cultural uniformity and an unreflexive adoption of an American modernity, but they did not just invent these things. On the contrary, they were responding to concrete facets of their material culture. While invention and response within cultural analysis cannot be separated, the space between these two things is of interest; to what extent did critics fabricate and ignore elements of the culture of which they spoke, and to what extent were their criticisms and fears reasonably founded, even perceptive?

Not all cultural critics of the 1980s were so quick to adopt a progressivist stance. I have suggested that *Myths of Oz* brought us full circle in the analysis of consumer society in Australia. There is another piece of work, however, that perhaps stands as a far better marker of a transition – as well as continuity – within the analysis and critique of post-war consumer cultures. In her now often-cited essay, 'Things to do with Shopping Centres', Meaghan Morris sought out a kind of 'middle way' in analysing the everyday use of the mall.[57] Morris accepted that shopping centres have a uniformity and are embroiled in attempts to manage the shopping spectacle, but she preferred to explore shopping centres as differentiated, as made into localised places – particularly by women. The importance of Morris's essay – or at least the one I want to focus on here – is that she rejected both the interpretation of consumption as mass manipulation and its celebration as resistant practice.[58] In interpreting consumption as variously characterised by both pleasure and boredom, escape and entrapment, Morris attempted to trace some of the local history connected with the rise of one particular centre as a means of illustrating the specificity and political complexity of shopping centre cultures.

As Morris acknowledged, it was very difficult to know how to grasp the ambiguities of shopping centre cultures and histories in analytical practice – a difficulty which to my mind made for a rather awkward mix between the theoretical and historical facets of the essay. Nevertheless, that essay represented a movement both away from and towards the whole mixed 'tradition' of post-war cultural critique in Australia. It moved away in rejecting talk of a generalised consumer culture and in refusing to position the consumer as a known subject; and it connected with a critical past in resuscitating a useful, though very problematic, mode of political ambivalence towards consumer environments and practices. Morris's essay suggested also the value of pursuing a cultural critique of consumption through a combination of theoretical, textual and historical analysis, an approach that was soon to be taken up in Australia.

Arguably, some of the most interesting work on consumption in Australia published during the 1990s has been historical. Writers such as Gail Reekie and Lesley Johnson have written in detail about the construction of feminine (and masculine) identities through retailing, marketing and advertising, and their analyses have been informed by a conceptualisation of that process as politically complex and historically framed.[59] Others, such as Beverley Kingston, while positively dismissive of a 'theoretical' or cultural studies approach, have nevertheless offered a detailed historical exploration of shopping as a changing social practice.[60]

Any mix of theory and history in relation to analysing consumption has inevitably come in for criticism given the often heated debate within Australia over the relationship between social and cultural theory and historical work.[61] I do not want to enter fully into this debate here, but I do wish to touch on a final related issue to do with the conceptualisation of complexity and contradiction that now informs critical/historical work on everyday life in Australia, including suburban and consumption cultures.

Within *Beasts of Suburbia* and *Suburban Dreaming*, both published in the mid-1990s, there was a conscious move from seeing suburban environments as emblematic of a knowable mass culture to a reading of the manner in which suburbia – and implicitly aspects of consumption – have been 'represented'.[62] Both these collections offered a range of 'partial' histories of specific suburban sites and practices, and deliberately positioned themselves in opposition to a tradition of anti-suburbanism in Australia.[63] They also rejected any pretence of generalising about suburban culture and concentrated instead on how the suburb has been spoken of by critics, historicised, painted, envisaged within commerce and government, portrayed in film and literature, conceived of within architecture and, occasionally, thought of by those who live suburban lives.

Yet the critical reception of these two collections was less than warm. In her review of *Beasts of Suburbia*, Janet McCalman angrily complained that (postmodern) theory was so dominant within this collection as to make what is offered remain unoriginal and superficial in terms of getting underneath the emotional and cultural surfaces of suburbia.[64] Similarly, Judith Brett, in reviewing both *Beasts of Suburbia* and *Suburban Dreaming*, accused these collections of not venturing very far into the suburbs of which they spoke, and of justifying this failure by interpreting history and cultural critique as offering fragments of interpretation rather than general histories.[65] Brett, too, saw this as connected with a postmodernism that absolved the intellectual of the responsibility to generalise; to move beyond the specific, the partial, or the fragmentary. Ironically, then, these two collections – with the notable exception of some contributions – were blamed for doing precisely what they accused past critics of doing; ignoring the nitty-gritty, the complexities, the lived realities, the underneath of suburban and consumer cultures.

It could be said of both these reviewers that they moved far too easily from talking about particular essays within the collections under review to characterising all such historical and critical writing as bland postmodernism and analytically shallow. Perhaps, too, they exaggerated the extent to which the everyday 'realities' of suburbia were being ignored by contemporary writers. Nevertheless, the reviews are of interest in the context of the present discussion because, in claiming that the post-war critique of suburbia has stood still, they articulate very well some impasses within contemporary social history and cultural studies. One such impasse is that complexity has been sometimes rigidly defined within recent cultural and historical analysis as embodied in an attention to specificity rather than to the (equally complex) connectedness between different social/cultural sites or historical moments. In many ways, the couplet of specificity/complexity has become positively fetishised within recent cultural critique. Another impasse is that at precisely the time when intellectuals have become interested in complexity and contradiction, there seems to have been a narrowing of the methodological means of producing historical/cultural analysis. Critics overall have come to utilise much the same way of generating interpretation; the analysis of written texts or artistic/media production in the context of often complex theoretical discussion.

McCalman and Brett, then, surely had a point. And a few years later the point still stands. Suburbia and consumption within recent critical and historical work do still serve at times as a backdrop for the exploration of other issues and intellectual concerns. It does still seem that there is a lot of talk about everyday suburban life in consumer Australia being offered – or talk about that talk – rather than much detailed exploration being undertaken. As a consequence contemporary historical and critical work on the cultures of everyday life can be a little thin in terms of research and leaves huge chunks of that life unspoken of precisely because a very partial analysis seems to be the only alternative envisaged. Theory is also sometimes invoked in recent historical work without explaining why it is useful and without questioning whether it is needed at all in getting across the point being made. Nor is there much recognition of the manner in which the utilisation of theory often seems to push historical narratives to one side, or even largely out of the picture.

To speak in these terms is, of course, to begin to tackle issues much wider than those to do with the post-war interpretation of consumption and suburbia in Australia. In raising these issues, however, I want to suggest that the difficulties over how to interpret consumer or suburban cultures remain so tangibly present because intellectuals (including this writer) are still playing out, still juggling with, those modes of thought – disdain, celebration and ambivalence – that have framed post-war intellectual criticism. Disdain for everyday participation in consumer cultures now seems entirely unacceptable and outright celebration positively naive. The one mode left is a critical ambivalence in the face of the complexities and political ambiguities of everyday life. But this has its problems too, not the least of which is that an attention to specificity, complexity, contradiction and ambiguity can undercut any attempt to move beyond a partial or fragmentary view (though not necessarily the tendency to make sweeping assumptions, as Judith Brett points out). At its worst, an attention to the contradictory complexities and the ambiguities of the historical moment can amount to saying nothing very much at all other than that things are complex. It can leave us with a seemingly endless parade of sometimes thinly researched 'partial readings' of everyday life as text. That is, it can leave us – to return to the opening image of this chapter – gazing at or perusing isolated representations of a consumer and suburban past and constructing possibly detailed but nevertheless distanced and disconnected interpretations.

This chapter has not been written simply as a 'review'; it has also been an attempt to extract a mixed and often disguised tradition of analysis within Australian intellectual work over the last three or four decades, a tradition concerning consumption and its interpretation. I have not wanted to take up a position outside or beyond that critique but rather to articulate how, as a historian and critic, I necessarily work within it.

There is, of course, a rule that academic writers are forced into in discussions such as this. It is that you should never be hesitant in your criticism, you should know what you think of other people's writing and write as if you know what they have said. I'm not averse to a bit of polemic, of articulating and holding an intellectual ground. But I hope I have not completely followed that rule. I think a touch of hesitancy is quite timely here, and the rule is a false one anyway. I have found some of this post-war scholarship much more complex and much harder to dismiss as simply elitist, wrong or out-of-date than I thought it would be when I first set out on this project.

I am conscious that I have picked my way very idiosyncratically through this 'tradition'. In doing so I have suggested a number of things. First, post-war cultural analysis in Australia has envisaged consumerism as crucially important in understanding Australian society, but it has largely ignored consumption as a social practice. It has both given consumption a central place in Australian culture but, until very recently, has said virtually nothing in detail about it. Second, while the post-war analysis of consumerism and suburbia can be understood as largely dismissive, there have also been elements of a populism and of a political ambivalence that suggest that we might question easy, progressivist demarcations between different analytical frameworks and theoretical languages; between different historical moments within cultural critique. Third, if the contemporary analysis of consumption – and suburbia with it – can be envisaged as now riven with an attention to specificity, complexity and ambiguity, then the critical ambivalence arising from this recognition presents difficulties in offering a firm political commentary on the present, in taking a more than partial, more than debilitatingly conditional position. In effect, Australian cultural critique, in exchanging a view of consumption as uniform for a view of it as complex, both lets go of a past tendency to dismiss the cultures of everyday life, but loses also one of its past strengths; the preparedness to take a position, and to confront broad questions about the effects and value of consumption cultures. This retreat from tackling broad issues within contemporary cultural analysis was a difficulty that I began to speak of in the introduction to this book, and it is one that I will return to in the conclusion. For now, we will turn to exploring a different form of talking about shopping and consumption in Australia than that offered by intellectuals.

Chapter 9
Everyday Shopping

Shopping is very much a subject of everyday discussion and reflection. To a lesser extent, so too are the benefits and hazards of living in a consumer society, of wanting, buying and deriving meaning from various consumer goods, services and experiences. Chapter six of this book began to explore something of this everyday realm by constructing a narrative of supermarket shopping based on a set of oral history interviews. In this chapter, as a means of bringing this history to a close, we once again engage – by way of interview material – with some of the everyday talk connected with supermarket shopping, this time in a contemporary context.[1]

For many of the people I spoke with as part of this study, any equation of everyday shopping practices with feelings of pleasure, leisure, community, sociability, self-fulfilment and empowerment was no straightforward matter, suggesting that retailers, and cultural commentators as well, have been too easily drawn into making risky assumptions about the nature of the shopping experience. Indeed, the very diversity of responses documented here, and the way in which people clearly juggle often totally contradictory feelings about consumption, suggests that the cultures of consumption and of everyday life are simply not that easy to grasp; not that easy to 'know'. This chapter seeks to document that 'lived contradiction', and this difficulty of knowing. Towards the end of the discussion, I will comment in a little more detail on the process of interpreting this interview material.

In-store Society

For Emma, a university student in her early twenties, the local Safeway, where she shops on a weekly basis, offers at least the possibility of combining necessity shopping with a bit of fun; you don't do much talking but you do mingle with others:

> There's lots of different people that go in there, and you're sort of forced to interact with each other in some sort of way, even if it's manoeuvring your trolley out of the way of their trolley or whatever . . . and it's good to have a bit of communication with other people across the board . . . and they're strangers.

Emma recognises that many people dislike supermarket shopping, but she made it clear during our conversation that having been brought up in rural Victoria she liked the particular type of anonymous, cosmopolitan interaction that her local, inner-urban supermarket offers.

Fay Hussey, over in Dandenong, is separated in age from Emma by over 40 years as well as numerous suburbs but, like Emma, she finds the supermarket quite a social experience. It is not, however, the gazing at others or the anonymity that Fay likes, it is the chance to *talk* with people. This is something that, as Emma noted, happened only rarely during her visits to the supermarket; people looked at each other but almost never conversed. This experiential difference between Emma and Fay may be due to the fact that shoppers at Fay's supermarket have a longer-term connection with each other. It may point also to a (perhaps generational) difference concerning the willingness of people to fully interact with other shoppers.

These two reactions to the supermarket clearly speak of a certain preparedness to find something vibrant, or at least something partially fulfilling, within the one-stop-shop. They posit the existence of an in-store society and undercut interpretations of the supermarket as an asocial or culturally empty environment. Emma's comments are particularly interesting because they suggest that the sociability of the supermarket is as much about the fact that people are physically brought together in the one place, as it is about them deliberately interacting. This is a notion of sociability based on being with others momentarily rather than knowing them over time.

Anthony, a postgraduate student in his early thirties for whom shopping is a bit of a chore, shared Emma's perception:

> The good thing about going to the supermarket is that you don't have to talk to anybody. That's why I'd hate to go to the Victoria Market, because I just don't want to, I wouldn't want to interact, or wouldn't want to have to ask what the price is. But, I reckon it's social [the supermarket] in the sense in which you're dealing with this collection of people who you can wander round with and look at, but feel under no obligation whatsoever to talk to. So it's

> social in the sense, in the sense that you're being surrounded by
> a group of people, and that's interesting.

What is being articulated here by both Emma and Anthony is clearly not
anti-social, but rather, a refusal to enter very far into 'circumstantial' social
relationships. The supermarket is seen here as a realm in which one can be
'autonomously present' with others, in which a deeper sociability is optional
– like the products on the shelves. In a sense the very autonomy guaranteed
by the supermarket, and promoted by the wider outside culture of which it is
a part, is embedded in a notion of social relationships as chosen rather than
given. This tentativeness towards an overly interactive form of shopping was
also expressed by Christopher, a public servant in his early thirties:

> It depends on how intrusive the interaction is [between retailer
> and shopper]. I don't really want to be friends with the person,
> unless you've had enough interactions to decide that you do like
> that person. But I wouldn't want that boundary crossed too early.
> And I don't want that demand of having to talk to someone every
> time I go in [to a shop].

 It is tempting to see this desire to be autonomously present with others as
a generational change in attitudes towards social interaction, particularly
since many of the older people I spoke with retained a quite different sense
of sociability. Certainly, a desire for autonomous presence may be a part of
broader post-war social and cultural transformations in the personal negotiation of public space. However, any notion of a uniform generational change
was undercut by the fact that some younger people I interviewed rejected the
supermarket on social grounds.
 For Sue, a secretary in her thirties, the experience of supermarket shopping is intensely frustrating:

> No I don't [like the supermarket]. I get very frustrated in super-
> markets. There are necessities there, like your washing powder
> and that sort of thing. But I do get, I get frustrated by the pack-
> aging and the advertising as well as the, just the whole experience
> I find very dull and tedious . . . There's no pleasure, I don't find it
> going up and down supermarket aisles with hundreds of other
> people and just picking off packages and boxes from the wall.

Based on her informal observations, Sue feels that many other people dislike
supermarket shopping as well and she finds it difficult to imagine how
anybody could set out to enjoy the experience. Cheryl, a supermarket cashier
for many years and now a tertiary student in her mid-twenties, feels much
the same way:

> Like, you've got it all for you, but there's no sort of real choice. It's all planned, every supermarket aisle is planned so that they know which ones to target and what's on special, they know what people want basically, and basically people buy everything, basically the same things . . . They're so much more modern. I don't like modern. I'm really anti-modern when it comes to that sort of stuff . . . There's no atmosphere because people don't talk.

This link between the very particular modernity of the supermarket and lack of atmosphere was articulated by a number of other people (of various generations) whose strategies of coping with the disappointments of everyday shopping – as we shall see below – revolved around minimising their use of the supermarket. These disappointments were based on certain expectations of the shopping experience embedded in a conception of sociability that relied on more than being autonomously present with others but translating that presence into a fuller, verbal interaction, and thus willingly compromising one's autonomy. This, then, is the sociability of talk rather than of the look, and is clearly understood by a number of people as a mode of interaction precluded by a retail environment, the supermarket, that is fundamentally dependent on the autonomous gaze.

Others, however, were less bothered by any lack of atmosphere or sociability within the supermarket, preferring to see everyday shopping in more practical terms. For Brian, a panel-beater in his mid-thirties, supermarket shopping is simply not about social atmosphere or interaction at all, it is about a functionality:

> Social atmosphere, no I've, it may have one, I've never thought of it. It's a shop. You go there, you do your shopping. It's a little larger than most shops, but it's nonetheless a shop.

It may be that this very functional view of everyday shopping is particularly male. But this is not necessarily the case. Such a view may equally be to do with class-framed attitudes towards the meanings surrounding the purchase of food and household goods. Expectations that everyday shopping could and should be enjoyable on a social level did not fit neatly into class demarcations, nor gendered ones, among the people I spoke with, but it was nevertheless the case that those who defined their background and everyday culture as working class more readily viewed shopping in quite utilitarian terms.

Zoe, a student in her twenties who has worked in retailing since she was 15, also looks on shopping quite functionally. For Zoe, who lives in the same working-class suburb as Brian, you don't go food shopping for atmosphere, you go to buy what you need. The supermarket, Zoe argues (with some resignation), is simply the most convenient place to do this; it's clean, cheap

and easy to get around but not much else. Having worked as a cashier now
for a number of years Zoe suggests that most other people, at least within the
supermarkets where she has worked, do not seek to actually enjoy supermarket shopping either. People simply go there and get out as soon as they
can. Observational studies of supermarket buying behaviour tend to confirm
this. One study in the late 1980s established that most supermarket shopping
involves locating and quickly selecting items, rather than browsing or talking
to staff and other customers.[2]

Zoe and others who worked in the supermarket spoke also of a generational difference connected with the enjoyment of supermarket shopping. Of
all Zoe's 'regulars', it is only some of the elderly people who seem to her to
derive real pleasure from the visit:

> I think it's because it's an outing for them, not a big one, but it
> does give them something to do . . . it's like a daily routine. They
> don't carry a lot when they come, so they've got to top-up
> everyday, so they may as well enjoy it while they're out there.

Similarly, Cheryl finds that some elderly people – more so than members of
other social groups – rely on the supermarket for forms of social interaction,
often going to the checkout operator they know. As Cheryl noted of one
elderly customer; 'One woman comes in and she says, "You're my family, this
is all I have, I've got no one else", and so she comes in and she's in her
seventies'. Of course neither Cheryl nor Zoe are suggesting that all elderly
people carve out a social life in the supermarket. Their observations, however, are astute ones and illustrate the continued importance of the physical
activity of shopping as a public interaction that offers at least some escape
from social isolation, particularly for social groups such as the elderly. Once
again, observational studies of the supermarket tend to confirm the greater
propensity of elderly shoppers to browse and spend more time in the store.[3]

But there are, of course, elderly critics of supermarket shopping for whom
the supermarket is far from a terrain of pleasure. Anetta Barr recognises that
everyday shopping is probably easier now than it was 50 years ago but insists
that; 'I don't think shopping for food is a pleasure, I really don't . . . I think
most people regard it as another chore'. Anetta, however, is a little torn
between two different responses to the contemporary supermarket. She likes
the variety and the ability to choose your own things, now that she has
become used to it, but regrets, as we saw in chapter six, the loss of a more
personal type of shopping. Muriel Norris seems to have much the same
fractured experience of supermarkets; for her the variety is good, the environments sometimes exciting, but the human relationships somewhat thin.

Overall, very few people I talked with, of whatever generation, class,
gender or ethnicity, saw the supermarket as a place to linger. In many

The contemporary supermarket: opening day, Woolworths, Casuarina Square, Darwin, November 1997

respects, social interactions within the supermarket were spoken of as an incidental rather than an integral part of the visit. As Gerard, a theatrical consultant in his late thirties, put it in response to being questioned about the social nature of the supermarket:

> It depends. Living in Prahran [Melbourne] you see lots of people you know, and if someone's in there I know, yeah, you have a yarn. Otherwise no. I'm in there to shop and get out again. Something's got to be done, you do it.

This comment seems to return us to a very functional view of supermarketing. Gerard, however, made this statement in the context of discussing his overall enjoyment of everyday shopping. For Gerard, it was the supermarket – despite the occasional in-store yarn – that interrupted that enjoyment, a position shared by Sue and Cheryl among others. Even the more favourable reactions of Emma, Fay, and Anthony were, as we shall see, offered in the context of them placing definite limits on just how personally and socially satisfying shopping, of any sort, could be.

Compared to What?

People always envisage and search out alternatives to what everyday life offers them. This is as true of shopping environments as it is of other aspects of everyday living. Thus some people I spoke with as part of this study did not merely express a dislike of supermarkets, they searched out other ways of shopping. As Cheryl put it:

> When I get sick of shopping at supermarkets I go back to the old way where . . . I just go to this shop or to this shop, or go to the market. I find that so much more exciting because there's so much more . . . people talking and there's social activity going on and that's, that's more REAL.

Sue also finds a shopping pleasure, and a social reality, outside the confines of the supermarket:

> I really enjoy, like the delicatessen, for example. I really enjoy going there and telling them that I liked that piece of ham, or that bit of pork, and sort of cheese, or [asking] what coffee might I buy for dinner, and can you tell me about this? And I like the exchange of information about food because it's a whole experience for me. I really enjoy food, and I like other people to sort of help me along with that.

Both these women are relatively young, their 'going back' to older forms of retailing is not a nostalgia for a retailing they have experienced, but a form imagined. Both women also purposefully seek out a more elaborate way of undertaking everyday shopping rather than always opting for the supposed convenience of the supermarket. Others spoke of these 'elaborated forms' of everyday shopping; of mixing and matching different commercial spaces and the possible social experiences they offered. Gerard, like Sue, has a quite extensive network of shops that he regularly visits on his weekly shopping trip, discriminating between retail outlets on the basis of both financial and social factors. Although he now no longer goes to the open-air market – which he regrets – he insists that:

> I still make that separation [from the supermarket] with fruit and vegetables at the green-grocers, and I go to the butcher for meat, and I go to the delicatessen for bacon and cheeses, though I do buy some cheeses from the supermarket. And the last thing I would do is buy fish from the supermarket.

These attempts to construct elaborated forms of everyday shopping are illustrative of the manner in which people make shopping a social or pleasurable experience precisely by rejecting and circumventing the claims of one particular environment, such as the supermarket or the shopping centre, to offer all that is needed. These responses illustrate that it is not everyday or 'necessity shopping' per se that is relegated to non-leisure status, but rather particular shopping environments which are seen to offer an overly constructed or less 'real' experience. It is the open-air market and smaller shops, then, that some people see as being *socially* different to corporate shopping environments. Sue, for example, drew a clear differentiation between a European shopping cosmopolitanism and an American retail sterility:

> I like the experience of the market. Well, it's the colour and it's the sound, and the idea, too, of being able to, to give your money to people who are small business owners. I really enjoy that and I think, too, the European feel about, about shopping in that atmosphere, as opposed to supermarket shopping which reminds me of that American-style shopping.

Gerard too, although he no longer visits the market for lack of time, thinks of market shopping as an enjoyable ritual in direct contrast to visiting the supermarket:

> I liked . . . the atmosphere [of the market], the quality, the selection, the price. And I remember it became a ritual. And an enjoyable ritual. I mean going to the supermarket to me, I do it really quickly.

One of the problems connected with recent work on retail spaces and consumer activities is that it has effectively ignored sentiments like these. Whether dismissive or celebratory of consumption practices, recent cultural analysis has tended to focus on the use of particular 'postmodern' shopping environments, not on those who don't use them or who attempt to limit their involvement with the hypermarket, the superstore and the mall. This has both exaggerated the importance of postmodern consumer spaces in people's lives and failed to come to grips with the critique of these environments implicit in the actions of people who deliberately stand outside them.

It is precisely the experiential gap between the relatively unplanned and the planned shopping environment, between the unpredictability of older shopping spaces and the much more predictable possibilities of wandering the supermarket aisles, that was so often commented on by those I interviewed. As Christopher summed things up:

> The market is mainly about looking around for what you need and searching for bargains. And also you're not always quite sure what you're going to find at the market, you may not be able to get something you've come for or you might discover something

you didn't know was there. But the supermarket's a little bit more, more predictable and controlled.

Similarly, for Gerard the supermarket actively broke down the complexities of the shopping experience, 'I hate shopping complexes, you know, sterile shopping is, is, forget it. And I think the supermarket is somewhere on the way to that'. Sue was even more forceful in her critique. As she scathingly observed:

> An evil necessity is the supermarket, and I think, I think, that the convenience of the supermarket itself forbids anybody else from trying to make shopping any other way.

Although some cultural analysts have been very reticent to see the supermarket or the shopping centre as less 'social' or 'entertaining' than alternative retail spaces, others outside these intellectual confines are clearly not so timid. The cultural analysis of consumption practices as creative and resistant has proved enormously hesitant in drawing such distinctions between consumer environments because of a fear of appearing dismissive towards those who *do* gain enjoyment from wandering the supermarket or the shopping centre. In a sense, this genre of critique has been hamstrung by its own populism, its own obsession with the complexity of specific everyday experiences, unable to see that while the pleasures of everyday shopping can be derived from a whole range of shopping spaces – the supermarket, the mall, the market, the small shop, the department store – these spaces are not necessarily thought of as offering the *same* possibilities of enjoyment, the *same* complexities of experience. Thus many of the people I spoke with as part of this study responded with either derision or laughter to the suggestion that visiting the supermarket was as socially rich or culturally complex an experience as visiting an open-air market or shopping within smaller shops where one was known. Even those who derived enjoyment from supermarket shopping (an enjoyment which I personally share) still spoke of the supermarket as an overly constructed and often sterile environment.

Sex and Desire in the Aisles

> With the males I've known throughout my life, I don't think I've ever been shopping with any of them. [laughter] . . . Most of the males I've known never go shopping for clothes, and the last thing they'll do is go shopping for food . . .

> Some men are catching-up, but some men just do not have a clue. Yeah, they just get lost, just general shopping, they just don't have a clue.

> For some reason men hate shopping. Every one that I've come in
> contact with does, and I don't really know why. I s'pose it's
> because when they go shopping with women, women often take
> so long to do things, whereas . . . my boyfriend . . . he just wants
> to get in there and get out.

These comments were made by three of the younger female interviewees in
response to a question about shopping and gender differences. Their responses reconfirm that classic and still very concrete division within consumption cultures between women who shop and men who don't. Although
all three women recognise that more men are now going shopping than in
the past, particularly for everyday goods, they have their suspicions as to how
much of a change has occurred.

As we noted in chapter seven, market research has suggested that the
number of men buying groceries in Australian supermarkets has increased
dramatically during the 1980s. Despite this fact, Zoe argued, quite astutely,
that we need to look beyond simply the *presence* of men in the supermarket
and ask more searching questions about what they are doing there. In this
respect, Zoe observed that men who accompany women in the supermarket
are not actively shopping at all:

> Even when I'm serving it's the woman, you can tell it's the
> woman's responsibility and the man's just there to give an
> opinion or is there to pay or the rest of it.

When it comes to the lone male shopper with trolley in hand there are also
some perceived problems. Both Zoe and Cheryl speak of the prevalence now
of a relatively new category of shopper; the 'helpless', or perhaps just lazy,
male. As Zoe commented:

> But also the men that come along will always, they'll always
> broadcast about how incompetent they are. Yeah, in the store.
> Like recently we've just had everything moved around . . . This
> elderly gentleman came past and said: 'Oh you know, you need
> someone directing us blokes around because I don't know where
> I am, I don't know what's going on'. [laughter].

Cheryl speaks of a similar incident, one in which her male customer played
directly on gender differences in shopping:

> One man said to me once: 'Well, you know, we just can't do
> it, we're not as good as women, we're just hopeless, can you
> help me?'. Playing the helpless male, which I thought was quite
> funny.

The skills of the male supermarket shopper were also brought into question by many other women I spoke to (and some of the men), particularly in relation to what has long been seen as the Achilles heel of the male shopper – the impulse buy. As Emma noted, echoing others:

> The boys I know, that I've shopped with or whatever, seem to not care so much about what they're putting in the trolley and how expensive it is even though they might not have a lot of money.

Despite the clear differentiation made by almost all the women I interviewed between the knowledgeable female shopper and the fumbling male aisle wanderer, there was some preparedness to recognise that a growing number of men – of various ages and socio-economic backgrounds – were learning; that they were becoming, as Cheryl noted, more price conscious and skilled at everyday shopping. Others such as Zoe tempered this by insisting that only certain men were being drawn into the supermarket as shoppers. Zoe thus spoke of *ethnic* differences connected with men accompanying women in the store in which she works:

> I find the more men that come and help – help, I'm not saying are responsible for, there's a difference – that come and help their wives are mainly Australian [Anglo-Celtic] men.

Once again, this confirms the findings of observational studies which have established that male supermarket shoppers are of a predominantly Anglo-Celtic background.[4] However, some caution is needed here, since within various non-Anglo-Celtic cultures in Australia there is a tradition of male involvement in everyday shopping activities. It may be then that non-Anglo-Celtic men undertake everyday shopping tasks but utilise small shops and open-air markets more so than the supermarket.

It seems that many of the men I spoke with as part of this study fell within that category of 'skilled' male shoppers identified by Cheryl and others. This perhaps explains why these men agreed to talk about shopping in the first place. Clearly, men like Gerard feel a real confidence in their everyday shopping skills. Yet when asked how he acquired these skills, Gerard suggests that it was not as a result of his upbringing but rather of his experience of living in shared households and of his friendships with women.

Other men I spoke with also talked about this very deliberate taking on of basic shopping skills once they had left the family home, skills developed either through association with women, living in group households or through a process of in-store self-education. Most conceded that they were still learning and that when it came to shopping for items such as clothes, they still felt out of their depth. Paul, a public servant in his early thirties, preferred necessity shopping above all else. This was in part because he took a pleasure in the foodstuffs bought but also because he felt more confident about shopping for everyday goods than for 'big ticket' items:

> I always liked shopping, . . . supermarket shopping. I like super-market shopping and I don't like other sorts of shopping. Well, I like grocery shopping, perhaps I should say. The weekly grocery shop. There's something, I don't know, in a way there's something soothing about the familiarity of it, but there's also something satisfying about coming home with all the different things . . . Whereas, like shopping for clothes or something, I guess it's a lot more of an unknown and I feel a lot less certain . . .

For some men shopping was a kind of secret world, only parts of which they had yet gained a knowledge of. Christopher, like Paul, felt confident about everyday shopping, but not so other forms of consumption:

> I don't feel very good at shopping, you know shopping for clothes. But I do like the idea of having nice clothes and wearing them, and looking good. But I just don't, it's like a secret that no one's let me in on, on how to do it.

For women, on the other hand, a knowledge of this secret world and the development of shopping skills were spoken of as involving much more than simply learning to shop. A number of the younger women I spoke to attempted to grapple with the manner in which shopping, particularly for everyday goods, was constructed as a coming of age activity during girlhood. Some fascinating vignettes came out during the interviews that traced something of the manner in which shopping was a means of both bonding between mother and daughter and a debut into domesticated womanhood. Prue, a retail worker and part-time student in her mid-twenties, recalled that as a teenager 'You felt good going shopping because it was a time when you were bonding with your mother'.

Claire, another student in her mid-twenties, also remembers the excitement and satisfaction she felt in her early teens when first given the responsibility of doing the family shopping:

> She [her mother] gave me the shopping list, and she gave me the money, and off I went and actually did the family shopping, all by myself . . . And I had to arrange for delivery because, I mean I

couldn't carry all the packages home and I wasn't going to go back five or six times and my brother was too small to carry things . . . And I remember thinking that was like, I was like, wow, I'm grown up now, I'm doing the shopping myself.

Emma recalled a similar feeling of independence and solidarity with her mother through the act of shopping as a teenager:

I actually, it was quite crazy, none of my friends used to do this. I wanted, I liked going and doing the shopping for Mum, the grocery shopping. And I used to like every Thursday or Friday, whenever Mum used to get paid, I would go and do the grocery shopping for Mum because I wanted to, because somehow I felt independent and I always saved Mum money as well, and so Mum didn't mind me doing it.

While some men I interviewed recounted similar experiences between father and son in relation to hardware shopping in particular, it was women who drew out the significance of domestic shopping as an entry into adult society, underlining the much closer relationship between routine consumption and constructed notions of the feminine.

The supermarket, of course, is not only a space for gender demarcations and family bonding, but for other forms of sexualised differentiation and interaction as well. One of the lesser myths of post-war modernity is the reputation of the supermarket as being a sexual space in more ways than one. Very few heterosexual people I spoke with recounted any great sexual frisson of wandering the supermarket aisles. Some had heard stories of friends being 'picked up' in the fruit and vegies section, or while working on a checkout register. But mostly, for heterosexuals, the supermarket was a space for a bit of a 'perve' or for simply confirming coupledom.

For some older women, in particular, the confirmation of coupledom through everyday shopping was understood in favourable terms. Both Anetta Barr and Muriel Norris find an enormous and very positive contrast between shopping in the past as a strictly female activity and the greater number of couples they now see shopping together in the supermarket and at shopping centres. Both remarked on how nice it was to see men and women doing something domestic *together*.

Other younger people, however, while sometimes enjoying shopping for food or clothes with a partner, were more cautious about the meaning and value of doing so. Prue, for example, regularly goes shopping to the supermarket and to the city stores with her boyfriend. Yet at the same time she places definite boundaries around the link between shopping and coupledom:

> I think it becomes a trap. You don't need to be spending money to
> be together. I mean you can just stay at home or you can go to the
> park or something.

Some of the men I spoke with were also rather sceptical of the value
of shopping with a female partner – particularly in the supermarket –
though for reasons which seemed more to do with a perceived difference in
men's and women's approaches to shopping than wanting or not wanting a
certain type of 'togetherness'. It struck me very clearly during the interviews
that when men do feel skilled as shoppers, they are often quite assured in
those skills and interpret shopping in extremely task-oriented and self-
sufficient terms. This could, of course, be interpreted as male arrogance,
but it is more complex than that. It relates to the manner in which some
men need to retain a firm sense of control over their consumer desires and
their participation in consumption environments. This sense of purpose
can at times lead to an absolute determination *not* to impulse buy, since
giving in to impulse is to be associated with a 'feminine' aimlessness or lack
of control.

Of course not all men who feel skilled at shopping see everyday consumption in a purely task-oriented way. Gerard, for example, does not shop with
his partner simply because she hates everyday shopping. But, as we have
seen already, he attempts to make his shopping trips into a complex social
experience. So, too, do some gay men, particularly when it comes to transforming the supermarket into a sexualised space.

Within gay cultures, both in Australia and overseas, the supermarket
has long held a sexualised status as a place to meet, or at least to view,
other gay men. This can be overemphasised, at least in the Australian
context. Supermarkets are not somehow made into gay venues or even gay
'beats'. Rather, within certain very select supermarkets aspects of a gay
culture are brought through the doors. This does not make supermarket
shopping any more fundamentally exciting for gay men as opposed to
heterosexual shoppers, it just adds a bit of spice. Indeed, for some gay men
the chance to 'perve' is the saving grace of the weekly shop. As one gay man
put it:

> For me, it's part of the social event. It's an added element, that I
> go to [the supermarket], and I know that often there'll be a
> percentage of gay men there, and so it just adds to the, well not
> excitement, it just adds to the event, adds to the sociability of it.
> Because, you know there's a possibility of seeing somebody that
> you find attractive . . . That may be all it is, in fact overwhelm-
> ingly that is all it is. But that in itself, there's some enjoyment in
> that. It takes away from the chore . . .

Other gay men I spoke with noted a certain solidarity and gentle subversion involved in making the supermarket into a gay space. As one interviewee put it:

> I guess it is also, I don't know, maybe not ironic, but just, like those coded signs that there's another gay man and yet you're in a very traditional suburban milieu. And it's just like seeing someone, like you're making a quick eye contact with someone at Church, or you know at Granny's funeral or something. It adds something too, yeah it's not exciting, but just the experience of it. It's not sort of like if you saw the same person at a gay venue, it would do the same thing for you, but it does in the supermarket.

As another gay man added: 'There's a feeling, there's a slight feeling of solidarity at [the supermarket]'. These men, however, were all speaking of one particular supermarket and were at pains to emphasise the subtlety of its gay status. Although there was the occasional story of the chat-up and of the relationship forged over the broccoli, the supermarket as a gay sexual space was usually envisaged as centred on the pleasure of the gaze. One lesbian woman I spoke to articulated this well:

> Yeah, I mean, yeah it's a perving area, [the supermarket] and I don't know if it is for the heterosexuals that go in there but I've really noticed before that, you know, if I'm walking around with Andrew [her gay housemate], or just watching some of the gay boys, they really look each other up and down, if you're passing them in the aisle or whatever, or you know across the fruit and veg section or whatever . . .

This woman made this observation in the context of discussing the absence of a similar supermarket culture among lesbian women; an absence tempered by what she saw as the increasing visibility of lesbian couples shopping together.

Flexible Demarcations, Shopping Delimited

We noted in a previous chapter that the demarcation between convenience and comparison shopping, between necessity and leisure shopping, is a false one. Shopping as frustration and pleasure exists on a continuum and is not simply a product of the type of shopping being undertaken. Even the physical environments of everyday consumption, while they may be seen to either facilitate or delimit the enjoyments to be gained from shopping, do not have the power to simply dictate the content of that experience. Pleasure and frustration can be felt within a whole range of shopping environments, traditional, modern and postmodern, even though certain environments might be seen to offer more possibilities than others. In this sense, whether we are shopping for luxuries or necessities, consuming for ourselves or others, the consumption experience can work, and equally, it can come unstuck.

Certainly many of the people I spoke with as part of this study did not make any simple distinction between necessity and leisure shopping and were sometimes reticent to speak of shopping as leisure at all.[5] Nor did people speak of shopping and the consumption of material goods as crucially important in terms of expressing their self-identity. In fact many people placed clear boundaries around how consumer experiences and products were incorporated into their everyday lives.

Prue was among the few people I spoke to who agreed with the demarcation between necessity and leisure consumption. She dislikes going to the supermarket but derives great pleasure from other forms of shopping like searching out clothes:

> I like, I just like buying, like having nice things, and nice things for the house, and that's the things that I enjoy. And I s'pose one of the reasons I don't enjoy supermarket shopping is because although it's a necessity to eat and what have you, it seems like such a waste of money.

Despite this seemingly unreserved acceptance of buying as fulfilment, however, shopping has real limits for Prue; it's enjoyable, but only if it does not replace other forms of leisure. Having worked previously in retailing, Prue has strong opinions on Sunday trading and her comments speak of these perceived limits to shopping pleasure:

> I really saw it [families shopping on Sunday] as this is what people do on their Sundays now, because the shops are open for Sunday trading, and it's really, I think that's really awful. I don't think it's necessary to have shops open on Sunday . . . You just don't need to. It's like having Coles open 24 hours, you just don't need it. But you think you do. You begin to think that you need it and when they close on Sunday, you feel like 'Oh no, the supermarket's closed what are we going to do?' . . . and I think Sunday shopping's just a bit extreme and it's not fair on the people that work.

Others, like Sue, were to some extent torn between two quite different positions when it came to shopping. On the one hand Sue liked the search for a bargain and, as we have already noted, certain types of food shopping, yet she felt quite unwilling to express herself through shopping generally. To Sue, there seemed to be something 'empty' about placing too much importance on shopping as a field of leisure. Most of the older people interviewed felt much the same way. Muriel Norris insisted that she had never seen shopping as leisure, preferring to spend her time at the local Historical Society or with the Country Women's Association: 'Never been one to sort of wander round the shops on my own. I usually know what I want, what I'm looking for and go and buy it'.[6] Fay Hussey is much the same: 'No it's necessary [shopping], it's a necessary part [of life] that's all . . . I've got other more interesting things I want to do . . . It doesn't really interest me'.

Fay added that she has always stayed away from 'sales' and was clear on the fact that she prefers to express herself through something she has made rather than bought. This distinction between production and consumption, although now unpopular within some contemporary cultural analysis, was mentioned by a number of other people as well. Although consumption has been theorised as 'another form of production', as equally creative and satisfying as making something material, some people I spoke with did not see it like this at all. Both Cheryl and Emma mentioned their preference for making clothes or at least buying and adapting 'op shop' clothes over purchasing what they saw as sterile mass-produced clothing. Likewise, Gerard linked his enjoyment of everyday shopping to what came out of it, not simply to the activity itself:

> I often shop because I have things I want to cook. And I think there's probably more control in the cooking and the creation of a dish [than going shopping].

Perhaps one of the most striking aspects of the interviews I conducted as part of this project was that the leisure and sociability expressed through shopping were constantly brought into question even by those for whom shopping was a regular pleasure. Prue, despite being apparently 'born to shop', drew a challenging distinction between the enjoyment of shopping and its status as leisure:

> I don't really think of it as leisure, I go shopping on Saturdays but it's not like that's what I do for leisure. I'd prefer to be down the beach or something. If we have the choice of going to the beach or going shopping we'll go to the beach . . . It's [shopping] kind of just something I do when I don't have anything else to do.

Zoe made an even more confronting observation, 'I think it's only because it exists [shopping] that we make it enjoyable, not so much that it actually is'.

The gay men I spoke with also dealt with the pleasures of shopping with some scepticism, despite the entrenched myth that like women, gay men love to 'shop-till-they-drop'. As one gay man put it:

> I just think it's underrated how much hard work it is consuming . . . It sounds like too much hard work, to you know go and get them, it's just a bit too much effort. And when I do get things . . . I usually buy them in about twenty minutes. The actual act of you know buying is too boring . . . I'm usually just relieved that I've done it . . . There's very little pleasure in the actual buying . . .

The efforts of these women and men to put shopping in its place was part of many people's thinking. When asked to place shopping in order of import-ance alongside other sources of pleasure and self-worth, no one I spoke with placed shopping of any sort very high on their list of priorities; family, home, relationships, friendships, work, vacations, day outings all came out much more favourably. The meaning and value of shopping were always delimited in terms of the supposed leisure and the possibilities for satisfaction that they offered.

The meanings of shopping were also delimited in terms of expressing one's identity. Although people recognised the obvious point that a personal identity was in some sense expressed through things bought and desired, consumption objects were certainly not seen as a means of *forging* the self. If anything, people were as suspicious of shopping as a realm of identity formation as they were of its status as leisure. As Zoe insisted:

> What I don't like about this society is precisely that, that that's how you express yourself, through the things you consume, and that's why I sort of put more value on other things such as personal characteristics.

Even though most people I spoke with would readily concede that they placed value on clothes, on items like cars and compact disks and on the interior decor of their houses, they were often insistent that this was not ultimately, or even mainly, how they wished to express who they were. For many people consumption seemed a too inactive or passive way of expressing themselves. Emma articulated this well, echoing the thoughts of others:

> I think you get a lot more out of life not from consumption but from maybe, maybe using yourself to get something out of life, using your head to get something out of life, and using the world to get something out of life, to enjoy life more . . .

These efforts to further delimit the meanings and importance of shopping related, as we shall see below, to people's wider concerns about living in a consumer society.

Consumption Critiqued, Empowerment Queried

Whether people like or dislike the supermarket, demarcate between necessity and leisure shopping, or seek a sense of pleasure through the shop, the very same people often express a quite detailed critique of 'consumer society'. Many of the people I spoke with expressed an ambivalence about consumption cultures, just as they were sometimes critical of particular shopping environments. People were drawn in some way to the material goods and experiences that a consumer economy offered, but felt concerned also and sometimes repelled by the selfishness, materialism, environmental damage and cultural emptiness they thought 'consumerism' encouraged.

Other qualitative studies of consumption cultures have spoken of similar feelings of ambivalence. In the early 1990s two British researchers, Peter K. Lunt and Sonia M. Livingstone, found that, on the one hand, consumption was celebrated by the people they interviewed as a terrain of personal choice and individual economic freedom. On the other hand, the very same people were highly critical of the materialism, loss of self-control and the undermining of community bonds that the rise of a consumer culture was seen to encourage.[7] That is, the people interviewed experienced a contradiction in living a consumer culture; they embraced consumption but felt also an ambivalence about the changes ushered in by consumer cultures in terms of fostering a materialistic and socially fragmented world over which people felt less and less control. As Lunt and Livingstone noted, within everyday life 'the basic debate about consumption and identity is ongoing – is involvement in material culture a liberation or an entrapment?'.[8]

The same question was dealt with by the people I spoke to as part of this study. Their responses to living within a 'consumer society' were often forceful and unguarded, precisely because they were not constrained by the need to fit their reactions into more formal debates within social and cultural theory.

> The first thing that came into my mind was selfish . . . It's just everything there at your fingertips, there's no thought at all, it's just that's what I want and I want to have it.

This is how Zoe began to explain what the term 'consumer society' meant to her. For Zoe, contemporary consumption cultures encourage a selfishness and a desire for immediate gratification. This is a view shared by some older people as well. Anetta Barr spoke of consumer society in much the same terms:

> I think that it doesn't make for a peaceful, contented life. I think people see things, they want things, they use it and throw it away . . . I don't think it does anything for people.

Clearly, Anetta sees consumption not only as selfish, but ultimately unsatisfying. During our conversation, Anetta spoke of people's participation in consumption cultures as a kind of restless searching for happiness and gratification that she felt could not ultimately be met by material things.

These two responses to living in a 'consumer society' suggest that people of widely varying ages and backgrounds can be highly critical of consumer cultures, though for different reasons. While Anetta tended to compare the present with a lost past in which community bonds were seen to be stronger, Zoe made no such historical comparisons. For Zoe consumption cultures did not signal something lost but something absent. Indeed, she posited a striking demarcation between everyday life and the economic marketplace when she insisted that, 'Consumerism is a substitute for living'.

This unease about living within a consumer society – and everyone I spoke to felt that they *were* living in such a society – was connected by some to notions of entrapment rather than individual selfishness. Sue, for example, spoke of consumer society as involved in 'normalising' an economic definition of life, 'The term consumer society conjures up for me the idea of, of spending as a normal course of life, that's it, it's something that we are here to do'. Others, like Prue, drew a direct link between the compulsory and normalising nature of paid work and the unequal consumer rewards it yielded:

> I think we do consume too much, and it just becomes a way of, it's just as controlling as work because it means that you have to work to be part, to be part of the consumer society and interact and partake in it. And it marginalises a lot of people as well, it's because consumer items have so much status as well . . . it just creates more inequalities, I think, in society, because people can't, it just makes it harder and harder for people to get involved.

Emma, as well, spoke of consumption as a treadmill of working and spending:

> To me the term [consumer society] means buy, buy, buy. And we work to consume, so it's like a machine in that we're working and

earning money which we just put back into it again . . . But we
have to sort of. I mean we have to, we don't have to buy food, we
could maybe live self-sufficiently, but it's almost vital to go up to
the supermarket.

These comments emphasise both the inequalities of consumption and
people's feelings of entrapment within consumption cultures. Despite Prue's
liking for 'nice things' she was highly critical of consumer culture in general,
just as she was wary of the leisure status of shopping. Prue experienced this
as a contradiction within herself and grappled with this ambivalence during
our conversation. Emma described much the same fractured experience of
consumption cultures and of a feeling that fewer and fewer viable alternatives were available to those who did not want to use spaces such as the
supermarket. Neither of these women felt powerless or purely manipulated
in relation to living within a consumer society, but both were intensely aware
of the possibility of themselves and others being drawn into a culture of
consumerism over which they felt only partial control.

This raises questions about the various ways in which people feel both
manipulated into living consumption cultures while also partially withstand-
ing being drawn too far in to them. When asked to comment on the notion of
consumption as embodying a culture of manipulation many people felt that
they were indeed subject to such manipulation, but within definite limits.
People tended to speak of both a power to refuse consumer ideologies and of
moments where they were drawn unwillingly into them. In fact some people
felt enormously frustrated by constantly, and sometimes unsuccessfully,
having to resist consumerism. This was particularly the case for younger
women, some of whom were enormously resentful of the forces that played
on them. As Emma put it:

Even so-called women's magazines like Cleo and Dolly or whatever, they say the best thing a girl can do when she's feeling down
is go shopping and I've actually done that before and it worked
which is really sad [laughter] . . . We think we have to go and buy
things to make us feel worthy somehow and that we've achieved
something by buying something . . . I just thought 'Oh that's,
that's very sad', that what those horrible women's magazines said
is true, 'cause I don't believe what they say, and I don't think it is
true, like, with shopping you go and solve all your problems.
Such a stereotype for a woman thing to do.

There is both humour and anger here, as well as a real mindfulness of the
limitations attached to the cultures Emma finds herself within. Her comments suggest also that 'giving in' to the ideologies of consumption is by no

means an unconscious process. Many people I talked with spoke of moments when they were drawn only half willingly into consuming as if viewing their actions from a distance. At the very moment of consuming people can know full well that the desire to consume may come not simply from themselves but from forces outside them. Even when manipulated, then, people are not necessarily duped. It is almost as if there is a shadow land surrounding particular acts of consumption, or a gap between not quite choosing to consume but not quite giving in to the cultural imperative to do so; not quite feeling in control within consumer environments, but not quite relinquishing a sense of power and refusal. When particular consumption decisions were spoken of in this way, as 'not quite conscious', people often spoke also of a sense of guilt or dissatisfaction. As Claire put it:

> I don't know, you buy something and you, you get that sort of initial 'oh great', you know, got something new to wear, or something new to put in the house. And then, then, you know, two hours later you're going 'Oh God, I shouldn't have spent the money. Oh God, I should have paid this, I should have saved it, I should have . . .'. Then it's like, 'Oh well it's here now'.

Anthony spoke, too, of a sense of emptiness on those occasions where shopping did not deliver on its promises:

> I think I get manipulated at times. I'm just thinking, like some- times I want to reward myself, so I'll go and buy . . . Like yester- day, I went to go and buy [a magazine] and I only went to buy it because I feel like I deserve it, and what I deserve is something gorgeous and glossy, you know. And then I buy it and then I end up feeling a bit empty [laughter], this is tragic [laughter], because it's failed to deliver whatever I thought it was going to give me . . . So I guess I feel a bit manipulated then . . . by some other force . . . It feels like it's something [that's] been done to me rather than me doing it.

In many respects, people's responses to the issue of manipulation suggested the continued importance of exploring the unconscious, semi-conscious and 'powerless' elements attached to the practices of consumption and consumer desire, instead of just assuming that manipulation does not occur or should be ignored in favour of exploring moments of resistance and empowerment.

And what of resistance and empowerment? What of the notion that through consumption practices people can resist, remake and partially escape the drudgeries of life and even the dominant ideologies of consumer capitalism. Few people I talked with seemed very enthusiastic about this idea. In fact I searched largely in vain for the resistant and empowering aspects of consumption of which some cultural analysts have spoken. What I did certainly find was a mindfulness about the possibilities and limitations of consumption and an ability to act in discriminating and purposeful ways as 'consumers'. This was sometimes interpreted as a power, but then only a limited one. Emma, once again:

> I don't, I don't feel a sense of power, I don't think it's power, no, definitely not. It's, I don't know what you'd call it, it's getting out into the world I guess and seeing lots of people and not being powerful, not being above anyone that's in the place, and not feeling powerful by taking a can off the shelf or, you know, buying something or whatever. I don't feel powerful in that way . . . No actually in the supermarket I don't feel powerful, but I'm just thinking now about when I buy clothes and I will go and dish out quite a bit of money for a dress or something, or anything. I think, yeah, I do feel a little bit, I don't know if power's the correct word, but I feel something, yeah empowered perhaps, yeah because I'm, I'm doing something for myself.

Others, like Prue, felt neither powerful nor manipulated: 'I don't feel a power no. But I don't really feel anything acting on me as well'. Zoe, on the other hand, was less guarded in dismissing the personally empowering potentialities of shopping:

> No, not really. I don't feel power, no, not really. If it wasn't around, if shopping wasn't around, I wouldn't know what I was missing, so therefore I wouldn't think I was missing anything enjoyable. Do you know what I mean?

Sue also rejected outright the notion that shopping and consumption were a terrain of personal empowerment. She argued that we consume mostly to fill a vacuum in our life. For her, consumption was thus largely disempowering rather than a realm of creativity: 'I wouldn't, I wouldn't consider it [shopping] an empowering process at all'. Brian also rejected the notion of shopping as empowering in no uncertain terms; though for reasons which returned, once again, to a utilitarian and perhaps class-based view of shopping. Brian was, in fact, witheringly critical of those who speculate about the politics of consumption from behind a desk:

> I would describe that argument as sounding very academic up yourself . . . No, because you go out and you get this sense of power, you control your own destiny. If you want to relate that to

the supermarket, that's not what's happening, you're going out to buy the bread so you can have your lunch tomorrow, you know simple survival. I can't see how any type of shopping is powerful. Perhaps some people can, but you've lost me on it . . . I would simply describe it as academic up yourself and forget about it.

For some people, like Paul, feeling empowered within consumer society was based on rejecting something of what it offered. Paul argued strongly, though with a touch of melodramatic humour, against the consumerism that he felt surrounded him:

Well, we do live in a consumer society. I've made a deliberate choice to do some things like not own a car, which is a big consumer item . . . and also not to have a television . . . which I think is one of the most vicious forms of consumer propaganda!

Perhaps the last word on consumption cultures, however, should go to Sue who was clear in her wish, as she put it, to be 'independent of the consumer circle', 'to stand outside it', rather than participate within it. Although most people did not articulate a wish to 'stand outside' as clearly or as strongly as this, and nor were they as firm in their opinions of consumption as Paul, few if any people I spoke with were happy to think of themselves as 'consumers'. This was not a process of denial; people accepted that they were involved in the consumption of material and cultural goods on a daily basis. Yet, at the same time, being a shopper or a consumer was not something to be entirely claimed. Somehow, consumption was felt to be inadequate as a means of self-expression and as an intrinsically valuable terrain of human agency.

In this chapter I have sought to construct a narrative of contemporary supermarket shopping using the words of others rather than purely my own. The everyday talk explored here has offered a glimpse – and just a glimpse – of people's reactions to the presence of the supermarket in their lives, and their thoughts about contemporary consumer environments and practices. This talk illustrates the social and cultural complexity of everyday shopping. As we have seen in this chapter, and in chapter six, the supermarket has been and continues to be envisaged by shoppers themselves as both exciting and mundane, sociable and sterile, as a place to be selectively used and to be avoided.

The interviews drawn on here, then, certainly confirm the notion, signalled in the introduction to this study, that people react in diverse ways to the consumer cultures they find themselves in. Moreover, people clearly think through the nature of their participation in those cultures. In a very real sense, people do not just simply act within consumer cultures in either accepting or resistant ways, but strive at times to stand outside them and to 'theorise' consumption itself. This is a process of thinking through which takes place not on paper but on the terrain of everyday life, and which is thus freed from the constraints of constantly having to justify its claims and hedge its bets with the footnotes of a more formal mode of theorising.

However, the contradictory texture and diversity of the responses documented here also suggest how difficult it is to generalise about people's participation in consumer cultures. This very diversity of response illustrates the manner in which the talk of others can be used to extend and to ground historical and cultural interpretation while rendering suspect any claim to an authentic knowledge of everyday life, any claim that the popular somehow legitimates a particular intellectual position.[9] Ultimately, then, it is the historian or theorist of consumption themselves who must take responsibility for what *they* think, not look to others – conceived as either a mindless mass or subversive popular – to legitimate it.

This is made even more apparent when confronting the problem of how to 'read' interview material. In chapter six I spoke of the difficulties in dealing with historical memory. In this chapter, we strike a similar difficulty connected with the manner in which, through conversation, people plot their participation in consumption cultures in a way which perhaps exaggerates a distancing and reorients, rather than simply reports, the meaning of past actions. This is not to suggest that people's statements are false or misleading, simply that the talk reviewed here does not exist outside those discourses of retailing and consumption discussed in chapters seven and eight. Rather, people speak about the pleasures and dissatisfactions of consumption cultures at the very moment of being immersed within them. Thus when people speak of efforts to delimit their involvement with those cultures, they invoke, I would argue, both an *actual* and an *imaginary* outside. Together, these two 'outsides' stand as a powerful critique of consumption itself, though a critique which evades firm identification.

Chapter 10

Towards the Exit

I began this book with an image of contemporary supermarket shopping in England where this study first took shape. I will open this closing chapter with another image, this time an Australian one. I visited many supermarkets as part of this study but it was my local Safeway that served as the constant reference point of my thinking about the rise of the one-stop-shop. I would go in to 'my' Safeway both as a consumer and as a historian. Recently, however, I visited it for the last time – not as a shopper but as someone formally piecing together its history and exploring its cultural meaning.

As I walked to Safeway, down Smith Street in the inner-Melbourne suburb of Collingwood, I could see materially, as I had done many times, something of the historical transformations that have been traced throughout this study. As I walked this street I could almost visualise the 15 000 shop assistants who marched in protest here in 1886. For a moment I could hear the shouts of those 'howling ruffians and unsexed women', as one contemporary observer labelled them, calling for shorter working hours. In looking up at one facade I realised, too, that I was passing the old Mac.Robertson's confectionery works. At the turn of the century this was an enormous manufacturing complex and its owner, Sir Macpherson Robertson, was looked on as a god of the Australian manufacturing industry. Now other gods occupy the place; Christian literature is sold there in renovated surroundings. A little further towards destination Safeway, I pass the very first Coles variety store, the one that opened in 1914. The store is no longer owned by Coles but it still sells bargains; it's an opportunity shop. Across the road from this 'op shop' is the Kentucky Fried Chicken store. If you look skyward above the red and white KFC logos, you notice a still-impressive late nineteenth-century warehouse

From grocery to takeaway: the Moran & Cato building, Smith Street, Collingwood, 1995

with the words 'Moran & Cato' tiled in relief along the top of the building. This was one of the first Moran & Cato storage depots, with a shop below. Now, the global takeaway food outlet is housed within the forgotten grocery store.

In terms of the history of Australian manufacturing, retailing and shopping, Smith Street is of considerable importance. In walking down this street today, however, its past glory is none too obvious. From the late nineteenth century on, the shops of Smith Street competed with the city centre for clientele, drawing customers from the surrounding inner suburbs. There was the big Foy and Gibson's department store here, as well as Moran & Cato and later Coles, and other chain stores like Crofts.

Over the last few years Smith Street has experienced a confused renaissance after quite a few decades of decline. Brunswick Street, close by, has grown rapidly over the last ten years or so and has been transformed into a centre of cafes, bookshops and gift stores. Smith Street, on the other hand, is still a patchwork of pubs, green-grocers, opportunity shops, cheap clothing shops (and some trendy designer ones as well), mixed-business Vietnamese stores, and a fast-growing number of cafes, suggesting that Brunswick Street 'culture' is moving east at a pace. There is, even now, only a partial coherence to Smith Street, which is perhaps one of its attractions.

There is one shop, in particular, that is pure anomaly even among this retailing hotchpotch. It's an old manchester store with a wooden counter that runs in a horseshoe shape around the floor. The high shelves behind the counter are stocked with sheets and towels and sundry other items. There are three brass-rimmed display windows fronting the store presenting a show of cushions, quilts and blankets. Inside, the light is dim and you can just make out the figures of the Italian proprietors moving behind the counter.

I have not been in this shop, and I have rarely seen anyone else in there either. I want to go in but I always lose my nerve at the moment I am about to enter. What pushes me away is not simply my own shyness but the fact that I have been brought up to think of shopping as a particular kind of activity. This is not a shop designed to accommodate the autonomous gaze or the unrestrained touch. It clearly provides only a certain framework for the expression of consumer desire. You are not going to be left on your own in this store; you are going to have to interact. Of course other stores, like the delicatessen or the butcher, have elements of the same counter-service culture. But there is usually some attempt within such stores to relax the customer by incorporating some limited self-service. In the old Smith Street manchester store there is no such compromise.

My own tentativeness, and I suspect that of others, towards entering this shop speaks of the transformations in retailing and shopping that have taken place in the post-war period. When self-service first appeared, as we have seen in previous chapters, many people were wary of it. Customers quite literally had to be taught what to do, how to use the self-service shop. The complete abandonment of the counter seemed both frustrating and exciting. In the self-service store you no longer had to interact with anybody, just with the products. Now, at the close of the twentieth century, that very framework of autonomy has become so much a part of shopping, and what was once a strange modernity so familiar, that it is the old, the counter, that appears uninviting. It is the old that I, and people of my age and younger, no longer know how to use.

To write this is not to indulge in nostalgia. I'm not sure I would want to return to an early counter-service form of shopping, even if this was possible. Counter service, after all, was often involved in class-specific notions of pro-prietorial servility and customer privilege as well as very particular gender relationships. But in terms of social and cultural transformation, it is extraordinary that just 40, even 30 years ago people would have had no hesitation in entering a counter-service shop. In fact, they may have taken a certain pleasure in the framework of desire it allowed and perhaps, too, enjoyed the interaction across the counter. Now, many people, including myself, think of that very interaction as threatening, constraining and something to be avoided.

Almost directly across the road from the old manchester store, I can enter into an entirely different retailing environment; the Safeway to which I have so often come. As the doors open just for me, and the temperature changes, I am 'welcomed' by an environment that is not necessarily any less social than an older form of retailing, but which is undoubtedly, as the slogans of the 1960s insisted, *a world away*. It is that difference, and the speed with which modern forms of retailing and shopping have become familiar, that this book has attempted to explore in historical and cultural terms.

That speed of change continues. The old manchester store has since been transformed into a cafe and its interior is being peopled once again. The final demise of one sociability gives rise to another.

What this book has offered is a history of supermarket retailing in Australia in the context of the changing cultures and practices of everyday shopping throughout the second half of the twentieth century. There are a number of themes running throughout this text concerning nationhood and modernity, the globalisation of retail forms, changing notions of masculinity and femininity, and consumption as expressive of the autonomous self. Above all, this book has sought to draw attention to the status of consumer cultures as *negotiated forms*; that is, as cultures that arise through an interaction between those who have something to sell, those who wander, use, interpret and sometimes refuse consumer spaces and products, and those who comment on this process.

In the introductory chapter, I drew a number of distinctions: between retail cultures and consumer cultures, between the new and the familiar, and between popular participation and everyday outsidedness. These distinctions have shaped the interpretations offered throughout this study.

In Part One I sought to provide a context for the rise of modern retailing and consumer cultures in Australia by offering a brief comparative history of retail transformations, food manufacturing, and the development of consumer cultures in nineteenth and early twentieth-century Britain and the United States. I traced also the development of a modern retail industry within colonial and early twentieth-century Australia, and explored in detail the early history of the counter-service grocery store.

Part One was designed to illustrate that, even before the rise of self-service, industrialising countries, including Australia, witnessed the gradual emergence of a culture of retailing that viewed consumption as an individual rather that collective practice. This retail culture, centred on the autonomous self, the discrete package and the abundant shelf, began to shape the parameters of the emerging 'consumer', and was understood by retailers as nothing short of revolutionary. Part One sought, in addition, to illustrate the link made by Australian retailers and manufacturers between the growth of the nation and commercial developments. This was connected with the emergence of a modernity in Australian retailing understood through the categories of Americanisation and scientific selling, and embodied in the establishment of retail chains. Finally, we began in Part One to examine the complex relationship between retailing and certain conceptions of femininity and masculinity.

In Part Two these themes were explored in more detail in relation to the rise of self-service and the supermarket. The provenance of the Australian supermarket was further contextualised through a brief discussion of the 'invention' and development of supermarketing in the United States and its transportation to post-war Britain. Here, I sought to illustrate the manner in which the supermarket has, in the post-war period, become an increasingly global phenomenon, whereby the supermarket has adapted to as well as remoulded particular national and local cultures.

This interplay between the global and the local was clearly evident in the demise of counter-service grocery retailing in Australia and in its replacement by self-service. During the 1950s and 1960s the nature of grocery retailing and of everyday shopping in Australia was fundamentally transformed. Part Two sought to illustrate in detail how this transformation was embedded in the struggle between the traditional and the modern in food retailing, between big and small business, and between different notions of how and what type of masculinity could be expressed through commerce.

Part Two also explored transformations in the notions of selfhood embodied in the rise of self-service and the supermarket. As part of this exploration I traced the manner in which the notion of consumer autonomy was reconfirmed through self-service and had, by the 1960s, become an integral part of the experience of everyday shopping in Australia. This experience, however, was discussed in terms other than those offered by post-war retailers. The exploration of early supermarketing in Australia was given greater depth by drawing on the memories of people who themselves experienced retail transformations first hand. Their observations suggested, among other things, that the power of post-war retailing to shape and control the experience of everyday shopping was by no means seamless or unproblematic.

As the autonomous consumer became embroiled in a transition from the new to the familiar throughout the post-war decades, autonomy became a definitive part of everyday shopping and, at the same time, began to lose some of its supposed magic. In the final section of the book, we have examined this process of dissolution, and brought the history of the Australian supermarket full circle. As people have become familiar with and ultimately bored by the supermarket, and as the framework of everyday life has altered in the later decades of the twentieth century, the stock super-marketing motifs of modernity, convenience and leisure have apparently come unstuck.

This has been the contradictory logic of large-scale retailing. At almost the very moment that everyday shopping became defined as an autonomous and leisurely activity, the potential enjoyments of shopping began to be altered and undermined by the very retail environments and cultures constructed. By the 1980s it was the perceived failure of the supermarket to offer an appealing shopping culture that came to occupy the minds of retailers, not its supposed magic. Retailers in this situation began, once again, to look for ways of 're-revolutionising' shopping as a ground of convenience, choice, comfort and sociability. In fact, only about 30 years after the establishment of the big corporate supermarket in Australia, retailers had begun talking of its partial abandonment.

Over the last three or four decades, retailing in Australia has thus been embroiled in an extraordinarily contradictory discourse. At one and the same time, retailing has sought to individuate the shopper as an autonomous consumer, but speak also the language of community. It has sought to connect shopping with the self, but construct also new social bonds through the very activity of the autonomous consumer wandering within ever larger, impersonal and clinically planned retail environments. This is a contradictory discourse that continues unabated.

What this study ultimately suggests, then, is that while involved in the reshaping of everyday life, the retail cultures constructed in the post-war period have been less coherent, less rational and scientific, less powerful in design and effect than retailers and cultural critics have believed them to be. In fact, the thinking of corporate retailers has often been rather ad hoc in nature and naive in outlook when it has come to understanding the consumer and the processes of consumption. This thinking has often been as much about imagined (and intensely masculine) futures – about the dream-worlds of *retailers* – as it has been about potential profits through the rationalisation of the retail industry. The rise and consolidation of the corporate supermarket in Australia have brought about enormous change in the nature of retailing and in our everyday life, as they have elsewhere in the world. Yet the supermarket's power to reshape that life has been as problematic as it has been effective.

For Australian intellectuals, as we have seen in chapter eight, the ongoing attempt by retailers to couple commerce and community has been anathema. For many critics, retailers have been seen as promoting a commercial individualism while constructing false communities and mundane pleasures into the bargain. Intellectuals have clearly played a significant part in constructing notions of Australia as a consumer society. However, there have been aspects of this critical tradition that have offered more populist explanations of consumption practices, or at the very least have suggested that a critical response to consumption must come to terms with the political ambiguities of people's participation in consumer cultures.

It is, in part, for this reason that intellectual work has been contrasted in the previous chapter with the contradictory talk of 'shoppers' themselves. In utilising the words and imaginings of others I have sought to suggest that, ultimately, the task of theorising consumption cannot rest on making sweeping generalisations about the 'manipulated masses', but nor can it rest on moving to the opposite theoretical pole and claiming the voice of the popular as speaking for a certain politics of participatory resistance and transgression. If anything, the people I spoke with as part of this study seemed to waver between quite different moments of being unconsciously drawn into and manipulated by the 'dreamworld' of consumer cultures, participating in those cultures in sometimes quite selective, critical and highly conscious ways, and refusing to participate in consumer cultures at all.

In recognising this difficulty of grasping and analysing the meanings of everyday consumption, this book has further sought to engage with recent debates concerning the interpretation of consumer cultures, making this as much a text about contemporary cultural theory as it is a work of narrative history. In the last few pages I want to return to theory and particularly to some of the issues raised in the introduction.

In the introduction to this book I spoke of recent attempts by cultural commentators and historians to move beyond a certain critical legacy, one which understood people's participation in consumption cultures as socially destructive, culturally bereft and politically suspect. Consumption in the West is still certainly viewed in these terms. However, less dismissive modes of interpreting consumption cultures have gained ground over the last two decades in particular. Drawing on less negative traditions of theorising consumption, many writers now speak of consumer cultures with a feel for the complexity and political ambiguities of people's consumption activities. This has not meant the abandonment of a critique of consumer capitalism, but rather involves an effort to grasp the manner in which people – even when fully participating in consumer cultures – evade being simply manipulated by the market.

Yet the introduction to this book also identified some problems with this interpretative shift, not the least of which has been the tendency of some writers to simply opt for a straightforward celebration of consumption practices as resistant, subversive, or in some way oppositional to the ideologies of consumer capitalism. Until very recently, a rather thinly conceptualised notion of resistant consumer practices has been privileged, within an array of studies, over an examination of the broader historical, cultural, social and global economic frameworks within which consumption takes place. This attempt to equate popular consumption practices with a politics of resist-ance, I have argued, has been expressive of both a critical timidity and an inability to fully confront the difficulties embedded in reformulating a radical critique of the present. Indeed, as a form of oppositional critique, the turn to the active consumer quickly became a politically lazy, and even politically negligent, analytical strategy. Moreover, as a form of analysis it failed to see that we do not have to be dismissive towards people in order to be critical of the economies, societies and cultures we all live within.

One way to move beyond the legacy of this critical strategy is, perhaps, to forget about 'the people' or 'the popular' altogether, rather than to continue trying to know what these are and to claim them in the name of a radical politics. This is not to suggest that historians and critics should abandon efforts to engage with the everyday aspects of people's lives, and to see those lives as engaged in political struggle. It is to see a politicised critique of the present as being engaged in little more than simply documenting the various ways in which people live creatively and resistantly within it. In political terms, historical and cultural critique reduced to this purely documentary role relegates to the back-burner the act of imagining different futures.

It is this imperative to go beyond the documentation of consumer practices that informs the present study. As is evident right throughout this book, I share an interest in the 'consumer' as an active agent who participates in the creation and critique of consumer cultures. But I have argued, too, that there is a further dynamic which tends to be elided by any exclusive emphasis on resistant participation. This is a recognition of the manner in which consumption practices are delimited by and encased within given retail environments, marketing logics, commercial cultures and a whole array of historically entrenched social, cultural, economic and political frameworks. These delimiting forces may not ultimately fully contain the practices of everyday life, but they do have a power to partially direct and constrain the meanings of individual acts of consumption. This is not to reinstate a theory of mass manipulation. It is simply to recognise that, while consumption activities are involved in the process of re-inscribing consumer environments and products with meaning, that re-inscription takes place on a terrain where certain meanings are always already inscribed on the pro-ducts consumed or the consumer spaces utilised. It would seem that neither the inscription of meaning by forces outside the individual, nor the re-inscription of meaning by an individual's actions can be privileged within any analysis of consumer cultures. Rather, both the processes of inscription and re-inscription are of interest, since it is in the dynamic between the two – the space in between, so to speak – where consumer cultures arise.

Given this very dynamic, everyday consumer activity has been understood in this study as a terrain of both action and thought, of active participation and active refusal, of working within and standing back from the given – and at times popular – frameworks within which people live their lives. As I argued in the introduction, it is this dual process of making do with *and* thinking through the consumer present, of both participating in *and* distancing oneself from given consumer frameworks that is of analytical and political interest. One of the things I have argued in this study is that people do not simply construct and live their identity solely through 'making do', in either resigned or resistant ways, with what is available to them under conditions of consumer capitalism. They are equally involved in delimiting their engagement with the consumer present and in living and/or imagining an *outside*. This is precisely because people may not always feel the potential to be empowered within given consumer frameworks. They may not always feel that those frameworks – popular or not – actually provide the pleasures, the possibilities for creativity or subversion, the terrains of unconstrained desire of which, ironically, both retailers and recent cultural analysts have so overconfidently spoken.

These comments return us to the issue of ambiguity and ambivalence. To speak of people standing both inside and outside consumer cultures, and as both subject to constraint and engaged in creativity when consuming, is to suggest that consumption as a social practice is enormously complex. I have attempted, throughout this book, to grapple with this complexity, and with the ambiguity of meanings embedded in retail and consumer cultures. I have wanted to retain a sense of the power held by a consumer capitalism 'over' the frameworks of everyday life, but to see that power as productive of something beyond itself, and as often not very effective in moulding how life is lived and thought about.

Yet recognition of this ambiguity can, as I have argued previously, lead to an intellectual and political ambivalence that can be enormously debilitating in formulating a clear response to life as presently lived. A critical ambivalence can be a way of saying nothing very much at all, other than that things are complex. For this reason, I don't want to end this book on a note of ambivalence. Having now spent a number of years studying the supermarket and the cultures of which it is a part, I feel a certain clarity of response. That response is based on a realisation that none of us are simply manipulated into an unquestioning acceptance of the consumer present. Yet, however belligerently, thoughtfully or resistantly we may act within that present, the given frameworks of a consumer capitalism *remain in place*. This is the central problem with which a radical historical and cultural analysis of consumption must in some way deal.

For my own part, then, the issue to be confronted is not only how people act within retail and consumer cultures, but the fact that those particular cultures are there and, in the process, displacing something else which could be put in their place. For my own part, I do not simply want to 'make do' with supermarkets and the retail and consumer cultures of which they are a part, I want to *undo* them. I cannot claim that 'the people', 'the popular', 'the everyday' agrees with or authenticates this position. However, I suspect that there might be some 'popular' sympathy with it. This is because, at the end of the day, I suspect many people know that it is simply not as easy to resist, undo, or remake 'the meanings of the market' as some cultural analysts have supposed.

Consumer environments and experiences – of which the supermarket is a central one – have a power to greatly delimit the possibilities for human interaction, satisfaction and co-operation, even though a human creativity seeps through and partially undoes those delimitations. Supermarkets, like all other retail forms, are never simply free-standing, entirely local environments, open to an endless free-play of meaning. On the contrary, they are always part of a broader economic, social and cultural framework of production, distribution, consumption and disposal in the West which is implicated in enormous damage to community, human relationships, the environment and other cultures. The central issue confronting the historian and critic of consumption, then, is not simply how passively or actively people live the present, not simply about condemning or celebrating the blandness or vibrancy of popular culture, but how all of us can think about and realise *other cultures*; how all of us can think about and realise modes of *living differently*. Those modes are precisely the things that are never to be found on the supermarket shelf. They cannot be bought. They can only be found outside the shop.

Notes

Introduction

1 See *Some Facts About J Sainsbury plc 1996*, Sainsbury's Corporate Relations Department, London, 1996; Tesco plc, *Annual Report and Accounts 1996*, Tesco plc, Cheshunt, 1996; ASDA, *Report and Accounts 1996*, ASDA Group plc, Leeds, 1996.

2 Subha Narayanan, 'Annual Report', *Retail World*, December 9–13, 1996, p. 15. Supermarkets and grocery stores in Australia are broadly divided within the industry into three groups; 'non-aligned independents' (small shops run by an individual, a family or a group), 'independents' (stores with similar ownership patterns as non-aligned independents but trading under a particular 'banner' identity and aligned with one major wholesaling company), and 'chain operators' (generally corporately owned networks of large stores).

3 A supermarket is now industry-defined worldwide as any store with a selling area of between 400 and 2500 square metres selling at least 70 per cent foodstuffs and everyday commodities. This is differentiated from a self-service store or superette, a food outlet with a selling area of between 120 and 400 square metres. See *Retail Trade International 1989/90 Volume One: Europe*, Euromonitor Publications, London, 1989, p. 7. The supermarket is further differentiated from the 'superstore' and the 'hypermarket', both of which are discussed in chapter seven of this book. These technical definitions do not necessarily correspond at all to the manner in which retailers have, in the past, utilised the term 'supermarket'. As such, this study is concerned to explore the supermarket conceptually rather than as a tightly defined retail entity.

4 See Narayanan, 'Annual Report'. As of December 1996 the breakdown of market shares in packaged groceries was Woolworths: 34.3 per cent, Coles Myer: 26.3 per

cent, 'independent' wholesalers (supplying 'banner group' stores): 23 per cent, Franklins: 15.2 per cent, and other retailers: 1.2 per cent. Supermarketing in Australia is the largest retailing activity, accounting for about one-third of all retail sales.

5   Gail Reekie, *Temptations: Sex, Selling and the Department Store*, Allen & Unwin, Sydney, 1993, 'Introduction'.

6   See Victorian Advisory Council on the Status of Women, *Who Shops in the Supermarket – Men or Women?*, Government Printer, Melbourne, 1981. The Australian Bureau of Statistics found that, in 1992, shopping was the one unpaid domestic task shared most equally between women and men, no doubt because it is one of the least mundane. Nevertheless, women still spent an average of 6.4 hours a week shopping compared to the male average of 4.1 hours. Cited in *The Age*, Wednesday 22 June 1994, p. 22.

7   On theorisations of consumption see Mike Featherstone, *Consumer Culture and Postmodernism*, Sage, London, 1991 (particularly ch. 2.); Robert Bocock, *Consumption*, Routledge, London, 1993; Martyn J. Lee, *Consumer Culture Reborn: The Cultural Politics of Consumption*, Routledge, London, 1993; and Daniel Miller, *Material Culture and Mass Consumption*, Blackwell, Oxford, 1991.

8   On the history of consumption see; Joan Thirsk, *Economic Policy and Projects: The Development of Consumer Society in Early Modern England*, Oxford University Press, Oxford, 1978; Neil McKendrick, John Brewer and J.H. Plumb, *The Birth of Consumer Society: The Commercialisation of Eighteenth-Century England*, Indiana University Press, Bloomington, 1982; Chandra Mukerji, *From Graven Images: Patterns of Modern Materialism*, Columbia University Press, New York, 1983; Colin Campbell, *The Romantic Ethic and the Spirit of Modern Consumerism*, Basil Blackwell, Oxford, 1987; Lorna Weatherill, *Consumer Behaviour and Material Culture in Britain 1660–1760*, Routledge, London, 1988; Carol Sharmas, *The Pre-Industrial Consumer in England and America*, Clarendon Press, Oxford, 1990; and John Brewer and Roy Porter (eds), *Consumption and the World of Goods*, Routledge, London, 1993.

9   It has been suggested that this 'new' interest in consumption has spanned the humanities and social sciences over the last decade, leading to the rise of 'consumption studies'. See Daniel Miller, 'Consumption as the Vanguard of History', in Daniel Miller (ed.), *Acknowledging Consumption: A Review of New Studies*, Routledge, London, 1995, pp. 1–57. Miller's self-styled 'polemic', although thought-provoking, wildly overstates the case for the importance of consumption studies and exaggerates the extent to which theorists and critics have previously 'ignored' consumption. This tendency to construct consumption as an 'absence' within Western intellectual discourse is evident also in Grant McCracken, *Culture and Consumption: New Approaches to the Symbolic Character of Consumer Goods and Activities*, Indiana University Press, Bloomington, 1990, ch. 1.

10 There are many works that could be cited here and it is not possible to provide an exhaustive list. See following notes for references to individual texts. Jim McGuigan provides a useful discussion of the 'cultural studies of consumption' in his *Cultural Populism*, Routledge, London, 1992.

11 The concept of 'making do' has been important within the cultural studies of consumption and is derived from the work of Michel de Certeau, *The Practice of Everyday Life*, University of California Press, Berkeley, 1984.

12 Feminist cultural studies has been instrumental in this reappraisal of consumption practices. See, for example, Erica Carter, 'Alice in Consumer Wonderland', in Angela McRobbie and Mica Nava (eds), *Gender and Generation*, Macmillan, London, 1984, pp. 185–214; Angela McRobbie, 'Postmodernism and Popular Culture', in Lisa Apignanesi (ed.), *Postmodernism*, Institute of Contemporary Arts, London, 1986, pp. 54–8; E. Ann Kaplan, *Rocking Around the Clock: Music Television, Postmodernism and Consumer Culture*, Methuen, London, 1987; and Ien Ang, *Watching Dallas: Soap Opera and the Melodramatic Imagination*, Methuen, London, 1985; and her *Desperately Seeking The Audience*, Routledge, London, 1991.

13 For an example of this differentiation between the 'new' and the 'old' positions see Mica Nava, 'Consumerism Reconsidered: Buying and Power', *Cultural Studies*, vol. 5, no. 2, May 1991, pp. 157–73. Other writers have spoken also of the manner in which this rather bland dichotomy has come to characterise contemporary debate. See, for example, Lesley Johnson, *The Modern Girl: Girlhood and Growing Up*, Allen & Unwin, Sydney, 1993, ch. 2; and more recently, Peter Miller and Nikolas Rose, 'Mobilizing the Consumer: Assembling the Subject of Consumption', *Theory, Culture and Society*, vol. 14, 1997, pp. 1–36.

14 On the 'negativity' of social theory, including postmodernism, see, for example, Featherstone, *Consumer Culture and Postmodernism*, ch. 2; and Daniel Miller, 'Consumption as the Vanguard of History'.

15 For a discussion of cultural studies as an academic discipline see Jim McGuigan, *Cultural Populism*; Graeme Turner, *British Cultural Studies*, Unwin Hyman, London, 1989; and John Frow and Meaghan Morris (eds), *Australian Cultural Studies: A Reader*, Allen & Unwin, Sydney, 1993, 'Introduction'.

16 For the manner in which consumption practices have become a subject of study within other disciplinary areas also, see the many useful bibliographic essays in Miller (ed.), *Acknowledging Consumption*. See also Roger Burrows and Catherine Marsh (eds), *Consumption and Class: Divisions and Change*, Macmillan, London, 1992; and Peter K. Lunt and Sonia M. Livingstone, *Mass Consumption and Personal Identity: Everyday Economic Experience*, Open University Press, Buckingham, 1992.

17 For a diverse selection of this work see John Fiske, Bob Hodge and Graeme Turner, *Myths of Oz: Reading Australian Popular Culture*, Allen & Unwin, Sydney, 1987; Meaghan Morris, 'Things To Do With Shopping Centres', in Susan Sheridan (ed.), *Grafts: Feminist Cultural Criticism*, Verso, London, 1988, pp. 193–225; John Fiske, *Reading the Popular*, Unwin Hyman, London, 1989; and some of the essays in Rob Shields (ed.), *Lifestyle Shopping: The Subject of Consumption*, Routledge, London, 1992. Note, however, that cultural studies has tended to focus on 'cultural consumption', that is, on the consumption of 'services' such as television and popular music rather than on shopping and the consumption of material goods, the activity with which we are most concerned in this study.

18 Frow and Morris (eds), *Australian Cultural Studies*, pp. xv–xvi.

19 See Meaghan Morris, *The Pirate's Fiancée: Feminism, Reading, Postmodernism*, Verso, London, 1988, p. 5.

20 This was particularly notable in the years 1988 to 1992. Compare, for example, Dick Hebdige, *Hiding in the Light: On Images and Things*, Routledge, London,

1988; John Fiske, *Understanding Popular Culture*, Unwin Hyman, London, 1989; and McCracken, *Culture and Consumption*. See also some of the essays in the following collections: Stuart Hall and Martin Jacques (eds), *New Times: The Changing Face of Politics in the 1990s*, Lawrence and Wishart/Marxism Today, London, 1989; Alan Tomlinson (ed.), *Consumption, Identity and Style: Marketing, Meanings and the Packaging of Pleasure*, Routledge, London, 1990; Cary Nelson, Paula A. Treichler and Lawrence Grossberg (eds), *Cultural Studies*, Routledge, New York, 1992; and Shields (ed.), *Lifestyle Shopping*.

21 I have written about this elsewhere in two articles which prefigure this larger study. See 'Youth and the Art of Subversion', *Arena*, no. 86, 1989, pp. 55–70; and 'A Stranger in Daimaru', *Meanjin*, vol. 53, no. 1, Autumn, 1994, pp. 85–95.

22 See, for example, Tania Modleski (ed.), *Studies in Entertainment*, Indiana University Press, Bloomington, 1986, 'Introduction'; Andrew Ross, *No Respect: Intellectuals and Popular Culture*, Routledge, New York, 1989; Meaghan Morris, 'Things to do with Shopping Centres', and her 'Banality in Cultural Studies', in Patricia Mellencamp (ed.), *The Logics of Television: Essays in Cultural Criticism*, Indiana University Press, Bloomington, 1990, pp. 14–43; and Yvonne Tasker, 'Having it All: Feminism and the Pleasures of the Popular', in Sarah Franklin, Celia Lury and Jackie Stacey (eds), *Off-Centre: Feminism and Cultural Studies*, Harper Collins, London, 1991, pp. 85–96.

23 See, for example, Angela McRobbie, 'New Times in Cultural Studies', *New Formations*, 13 (Spring), 1991, pp. 1–17, and her 'Window Shopping', *Red Pepper*, London, 1996 p. 25; and Graeme Turner, '"It Works for Me": British Cultural Studies, Australian Cultural Studies, Australian Film', in Cary Nelson, Paula A. Treichler and Lawrence Grossberg, (eds), *Cultural Studies*, Routledge, New York, 1992, pp. 640–53.

24 McGuigan, *Cultural Populism*.

25 This has recently been explored by Angela McRobbie in 'Bridging the Gap', *Feminist Review*, no. 55, Spring 1997, pp. 73–89.

26 Interestingly, within North American cultural studies there has been a continuing critique of consumption cultures evident, for example, in the work of Stuart Ewen, *All Consuming Images: The Politics of Style in Contemporary Culture*, Basic Books, New York, 1988. Within recent British social theory there has been a similarly circumspect approach to consumption practices and spaces such as in David Chaney, 'Dystopia in Gateshead: The MetroCentre as a Cultural Form', *Theory, Culture and Society*, vol. 7, 1991, pp. 49–68.

27 For a useful discussion of this tendency within cultural studies see Jean-Christophe Agnew, 'Coming Up for Air: Consumer Culture in Historical Perspective', in Brewer and Porter (eds), *Consumption and the World of Goods*, pp. 19–39.

28 Rachel Bowlby, 'Scenes from Consumer Psychology', *Critical Quarterly*, vol. 24, no. 4, Winter, 1992, p. 63. See also her *Shopping With Freud*, Routledge, London, 1993.

29 Johnson, *The Modern Girl*, ch. 2.

30 See respectively, Rob Shields, 'Spaces for the Subject of Consumption', in his *Lifestyle Shopping*, p. 2; and Janice Radway, 'Mail Order Culture and its Critics: The Book-of-the-Month Club, Commodification and Consumption, and the Problem of Cultural Authority', in Cary Nelson et al. (eds), *Cultural Studies*, pp. 512–30.

31 On the latter theme see Gary Foley, 'White Myths Damage Our Souls', *The Age*, 21 July 1993, p. 15. In undertaking this project I planned to briefly explore the impact of consumption on indigenous Australians. However, this effort quickly appeared tokenistic and inappropriate to this particular study, not least because of the range of themes already covered in the text. I have since had the opportunity to explore some issues of food shopping within indigenous communities in a more practical, co-operative and less academic way. See Kim Humphery, Mervyn Dixon Japanangka and James Marrawal, *From the Bush to the Store: Diabetes in Two Remote Northern Territory Aboriginal Communities* (Territory Health Services/ Diabetes Australia, forthcoming, 1998).

32 Carolyn Steedman, 'Culture, Cultural Studies, and Historians', in Cary Nelson et al. (eds), *Cultural Studies*, pp. 515–16.

33 Ann Curthoys, 'Labour History and Cultural Studies', *Labour History*, no. 67, November 1994, p. 18. See also Graeme Turner, 'Discipline Wars: Australian Studies, Cultural Studies and the Analysis of National Culture', in Graeme Turner (ed.), *Fabrications: Journal of Australian Studies*, no. 50/51, University of Queensland Press, St Lucia, 1996, pp. 6–17.

1 The Discovery of the Consumer

1 Elizabeth Levett, 'The Consumer in History', in Percy Redfern (ed.), *Self and Society: Social and Economic Problems from the Hitherto Neglected Point of View of the Consumer*, vol. 2, Ernest Benn, London, 1930, p. 1 (separately paginated pamphlet).

2 Percy Redfern, 'Introduction', ibid., vol. 1.

3 Harold J. Laski, 'The Recovery of Citizenship', in ibid., p. 5 (separately paginated pamphlet).

4 Beatrice Webb, 'The Discovery of the Consumer', in ibid. Recently, there has been a partial, though somewhat different, 'return' to this linkage between consumption and politicised citizenship in Miller, 'Consumption as the Vanguard of History'. As the title suggests, Miller polemically argues for a view of the 'empowered' consumer as the new agent of radical social change.

5 Webb, ibid.

6 See Robert N. Mayer, *The Consumer Movement: Guardians of the Marketplace*, Twayne, Boston, 1989; and David Halpin (ed.), *Consumers' Choice: 25 Years of the Australian Consumers' Association*, ACA, Marrickville, 1984.

7 James B. Jefferys, *Retail Trading In Britain, 1850–1950*, Cambridge University Press, Cambridge, 1954. See also James Jefferys and David Knee, *Retailing in Europe: Present Structure and Future Trends*, Macmillan, London, 1962

8 See W.G. McClelland, *Studies in Retailing*, Blackwell, Oxford, 1964; Alison Adburgham, *Shops and Shopkeeping, 1800–1914*, Allen & Unwin, London, 1964; Christina Fulop, *Competition for Consumers: A Study of Changing Channels of Distribution*, Institute of Economic Affairs/Andre Deutsch, London, 1964; Dorothy Davis, *A History of Shopping*, Routledge and Kegan Paul, London, 1966; Peter Mathias, *Retailing Revolution: A History of Multiple Retailing in the Food Trades Based upon the Allied Suppliers Group of Companies*, Longman, London, 1967.

9 David Alexander, *Retailing in England During the Industrial Revolution*, Athlone Press, University of London, London, 1970; Gareth Shaw, 'The Evolution and

Impact of Large-Scale Retailing in Britain', in John Benson and Gareth Shaw (eds), *The Evolution of Retail Systems, c. 1800–1914*, Leicester University Press, London, 1992, pp. 135–65. On retailing and consumption generally see Hamish Fraser, *The Coming of the Mass Market, 1850–1914*, Archon, Connecticut, 1981; John A. Dawson, *Commercial Distribution in Europe*, Croom Helm, London, 1982; and Benson and Shaw, ibid.

10 Sharmas, *The Pre-Industrial Consumer*; Hoh-Cheung and Lorna H. Mui, *Shops and Shopkeeping in Eighteenth-Century England*, McGill-Queen's University Press/Routledge, London, 1989. See also Michael J. Winstanley, *The Shopkeeper's World, 1830–1914*, Manchester University Press, Manchester, 1983.

11 Rachel Bowlby, *Just Looking: Consumer Culture in Dreiser, Gissing and Zola*, Methuen, New York and London, 1985, p. 2.

12 Rosalind H. Williams, *Dream Worlds of Mass Consumption in Late Nineteenth-Century France*, University of California Press, Berkeley and Los Angeles, 1982.

13 Michael B. Miller, *The Bon Marché: Bourgeois Culture and the Department Store, 1869–1920*, Allen & Unwin, London, 1981, p. 165.

14 ibid. 'Introduction'. For the department store's impact on gender relations see Reekie, *Temptations*; and Susan Porter Benson, *Counter Cultures: Saleswomen, Managers and Customers in American Department Stores 1890–1940*, University of Illinois Press, Urbana and Chicago, 1986.

15 Thomas Richards, *The Commodity Culture of Victorian England: Advertising and Spectacle 1851–1914*, Stanford University Press, Stanford, 1990.

16 ibid., p. 1.

17 See Richard Wightman Fox and T.J. Jackson Lears (eds), *The Culture of Consumption: Critical Essays in American History 1880–1980*, Pantheon, New York, 1983; Daniel Horowitz, *The Morality of Spending: Attitudes Towards the Consumer Society in America 1875–1940*, Johns Hopkins University Press, Baltimore, 1985; Susan Strasser, *Satisfaction Guaranteed: The Making of the American Mass Market*, Pantheon, New York, 1989; and Ewen, *All Consuming Images*.

18 On the importance of foodstuffs in the rise of consumer society see Mary Douglas and Baron Isherwood, *The World of Goods: Towards an Anthropology of Consumption*, Allen Lane, London, 1979; Diane Barthel, 'Modernism and Marketing: The Chocolate Box Revisited', *Theory, Culture and Society*, vol. 6, 1989, p. 431; and Sidney Mintz, 'The Changing Role of Food in the Study of Consumption', in Brewer and Porter (eds), *The World of Goods*, pp. 261–73.

19 Fraser, *The Coming of the Mass Market*, p. 30.

20 Sharmas, *The Pre-Industrial Consumer*, p. 127.

21 Fraser, *The Coming of the Mass Market*, p. 40.

22 ibid., p. 41.

23 ibid., pp. 167–68.

24 Strasser, *Satisfaction Guaranteed*, 'Introduction'. See also Richard S. Tedlow, *New and Improved: The Story of Mass Marketing in America*, Basic Books, New York, 1990.

25 Tedlow, ibid., p. 14.

26 Williams, *Dream Worlds*, p. 84.

27 Barthel, 'Modernism and Marketing', p. 431.

28 Cited in David Trotter, 'Too Much of a Good Thing: Fiction and the Economy of Abundance', *Critical Quarterly*, vol. 34, no. 4, Winter, 1992, p. 28.

29 Glenna Matthews, *"Just a Housewife": The Rise and Fall of Domesticity in America*, Oxford University Press, New York, 1987, p. 189.

30 Susan Willis, *A Primer For Daily Life*, Routledge, London, 1991, p. 2.

31 Strasser, *Satisfaction Guaranteed*, p. 15.

32 Davis, *A History of Shopping*, p. 253.

33 Matthews, *"Just a Housewife"*. See also Gabriella Turnaturi, 'Between Public and Private: The Birth of the Professional Housewife and the Female Consumer', in Anne Showstack Sassoon (ed.), *Women and the State: The Shifting Boundaries of Public and Private*, Hutchinson, London, 1987, pp. 225–78. As discussed later, this process of 'de-skilling' should not be exaggerated.

34 See Ann Game and Rosemary Pringle, *Gender at Work*, George Allen & Unwin, Sydney, 1983; Jill Julius Matthews, *Good and Mad Women: The Historical Construction of Femininity in Twentieth-Century Australia*, Allen & Unwin, Sydney, 1984; Kereen Reiger, *The Disenchantment of the Home: Modernizing the Australian Family 1850–1940*, Oxford University Press, Melbourne, 1985.

35 On co-operative retailing see Davis, *A History of Shopping*, Chapter XIII; and Jefferys, *Retail Trading in Britain*, Chapter V.

36 Fraser, *The Coming of the Mass Market*, pp. 124–7; Jefferys, ibid., p. 19 and p. 163.

37 Davis, *A History of Shopping*, p. 281.

38 ibid., pp. 281–4; Fraser, *The Coming of the Mass Market*, pp. 113–14.

39 Davis, ibid., p. 283.

40 Fraser, *The Coming of the Mass Market*, p. 112.

41 *J.S. 100: The Story of Sainsbury's*, J. Sainsbury Ltd, London, 1969, p. 44.

42 Jefferys, *Retail Trading in Britain*, p. 137.

43 Shaw, 'The Evolution and Impact of Large-Scale Retailing', p. 137.

44 Jefferys, *Retail Trading in Britain*, p. 163.

45 Fraser, *The Coming of the Mass Market*, p. 115.

46 Jefferys, *Retail Trading in Britain*, p. 65.

47 See Godfrey Lebhar, *Chain Stores in America, 1859–1962* (3rd edn), Chain Store Publishing Corp., New York, 1963; and George Laycock, *The Kroger Story: A Century of Innovation*, Kroger Co., Cincinnati, 1983, p. 37.

48 Lebhar, ibid., p. 31.

49 Bowlby, *Shopping With Freud*, pp. 97–8.

50 Arjun Appadurai (ed.), *The Social Life of Things: Commodities in Cultural Perspective*, Cambridge University Press, New York, 1986, 'Introduction', p. 56.

51 See: Greg Whitwell, *Making the Market: The Rise of Consumer Society*, McPhee Gribble, Melbourne, 1989; Frances Pollon, *Shopkeepers and Shoppers: A Social History of Retailing in New South Wales*, Retail Traders' Association of New South Wales, Sydney 1989; Beverley Kingston, *Basket, Bag and Trolley: A History of Shopping in Australia*, Oxford University Press, Melbourne, 1994; and Reekie, *Temptations*. Other related work is cited throughout this book.

52 Cited in Michael Collins, 'A Brief History of Retailing, Part 2: The Development of Australian Retailing (1800–1990)', in *Retail Management Principles Reader*, Australian Centre for Retail Studies, Monash University, Melbourne, 1991 (no page numbers given).

53 Cited in Michael Cannon, *Life in the Cities: Australia in the Victorian Age*, vol. 3, Currey O'Neil, Melbourne, 1983, p. 32.

54 Clara Aspinall cited in James Grant and Geoffrey Serle (eds), *The Melbourne Scene 1803–1956*, Hale & Iremonger, Sydney, 1983, p. 115. See also Kingston, *Basket, Bag and Trolley*, pp. 18–22.

55 Graeme Davison, 'Exhibitions', *Australian Cultural History*, no. 2, 1982/83, pp. 5–21.

56 Geoffrey Bolton, *The Oxford History of Australia: The Middle Way, 1942–1988*, Oxford University Press, Melbourne, 1993, p. 90.

57 See Ronald W. Gibbins, 'American Influence on Commercial Practice', in Richard Preston (ed.), *Contemporary Australia: Studies in History, Politics and Economics*, Duke University Press, Durham, 1969, pp. 498–520; John Spierings, 'Magic and Science: Aspects of Business Management, Advertising and Retailing, 1918–40', PhD thesis, University of Melbourne, 1989. On the relationship between Australia and the United States generally see Philip Bell and Roger Bell, *Implicated: The United States in Australia*, Oxford University Press, Melbourne, 1993.

58 Stuart Macintyre, *The Oxford History of Australia: The Succeeding Age, 1901–1942*, Oxford University Press, Melbourne, 1993, pp. 34–6. Aboriginal people were not included in early official Commonwealth population counts since they were not given even the basic status of citizenship.

59 See David Harris, 'A Great Ring of Landlords?', in Verity Burgmann and Jenny Lee (eds), *A People's History of Australia: Making A Life*, Penguin, Melbourne, 1988, pp. 39–55; and D.T. Merrett, 'Australian Capital Cities in the Twentieth Century', in J.W. McCarty and C.B. Schedvin (eds), *Australian Capital Cities*, Sydney University Press, 1978, p. 172.

60 Harris, ibid. See also Bernard Barrett, *The Inner Suburbs: The Evolution of an Industrial Era*, Melbourne University Press, Melbourne, 1971; and Graeme Davison, *The Rise and Fall of Marvellous Melbourne*, Melbourne University Press, Melbourne, 1978.

61 Harris, ibid.

62 ibid., p. 45.

63 Reekie, *Temptations*. See also, Jennifer MacCulloch, ' "This Store is Our World": Female Shop Assistants in Sydney to 1930', in Jill Roe (ed.), *Twentieth-Century Sydney: Studies in Urban and Social History*, Hale & Iremonger, Sydney, 1980, pp. 166–77.

64 Reekie, ibid., p. xix; Kingston, *Basket, Bag and Trolley*, pp. 27–30; and Howard Wolfers, 'The Big Stores Between the Wars', in Jill Roe (ed.), ibid., pp. 18–33.

65 See Kingston, ibid., pp. 26–7; and Andrew McCann, 'Melbourne's Royal Arcade and the Empty Time of Fashion', *Australian Historical Studies*, no. 107, October 1996, pp. 343–55.

66 'The Coles Story', *Annual Report*, G.J. Coles & Coy Limited, Melbourne, 1964 (no page numbers given).

67 Advertisement, 4 December 1924, cited in *How Woolworths Started and Grew: A Brief History of Woolworths Limited*, Public Relations Department, Woolworths Limited, Sydney, n.d., c.1989, p. 2.

68 ibid.

69 On discourses of scientific management see Lucy Taksa, 'All a Matter of Timing: The Diffusion of Scientific Management in New South Wales, Prior to 1921', PhD thesis, University of New South Wales, 1993; and Spierings, 'Magic and Science'.

On commercialism and masculinity see Michael Roper, 'Yesterday's Model: Product Fetishism and the British Company Man, 1945–85', in Michael Roper and John Tosh (eds), *Manful Assertions: Masculinities in Britain since 1800*, Routledge, London, 1991, pp. 190–211.

70 Whitwell, *Making the Market*, p. 14.

71 See George Patterson, *Life Has Been Wonderful: Fifty Years of Advertising At Home and Abroad*, Ure Smith, Sydney, 1956. On market research see Gail Reekie, 'Market Research and the Post-War Housewife', *Australian Feminist Studies*, no. 14, Summer 1991, pp. 15–27.

72 Peter Spearritt, *Sydney Since the Twenties*, Hale & Iremonger, Sydney, 1978, p. 45.

73 M. Barnard Eldershaw, *Tomorrow and Tomorrow*, Georgian House, Melbourne, 1947, pp. 46–7.

74 Rodney Maddock and Frank Stilwell, 'Boom and Recession', in Ann Curthoys, A.W. Martin and Tim Rowse (eds), *Australians From 1939*, Fairfax, Syme and Weldon, Sydney, 1987, p. 255.

2 Really Modern Retailing

1 Hal Porter, *The Watcher on the Cast-Iron Balcony*, Faber and Faber, London, 1963, pp. 21–2.

2 Cited in 'A British Manufacturer's Impressions of the Australian Grocery Trade', *The Australasian Grocer*, 24 September 1901, p. 118.

3 The term 'cash and carry' referred to the policy of requiring immediate payment for the goods and abandoning delivery services. Cash and carry grocery stores were operating in the larger Australian cities by the 1890s, and possibly earlier. The concept of self-service entailed open shelves and was introduced considerably later than cash and carry.

4 Anne Gollan, 'Salt Pork to Take Away', in Burgmann and Lee (eds), *Making a Life*, p. 7.

5 J.B. Cooper, *Victorian Commerce: 1834–1934*, Robertson and Mullens, Melbourne, 1934, p. 129.

6 K.T.H. Farrer, *A Settlement Amply Supplied: Food Technology in Nineteenth-Century Australia*, Melbourne University Press, Melbourne, 1980, p. 154 (The Henry Jones company later became known as IXL). On the history of food manufacturing and consumption in Australia see also R.C. Hutchinson, *Food for the People of Australia*, Angus & Robertson, Sydney, 1958; G.J.R Linge, *Industrial Awakening: A Geography of Australian Manufacturing 1788–1890*, Australian National University Press, Canberra, 1979; and Robin Walker and Dave Roberts, *From Scarcity to Surfeit: A History of Food and Nutrition in New South Wales*, New South Wales University Press, Kensington, 1988.

7 See Ambrose Pratt (ed.), *The National Handbook of Australia's Industries*, Specialty Press, Melbourne, 1934, p. 167.

8 ibid., pp. 199, 280

9 See Michael Symons, *One Continuous Picnic: A History of Eating in Australia*, Duck Press, Adelaide, 1982, p. 100.

10 Pratt (ed.), *The Handbook of Australia's Industries*, p. 329.

11 ibid, pp. 268–72.

12 ibid., p. 329.

13 Jenny Lee, 'A Redivision of Labour: Women and Wage Regulation in Victoria 1896–1903', in Susan Magarey, Sue Rowley and Susan Sheridan (eds), *Debutante Nation: Feminism Contests the 1890s*, Allen & Unwin, Sydney, 1993, p. 34.

14 Graeme Snooks, 'Manufacturing', in Wray Vamplew (ed.), *Australian Historical Statistics*, Fairfax, Syme & Weldon Associates, Sydney, 1987, p. 290.

15 Symons, *One Continuous Picnic*, p. 130.

16 Cadbury, *Creating the Great Taste: The Story of Cadbury and Chocolate Making*, Cadbury, Melbourne, n.d., c.1994 (no page numbers given).

17 Kellogg, *The History of Kellogg Company*, Kellogg (Aust) Pty Ltd, Sydney, n.d., c.1990 (no page numbers given).

18 Heinz Australia, 'The Heinz Story – a Proud Record of Manufacturing in Australia', Heinz (Australia), Melbourne, n.d., c.1992, p. 1.

19 Kraft Foods Limited, *The Kraft Story in Australia*, Kraft Foods Ltd, Melbourne, n.d.

20 K.R. Cramp, cited in Symons, *One Continuous Picnic*, p. 162.

21 These slogans are taken from advertisements appearing in the *Moran & Cato Price List*, 1921. Moran & Cato papers, La Trobe Library, Melbourne, MS10325.

22 Richard White, *Inventing Australia: Images and Identity 1688–1980*, George Allen & Unwin, Sydney, 1981, pp. 148–51.

23 Pratt (ed.), *The Handbook of Australia's Industries*, p. 8.

24 ibid., p. 7.

25 Symons, *One Continuous Picnic*, p. 100; and Peters, 'Peters Ice Cream Story', Peters Foods, Melbourne, n.d., c.1991.

26 Symons, ibid., p. 130; and *The Kraft Story in Australia*.

27 George Johnston, *Clean Straw For Nothing*, Collins/Fontana, Melbourne, 1969, p. 22.

28 See Tom Cairns, 'As it Was: Work as a Grocer Boy Saw it in Middle Park 1933–1939', typescript notes, La Trobe Library, Melbourne, MS 12750, Box 3530/2.

29 'Weekly Order book of Mrs J.C. Robinson', La Trobe Library, Melbourne, PA 93/89 (unprocessed acquisition).

30 Commonwealth of Australia, *Report of the Committee of Economic Enquiry*, vol. 1 (J. Vernon, Chairman), Government Printer, Canberra, 1965, pp. 116–17.

31 ibid.

32 ibid., vol. 2, Table E.12, p. 573.

33 Hutchinson, *Food for the People*, pp. 34–5.

34 See 'Fifty Years of Trade Organisations in Australia', *The Australasian Grocer*, 20 February 1925, p. 1099.

35 'The Australian Grocery Trade', *The Australasian Grocer's Journal*, 22 March 1892, p. 72.

36 *The Australasian Grocer*, 24 June 1902, pp. 194–5.

37 See the following articles all in *The Australasian Grocer*: 'A Glimpse up North', 20 June 1921, p. 153; 'The Trade in Western Australia', 20 July 1921, p. 209; 'Retail Trade Conditions in Sydney', 20 August 1921, p. 293; 'Impressions of Launceston, Tasmania', 20 April 1922, p. 1029.

38 Annual Report of the Grocers' Association of Victoria, 1923, in *The Australasian Grocer*, 20 May 1924, p. 39.

39 Kingston, *Basket, Bag and Trolley*, p. 44.
40 Cited in Robin Walker, 'Aspects of Working-Class Life in Industrial Sydney in 1913', *Labour History*, no. 58, May 1990, p. 41. See also Walker and Roberts, *From Scarcity to Surfeit*, pp. 136–8.
41 See Jill Matthews, 'Education for Femininity: Domestic Arts Education in South Australia', *Labour History*, no. 47, November 1983, pp. 30–53; Reiger, *The Disenchantment of The Home*; and Marilyn Lake, 'Historical Homes', in John Rickard and Peter Spearritt (eds), *Packaging the Past: Public Histories*, Melbourne University Press, Melbourne, 1991, pp. 46–54.
42 Turnaturi, 'Between Public and Private'.
43 Reiger, *The Disenchantment of the Home*, p. 53.
44 Reekie, *Temptations*, ch. 7
45 *The Grocers' Assistant*, 20 October 1915, vol. 5, no. 2 (cover).
46 For a discussion of the arrangement and management of the grocery store see W.A. Robjohns, *Grocery Commodities: A Textbook for the Australian Grocery Trade*, Retail Storekeepers Association of South Australia, Adelaide, 1939; and Cairns, 'As it Was'.
47 Cairns, ibid.
48 See 'Starting at the Grocery Trade', *The Grocers' Assistant*, vol. 5, no. 4, 20 December 1915 (cover).
49 'On the Counter', *The Grocers' Assistant*, vol. 5, no. 7, 20 March 1916 (cover).
50 ibid.
51 Cairns, 'As it Was', p. 1. Cairns started work at the age of 13. The uniform was a short white coat and a long white apron.
52 Assistants were either apprentices – trained under agreements of indentured service – or employed under a scheme of 'improvership' in which continued employment was not guaranteed. See 'Apprenticeship v. Improvership', *The Grocers' Assistant*, vol. 5, no. 3, 20 November 1915 (cover).
53 Cairns, 'As it Was', p. 2.
54 See Cannon, *Life in the Cities*, p. 28.
55 On female retail workers see Jennifer MacCulloch, ' "This Store is Our World" '; Game and Pringle, *Gender at Work*, ch. 3; and Edna Ryan and Ann Conlon, *Gentle Invaders: Australian Women at Work*, Penguin, Melbourne, 1989, pp. 62–3.
56 'Female Labour in the Grocery Trade', *The Grocers' Assistant*, vol. 5, no. 9, 20 May 1916 (cover).
57 Branch Letters, 1945 and following years, Crofts Stores papers, Melbourne University Archives.
58 This point is discussed in Kingston, *Basket, Bag and Trolley*, pp. 114–15.
59 'Chain Stores, Report of the Industrial Commission of New South Wales upon Matters relating to the management, control and operations of General Chain Stores in New South Wales', *New South Wales Parliamentary Papers*, 1939. p. 63.
60 C.H. Stanwix, 'Overcoming Chain-Store Competition', *Rydges*, February 1939, pp. 105–7.
61 *The Australasian Grocer*, 24 September 1901, p. 118.
62 On the relative lack of consumer co-operation in Australia see Ray Markey, 'New South Wales Trade Unions and the "Co-operative Principle" in the 1890s', *Labour History*, no. 49, November, 1985, pp. 51–60.

63 See Godfrey Lebhar, *Chain Stores in America*. Australian legislation limiting the operation of the chains had already been introduced, without much effect, in Victoria in 1904.

64 *Retail Merchandiser and Chain Store Review* (official organ of the Bureau of Modern Merchandising), May 1937, p. 6.

65 'Chain Stores, Report'.

66 ibid., pp. 71–2.

67 See 'Some Notes on the Early History of Moran & Cato', 22/5/1968, typescript, Moran & Cato Papers. See also Una B. Porter (ed.), *Growing Together: Letters Between Frederick John Cato and Frances Bethune, 1881–1884*, privately published, Melbourne, 1981.

68 See *Crofts Stores 30th Anniversary Cookerybook and Household Guide, 1936*, Crofts Stores papers.

69 'Early History of Moran & Cato'. See also, in the same manuscript collection, *Moran & Cato: Price List*, 1921 for an indication of the variety of products then sold.

70 Branch Letters, 1939–1968, Crofts Stores papers.

71 'Window Plan Book' 1935, in ibid.

72 See material relating to staff matters, in ibid.

73 Winifred Taylor, 'Trends in Retail Training', *Rydges*, May 1939, pp. 343–5. Taylor was the first principal of the Institute.

74 See Reekie, *Temptations*, ch. 3, for a useful discussion of this.

75 *The Grocers' Assistant*, vol. 5, no. 5, 20 January 1916 (cover).

76 Marilyn Lake, 'The Politics of Respectability: Identifying the Masculinist Context', reprinted in Magarey, Rowley and Sheridan (eds), *Debutante Nation*, pp. 1–15.

77 *The Grocers' Assistant*, 20 December 1916 (cover).

78 *The Grocers' Assistant*, 20 January 1917 (cover).

79 *Hints on Better Salesmanship*, Moran & Cato Company, n.d., c.1920, p. 16. Moran & Cato papers.

80 ibid., p. 11.

81 ibid., p. 7.

82 See, for example, Judy Wajcman, *Feminism Confronts Technology*, Polity, Cambridge, 1991, p. 22.

3　Engineering the Shop

1 M.E. Gagg, *Shopping with Mother*, J.H. Wingfield (illus.), Wills and Hepworth, Loughborough, 1958.

2 Jeanne Bendick, *The First Book of Supermarkets*, Franklin Watts, New York, 1954.

3 ibid., p. 36.

4 *Life*, 3 January 1955 (cover).

5 For a selection of work on globalisation, see Mike Featherstone, Scott Lash and Roland Robertson (eds), *Global Modernities*, Sage, London, 1995.

6 McClelland, *Studies in Retailing*, p. 38.

7 ibid., p. 42.

8 Georg Lukacs, *History and Class Consciousness*, Merlin Press, London, 1968; Walter Benjamin, 'The Work of Art in the Age of Mechanical Reproduction', in

Walter Benjamin, *Illuminations*, Hannah Arendt (ed.), Harry Zohn (trans.), Wolf/Harcourt, Brace & World, New York, 1973; Theodor W. Adorno and Max Horkheimer, 'The Culture Industry: Enlightenment as Mass Deception', in Max Horkheimer and Theodor W. Adorno, *The Dialectic of Enlightenment*, John Cumming (trans.), Continuum, New York, 1982.

9 Karl Marx, *Capital: A Critique of Political Economy*, vol. 1, Ben Fowkes (trans.), Penguin, Harmondsworth, 1982, ch. 1.

10 Lukacs, *History and Class Consciousness*, p. 91.

11 Adorno and Horkheimer, 'The Culture Industry'; see also Theodor W. Adorno, *The Culture Industry: Selected Essays on Mass Culture*, J.M. Bernstein (ed.), Routledge, London, 1991. This collection suggests the need for caution in overemphasising Adorno's apparent 'elitism'.

12 Walter Benjamin, *Charles Baudelaire: A Lyric Poet in the Era of High Capitalism*, Verso, London, 1983. Within recent cultural studies Benjamin has often been favourably contrasted with the apparent elitism of other Marxist critics.

13 Thorstein Veblen, *The Theory of the Leisure Class: An Economic Study of Institutions*, Random House, New York, 1934.

14 Georg Simmel, *The Philosophy of Money*, David Frisby (ed.), Tom Bottomore, David Frisby and Kaethe Mengelberg (trans.), Routledge, London, 1990.

15 Vance Packard, *The Hidden Persuaders*, Penguin, Harmondsworth, 1957; John Kenneth Galbraith, *The Affluent Society*, Andre Deutsch, London, 1984; F.R. Leavis, 'Mass Civilisation and Minority Culture', in his *Education and the University*, Cambridge University Press, Cambridge, 1979; Richard Hoggart, *The Uses of Literacy*, Penguin, Harmondsworth, 1980.

16 McClelland, *Studies in Retailing*, p. 45.

17 ibid., pp. 46–7.

18 Cited in ibid., p. 47.

19 The 'classic' studies of the supermarket in the United States are provided by M.M. Zimmerman, *The Supermarket: A Revolution in Distribution*, McGraw Hill, New York, 1955; and Frank J. Charvat, *Supermarketing*, Macmillan, New York, 1961. See also Lebhar, *Chain Stores in America*; Rom J. Markin, *The Supermarket: An Analysis of Growth, Development and Change*, Washington State University Press, 1968; Randolph McAusland, *Supermarkets: 50 Years of Progress*, Food Marketing Institute, Washington, 1980; and Tedlow, *New and Improved*.

20 Lebhar, ibid., p. 34.

21 ibid.

22 See Tedlow, *New and Improved*, pp. 234–5; and Frank Charvat, *Supermarketing*, pp. 6–13.

23 Strasser, *Satisfaction Guaranteed*, p. 231.

24 Cited in ibid, p. 203.

25 Carl W. Dipman (ed.), *Self-Service Food Stores*, Progressive Grocer, New York, 1946, p. 9.

26 ibid., p. 6.

27 Markin, *The Supermarket*, pp. 10–12.

28 See Lebhar, *Chain Stores*, pp. 226–8; Markin, ibid., ch. 1; and Tedlow, *New and Improved*, pp. 226–38.

29 Tedlow, ibid., p. 233.

30 Cited in ibid., p. 188.
31 See ibid., p. 240; and Charvat, *Supermarketing*, p. 3.
32 Charvat, ibid., p. 18.
33 Cited in Markin, *The Supermarket*, p. 12.
34 Tedlow, *New and Improved*, pp. 241–2.
35 Safeway Stores Incorporated, *Our 50th Year, Annual Report, 1975*, Safeway Stores Inc., Oakland, 1976, pp. 4–8.
36 Charvat, *Supermarketing*, p. 27.
37 Tedlow, *New and Improved*, pp. 230–1.
38 ibid., pp. 231–2.
39 Markin, *The Supermarket*, ch. 3.
40 McAusland, *Supermarkets*, p. 59.
41 Charvat, *Supermarketing*, p. 29.
42 McAusland, *Supermarkets*, p. 39.
43 Edward A. Brand, *Modern Supermarket Operation*, Fairchild, New York, 1973 (first published 1963).
44 ibid., p. 162.
45 ibid., p. 164.
46 ibid., p. 171.
47 ibid.
48 Cited in Markin, *The Supermarket*, p. 57.
49 Safeway, *Our 50th Year*, p. 10; Lebhar, *Chain Stores*, p. 31.
50 See Jennifer Cross, *The Supermarket Trap: The Consumer and the Food Industry*, Indiana University Press, Bloomington, 1976, p. 29.
51 McAusland, *Supermarkets*, p. 83.
52 Cross, *The Supermarket Trap*, p. 33.
53 ibid., p. 70.
54 ibid., p. 4.
55 Daniel J. Boorstin, 'The Consumption Community', in Grant S. McClellan (ed.), *The Consuming Public*, H.W. Wilson, New York, 1968, p. 9.
56 ibid., p. 19.
57 Herbert Marcuse, *One-Dimensional Man: Studies in the Ideology of Advanced Industrial Society*, Routledge & Kegan Paul, London, 1968.
58 ibid., p. 12.
59 Betty Friedan, *The Feminine Mystique*, Penguin, Harmondsworth, 1965.
60 David Powell, *Counter Revolution: The Tesco Story*, Grafton, London, 1991, p. 51. See also Frank Whitford, 'The Grocer's Tale', in *Sainsbury's 125 Years Celebration Supplement: Sainsbury's Magazine*, New Crane Publishing, London, 1994, pp. 6–13. Whitford suggests that co-operative stores began experimenting with semi-self-service during the 1920s.
61 Mathias, *Retailing Revolution*, p. xii.
62 Fulop, *Competition for Consumers*, p. 19.
63 See Jefferys and Knee, *Retailing in Europe*, p. 20.
64 McClelland, *Studies in Retailing*, p. 8.
65 Cited in Powell, *Counter Revolution*, p. 65.
66 *J.S. 100*, p. 59.
67 Powell, *Counter Revolution*, pp. 66–8.

68   ibid., p. 78

69   On the link between labour costs and the rise of self-service in Britain, see Fulop, *Competition for Consumers*, p. 25.

70   *J.S. 100*, p. 60.

71   Sainsbury's, 'History of The Company', Sainsbury plc, London, 1991.

72   *J.S. 100*, p. 61.

73   Tesco, 'Abbreviated History and Fact Sheet', Tesco plc, Customer Service Department, Cheshunt, January 1990.

74   *J.S. Journal* (House magazine of J. Sainsbury Ltd), January 1960, p. 4 (British Library, London, Pp. 5793 RAD).

75   *J.S. 100*, p. 74. Sainsbury's and other chains such as Tesco had long cemented this corporate identification by the early introduction of 'house brands', manufactured in their own food production plants. By the 1960s, there were over 1000 Sainsbury labelled products.

76   McClelland, *Studies in Retailing*, p. 166.

77   See Fulop, *Competition for Consumers*, pp. 179–82. Such training schemes were male dominated and management-focused.

78   ibid., p. 27.

79   *J.S. Journal*, October 1959, pp. 6–7.

80   *J.S. Journal*, November 1959, p. 2. For more of the same see also *Family: Sainsbury's Magazine for Every Woman*, no. 1, Autumn 1961 (British Library, London, Pp. 5109 bs).

81   See Safeway, *Checkout* (The House Journal of Safeway Food Stores Ltd), UK Division, Safeway Stores Inc., London, October/November, 1983, p. 3.

82   ibid., p. 16.

83   ibid., pp. 12–15.

84   Tesco, 'Abbreviated History and Fact Sheet'. Tesco increased market share also through the introduction of Green Shield 'trading stamps' in 1963, a scheme through which customers accumulated a set number of stamps which could then be exchanged for a 'free gift'. Other companies followed suit.

85   Dawson, *Commercial Distribution in Europe*, p. 73.

86   The ASDA company claims 'pioneer' status in the establishment in Britain of superstore retailing. See ASDA, 'Information Pack', ASDA Stores Ltd, Leeds, n.d., c.1996/7.

87   Fulop, *Competition for Consumers*, p. 176; and Jordan Dataquest, *British Supermarkets*, Jordan Dataquest, Ltd, London, 1977, p. 1 (British Library, London, P. 513/2228).

88   Fulop, ibid., p. 23, notes that between 1966 and 1971 the number of grocery stores in Britain fell by 12.8 per cent, falling a further 36 per cent between 1971 and 1976. In the United States there was an even more dramatic drop of 31 per cent in the number of grocery stores between 1935 and 1958, a trend which continued during the 1960s and 1970s. See Jefferys and Knee, *Retailing in Europe*, p. 108.

89   Although co-operatives are still a significant part of British retailing, since 1965 the number of co-operative societies in Britain has declined from 704 to 100 in 1986. See *Retail Trade International*, vol. 1, p. 636.

90   Jefferys and Knee, *Retailing in Europe*, p. 107.

91   Powell, *Counter Revolution*, p. 128.

92 Guy Debord, *Society of the Spectacle*, Rebel Press/Aim Publications, London, 1987.
93 Henri Lefebvre, *Everyday Life in the Modern World*, Allen Lane, London, 1971, p. 60.

4 She Likes to Look

1 Gavin Casey, *Amid the Plenty: A Novel of Today*, Australasian Book Society, Sydney, 1962, p. 1.
2 ibid., p. 4.
3 Commonwealth Bureau of Census and Statistics, *Official Yearbook of the Commonwealth of Australia*, no. 39, Canberra, 1953, p. 1308.
4 Commonwealth Bureau of Census and Statistics, *Official Yearbook of the Commonwealth of Australia*, no. 50, Canberra, 1964, pp. 1241–5. The breakdown by state of self-service stores was: New South Wales, 1668; Victoria, 1385; Queensland, 751; South Australia, 431; Western Australia, 429; and Tasmania, 161. Most of these stores were in the metropolitan centres. Sydney, for example, had 910 self-service stores and Melbourne had 892.
5 J.L.J. Wilson (ed.), *Current Affairs Bulletin: The Merchandising Revolution*, vol. 31, no. 11, 15 April 1963, p. 164.
6 *The Australasian Grocer*, August 1958, p. 9.
7 *The Australasian Grocer*, July 1958, p. 97.
8 On packaging versus 'nakedness' see the *Sydney Morning Herald*, 8 July 1957, p. 58.
9 'Convenience the Keynote for the Coming Era of Retail Trade', *Australian Financial Review*, 11 July 1957, pp. 1–4.
10 *Retail World*, vol. 41, no. 13, 29 June 1988.
11 *The Australasian Grocer*, 20 August 1921, p. 293.
12 'Cash and Carry System: A Visit to Sydney's Largest Experiment', *The Australasian Grocer*, 21 August 1922, p. 351.
13 *The Australasian Grocer*, 21 January 1924, p. 831.
14 See 'Pick Me Up and Take Me Home: Self-Service in Retail Stores', *Rydges*, March 1948, pp. 241–2. The David Jones Food Hall even utilised an 'express' checkout lane for five items or less.
15 See *Keeping Brunswick's Heritage: A Report on the Review of the Brunswick Conservation Study*, vol. 2, Context Pty Ltd, Melbourne, 1990, pp. 89–90.
16 On rationing, see Hutchinson, *Food for the People of Australia*, pp. 12–17; Walker and Roberts, *From Scarcity to Surfeit*, ch. 9. Note, however, that war-time restrictions sometimes worked in favour of the development of cash and carry since deliveries became less common because of petrol rationing.
17 See Kingston, *Basket, Bag and Trolley*, pp. 77–9, for a discussion of war-time restrictions.
18 Whitwell, *Making the Market*, pp. 25–6.
19 *Report of the Committee of Economic Enquiry*, vol. 2, p. 587, Table E.42. On the same page, Table E.44 indicates that, by 1962, 93 per cent of Australian households owned a refrigerator, 78 per cent a washing machine, 75 per cent a vacuum cleaner, 60 per cent a television set, 4 per cent a deep freezer, and 5 per cent an air-conditioner.

20 ibid, vol. 1, p. 117, Table 6.6. This contrasted with the United Kingdom where 28.2 per cent of consumption expenditure went on food in 1962. In the United States and Canada the figures were 21 per cent and 22 per cent respectively. See, ibid., vol. 2, p. 586, Table E.41.

21 ibid, p. 585, Table E.39.

22 Commonwealth Bureau of Census and Statistics, *Official Yearbook of the Commonwealth of Australia*, vol. 46, Canberra, 1960, p. 1161, and no. 50, p. 1241.

23 The level of manufactured sugar products, for example, rose from 36 per cent of all sugar related products in 1939 to 58 per cent in 1961. See *Report of Committee of Economic Enquiry*, vol. 2, p. 573, Table E.12.

24 On frozen foods see Symons, *One Continuous Picnic*, pp. 207–8; and Edgell-Birds Eye, 'Company Profile', Edgell-Birds Eye, Sydney, n.d., c.1994.

25 'The Supermarket Diet', *Nation*, 16 January 1960, pp. 17–19.

26 Kevin Blackburn, 'The "Consumer's Ethic" of Australian Advertising Agencies 1950–1965', *Journal of Australian Studies*, no. 32, March 1992, p. 63. Advertising was further professionally organised in the post-war period with the establishment of the Australian Association of Advertising Agencies and the Advertising Institute of Australia. See Patterson, *Life Has Been Wonderful*. For earlier accounts see W.A. McNair, *Radio Advertising in Australia*, Angus & Robertson, Sydney, 1937; and Herbert N. Casson, *How to Make Advertising Pay*, Angus & Robertson, Sydney, 1939.

27 Sydney *Sun-Herald*, 1 June 1958, p. 100.

28 On the making of modern self-identity, see Anthony Giddens, *Modernity and Self-Identity: Self and Society in the Late Modern Age*, Polity, Cambridge, 1991. For an Australian discussion of modernity and the self, see Geoff Sharp, 'Constitutive Abstraction and Social Practice', *Arena*, no. 70, 1985, pp. 48–83, and his 'Extended Forms of the Social: Technological Mediation and Self-Formation', *Arena Journal*, New Series, no. 1, 1993, pp. 221–37. See also Marshall Berman, *"All That is Solid Melts Into Air": The Experience of Modernity*, Verso, London, 1982.

29 *The Australasian Grocer*, 30 September 1949, p. 441.

30 *The Australasian Grocer*, 20 February 1954, p. 1009.

31 'Supermarkets: For or Against?', Sydney *Sun-Herald*, 10 August 1958, p. 107.

32 ibid.

33 See Judith Smart, 'Feminists, Food and the Fair Price: The Cost of Living Demonstrations in Melbourne, August–September 1917', *Labour History*, no. 50, May 1986, pp. 113-31; Reekie, *Temptations*, ch. 7; Kingston, *Basket, Bag and Trolley*, ch. 6; and Halpin (ed.), *Consumers' Choice*.

34 *The Australasian Grocer*, 20 February 1951, p. 980.

35 *The Australasian Grocer*, 20 February 1956, p. 1171.

36 *The Australasian Grocer*, 21 November 1949, p. 707.

37 *The Australasian Grocer*, June 1957, p. 29.

38 *The Australasian Grocer*, 20 July 1954, p. 274.

39 See 'Emotional Selling', *Rydges*, 1 March 1956, p. 251.

40 D.A. Cruickschank, 'Proper Packaging Means Modern Merchandising', *Rydges*, 1 November 1957, pp. 1070–1.

41 'Let's Talk Business: What Makes a Good Package', *Rydges*, 1 December 1956, p. 1245.

42 Cruickschank, 'Proper Packaging'.

43 See 'Self-Service Stores' (photograph album with list of store openings), Crofts Stores papers.

44 ibid., Advertising Material c.1930s–1950s.

45 Wilson (ed.), 'The Merchandising Revolution', p. 171. Chain stores were most dominant in New South Wales, home to 54.7 per cent of chain stores in Australia and only 6.8 per cent of group stores by the early 1960s.

46 Composite Buyers, 'Composite Buyers – A Brief History', Composite Buyers Ltd, Melbourne, n.d., c.1993.

47 Foodland, 'The First Three Months', 1958, in Crofts Stores papers, Advertising Material.

48 Wilson (ed.), 'The Merchandising Revolution', p. 173.

49 See Game and Pringle, *Gender At Work*, p. 62.

50 *Australian Financial Review*, 11 July 1957, pp. 1–4.

51 ibid.

52 Alex Paton, 'Grocers Were Born Free . . . And Are Now Everywhere in Chains', *Nation*, 28 March 1959, pp. 11–12. Profit margins in the large supermarket would, by the 1980s, be down to about 1–2 per cent.

53 ibid., p. 11.

54 Roper, 'Yesterday's Model'.

55 Paton, 'Grocers Were Born Free', p. 12.

56 *The Australasian Grocer*, June 1957, p. 43. See also Thomas J. Store, 'Retailing Considerations', *Rydges*, 1 April 1956, pp. 357–8, which offered a similar comparison of service and self-service.

57 Emile Durkheim, 'Rules for the Classification of Social Types', in his *The Rules of Sociological Method*, Free Press, New York, 1966, pp. 79–80.

58 See Reekie, 'Market Research and the Post-War Housewife'. The first Australian market research organisation was established by Sylvia Ashby in 1936. The Market Research Society of Australia was formed in the 1950s, and in the same decade major consumer surveys were launched such as the Ashby Consumer Panel. By the mid-1960s there were about 50 market research organisations in Australia. See also Karen Hutchings, 'The Battle for Consumer Power: Post-War Women and Advertising', in Graeme Turner (ed.), *Fabrications: Journal of Australian Studies*, no. 50/51, University of Queensland Press, St Lucia, 1996, pp. 66–77.

59 ibid.

60 *The Australasian Grocer*, January 1960, pp. 82–3.

61 Blackburn, 'The "Consumer's Ethic"', p. 66.

62 Stella Lees and June Senyard, *The 1950s : How Australia Became a Modern Society, and Everyone Got a House and a Car*, Hyland House, Melbourne, 1987, p. 70.

63 J.C. Timms, *Greater Retail Turnover*, Pitman, Melbourne, 1939.

64 'Emotional Selling', p. 251.

65 *The Australasian Grocer*, 20 October 1955, p. 653.

66 David T. Bottomley, *Introduction to Market Analysis* (revised ed.), Market Research Society of Australia, Melbourne 1964, p. 104.

67 Jenny Ryan, 'Women, Modernity and the City', *Theory, Culture and Society*, vol. 11, 1994, pp. 35–63. Ryan argues that what is universalised within theories of

modernity from Simmel to Berman, Harvey and Giddens is, in fact, the experience of the white, heterosexual male. See also, Rita Felski, *The Gender of Modernity*, Harvard University Press, London and Cambridge MA, 1995.

68 Johnson, *The Modern Girl*, p. 3.
69 ibid., p. 116.
70 Reekie, 'Market Research and the Post-War Housewife', p. 19. As Reekie points out, this was very probably an over-estimation and exaggerates the dominance of women in consumer decision-making.
71 See, for example, Andreas Huyssen, 'Mass Culture as Woman: Modernism's Other', in Tania Modleski (ed.), *Studies in Entertainment*, pp. 188–207.
72 Jean Duruz has made a similar point in suggesting that Australian men during the 1960s may have defined themselves, in part, through suburban living. See her 'Suburban Houses Revisited', in Kate Darian-Smith and Paula Hamilton (eds), *Memory and History in Twentieth-Century Australia*, Oxford University Press, Melbourne, 1994, p. 180.
73 'Shoplifting . . . How to Reduce Losses', in *The Australasian Grocer* (National Retailing, supplement), October 1961, p. 41.
74 On shoplifting in Australia see Reekie, *Temptations*, ch. 6; and Kingston, *Basket, Bag and Trolley*, pp. 70–6. For a 'criminological' approach, characteristic of the 1950s and 60s, see Mary Owen Cameron, *The Booster and the Snitch: Department Store Shoplifting*, Collier Macmillan, London, 1964.
75 See 'Shoplifting', *The Australasian Grocer*, January 1959, p. 9.
76 See Elaine S. Abelson, *When Ladies Go A-Thieving: Middle-Class Shoplifters in the Victorian Department Store*, Oxford University Press, New York, 1989; and Daniel J. Murphy, *Customers and Thieves: An Ethnography of Shoplifting*, Gower, London, 1986, ch. 4.
77 *Retail World*, 3 May 1967, p. 7.
78 Sydney *Sun-Herald*, 9 March 1958, p. 96.
79 National Association of Retail Grocers' Associations, *Food Store Operator's Manual*, NARGA, Melbourne, 1971, p. 94.
80 *Retail World*, 3 May 1967, p. 67.
81 These figures are cited in Dennis Challinger, 'Official Facts About Shoplifting', in D. Challinger (ed.), *Studies in Shoplifting*, Australian Crime Prevention Council, Melbourne, 1977, pp. 1–13.
82 Dennis Challinger, 'Reflections on Shoplifting', in ibid., pp. 105–18.
83 *The Australasian Grocer*, March 1960, p. 13.

5 Tomorrow's Shop Today

1 *Sydney Morning Herald*, 26 February 1957, p. 11.
2 *Colesanco*, vol. 4, no. 3, December 1963 (cover).
3 Coles, *Annual Report*, 1963, p. 3.
4 Bolton, *The Middle Way*, p. 106.
5 Barnard Eldershaw, *Tomorrow and Tomorrow*, p. 180.
6 Dymphna Cusack and Florence James, *Come In Spinner*, William Heinemann, Melbourne, 1957, pp. 98–9.
7 Coles, *Annual Report*, 1959, p. 6.

8   ibid.
9   ibid.
10 *The Australasian Grocer*, November 1958, p. 53.
11 ibid. See also Seedman's Supermarkets, 'Consolidated Trading Statements', in Mutual Stores papers, Melbourne University Archives.
12 J. Oliver, 'The Modern Touch: An Australian Supermarket', *Rydges*, March 1948, p. 240.
13 Norman Tieck, 'Better Service, Higher Profits, Lower Costs', *Rydges*, March 1952, p. 237.
14 ibid. See also his 'Better Business From a Supermarket', *Rydges*, April 1952, pp. 351–7; and 'How to Run a Supermarket', *Rydges*, May 1952, pp. 502–7.
15 Tieck, 'Better Service', p. 234.
16 Tieck, 'How To Run a Supermarket', p. 507.
17 'Editorial', *Rydges*, March 1964, p. 183.
18 ibid.
19 *Rydges*, January 1959 (cover).
20 See M.M. Henderson, 'Making Men', *Rydges*, August 1956, pp. 813–15.
21 Michael Baume, 'The Place of Women in Business and the Professions', *Rydges*, March 1960, pp. 224–6.
22 See Stuart Rosewarne, 'The Political Economy of Retailing into the Eighties – Part 2', *Journal of Australian Political Economy*, no. 16, March 1984, p. 75. By 1969, 12 170 men and 16 126 women were employed in Australia's 657 supermarkets. Women thus comprised 57 per cent of the supermarket workforce. See Commonwealth Bureau of Census and Statistics, *Economic Censuses 1968–69: Retail Establishments and Selected Service Establishments in Australia*, Final Bulletin, Canberra, 1973.
23 Rosewarne, ibid., p. 77.
24 ibid. This was in part due to a growth in the temporary employment of teenage boys.
25 For a potted history of the SDA, the origins of which go back to 1918, see SDA, 'Trade Union Information Kit on The Shop, Distributive and Allied Employees' Association', SDA, Melbourne, n.d., p. 6.
26 Game and Pringle, *Gender at Work*, p. 59.
27 Rosewarne, 'The Political Economy of Retailing', p. 79. Rosewarne suggests that the SDA leadership was more intent on increasing the size of the union and therefore its influence within the labour movement.
28 The SDA became more active during the 1980s and less male dominated, but remains avowedly 'moderate' and strongly pro-family. See SDA, 'Trade Union Information Kit', p. 8.
29 See Whitwell, *Making the Market*, p. 46.
30 ibid., p. 25.
31 *Report of Committee of Economic Enquiry*, vol. 1, p. 111.
32 ibid., vol. 2, p. 882, Table G.28.
33 ibid., vol. 1, p. 64 and p. 74. Between 1947 and 1961 net immigration increased the population by over 1.2 million, while births increased it by a further 1.7 million.

34 See W.E. Norton and P.J. Kennedy, *Australian Economic Statistics 1949–50 to 1984–85: 1 Tables*, Reserve Bank of Australia, Occasional Paper no. 8A, Canberra, November 1985, p. 132 (Table 5.9b Private Final Consumption Expenditure).

35 Mark Peel has explored this process of spatial management in detail in relation to the South Australian 'new town' of Elizabeth in his 'Elizabeth: From the City of the Future to a Suburb with a Past', PhD thesis, University of Melbourne, 1992.

36 See ibid., ch. 5 for a useful discussion of some of this material in the context of Australian suburbanisation. Some of the more influential texts in this area include Edward M. Soja, *Postmodern Geographies: The Reassertion of Space in Critical Social Theory*, London, 1989; and David Harvey, *The Urban Experience*, Blackwell, Oxford, 1989.

37 See David Harvey, *The Condition of Postmodernity: An Enquiry Into the Origins of Cultural Change*, Blackwell, Oxford, 1991, ch. 14 for a discussion of time and space as a source of social power.

38 See Ryan, 'Women, Modernity and the City'; and Rob Shields, *Places on The Margin: Alternative Geographies of Modernity*, Routledge, London, 1991.

39 'The Coles Story'; and G.J. Coles & Coy Limited, *Annual Report*, 1960, p. 7.

40 *Food Store News and Self-Service Journal*, 15 December 1962, p. 8.

41 Malcolm Taylor, *Twenty-One Years of Australian Safeway 1963–1984*, Safeway, Melbourne, c.1984, p. 7.

42 *Colesanco*, vol. 4, no. 1, May 1963 (cover).

43 *Colesanco*, vol. 4, no. 3, December 1963 (cover).

44 Nan Hutton, 'The Pleasures of Shopping', *Walkabout*, December 1963, p. 54.

45 Tieck, 'Better Business from a Supermarket', p. 357.

46 'Why Customers Buy', *Rydges*, May 1967, pp. 11–13.

47 J.R. Gibbons, 'Some Fundamentals about Motivation Research', *Rydges*, January 1965, pp. 19–20; See also R.C. Chapman, 'Consumer Depth Probing', *Rydges*, August 1964, pp. 687–8.

48 'Home Habits that Save you Money', *The Australian Women's Weekly*, 21 February 1962, p. 29.

49 *Food Store News and Self-Service Journal*, 15 August 1961, p. 16.

50 R.J. Johnston and P.J. Rimmer, *Retailing In Melbourne*, Department of Human Geography, Australian National University, Canberra, 1969, ch. VI.

51 *Retail World*, December 1968, pp. 2–3.

52 Taylor, *Twenty-One Years of Australian Safeway*, p. 11.

53 See *The Australasian Grocer*, 20 November 1963, p. 45; and Sandra Jobson, 'The Lure of the Supermarkets', *Sydney Morning Herald*, 9 June 1970, p. 6.

54 Cited in Reekie, *Temptations*, p. 134.

55 For a discussion of planning methods see Johnston and Rimmer, *Retailing In Melbourne*, pp. 1–10.

56 'The Coles Story'.

57 G.J. Coles & Coy Limited, *Annual Report*, 1958, p. 7.

58 *Colesanco*, vol. 3, no. 1, June 1962 (Cover), 'Coles Food Markets are Here'.

59 G.J. Coles & Coy Limited, *Annual Report*, 1960, p. 5.

60 *Colesanco*, vol. 2, no. 1, December 1960, p. 5.

61 *Colesanco*, vol. 3, no. 3, December 1962 (cover).

62 G.J. Coles & Coy Limited, *Annual Report*, 1964, p. 3
63 ibid.
64 *How Woolworths Started and Grew*, p. 3
65 ibid.
66 ibid.
67 *Retail World*, vol. 20, no. 26, 13 December 1967, p. 1.
68 See Taylor, *Twenty-One Years of Australian Safeway*, p. 3.
69 ibid., p. 5.
70 ibid., p. 9.
71 ibid., p. 11.
72 'Annual Report of the Grocery Industry 1968–69', *Retail World*, 11 December 1968, p. 2.
73 Commonwealth Bureau of Census and Statistics, *Economic Censuses 1968–69*.
74 ibid. Self-service stores as a whole by 1964 accounted for only 21.5 per cent of grocery stores, but took 60.7 per cent of the trade. See 'Annual Report of the Grocery Industry 1968–69', p. 3.
75 'Annual Report of the Grocery Industry 1968–69', ibid.
76 *Colesanco*, vol. 6, no. 2, September 1964, p. 6.
77 *Colesanco*, vol. 8, no. 2, p. 2.
78 Geoff Farries, 'Shopping Centres: An Important Retail Trend', *Rydges*, August 1960, pp. 793–5.
79 ibid.
80 Johnston and Rimmer, *Retailing in Melbourne*, p. 23.
81 Desmond Crowley (ed.), 'Shopping Centres', *Current Affairs Bulletin*, vol. 40, no. 2, 19 June, 1967 p. 20 (no author given).
82 See 'Convenience the Keynote for the Coming Era of Retail Trade', *Australian Financial Review*, 11 July 1957, pp. 1–4.
83 'Melbourne to Get Huge Regional Shopping Centre', *Australian Financial Review*, 2 June 1960, p. 8.
84 Myer Emporium, 'Northland Shopping Centre', n.d., c.1964, La Trobe Library, Melbourne.
85 ibid.
86 Roger Aldridge and Michael Darling, 'The Mega-Emporiums: Can Shopping Ever be the Same Again?', *The Age*, 30 August 1968, p. 4.
87 Crowley (ed.), 'Shopping Centres', p. 19.
88 ibid., p. 22.
89 G.J. Coles & Coy Limited, *Annual Report*, 1966, pp. 4–5.
90 Aldridge and Darling, 'The Mega-Emporiums'.
91 Johnston and Rimmer, *Retailing In Melbourne*, p. 28. See also P.J. Smailes, *The Impact of Planned Shopping Centres in a Sector of Metropolitan Adelaide*, Department of Geography, University of Sydney/Geographical Society of New South Wales, May 1969.
92 See Sandra Jobson, 'Is the Little Shop all Wrapped-Up?', *Sydney Morning Herald*, 8 June 1970, p. 4.
93 Yvonne Preston, 'Are We Becoming Over-Shopped?', *Australian Financial Review*, 29 June 1966, pp. 2–3.
94 ibid.

95 Norman Edwards, 'Shopping Centres', *Architecture in Australia*, February 1969, p. 69.

96 Cited in 'Shopping Centres', p. 29.

97 Sandra Jobson, 'The Lure of The Supermarket', *Sydney Morning Herald*, 9 June 1970, p. 6; and her 'Shopping – as a Way of Life', *Sydney Morning Herald*, 10 June 1970, p. 6.

98 'Shopping Centres', p. 29.

99 G.W. Smith, 'The Market Place: Progress or the Erosion of a Social Institution?' in *Architecture in Australia*, February 1969, p. 79.

100 Jobson, 'The Lure of the Supermarkets'.

101 John Kay, 'What Makes Women Buy', *Rydges*, August 1968, pp. 17–18.

6 Living the Transformation

1 A list of those interviewed specifically for this study is provided in the bibliography. Unless otherwise stated, all quotations in this chapter are derived from those discussions. All those interviewed in Dandenong requested that their real names be used and formally consented to participate in the project. The interviews themselves were qualitative and followed a detailed, but flexible, interview schedule. The questions were open-ended and designed to explore both memories of everyday shopping and attitudes towards consumer culture. Each interview lasted from one to two hours and was tape-recorded and later transcribed. No effort was made to seek a 'representative sample' of interviewees. Rather, select issues were explored in detail with a small number of people on a one-to-one basis. A more detailed discussion of the interview methodology and the interview schedule is provided in the thesis upon which this book is based.

2 For a small selection of recent work on oral history and the relationship between history and memory see Raphael Samuel and Paul Thompson (eds), *The Myths We Live By*, Routledge, London, 1990; Sherna Berger Gluck and Daphne Patai (eds), *Women's Words: The Feminist Practice of Oral History*, Routledge, London and New York, 1991; Jacques Le Goff, *History and Memory*, (trans.) S. Rendall and E. Claman, Columbia University Press, New York, 1992; Elizabeth Tonkin, *Narrating Our Pasts: The Social Construction of Oral History*, Cambridge University Press, 1992; and Darian-Smith and Hamilton, *Memory and History in Twentieth-Century Australia*.

3 For a useful critique of oral history, see John Murphy, 'The Voice of Memory: History, Autobiography and Oral Memory', *Historical Studies*, vol. 22, no. 87, October 1986, pp. 157–75

4 On the relationship between practices and representations in historical interpretation see Roger Chartier, *Cultural History: Between Practices and Representations*, (trans.) L.G. Cochrane, Oxford University Press, Oxford, 1988.

5 For a brief history of Dandenong, see Lesley Alves, *Destination Dandenong*, Heritage Hill, Dandenong, c.1990.

6 Interview with Kevin Synott, Benga Oral History Centre, Heritage Hill, Dandenong (hereafter referred to as Benga), tape no. 26/92. All Benga interviews referred to were conducted by staff at the centre and were not specific to this study.

7   Interview with Evelyn Mitchell, Benga, tape no. 33/88. All further references to Evelyn Mitchell are based on this interview.
8   Interview with Edna and Albert Bramley, Benga, tape no. 3/88. All further references to Edna and Albert Bramley are based on this interview.
9   On the continued use of the open-air market in Melbourne, see Stephen Knight, 'Victoria at the Market' in his *The Selling of the Australian Mind: From First Fleet to Third Mercedes*, Heinemann, Melbourne, 1990. Note that Knight continues to subscribe to a view of the supermarket, as opposed to the market, as a sterile cathedral of consumerism.
10 Cairns, 'As it Was', p. 3.
11 Reekie, *Temptations*, 'Introduction'.
12 Interview with Anetta Barr, Benga, tape no. 33/90.
13 Interview with Maurie Jarvis, Benga, tape no. 37/90.
14 Kitty Rynsent, cited in Alves, *Destination Dandenong*, p. 17.
15 Interview with Lily Midro, Benga, tape no. 5/93.
16 Interview with Jean Cusson, Benga, tape no. 28/90.
17 Interview with Dorothy Hart, Benga, tape no. 25/88.
18 'Australia's Largest Supermarket', *Colesanco*, vol. 4, no. 3, December 1963, p. 1.
19 ibid.
20 ibid.

7 Magic Futures

1   G.J. Coles & Coy Limited, *Annual Report*, 1969, p. 15.
2   G.J. Coles & Coy Limited, *Annual Report*, 1974, p. 2.
3   *How Woolworths Started and Grew*, pp. 4–5.
4   Michael Collins, 'The Rise and Fall of Woolworths 1924–1986', unpublished paper, Australian Centre for Retail Studies, 1993, Table 3.
5   See Collins, 'A Brief History of Retailing, Part 2', p. 50.
6   ibid.
7   Norton and Kennedy, *Australian Economic Statistics*, p. 145 and p. 200.
8   Computerised stock control was introduced by Woolworths in 1975 and at Coles in 1979. See *How Woolworths Started and Grew*, p. 5; and G.J. Coles & Coy Limited, *Annual Report*, 1979. On the concentration of ownership within grocery retailing see Stuart Rosewarne, 'The Political Economy of Retailing into the Eighties – Part 1', *Journal of Australian Political Economy*, no. 15, 1983, pp. 18–38.
9   On post-Fordism, and its relationship to the concept of post-industrialism, see Hall and Jacques (eds), *New Times*, 'Introduction'. This concept has been developed in the context of wider debates about the perceived social and cultural transformations embedded in the rise of postmodernity. Other writers have spoken of the emergence of 'disorganised capitalism', and of 'flexible accumulation'. See, for example, Scott Lash and John Urry, *The End of Organised Capitalism*, Polity, Cambridge, 1987; and Harvey, *The Condition of Postmodernity*, ch. 9.
10 On this trend in Australia see Norton and Kennedy, *Australian Economic Statistics*, p. 101.
11 For a useful critique of post-Fordism and related concepts of economic change see Lee, *Consumer Culture Reborn*.

12 A hypermarket is industry-defined as a store with a sales space of over 5000 square metres and at least 35 per cent of selling space devoted to non-food items. See *Retail Trade International*, vol. 1, p. 6.

13 Taylor, *Twenty-One Years of Australian Safeway*, pp. 18-20. Linden Brown in his *Competitive Marketing Strategy*, Nelson, Sydney, 1990, p. 259, suggests that the first hypermarket proper was opened in Brisbane in 1984 with a selling space of 10 000 square metres and 89 checkouts.

14 A grocery superstore is industry-defined as having a sales space of 2500 square metres or more and selling mainly foodstuffs. See *Retail Trade International*, vol. 1, p. 7. On the rise and social impact of large supermarkets and superstores in Britain, see A.G. Hallsworth, *The Human Impact of Hypermarts and Superstores*, Avebury, Aldershot, 1988; and Carl Gardner and Julie Sheppard, *Consuming Passions: The Rise of Retail Culture*, Unwin Hyman, London, 1989, ch. 7.

15 There is now an enormous body of work on postmodernism and postmodernity. For some of the key texts see Jean-Francois Lyotard, *The Postmodern Condition: A Report on Knowledge*, trans. G. Bennington and B. Massumi, Manchester University Press, Manchester, 1989; and Jean Baudrillard, *Selected Writings*, Mark Poster (ed.), Polity, Cambridge, 1988. See also Fredric Jameson, *Postmodernism, or the Cultural Logic of Late Capitalism*, Verso, London, 1991.

16 See Jameson, ibid. See also his 'Postmodernism or the Cultural Logic of Late Capitalism', *New Left Review*, no. 146, July–August 1984, pp. 53–93; and 'Postmodernism and Consumer Society', in E. Ann Kaplan (ed), *Postmodernism and Its Discontents*, Verso, 1988, pp. 13–29.

17 For a taste of this see Jean Baudrillard, 'The Ecstasy of Communication', in Hal Foster (ed.), *The Anti-Aesthetic: Essays on Postmodern Culture*, Bay Press, Washington, 1985, pp. 126–34. See also Baudrillard's later essays in his *Selected Writings*.

18 The shopping mall is a popular theme within recent cultural criticism, and Jameson's influence can be seen in some of this work. See, for example, Margaret Crawford, 'The World in a Shopping Mall', in Michael Sorkin (ed.), *Variations on a Theme Park: The New American City and the End of Public Space*, Noonday, New York, 1992, pp. 3–30; and Lauren Langman, 'Neon Cages: Shopping For Subjectivity', in Shields (ed.), *Lifestyle Shopping*, pp. 40–82.

19 On the Australian shopping centre, see Morris, 'Things to do with Shopping Centres'; Gail Reekie, 'Changes in the Adamless Eden: The Spatial and Sexual Transformation of a Brisbane Department Store 1930–90', in Shields (ed.), ibid., pp. 170–94; Kingston, *Basket, Bag and Trolley*, ch. 6; and my 'A Stranger in Daimaru'.

20 The move by British supermarket chains (particularly Sainsbury's and Tesco) into house brands served as a model here. See Gardner and Sheppard, *Consuming Passions*, ch. 7.

21 Collins, 'A Brief History of Retailing: Part 2', p. 51.

22 Brown, *Competitive Marketing Strategy*, p. 248.

23 ibid.

24 See for example, Sean Nixon, 'Have you got the Look?: Masculinities and Shopping Spectacle', in Rob Shields (ed.), *Lifestyle Shopping*, pp. 149–69; and Reekie, 'Changes in the Adamless Eden'.

25   Reekie, ibid., pp. 189–92.
26   Victorian Advisory Council on the Status of Women, *Who Shops in the Super-market: Men or Women?*, Melbourne, 1981, p. 2.
27   ibid., p. 5
28   This study was reported on by Georgina Windsor and Jennifer Forshaw in 'Supermarket Invasion by Mrs Men an Ad Bonanza', *The Australian*, 3 August 1994, p. 3. The main reason given for this increase in male shoppers was the rise in one-parent families throughout the 1980s.
29   See Jo S. Cathro, *Men: Food for Thought?: The Male Influence on Shopping and Food Choice*, Consumer Focus no. 5, Leatherhead Food R.A., 1991, p. 27.
30   ibid., p. 8.
31   Collins, 'A Brief History of Retailing: Part 2', p. 51.
32   See *Retail Trade International*, vol. 2, pp. 60–1. In 1985 the American Safeway company sold its 126 Australian supermarkets to Woolworths thereby boosting the market position of the company.
33   ibid., p. 61. AAW was formed in 1983 through the amalgamation of four leading voluntary groups; Davids, Foodland, Queensland Independent Wholesalers and Independent Grocers Co-operative. AAW traded under such 'banners' as Jewel, Food Stop, Scoop, Cut Price, 7 Eleven, Four Square and Serv-Wel. Composite Buyers traded under various banners including Payless, Rite-Way, Tuckerbag, Goodfellows and Budget-Rite.
34   ibid., p. 49. The Australian retail industry as a whole was also becoming further concentrated in terms of ownership, particularly with the merger of Coles and Myer in 1985.
35   ibid.
36   Bevan Bradbury, 'The Excitement of Retailing', in Collins (ed.), *Retail Management Principles*, p. 6.
37   Collins, 'A Brief History of Retailing: Part 2', p. 58.
38   Brown, *Competitive Marketing Strategy*, p. 240.
39   Philip Luker, *Inside The Food Industry*, Philip Luker and Staff, Sydney, n.d., c.1988, p. 11.
40   Brown, *Competitive Marketing Strategy*, p. 242. It may seem surprising, at first, that 59% of those who visit the supermarket do not purchase anything; this percentage comprises those who accompany the main purchaser, many of whom are children.
41   ibid., Table 9.5.
42   Collins, 'A Brief History of Retailing: Part 2', p. 50.
43   Australian Bureau of Statistics, *Retailing In Australia 1991–1992*, ABS Catalogue no. 8613.0, Australian Bureau of Statistics, Canberra, 1992, pp. 5–6.
44   ibid., p. 10. From 1980 to 1992, however, the number of retail stores overall increased by 18 per cent Australia-wide to 172 000.
45   ibid.
46   ibid., p. 2. Turnover of supermarkets and grocery stores in Australia reached $26 billion by 1991–92. The number of people employed in retailing as a whole by June 1992 was 1.1 million or 13.5 per cent of Australia's employed workforce.
47   ibid., p. 7.
48   Coles Myer Ltd, *Annual Report*, 1992, p. 31. This mirrored the male-domination of Australian executive culture. See Amanda Sinclair, *Trials at the Top: Chief*

Executives Talk about Men, Women and the Australian Executive Culture, The Australian Centre, University of Melbourne, Melbourne, 1994.

49 By 1994 the two large wholesalers Davids Ltd and Foodland Associated Ltd, which supply independent, 'banner group' stores with goods, had merged, making the ownership of the Australian groceries market even more highly concentrated.

50 Coles Supermarkets, 'Customer Information Kit', Coles Supermarkets, Melbourne, 1992 (no page numbers given).

51 Woolworths Limited, *A Company Perspective 1987–1992*, Woolworths Limited, Sydney, 1992. See also Heather Eiszele, 'Woolies on Supermarket Splurge', *The Australian*, 3 February 1993, p. 30.

52 Woolworths Limited, *Annual Report*, 1996, p. 13, and Woolworths Limited Internet Site: http://www.woolworths.com.au, June 1997; Australian Financial Review Net Services: http://www.afr.com.au, report on supermarket sales, 27 May 1997.

53 Coles Myer Ltd Internet Site: htpp://www.colesmyer.com.au and Coles Supermarkets Internet Site: http://www.coles.com.au, May 1997; AFR Net Services, ibid. Note that Franklins by mid-1997 had lost market share (taking 13.2 per cent of supermarket sales) as had the Davids/Foodland group (taking 20.8 per cent of sales).

54 David McKenzie, 'Keating Bags Major Retailers', *The Age*, 4 October 1994, p. 1. The Australian Supermarket Institute was formed in 1989 to act as the peak supermarket body in Australia. It represents the large corporate chains and a range of independent wholesalers. See, *ASI: Australian Supermarket Institute*, ASI, Sydney, n.d., c.1994.

55 McKenzie, ibid.

56 See Tim Graham and Kathleen Buchanan, 'Huge Expansion will change the face of Melbourne's Regional Shopping Centres', *The Age*, 2 June 1993.

57 See Alex Messina, 'Strip Shopping Centres Face a Growing Threat', *The Age*, 3 June 1993.

58 'Retailers Against More Big Centres', *The Age*, 14 January 1997, p. A3.

59 Katrina Strickland, 'Mixed Business', *The Australian*, 10 March 1997.

60 By 1995 Woolworths considered 'electronic trading' an integral part of its expansion plans and was piloting a scheme to give remote areas in Australia access to 10 000 products by way of home computers. See Woolworths Limited, *A Profile of Our Company*, Woolworths Limited, Sydney, n.d., 1995, p. 5.

61 *The Investigators* (segment on the future of supermarket shopping), Australian Broadcasting Corporation, aired on ABC television, Melbourne, March 1994.

62 Ruthven made this statement on the television program *Lateline: Retailing The Future*, Australian Broadcasting Corporation, aired on ABC television, Melbourne, September 1994.

63 ibid.

64 Susan Horsburgh, 'Shopping is Becoming a Leisure Experience', *The Weekend Australian*, 4–5 December 1993 (property section), p. 1.

65 ibid., p. 2. By 1993 Woolworths had taken the notion of ownership to new heights. Its public float of the company, with prospectuses available at the checkout, turned out to be the most successful public float in Australian history.

66 Collins, 'A Brief History of Retailing, Part 2', pp. 56–60.

67 Richard Gluyas, 'Sector Must Rise to the Challenge of Changing Patterns', *The Australian*, 15 January 1997, p. 19.

68 There is not space here to explore the political economy of retailing in terms of the contemporary 'globalisation' and 'delocalisation' of food products. This has been the subject of some fascinating recent scholarship. See Ben Fine, 'From Political Economy to Consumption', in Miller (ed.), *Acknowledging Consumption*, pp. 127–63; Ian Cook and Philip Crang, 'The World on a Plate: Culinary Culture, Displacement and Geographical Knowledges', *Journal of Material Culture*, vol. 1, July 1996, pp. 131–53; and on Australia, Jane Dixon, 'Kitchen Kultures', *Arena Magazine*, no. 19, October–November 1995, pp. 35–8.

69 Cited in Andrew White, 'Woolies Bucks Retail Slump', *The Australian*, 15 January 1997, p. 19.

70 Enrica Longo, 'Cooks, Elitists, A Market and its Lovers', *The Age* (Metro section), 20 November 1996, p. 3.

71 See Rochelle Burbury, 'Customer always right – now more than ever', *The Australian*, 14–15 June 1997, p. 5. Burbury cites a study by Grey Advertising titled 'Who's Afraid of the Promiscuous Female Shopper?'.

72 I have discussed some of these issues more fully in my 'A Stranger in Daimaru'. For the 'classic' statement on green consumption see John Elkington and Julia Hailes (eds), *The Green Consumer Guide*, Gollancz, London, 1989, 'Introduction'. See also Fred Steward, 'Green Times', and Stewart Hall and David Held, 'Citizens and Citizenship', both in Hall and Jacques (eds), *New Times*, pp. 65–75; and pp. 173–88 respectively; and David Evans, *Sexual Citizenship: The Material Construction of Sexualities*, Routledge, London, 1993.

73 Hugh Mackay, 'Responding to the Consumer of the 1990s', in Society of Consumer Affairs Professionals in Business Inc. *1991 Conference Papers*, SOCAP, Geelong, 1991 (no page numbers).

74 Suzy Freeman-Greene, 'Shopping Daze', *The Age*, 11 October, 1993, p. 11. See also her earlier article 'This Shopping Life', *The Age* (Saturday Extra), 9 October, 1993, pp. 1, 6.

75 This is evident also in Sarah Gibson's exploration of the activities and thoughts of various inveterate shoppers in her *Born To Shop*, Inside Outside Productions, Australian Film Commission/Australian Broadcasting Corporation, 1991.

76 See Margaret Cook, 'Born to Shop', *The Age*, 21 December 1994, p. 15.

77 Foley, 'White Myths Damage our Souls'.

78 Richard Neville, 'Who Challenges the Real Sacred Cow?', *The Age*, 17 March 1994, pp. 15–16.

79 Kate Legge, 'The Kitchen Sinks', *The Australian*, 31 May–1 June 1997, p. 5

8 Strangers in Paradise

1 On critical responses to suburbia in Australia see Alan Gilbert, 'The Roots of Anti-Suburbanism in Australia', *Australian Cultural History*, no. 4, 1985, pp. 54–70; Tim Rowse, 'Heaven and a Hills Hoist: Australian Critics on Suburbia', *Meanjin*, vol. 37, no. 1, April 1978, pp. 3–13. See also the essays in Sarah Ferber, Chris Healy and Chris McAuliffe (eds), *Beasts of Suburbia: Reinterpreting Cultures in Australian Suburbs*, Melbourne University Press, Melbourne, 1994; and in Louise Johnson

(ed.), *Suburban Dreaming: An Interdisciplinary Approach to Australian Cities*, Deakin University Press, Geelong, 1994. On literary responses to suburbia see Beate Joseph, 'Images of Suburbia: Bruce Dawe, Bruce Beaver, Gwen Harwood and Vincent Buckley', *Quadrant*, April 1978, pp. 64–7; Robin Gerster, 'Gerrymander: The Place of Suburbia in Australian Fiction', *Meanjin*, 3, 1990, pp. 565–75; and Frances Devlin Glass, ' "Mythologising Spaces": Representing the City in Australian Literature', in Johnson (ed.), ibid., pp. 160–80.

2 The Australian 'consumer movement', represented in Australia by the Australian Federation of Consumer Organisations, has also offered an ongoing analysis of retailing and consumption, though within the framework of consumer rights rather than cultural critique. A discussion of organised consumer activism in Australia is not offered here. See, however, John Goldring, *Consumers or Victims*, George Allen & Unwin, Sydney, 1982; and Halpin (ed.), *Consumers' Choice*.

3 Donald Horne, *The Lucky Country*, Penguin, Ringwood, 1964, p. 29.

4 Robin Boyd, *The Australian Ugliness*, Cheshire, Melbourne, 1961, p. 2.

5 ibid., pp. 63–4.

6 ibid., p. 65.

7 Robin Boyd, *Artificial Australia: The Boyer Lectures 1967*, Australian Broadcasting Commission, 1967, p. 80.

8 ibid., p. 48.

9 See for example the introduction to George Caiger (ed.), *The Australian Way of Life*, Books for Libraries, New York, 1953. See also many of the essays in W.V. Aughterson (ed.), *Taking Stock: Aspects of Mid-Century Life in Australia*, Cheshire, Melbourne, 1953.

10 John Douglas Pringle, *Australian Accent*, Chatto and Windus, London, 1965, pp. 116–17.

11 Peter Coleman (ed.), *Australian Civilisation*, Cheshire, Melbourne, 1962. This was a collection of papers from a symposium organised in support of 'Cultural Freedom', the anti-communist grouping connected with the production of Australia's main journal of conservative critique, *Quadrant*.

12 A foretaste of the kind of rabid condemnation of Australian popular culture embodied in many of the contributions was evident in the title of T. Andrzejaczek's article 'Suburbia – A Cultural Defeat', *Quadrant*, vol. 2, no. 1, Summer 1957–58, pp. 25–30.

13 Max Harris, 'Morals and Manners', in Coleman (ed.), *Australian Civilisation*, p. 53.

14 ibid.

15 Ronald Conway, *The Great Australian Stupor: An Interpretation of the Australian Way of Life*, Sun Books, Melbourne, 1974 (first published 1971).

16 ibid., p. 233.

17 ibid. Conway's critique of suburbia became even sillier in his *Land of the Long Weekend*, Sun Books, Melbourne, 1978.

18 John Carroll, 'Automobile Culture and Citizenship', *Quadrant*, March 1979, p. 11.

19 See John Carroll, 'The Sceptic Turns Consumer: An Outline of Australian Culture', *Quadrant*, October 1978, p. 11.

20 ibid.

21 See John Carroll, 'Shopping World: An Afternoon in the Palace of Modern Consumption', *Quadrant*, August 1979, pp. 11–15.

22 ibid., p. 13.
23 Horne, *The Lucky Country*, p. 27.
24 See Meaghan Morris, 'On The Beach', in Nelson, Treichler and Grossberg (eds), *Cultural Studies*, pp. 450–78.
25 Horne, *The Lucky Country*, p. 22.
26 Donald Horne, *Money Made Us*, Penguin, Ringwood, 1976, p. 217.
27 ibid., pp. 218–25.
28 Craig McGregor, *Profile of Australia*, Penguin, Ringwood, 1968 (first published 1966). See also his *People, Politics and Pop: Australians in the Sixties*, Ure Smith, Sydney, 1968.
29 Craig McGregor, 'Pop Goes the Culture: Academic and Other Prognostications', *Meanjin*, vol. 39, no. 1, April 1980, pp. 3–4.
30 ibid., p. 4.
31 Hugh Stretton, *Ideas for Australian Cities*, Georgian House, Melbourne, 1975 (first published 1970), p. 9.
32 Ian Turner, 'The Life of the Legend', in his *Room For Manoeuvre: Writings on History, Politics, Ideas and Play*, Drummond, Melbourne, 1982, p. 36. This essay first appeared in *Meanjin* in 1959.
33 Allan Ashbolt, 'Godzone 3/Myth and Reality', *Meanjin*, vol. xxv, no. 4, 1966, pp. 373–4.
34 Peter Groenewegen, 'Consumer Capitalism', in J. Playford and D. Kirsner (eds), *Australian Capitalism*, Penguin, Melbourne, 1973, pp. 84–107.
35 John Docker, *Australian Cultural Elites: Intellectual Traditions in Sydney and Melbourne*, Angus & Robertson, Sydney, 1974.
36 Julie Rigg, 'The Loneliness of the Long Distance Housewife: Mrs Consumer', in Julie Rigg (ed.), *In Her Own Right: Women of Australia*, Nelson, Melbourne, 1969, pp. 135–49.
37 ibid., pp. 142–3.
38 Anne Summers, *Damned Whores and God's Police: The Colonization of Women in Australia*, Penguin, Ringwood, 1975, p. 435.
39 ibid.
40 Ann Game and Rosemary Pringle, 'Sexuality and the Suburban Dream', *Australia and New Zealand Journal of Sociology*, vol. 15, no. 2, July 1979, pp. 4–15.
41 ibid., p. 10.
42 ibid., p. 9.
43 Rosemary Pringle, 'Women and Consumer Capitalism', in Cora V. Baldock and Bettina Cass (eds), *Women, Social Welfare and the State in Australia*, Allen & Unwin, Sydney, 1983, pp. 85–103. See also Game and Pringle, *Gender at Work*, particularly ch. 6
44 Pringle, ibid., p. 91
45 This interest in consumption as social and symbolic practice was reflected also in urban and social research. See, for example, Department of Environment, Housing and Community Development, *The Shopping Centre as a Community Leisure Resource*, Australian Government Publishing Service, Canberra, 1978; and Shirley Horne, *A Study of Milk Bars and Corner Shops In Melbourne: Shopping as a Social Activity*, Department of Social Studies, University of Melbourne, Melbourne, 1984.

46 Gerry Gill, 'The Signs of Consumerism', *Arena*, no. 53, 1979, pp. 28–39.
47 John Docker, 'In Defence of Popular Culture', *Arena*, no. 60, 1982, pp. 72–87.
48 Anthony Ashbolt, 'Against Left Optimism: A Reply to John Docker', *Arena*, no. 61, 1982, pp. 134–40.
49 Ingrid Hagstrom, 'Popular Culture Undefined', *Arena*, no. 61, 1982, pp. 141–8.
50 John Docker, 'Popular Culture and its Marxist Critics', *Arena*, no. 65, 1983, pp. 105–9. For a more lengthy critique of attitudes towards suburbia within intellectual work, see also his *In A Critical Condition: Reading Australian Literature*, Penguin, Ringwood, 1984.
51 John Docker continued to defend popular culture, and to conceptualise it as working class, in his 'Popular Culture and Bourgeois Values', in Verity Burgmann and Jenny Lee (eds), *Constructing a Culture: A People's History of Australia since 1788*, McPhee Gribble/Penguin, Melbourne, 1988, pp. 241–58. See also his *Postmodernism and Popular Culture*, Cambridge University Press, Melbourne, 1994.
52 Ian Turner, 'The Bastards from the Bush: Some Comments on Class and Culture', in E.L. Wheelwright and Ken Buckley, *Essays in the Political Economy of Australian Capitalism*, vol. 3, Australia & New Zealand Book Co., Sydney, 1978, pp. 167–89.
53 Fiske, Hodge and Turner, *Myths of Oz*.
54 ibid., p. 103 passim.
55 See Frow and Morris (eds), *Australian Cultural Studies*, 'Introduction'.
56 ibid., 'Introduction'.
57 Morris, 'Things To Do With Shopping Centres'.
58 ibid., pp. 196–7.
59 See Reekie, *Temptations*, and Johnson, *The Modern Girl*.
60 Kingston, *Basket, Bag and Trolley*.
61 In her review of *The Modern Girl* (*Australian Historical Studies*, no. 102, April 1994, pp. 129–30) Katie Holmes suggests, for example, that one problem with the book is that the theory seems to displace the history.
62 See Ferber, Healy and McAuliffe (eds), *Beasts of Suburbia*; and Johnson (ed.), *Suburban Dreaming*.
63 As collections they are also very partial themselves; only *Suburban Dreaming*, for example, includes an essay on shopping and consumption: Peter Spearritt, 'I Shop Therefore I Am', pp. 129–40.
64 Janet McCalman, 'Suburbia from the Sandpit', *Meanjin*, vol. 53, no. 3, Spring, 1994, pp. 548–53.
65 Judith Brett, 'The Circus is in Town', *Arena Magazine*, no. 15, February/March 1995, pp. 48–50.

9 Everyday Shopping

1 This chapter is based on both the oral history interviews that form the basis of chapter six and a further series of qualitative interviews designed to explore everyday thinking about supermarket shopping and consumer culture. Once again, the questions asked were open-ended and based on a detailed interview schedule, with each interview lasting from one to two hours. Likewise, no effort was made to seek a 'representative sample' of interviewees. Although a list of those

interviewed is included in the bibliography, in this chapter an anonymity is preserved by the use of fictitious names (other than for those of the Dandenong group) and certain personal details have been altered. This is in accordance with the wishes of most interviewees.

2 M.I. Halliday and R.C. Cameron, *Observational Study of Supermarket Buying Behaviour*, Faculty of Business Working Papers Series, New South Wales Institute of Technology, Sydney, 1987, p. 16.

3 ibid., pp. 28, 32. Clearly, this is linked also to other factors such as increased leisure time through retirement. On the quite different 'in-store' behaviour of children see Matthew R. Sanders and Allen C. Hunter, 'An Ecological Analysis of Children's Behaviour in Supermarkets', in *Australian Journal of Psychology*, vol. 36, no. 3, 1984, pp. 415–27.

4 Victorian Advisory Council on the Status of Women, *Who Shops in the Supermarket: Men or Women?*, p. 4

5 A similar reticence was found by the authors of *The Shopping Centre as a Community Leisure Resource*, p. 8. However, the report did not fully explore why some people interviewed differentiated between shopping and leisure in this way.

6 In her study on the meanings of home and suburb in post-war Australia, Jean Duruz, in 'Laminex Dreams', *Meanjin*, vol. 53, no. 1, 1994, pp. 99–110, found that the women she interviewed similarly rejected a characterisation of suburban life as dominated by shopping.

7 Lunt and Livingstone, *Mass Consumption and Personal Identity*, pp. 144–50. This study was based on a survey of 279 people, on a number of 'focus group' discussions, and on 20 individual qualitative interviews.

8 ibid., p. 149.

9 For a useful critique of the sometimes shallow and populist use of 'ethnographic methods' within cultural studies, see Virginia Nightingale, 'What's "Ethnographic" About Ethnographic Audience Research?', in Frow and Morris (eds), *Australian Cultural Studies*, pp. 149–61.

Bibliography

Abbreviations

BL   British Library, London
CMA Coles Myer Archives, Melbourne
LaT   La Trobe Library, Melbourne
SLV   State Library of Victoria
UMA University of Melbourne Archives

Retail Companies: Company Literature and Manuscript Material

ASDA

ASDA, *Report and Accounts 1996*, ASDA Group plc, Leeds, 1996.
ASDA, 'Information Pack', ASDA Stores Ltd, Leeds, n.d., c.1996/97.

Coles Myer

G.J. Coles & Coy Limited, *Annual Report*, 1958–1979 (CMA).
Coles Myer Ltd, *Annual Report*, 1986–1996.
Colesanco (Staff Magazine of G.J. Coles & Coy Limited), 1958–1983 (SLV and CMA).
Coles Supermarkets, 'Customer Information Kit', Coles Supermarkets, Melbourne, 1992.
'The Coles Story', *Annual Report*, G.J. Coles & Coy Limited, Melbourne,1964.
Coles Myer, Internet Site: http://www.colesmyer.com.au
Coles Supermarkets, Internet Site: http://www.coles.com.au

Crofts Stores

Crofts Stores paper, UMA:
    Advertising material, c.1930–1950s.
    Branch Letters, 1939–1968.
    Crofts Stores 30th Anniversary Cookerybook and Household Guide, 1936.
    'Self Service Stores' (photograph album with list of store openings), 1951–1954.
    Material relating to staff matters, 1940s.
    'Window Plan Book', 1935.

Kroger Company

Kroger, Annual Report, 1993, Kroger Co., Cincinnati, 1993.
Barney Builds a Business: The Story of the Founding of the Kroger Co., Kroger Co., Cincinnati, n.d.
Laycock, George, *The Kroger Story: A Century of Innovation*, Kroger Co., Cincinnati, 1983.

Moran & Cato

Moran & Cato papers, MS 10325, LaT:
    Moran & Cato shop fliers, 1887–1894.
    Hints on Better Salesmanship, Moran & Cato, Melbourne, n.d., c.1920.
    Moran & Cato Price List, 1921–1923.
    'Some Notes on the Early History of Moran and Cato' (typescript), 22 May 1968.
Permewan Wright Papers, MS12283, LaT:
    Minutes of Company Shareholder Meetings, 1946–1969.

Safeway (UK and USA)

Safeway Stores Incorporated, *Our 50th Year: Annual Report 1975*, Safeway Stores Inc., Oakland, 1976.
Safeway, *Checkout* (The House Journal of Safeway Food Stores Ltd), UK Division, Safeway Stores Inc., London, October/November, 1983.
Argyll Group plc, *Report and Accounts*, 1994, Argyll Group plc, Middlesex, 1994.

Sainsbury's

Family: Sainsbury's Magazine For Every Woman, no. 1, Autumn 1961 (PP. 5109 bs, BL).
Sainsbury's, 'History of the Company', Sainsbury plc, London, 1991.
J.S. Journal (House Magazine of J. Sainsbury Ltd), 1957–1962 (PP5793 RAD, BL).
J.S. 100: The Story of Sainsbury's, J. Sainsbury Ltd, London, 1969 (BL).
Some Facts About J. Sainsbury plc 1996, Sainsbury's Corporate Relations Department, London, 1996.
Whitford, Frank, 'The Grocer's Tale', in *Sainsbury's 125 Years Celebration Supplement: Sainsbury's Magazine*, New Crane Publishing, London, 1994, pp. 6–13.

Tesco

Tesco plc, 'Abbreviated History and Facts Sheet', Tesco plc, Customer Service Department, 1990.
Tesco plc, *Annual Report & Accounts*, 1991 and 1996.
This is TESCO, Tesco Public Affairs Department, Cheshunt, 1990.

Woolworths

Woolworths Limited, *Annual Report*, 1959–1996.
Woolworths Limited, *A Company Perspective 1987–1992*, Woolworths Limited, Sydney, 1992.
Taylor, Malcolm (ed.), *Twenty-One Years of Australian Safeway 1963–1984*, Australian Safeway, Melbourne, 1984.
How Woolworths Started and Grew: A Brief History of Woolworths Limited, Public Relations Department, Woolworths Limited, Sydney, n.d., c.1989.
Woolworths Limited, *Company Profile*, Woolworths Limited, Sydney, n.d., c.1992.
Woolworths Limited, *A Profile of Our Company*, Woolworths Limited, Sydney, 1995.
Woolworths Limited, Internet Site: http://www.woolworths.com.au

Other Manuscript Material and Company and Union Literature

ASI, *Australian Supermarket Institute*, ASI, Sydney, n.d., c.1994.
Cadbury, *Creating the Great Taste: The Story of Cadbury and Chocolate Making*, Cadbury, Melbourne, n.d., c.1994.
Cairns, Tom, 'As It Was: Work as a Grocer Boy saw it in Middle Park 1933–1939' (typescript), (MS 12750, Box 3530/2, LaT).
Cathro, Jo S., *Men: Food For Thought? The Male Influence on Shopping and Food Choice*, Consumer Focus, no. 5, Leatherhead Food R.A., 1991.
Composite Buyers, 'Composite Buyers – A Brief History', Composite Buyers Ltd, Melbourne, n.d., c.1993.
Edgell-Birds Eye, 'Company Profile', Edgell-Birds Eye, Sydney, n.d., c.1994.
Foodland, 'Foodland Confidential News Report', nos 3–50, 1958 (in Crofts Stores papers, 'Advertising Material', UMA).
Foodland, 'The First Three Months', 1958 (in Crofts Stores papers, UMA).
Heinz Australia. 'The Heinz Story – A Proud Record of Manufacturing in Australia', Heinz (Australia), Melbourne, n.d., c.1992.
Kellogg, *The History of Kellogg Company*, Kellogg (Australia) Pty Ltd, Sydney, n.d., c.1990.
Kraft Foods Limited, *The Kraft Story in Australia*, Kraft Foods Ltd, Melbourne, n.d.
Myer Emporium, 'Northland Shopping Centre', n.d., c.1964 (LaT).
National Association of Retail Grocers' Associations, *Food Store Operator's Manual*, NARGA, Melbourne, 1971.
Peters, 'Peters Ice Cream Story', Peters Foods, Melbourne, n.d., c.1991.
Retailers Council of Australia, 'An Introduction', RCA, Melbourne, n.d.
Robinson, J.C., 'Weekly Order Book of Mrs J.C. Robinson' (PA 93/89, LaT).
Seedman's Supermarkets, 'Consolidated Trading Statements', 1959, 1960–61 (in Mutual Store Papers, UMA).

SDA, 'Trade Union Information Kit on The Shop, Distributive and Allied Employees' Association', Shop, Distributive and Allied Employees' Association, Melbourne, n.d.

Oral History and Qualitative Interviews

From the collection of Benga Oral History Centre, Dandenong

Anetta Barr, Tape no. 33/90
Edna and Albert Bramley, Tape no. 3/88
Jean Cusson, Tape no. 28/90
Dorothy Hart, Tape no. 25/88
Maurie Jarvis, Tape no. 37/90
Lily Midro, Tape no. 5/93
Evelyn Mitchell, Tape no. 33/88
Kevin Synott, Tape no. 26/92

Conducted for the Shelf-Life Project

Anetta Barr, 20/12/94
Yvonne Boulos, 1/12/94
Michael Casey, 30/3/95
John Crichton, 29/12/94
Joy Dempsey, 3/3/95
Russell Field, 8/3/95
Lawrence Gallagher, 30/3/95
Simone Howard, 8/12/94
Fay Hussey, 28/12/94
Samantha Jackman, 1/12/94
Nicole James, 8/12/94
Jack Lightfoot, 20/2/95
Peter McAuliffe, 12/12/94
Sharron McConville, 7/12/94
Lily Midro, 9/1/95
Muriel Norris, 21/12/94
Robert Reynolds, 30/3/95
Jane Whelan, 19/12/94

Government Publications: Federal and State

Australian Bureau of Statistics, *Census of Retail Establishments and Selected Service Establishments, Australia 1979–80*, ABS, Canberra, 1981.
Australian Bureau of Statistics, *Retailing in Australia 1991–1992*, ABS Catalogue no. 8613.0, ABS, Canberra, 1992.
'Chain Stores: Report of the Industrial Commission of New South Wales upon Matters Relating to the Management, Control and Operations of General Chain Stores in New South Wales', *New South Wales Parliamentary Papers*, 1939.

Commonwealth of Australia, *Report of the Committee of Economic Enquiry*, vols. 1 & 2, Government Printer, Canberra, 1965.

Commonwealth Bureau of Census and Statistics, *Official Yearbook of the Commonwealth of Australia*, Government Printer, Canberra, editions: 1953–64.

Commonwealth Bureau of Census and Statistics, *Economic Censuses 1968–69: Retail Establishments and Selected Service Establishments in Australia*, Final Bulletin, Canberra, 1973.

Department of Environment, Housing and Community Development. *The Shopping Centre as a Community Leisure Resource*, Australian Government Publishing Service, Canberra, 1978.

Norton, W.E. and Kennedy, P.J., *Australian Economic Statistics 1949–50 to 1984–85: Tables*, Reserve Bank of Australia, Occasional Paper no. 8A, Canberra, November 1985.

Report of the Technical Advisory Committee on Retailing, A Report Submitted to the Victorian Government and the Melbourne Metropolitan Board of Works, Government Printer, Melbourne, June 1980.

South Australian Council on Technological Change, *Scanning in Supermarkets: Employment Effects in South Australia*, Department of Industrial Affairs and Employment, Adelaide, 1982.

Victorian Advisory Council on the Status of Women, *Who Shops in the Supermarket: Men or Women?*, Government Printer, Melbourne, 1981.

Trade Journals, Newspapers and Magazines

Australian Financial Review, 1957–66, 1993–97.
Australian Financial Review Net Services: http://afr.com.au, 1997.
Food Store News and Self-Service Journal, 1961–62. (SLV)
Grocery and Storekeeping News, 1936–37. (SLV)
Nation, 1959–60.
Retail Merchandiser and Chain Store Review, 1937–41. (SLV)
Retail World, 1967–96. (SLV)
Rydges, 1939–70.
Sydney Morning Herald, 1954–70.
The Age, 1968–97.
The Australian, 1993–97.
The Australasian Grocer, 1901–1904, 1921–25, 1945–64. (SLV)
The Australasian Grocer's Journal, 1889–96. (SLV)
The Australian Women's Weekly, 1960–69.
The Grocers' Assistant, 1914–17. (SLV)
Sun-Herald, Sydney, 1958–60.
Walkabout, 1963.

Books

Abelson, Elaine S., *When Ladies Go A-Thieving: Middle-Class Shoplifters in the Victorian Department Store*, Oxford University Press, New York, 1989.

Adburgham, Alison, *Shops and Shopping 1800–1914. Where, and in What Manner the Well-Dressed English Woman Bought Her Clothes*, George Allen & Unwin, London, 1964.

Adorno, Theodor W., *The Culture Industry: Selected Essays on Mass Culture*, J.M. Bernstein (ed.), Routledge, London, 1991.

Alexander, David, *Retailing in England During the Industrial Revolution*, Athlone Press, University of London, London, 1970.

Alves, Lesley, *Destination Dandenong*, Heritage Hill, Dandenong, c.1990.

Ang, Ien, *Watching Dallas: Soap Opera and the Melodramatic Imagination*, Methuen, London, 1985.

—— , *Desperately Seeking the Audience*, Routledge, London, 1991.

Appadurai, Arjun (ed.), *The Social Life of Things: Commodities in Cultural Perspective*, Cambridge University Press, New York, 1986.

Aughterson, W.V. (ed.), *Taking Stock: Aspects of Mid-Century Life in Australia*, Cheshire, Melbourne, 1953.

Barnard Eldershaw, M., *Tomorrow and Tomorrow*, Georgian House, Melbourne, 1947.

Barrett, Bernard, *The Inner Suburbs: The Evolution of an Industrial Era*, Melbourne University Press, Melbourne, 1971.

Baudrillard, Jean, *Selected Writings*, Mark Poster (ed.), Polity, Cambridge, 1988.

Bell, Philip and Bell, Roger, *Implicated: The United States in Australia*, Oxford University Press, Melbourne, 1993.

Bendick, Jeanne, *The First Book of Supermarkets*, Franklin Watts, New York, 1954.

Benjamin, Walter, *Charles Baudelaire: A Lyric Poet in the Era of High Capitalism*, Verso, London, 1983.

Benson, John and Shaw, Gareth (eds), *The Evolution of Retail Systems, c.1800–1914*, Leicester University Press, London, 1992.

Benson, Susan Porter, *Counter Cultures: Saleswomen, Managers and Customers in American Department Stores 1890–1940*, University of Illinois Press, Urbana and Chicago, 1986.

Berman, Marshall, *"All That is Solid Melts Into Air": The Experience of Modernity*. Verso, London, 1982.

Bocock, Robert, *Consumption*, Routledge, London, 1993.

Bolton, Geoffrey, *The Oxford History of Australia: The Middle Way 1942–1988*, Oxford University Press, Melbourne, 1993.

Bottomley, David T., *Introduction to Market Analysis* (revised ed.), Market Research Society of Australia, Melbourne, 1964.

Bowlby, Rachel, *Just Looking: Consumer Culture in Dreiser, Gissing and Zola*, Methuen, New York and London, 1985.

—— , *Shopping With Freud*, Routledge, London, 1993.

Boyd, Robin, *The Australian Ugliness*, Cheshire, Melbourne, 1961.

—— , *Artificial Australia: The Boyer Lectures 1967*, Australian Broadcasting Commission, 1967.

Brand, Edward A., *Modern Supermarket Operation*, Fairchild, New York, 1973.

Brewer, John and Porter, Roy (eds), *Consumption and the World of Goods*, Routledge, London, 1993.

Brown, Linden, *Competitive Marketing Strategy*, Nelson, Sydney, 1990.

Burrows, Roger and Marsh, Catherine (eds), *Consumption and Class: Divisions and Change*, Macmillan, London, 1992.

Caiger, George (ed.), *The Australian Way of Life*, Books for Libraries, New York, 1953.

Cameron, Mary Owen, *The Booster and the Snitch: Department Store Shoplifting*, Collier Macmillan, London, 1964.

Campbell, Colin, *The Romantic Ethic and the Spirit of Modern Consumerism*, Basil Blackwell, Oxford, 1987.

Cannon, Michael, *Life in the Cities: Australia in the Victorian Age: 3*, Currey O'Neil, Melbourne, 1983.

Casey, Gavin, *Amid the Plenty: A Novel of Today*, Australasian Book Society, Sydney, 1962.

Casson, Herbert N., *How to Make Advertising Pay*, Angus & Robertson, Sydney, 1939.

Challinger, Dennis (ed.), *Studies in Shoplifting*, Australian Crime Prevention Council, Melbourne, 1977.

—— , *Stop Stealing From Our Shops: Retail Theft in Australia*, National Crime Prevention Council, Canberra, 1989.

Chartier, Roger, *Cultural History: Between Practices and Representations*, (trans.) L.G. Cochrane, Oxford University Press, Oxford, 1988.

Charvat, Frank J., *Supermarketing*, Macmillan, New York, 1961.

Coleman, Peter (ed.), *Australian Civilisation*, Cheshire, Melbourne, 1962.

Conway, Ronald, *The Great Australian Stupor: An Interpretation of the Australian Way of Life*, Sun Books, Melbourne, 1974.

—— , *Land of the Long Weekend*, Sun Books, Melbourne, 1978.

Cooper, J.B., *Victorian Commerce 1834–1934*, Robertson and Mullens, Melbourne, 1934.

Cross, Jennifer, *The Supermarket Trap: The Consumer and the Food Industry*, Indiana University Press, Bloomington, 1976.

Cusack, Dymphna and James, Florence, *Come In Spinner*, Heinemann, Melbourne, 1957.

Darian-Smith, Kate and Hamilton, Paula, *Memory and History in Twentieth-Century Australia*, Oxford University Press, Melbourne, 1994.

Davis, Dorothy, *A History of Shopping*, Routledge & Kegan Paul, London, 1966.

Davison, Graeme, *The Rise and Fall of Marvellous Melbourne*, Melbourne University Press, Melbourne, 1978.

Dawson, John A., *Commercial Distribution in Europe*, Croom Helm, London, 1982.

Debord, Guy, *Society of the Spectacle*, Rebel Press/Aim Publications, London, 1987.

de Certeau, Michel, *The Practice of Everyday Life*, University of California Press, Berkeley, 1984.

Dipman, Carl W., *Self-Service Food Stores*, Progressive Grocer, New York, 1946.

Docker, John, *Australian Cultural Elites: Intellectual Traditions in Sydney and Melbourne*, Angus & Robertson, Sydney, 1974.

—— , *In A Critical Condition: Reading Australian Literature*, Penguin, Ringwood, 1984.

—— , *Postmodernism and Popular Culture*, Cambridge University Press, Melbourne, 1994.

Douglas, Mary, and Isherwood, Baron, *The World of Goods: Towards an Anthropology of Consumption*, Allen Lane, London, 1979.

Durkheim, Emile, *The Rules of Sociological Method*, Free Press, New York, 1966.

Elkington, John and Hailes, Julia (eds), *The Green Consumer Guide*, Gollancz, London, 1989.

Evans, David T., *Sexual Citizenship: The Material Construction of Sexualities*, Routledge, London, 1993.

Ewen, Stuart, *All Consuming Images: The Politics of Style in Contemporary Culture*, Basic Books, New York, 1988.

Farrer, K.T.H., *A Settlement Amply Supplied: Food Technology in Nineteenth-Century Australia*, Melbourne University Press, Melbourne, 1980.

Featherstone, Mike, *Consumer Culture and Postmodernism*, Sage, London, 1991.

Featherstone, Mike, Lash, Scott and Robertson, Roland (eds), *Global Modernities*, Sage, London, 1995.

Felski, Rita, *The Gender of Modernity*, Harvard University Press, London and Cambridge MA, 1995.

Ferber, Sarah, Healy, Chris and McAuliffe, Chris (eds), *Beasts of Suburbia: Reinterpreting Cultures in Australian Suburbs*, Melbourne University Press, Melbourne, 1994.

Fiske, John, *Understanding Popular Culture*, Unwin Hyman, London, 1989.

—— , *Reading the Popular*, Unwin Hyman, London, 1989.

Fiske, John, Hodge, Bob and Turner, Graeme, *Myths of Oz: Reading Australian Popular Culture*, Allen & Unwin, Sydney, 1987.

Fox, Richard Wightman and Lears, T.J. Jackson (eds), *The Culture of Consumption: Critical Essays in American History 1880–1980*, Pantheon, New York, 1983.

Fraser, Hamish W., *The Coming of the Mass Market, 1850–1914*, Archon, Connecticut, 1981.

Friedan, Betty, *The Feminine Mystique*, Penguin, Harmondsworth, 1965.

Frow, John and Morris, Meaghan, *Australian Cultural Studies: A Reader*, Allen & Unwin, Sydney, 1993.

Fulop, Christina, *Competition For Consumers: A Study of Changing Channels of Distribution*, Institute of Economic Affairs/Andre Deutsch, London, 1964.

Gagg, M.E., *Shopping With Mother*, J.H. Wingfield (illus.), Wills and Hepworth, Loughborough, 1958.

Galbraith, John Kenneth, *The Affluent Society*, Andre Deutsch, London, 1984.

Game, Ann and Pringle, Rosemary, *Gender at Work*, George Allen & Unwin, Sydney, 1983.

Gardner, Carl and Sheppard, Julie, *Consuming Passions: The Rise of Retail Culture*, Unwin Hyman, London, 1989.

George Patterson Pty Ltd, *The Patterson Report: or 'Wooing the Australian Woman'*, George Patterson Pty Ltd, Sydney, 1972.

Giddens, Anthony, *Modernity and Self-Identity: Self and Society in the Late Modern Age*, Polity, Cambridge, 1991.

Gluck, Sherna Berger and Patai, Daphne (eds), *Women's Words: The Feminist Practice of Oral History*, Routledge, London and New York, 1991.

Goldring, John, *Consumers or Victims?*, George Allen & Unwin, Sydney, 1982.

Grant, James and Serle, Geoffrey (eds), *The Melbourne Scene 1803–1956*, Hale & Iremonger, Sydney, 1983.

Hall, Stuart and Jacques, Martin, *New Times: The Changing Face of Politics in the 1990s*, Lawrence & Wishart/Marxism Today, London, 1989.

Halliday, M.I. and Cameron, R.C., *Observational Study of Supermarket Buying Behaviour*, Faculty of Business Working Papers Series, New South Wales Institute of Technology, Sydney, 1987.

Hallsworth, A.G., *The Human Impact of Hypermarkets and Superstores*, Avebury, Aldershot, 1988.

Halpin, David (ed.), *Consumers' Choice: 25 Years of the Australian Consumers' Association*, ACA, Marrickville, 1984.

Harvey, David, *The Urban Experience*, Blackwell, Oxford, 1989.

—— , *The Condition of Postmodernity: An Enquiry Into the Origins of Cultural Change*, Blackwell, Oxford, 1991.

Hebdige, Dick, *Hiding in the Light: On Images and Things*, Routledge, London, 1988.

Hoggart, Richard, *The Uses of Literacy*, Penguin, Harmondsworth, 1980.

Horne, Donald, *The Lucky Country*, Penguin, Ringwood, 1964.

—— , *Money Made Us*, Penguin, Ringwood, 1976.

Horne, Shirley, *A Study of Milk Bars and Corner Shops in Melbourne: Shopping as a Social Activity*, Department of Social Studies, University of Melbourne, Melbourne, 1984.

Horowitz, Daniel, *The Morality of Spending. Attitudes Towards the Consumer Society in America 1875–1940*, Johns Hopkins University Press, Baltimore, 1985.

Hutchinson, R.C., *Food For the People of Australia*, Angus & Robertson, Sydney, 1958.

Jameson, Fredric, *Postmodernism, or the Cultural Logic of Late Capitalism*, Verso, London, 1991.

Jefferys, James B., *Retail Trading In Britain 1850–1950*, Cambridge University Press, Cambridge, 1954.

Jefferys, James and Knee, Derek, *Retailing In Europe: Present Structure and Future Trends*, Macmillan, London, 1962.

Johnson, Lesley, *The Modern Girl: Girlhood and Growing Up*, Allen & Unwin, Sydney, 1993.

Johnson, Louise (ed.), *Suburban Dreaming: An Interdisciplinary Approach to Australian Cities*, Deakin University Press, Geelong, 1994.

Johnston, George, *Clean Straw For Nothing*, Collins/Fontana, Melbourne, 1969.

Johnston, R.J. and Rimmer, P.J., *Retailing In Melbourne*, Department of Human Geography, Australian National University, Canberra, 1969.

Jordan Dataquest, *British Supermarkets*, Jordan Dataquest Ltd, London, 1977.

Kaplan, E. Ann, *Rocking Around the Clock: Music Television, Postmodernism and Consumer Culture*, Methuen, London, 1987.

Keeping Brunswick's Heritage: A Report on the Review of the Brunswick Conservation Study, vol. 2, Context Pty Ltd, Melbourne, 1990.

Kingston, Beverley, *Basket, Bag and Trolley: A History of Shopping in Australia*, Oxford University Press, Melbourne, 1994.

Knight, Stephen, *The Selling of the Australian Mind: From First Fleet to Third Mercedes*, Heinemann, Melbourne, 1990.

Kowinski, William Severini, *The Malling of America: An Inside Look at the Great Consumer Paradise*, New York, 1985.

Lash, Scott and Urry, John, *The End of Organised Capitalism*, Polity, Cambridge, 1987.

Lebhar, Godfrey M., *Chain Stores in America, 1859–1962* (3rd ed.), Chain Store Publishing Corporation, New York, 1963.

Le Goff, Jacques, *History and Memory*, S. Rendall and E. Claman (trans.), Columbia University Press, New York, 1992.

Lee, Martyn J., *Consumer Culture Reborn: The Cultural Politics of Consumption*, Routledge, London, 1993.

Lees, Stella and Senyard, June, *The 1950s: How Australia Became a Modern Society, and Everyone Got a House and Car*, Hyland House, Melbourne, 1987.

Lefebvre, Henri, *Everyday Life in the Modern World*, Allen Lane, London, 1971.

Linge, G.J.R., *Industrial Awakening: A Geography of Australian Manufacturing 1788–1890*, Australian National University Press, Canberra, 1979.

Lukacs, Georg, *History and Class Consciousness*, Merlin Press, London, 1968.

Luker, Philip, *Inside the Food Industry*, Philip Luker and Staff, Sydney, c.1988.

Lunt, Peter K. and Livingstone, Sonia M., *Mass Consumption and Personal Identity: Everyday Economic Experience*, Open University Press, Buckingham, 1992.

Lyotard, Jean-Francois, *The Postmodern Condition: A Report on Knowledge*, trans. Geoff Bennington and Brian Massumi, Manchester University Press, Manchester, 1989.

McAusland, Randolph, *Supermarkets: 50 Years of Progress*, Food Marketing Institute, Washington, 1980.

McClelland, W.G., *Studies in Retailing*, Basil Blackwell, Oxford, 1964.

McCracken, Grant, *Culture and Consumption: New Approaches to the Symbolic Character of Consumer Goods and Activities*, Indiana University Press, Bloomington, 1990.

McGregor, Craig, *Profile of Australia*, Penguin, Ringwood, 1968.

—— , *People, Politics and Pop: Australians in the Sixties*, Ure Smith, Sydney, 1968.

McGuigan, Jim, *Cultural Populism*, Routledge, London, 1992.

McKendrick, Neil, Brewer, John and Plumb, J.H., *The Birth of Consumer Society: The Commercialisation of Eighteenth-Century England*, Indiana University Press, Bloomington, 1982.

McNair, W.A., *Radio Advertising in Australia*, Angus & Robertson, Sydney, 1937.

Macintyre Stuart, *The Oxford History of Australia: The Succeeding Age 1901–1942*, Oxford University Press, Melbourne, 1993.

Marcuse, Herbert, *One-Dimensional Man: Studies in the Ideology of Advanced Industrial Society*, Routledge & Kegan Paul, London, 1968.

Markin, Rom J., *The Supermarket: An Analysis of Growth, Development and Change*, Washington State University Press, Washington, 1968.

Marx, Karl, *Capital: A Critique of Political Economy*, vol. 1, Ben Fowkes (trans.), Penguin, London, 1982.

Mathias, Peter, *Retailing Revolution: A History of Multiple Retailing in the Food Trades Based Upon the Allied Suppliers Group of Companies*, Longman, London, 1967.

Matthews, Glenna, *"Just a Housewife": The Rise and Fall of Domesticity in America*, Oxford University Press, New York, 1987.

Matthews, Jill Julius, *Good and Mad Women: The Historical Construction of Femininity in Twentieth-Century Australia*, George Allen & Unwin, Sydney, 1984.

Mayer, Robert N., *The Consumer Movement: Guardians of the Marketplace*, Twayne, Boston, 1989.

Miller, Daniel, *Material Culture and Mass Consumption*, Basil Blackwell, Oxford, 1991.

Miller, Daniel (ed.), *Acknowledging Consumption: A Review of New Studies*, Routledge, London, 1995.

Miller, Michael B., *The Bon Marché: Bourgeois Culture and the Department Store, 1869–1920*, Allen & Unwin, London, 1981.

Modleski, Tania (ed.), *Studies in Entertainment*, Indiana University Press, Bloomington, 1986.

Morris, Meaghan, *The Pirate's Fiancée: Feminism, Reading, Postmodernism*, Verso, London, 1988.

Mui, Hoh-Cheung and Mui, Lorna H., *Shops and Shopkeeping in Eighteenth-Century England*, McGill-Queen's University Press/Routledge, London, 1989.

Mukerji, Chandra, *From Graven Images: Patterns of Modern Materialism*, Columbia University Press, New York, 1983.

Murphy, Daniel J., *Customers and Thieves: An Ethnography of Shoplifting*, Gower, London, 1986.

Nelson, Cary, Treichler, Paula A. and Grossberg, Lawrence, *Cultural Studies*, Routledge, New York, 1992.

Packard, Vance, *The Hidden Persuaders*, Penguin, Harmondsworth, 1957.

Patterson, George, *Life Has Been Wonderful: Fifty Years of Advertising at Home and Abroad*, Ure Smith, Sydney, 1956.

Pollon, Frances, *Shopkeepers and Shoppers: A Social History of Retailing in New South Wales from 1788*, Retail Traders' Association of New South Wales, Sydney, 1989.

Porter, Hal, *The Watcher on the Cast-Iron Balcony*, Faber & Faber, London, 1963.

Porter, Una B. (ed.), *Growing Together: Letters Between Frederick John Cato and Frances Bethune, 1881–1884*, privately published, Melbourne, 1981.

Powell, David, *Counter Revolution: The Tesco Story*, Grafton, London, 1991.

Pratt, Ambrose (ed.), *The National Handbook of Australia's Industries*, Specialty Press, Melbourne, 1934.

Pringle, John Douglas, *Australian Accent*, Chatto and Windus, London, 1965.

Redfern, Percy (ed.), *Self and Society: Social and Economic Problems from the Hitherto Neglected Point of View of the Consumer* (2 vols), Ernest Benn, London, 1930.

Reekie, Gail, *Temptations: Sex, Selling and the Department Store*, Allen & Unwin, Sydney, 1993.

Reiger, Kerreen M., *The Disenchantment of the Home: Modernizing the Australian Family 1880–1940*, Oxford University Press, Melbourne, 1985.

Retail Trade International 1989/90 Volume One: Europe, Euromonitor Publications, London, 1989.

Retail Trade International 1989/90 Volume Two: International, Euromonitor Publications, London, 1989.

Richards, Thomas, *The Commodity Culture of Victorian England: Advertising and Spectacle 1851–1914*, Stanford University Press, Stanford, 1990.

Robjohns, W.A., *Grocery Commodities: A Textbook for the Australian Grocery Trade*, Retail Storekeepers Association of South Australia, Adelaide, 1939.

Ross, Andrew, *No Respect: Intellectuals and Popular Culture*, Routledge, New York, 1989.

Ryan, Edna and Conlon, Anne, *Gentle Invaders: Australian Women at Work*, Penguin, Melbourne, 1989.

Samuel, Raphael and Thompson, P. (eds), *The Myths We Live By*, Routledge, London, 1990.

Sharmas, Carol, *The Pre-Industrial Consumer in England and America*, Clarendon Press, Oxford, 1990.

Shields, Rob, *Places on the Margin: Alternative Geographies of Modernity*, Routledge, London, 1991.

Shields, Rob (ed.), *Lifestyle Shopping: The Subject of Consumption*, Routledge, London, 1992.

Simmel, Georg, *The Philosophy of Money*, David Frisby (ed.), Tom Bottomore, David Frisby and Kaethe Mengelberg (trans.), Routledge, London, 1990.

Sinclair, Amanda, *Trials at the Top: Chief Executives Talk about Men, Women and the Australian Executive Culture*, The Australian Centre, University of Melbourne, Melbourne, 1994.

Smailes, P.J., *The Impact of Planned Shopping Centres in a Sector of Metropolitan Adelaide*, Department of Geography, University of Sydney/Geographical Society of New South Wales, May 1969.

Soja, Edward M., *Postmodern Geographies: The Reassertion of Space in Critical Social Theory*, London, 1989.

Spearritt, Peter, *Sydney Since the Twenties*, Hale & Iremonger, Sydney, 1978.

Strasser, Susan, *Satisfaction Guaranteed: The Making of the American Mass Market*, Pantheon, New York, 1989.

Stretton, Hugh, *Ideas for Australian Cities*, Georgian House, Melbourne, 1975.

Summers, Anne, *Damned Whores and God's Police: The Colonization of Women in Australia*, Penguin, Ringwood, 1975.

Symons, Michael, *One Continuous Picnic: A History of Eating in Australia*, Duck Press, Adelaide, 1982.

Tedlow, Richard S., *New and Improved: The Story of Mass Marketing in America*, Basic Books, New York, 1990.

Thirsk, Joan, *Economic Policy and Projects: The Development of a Consumer Society in Early Modern England*, Oxford University Press, Oxford, 1978.

Timms, J.C., *Greater Retail Turnover*, Pitman, Melbourne, 1939.

Tomlinson, Alan (ed.), *Consumption, Identity and Style: Marketing, Meanings and the Packaging of Pleasure*, Routledge, London, 1990.

Tonkin, Elizabeth, *Narrating Our Pasts: The Social Construction of Oral History*, Cambridge University Press, Cambridge, 1992.

Turner, Graeme, *British Cultural Studies*, Unwin Hyman, London, 1989.

Veblen, Thorstein, *The Theory of the Leisure Class: An Economic Study of Institutions*, Random House, New York, 1934.

Wajcman, Judy, *Feminism Confronts Technology*, Polity, Cambridge, 1991.

Walker, Robin and Roberts, Dave, *From Scarcity to Surfeit: A History of Food and Nutrition in New South Wales*, New South Wales University Press, Kensington, 1988.

Weatherill, Lorna, *Consumer Behaviour and Material Culture in Britain 1660–1760*, Routledge, London, 1988.

White, Richard, *Inventing Australia: Images and Identity 1688–1980*, George Allen & Unwin, Sydney, 1981.

Whitwell, Greg, *Making the Market: The Rise of Consumer Society*, McPhee Gribble, Melbourne, 1989.

Williams, Rosalind, H., *Dream Worlds: Mass Consumption in Late Nineteenth-Century France*, University of California Press, Berkeley and Los Angeles, 1982.

Williamson, Judith, *Consuming Passions: The Dynamics of Popular Culture*, London, 1986.

Willis, Susan, *A Primer For Daily Life*, Routledge, London, 1991.

Winstanley, Michael, *The Shopkeeper's World, 1830–1914*, Manchester University Press, Manchester, 1983.

Zimmerman, M.M., *The Supermarket: A Revolution in Distribution*, McGraw Hill, New York, 1955.

Articles

Adorno, Theodor W. and Horkheimer, Max, 'The Culture Industry: Enlightenment as Mass Deception', in Max Horkheimer and Theodor W. Adorno, *The Dialectic of Enlightenment*, John Cumming (trans.), Continuum, New York, 1982.

Agnew, Jean-Christophe, 'Coming Up For Air: Consumer Culture in Historical Perspective', in John Brewer and Roy Porter (eds), *Consumption and the World of Goods*, Routledge, London and New York, 1993, pp. 19–39.

Andrzejaczek, T., 'Suburbia – A Cultural Defeat', *Quadrant*, vol. 2, no. 1, Summer 1957–58, pp. 25–30.

Ashbolt, Allan, 'Godzone 3/ Myth and Reality', *Meanjin*, vol. xxv, no. 4, 1966, pp. 373–88.

Ashbolt, Anthony, 'Against Left Optimism: A Reply to John Docker', *Arena*, no. 61, 1982, pp. 134–40.

Baars, Ann Marie, 'The Nature and Distribution of Retailing Activities in Perth Central Ward Between 1888 and 1904', *Australia 1888 Bulletin*, November 1983, pp. 3–17.

Barthel, Dianne, 'Modernism and Marketing: The Chocolate Box Revisited', *Theory, Culture and Society*, vol. 6, 1989, pp. 429–38.

Baudrillard, Jean, 'The Ecstasy of Communication', in Hal Foster (ed.), *The Anti-Aesthetic: Essays on Postmodern Culture*, Bay Press, Washington, 1983, pp. 126–34.

Benjamin, Walter, 'The Work of Art in the Age of Mechanical Reproduction', in Walter Benjamin, *Illuminations*, Hannah Arendt (ed.), Harry Zohn (trans.), Wolf/ Harcourt, Brace & World, New York, 1973.

Blackburn, Kevin, 'The "Consumer's Ethic" of Australian Advertising Agencies 1950–1965', *Journal of Australian Studies*, no. 32, March 1992, pp. 60–74.

Boorstin, Daniel J. 'The Consumption Community', in Grant S. McClellan (ed.), *The Consuming Public*, H.W. Wilson, New York, 1968, pp. 9–24.

Bowlby, Rachel, 'Scenes from Consumer Psychology', *Critical Quarterly*, vol. 24, no. 4, Winter, 1992, pp. 51–64.

Brett, Judith, 'The Circus is in Town', *Arena Magazine*, no. 15, February/March 1995, pp. 48–50.

Carroll, John, 'The Sceptic Turns Consumer: An Outline of Australian Culture', *Quadrant*, October 1978, pp. 11–15.

—— , 'Automobile Culture and Citizenship', *Quadrant*, March 1979, pp. 10–13.

—— , 'Shopping World: An Afternoon in the Palace of Modern Consumption', *Quadrant*, August 1979, pp. 11–15.

Carter, Erica, 'Alice in Consumer Wonderland', in Angela McRobbie and Mica Nava (eds), *Gender and Generation*, Macmillan, London, 1984, pp. 185–214.

Chaney, David, 'Dystopia in Gateshead: The MetroCentre as a Cultural Form', *Theory, Culture and Society*, vol. 7, 1991, pp. 49–68.

Collins, Michael, 'A Brief History of Retailing, Part 2: The Development of Australian Retailing (1800–1990)', in Michael Collins (ed.), *Retail Management Principles Reader*, Australian Centre for Retail Studies, Monash University, Melbourne, 1991.

Cook, Ian and Crang, Philip, 'The World on a Plate: Culinary Culture, Displacement and Geographical Knowledges', *Journal of Material Culture*, vol. 1, July 1996, pp. 131–53.

Cott, Nancy F., 'On Men's and Women's History', in Marc C. Carnes and Clyde Griffen (eds), *Meanings for Manhood: Constructions of Masculinity in Victorian America*, University of Chicago Press, Chicago, 1990, pp. 205–11.

Crawford, Margaret, 'The World in a Shopping Mall', in Michael Sorkin (ed.), *Variations on a Theme Park: The New American City and the End of Public Space*, Noonday, New York, 1992, pp. 3–30.

Crowley, Desmond (ed.), *Current Affairs Bulletin: Shopping Centres*, vol. 40, no. 2, 19 June 1967.

Curthoys, Ann, 'Labour History and Cultural Studies', *Labour History*, no. 67, November 1994, pp. 12–22.

Davison, Graeme, 'Exhibitions', *Australian Cultural History*, no. 2, 1982/83, pp. 5–21.

Dixon, Jane, 'Kitchen Kultures', *Arena Magazine*, no. 19, October–November 1995, pp. 35–8.

Docker, John, 'In Defence of Popular Culture', *Arena*, no. 60, 1982, pp. 72–87.

—— , 'Popular Culture and its Marxist Critics', *Arena*, no. 65, 1983, pp. 105–9.

—— , 'Popular Culture and Bourgeois Values', in Verity Burgmann and Jenny Lee (eds), *Constructing a Culture: A People's History of Australia since 1788*, McPhee Gribble/Penguin, Melbourne, 1988, pp. 241–58.

Duruz, Jean, 'Suburban Homes Revisited', in Kate Darian-Smith and Paula Hamilton (eds), *Memory and History in Twentieth-Century Australia*, Oxford University Press, Melbourne, 1994, pp. 174–91.

—— , 'Laminex Dreams: Women, Suburban Comfort and the Negotiation of Meanings', *Meanjin*, vol. 53, no. 1, 1994, pp. 99–110.

Edwards, N., 'Shopping Centres', *Architecture in Australia*, February 1969, pp. 68–9.

Fine, Ben, 'From Political Economy to Consumption', in Daniel Miller (ed.), *Acknowledging Consumption: A Review of New Studies*, Routledge, London, 1995, pp. 127–63.

Game, Ann and Pringle, Rosemary, 'Sexuality and the Suburban Dream', *Australia and New Zealand Journal of Sociology*, vol. 15, no. 2, July 1979, pp. 4–15.

Gerster, Robin, 'Gerrymander: The Place of Suburbia in Australian Fiction', *Meanjin*, 3, 1990, pp. 565–75.

Gibbins, Ronald W., 'American Influence on Commercial Practice', in Richard Preston (ed.), *Contemporary Australia: Studies in History, Politics and Economics*, Duke University Press, Durham, 1969, pp. 498–520.

Gilbert, Alan, 'The Roots of Anti-Suburbanism in Australia', *Australian Cultural History*, no. 4, 1985, pp. 54–70.

Gill, Gerry, 'The Signs of Consumerism', *Arena*, no. 53, 1979, pp. 28–39.

Glass, Frances Devlin, 'Mythologising Spaces: Representing the City in Australian Literature', in Louise Johnson (ed.), *Suburban Dreaming: An Interdisciplinary*

Approach to Australian Cities, Deakin University Press, Geelong, 1994, pp. 160–80.

Gollan, Anne, 'Salt Pork to Take Away', in Verity Burgmann and Jenny Lee (eds), *Making A Life: A People's History of Australia Since 1788*, McPhee Gribble/Penguin, 1988, pp. 1–17.

Groenewegen, Peter, 'Consumer Capitalism', in J. Playford and D. Kirsner (eds), *Australian Capitalism*, Penguin, Melbourne, 1973, pp. 84–107.

Hagstrom, Ingrid, 'Popular Culture Undefined', *Arena*, no. 61, 1982, pp. 141–8.

Hall, Stewart and Held, David, 'Citizens and Citizenship', in Stuart Hall and Martin Jacques (eds), *New Times: The Changing Face of Politics in the 1990s*, Lawrence & Wishart/Marxism Today, London, 1990, pp. 173–88.

Harris, David, 'A Great Ring of Landlords?', in Verity Burgmann and Jenny Lee (eds), *Making a Life: A People's History of Australia Since 1788*, Penguin, 1988, pp. 39–55.

Harris, Max, 'Morals and Manners', in Peter Coleman (ed.), *Australian Civilisation*, Cheshire, Melbourne, 1962, pp. 47–67.

Holmes, Katie, 'The Modern Girl', *Australian Historical Studies*, no. 102, April 1994, pp. 129–30.

Humphery, Kim, 'Youth and the Art of Subversion', *Arena*, no. 86, Autumn 1989, pp. 55–70.

——, 'A Stranger in Daimaru', *Meanjin*, vol. 53, no. 1, Autumn, 1994, pp. 85–95.

——, 'Talking Shop', *Arena Magazine*, no. 19, October–November 1995, pp. 30–4.

Hutchings, Karen, 'The Battle for Consumer Power: Post-War Women and Advertising', in Graeme Turner (ed.), *Fabrications: Journal of Australian Studies*, no. 50/51, University of Queensland Press, St Lucia, 1996, pp. 66–77.

Huyssen, Andreas, 'Mass Culture as Woman: Modernism's Other', in Tania Modleski (ed.), *Studies in Entertainment*, Indiana University Press, Bloomington, 1986, pp. 188–207.

Jameson, Fredric, 'Postmodernism or the Cultural Logic of Late Capitalism', *New Left Review*, no. 146, July–August 1984, pp. 53–93.

——, 'Postmodernism and Consumer Society', in E. Ann Kaplan (ed.), *Postmodernism and its Discontents*, Verso, London, 1988, pp. 13–29.

Joseph, Beate, 'Images of Suburbia: Bruce Dawe, Bruce Beaver, Gwen Harwood and Vincent Buckley', *Quadrant*, April 1978, pp. 64–7.

Lake, Marilyn, 'Historical Homes', in John Rickard and Peter Spearritt (eds), *Packaging the Past*, Melbourne University Press, Melbourne, 1991, pp. 46–54.

——, 'The Politics of Respectability: Identifying the Masculinist Context', in Susan Magarey, Sue Rowley and Susan Sheridan (eds), *Debutante Nation: Feminism Contests the 1890s*, Allen & Unwin, Sydney, 1993, pp. 1–15.

Langman, Lauren, 'Neon Cages: Shopping for Subjectivity', in Rob Shields (ed.), *Lifestyle Shopping: The Subject of Consumption*, Routledge, London, 1992, pp. 40–82.

Laski, Harold J., 'The Recovery of Citizenship', in Percy Redfern (ed.), *Self and Society: Social and Economic Problems from the Hitherto Neglected Point of View of the Consumer*, vol. 1, Ernest Benn, London, 1930 (pamphlet).

Leavis, F.R., 'Mass Civilisation and Minority Culture', in F.R. Leavis, *Education and the University*, Cambridge University Press, Cambridge, 1979.

Lee, Jenny, 'A Redivision of Labour: Women and Wage Regulation in Victoria 1896–1903', in Susan Magarey, Sue Rowley and Susan Sheridan (eds), *Debutante Nation: Feminism Contests the 1890s*, Allen & Unwin, Sydney, 1993, pp. 27–37.

Levett, Elizabeth, 'The Consumer in History', in Percy Redfern (ed.), *Self and Society: Social and Economic Problems from the Hitherto Neglected Point of View of the Consumer*, vol. 2., Ernest Benn, London, 1930 (pamphlet).

McCalman, Janet, 'Suburbia from the Sandpit', *Meanjin*, vol. 53, no. 3, Spring, 1994, pp. 548–53.

McCann, Andrew, 'Melbourne's Royal Arcade and the Empty Time of Fashion', *Australian Historical Studies*, no. 107, October 1996, pp. 343–55.

MacCulloch, Jennifer, ' "This Store is Our World": Female Shop Assistants in Sydney to 1930', in Jill Roe (ed.), *Twentieth-Century Sydney: Studies in Urban and Social History*, Hale & Iremonger, 1980, pp. 166–77.

McGregor, Craig, 'Pop Goes the Culture: Academic and Other Prognostications', *Meanjin*, vol. 39, no. 1, April 1980, pp. 3–11.

McRobbie, Angela, 'Postmodernism and Popular Culture', in Lisa Apignanesi (ed.), *Postmodernism*, Institute of Contemporary Arts, London, 1986, pp. 54–8.

—— , 'New Times in Cultural Studies', *New Formations*, 13 (Spring), 1991, pp. 1–17.

—— , 'Window Shopping', *Red Pepper*, London, no. 25, June 1996, p. 25.

—— , 'Bridging The Gap', *Feminist Review*, no. 55, Spring 1997, pp. 73–89.

Mackay, Hugh, 'Responding to the Consumer of the 1990's', in Society of Consumer Affairs Professionals in Business Inc., *1991 Conference Papers*, SOCAP, Geelong, 1991 (no page nos.).

Maddock, Rodney and Stilwell, Frank, 'Boom and Recession', in Ann Curthoys, A.W. Martin and Tim Rowse (eds), *Australians from 1939*, Fairfax, Syme and Weldon, Sydney, 1987, pp. 255–71.

Markey, Ray, 'New South Wales Trade Unions and the "Co-operative Principle" in the 1890s', *Labour History*, no. 49, November 1985, pp. 51–60.

Matthews, Jill, 'Education for Femininity: Domestic Arts Education in South Australia', *Labour History*, no. 47, November 1983, pp. 30–53.

Merrett, D.T., 'Australian Capital Cities in the Twentieth Century', in J.W. McCarty and C.B. Schedvin (eds), *Australian Capital Cities*, Sydney University Press, Sydney, 1978, pp. 171–98.

Miller, Daniel. 'Consumption as the Vanguard of History', in Daniel Miller (ed.), *Acknowledging Consumption: A Review of New Studies*, Routledge, London, 1995, pp. 1–57.

Miller, Peter and Rose, Nikolas, 'Mobilizing the Consumer: Assembling the Subject of Consumption', *Theory, Culture and Society*, vol. 14, 1997, pp. 1–36.

Mintz, Sidney W., 'The Changing Roles of Food in the Study of Consumption', in John Brewer and Roy Porter (eds), *Consumption and the World of Goods*, Routledge, London and New York, 1993, pp. 261–73.

Morris, Meaghan, 'Things to Do With Shopping Centres', in Susan Sheridan (ed.), *Grafts: Feminist Cultural Criticism*, Verso, London, 1988, pp. 193–225.

—— , 'Banality in Cultural Studies', in Patricia Mellencamp (ed.), *The Logics of Television: Essays in Cultural Criticism*, Indiana University Press, Bloomington, 1990, pp. 14–43.

—— , 'On the Beach', in Cary Nelson, Paula A. Treichler and Lawrence Grossberg (eds), *Cultural Studies*, Routledge, New York, 1992, pp. 450–78.

Mort, Frank, 'The Politics of Consumption', in Stuart Hall and Martin Jacques (eds), *New Times: The Changing Face of Politics in the 1990s*, Lawrence & Wishart/ Marxism Today, London, 1989, pp. 160–72.

Murphy, John, 'The Voice of Memory: History, Autobiography and Oral Memory', *Historical Studies*, vol. 22, no. 87, October 1986, pp. 157–75.

Nava, Mica, 'Consumerism Reconsidered: Buying and Power', *Cultural Studies*, vol. 5, no. 2, May 1991, pp. 157–73.

Nightingale, Virginia, 'What's "Ethnographic" about Ethnographic Audience Research?', in John Frow and Meaghan Morris (eds), *Australian Cultural Studies: A Reader*, Allen & Unwin, Sydney, 1993, pp. 149–61.

Nixon, Sean, 'Have You Got the Look?: Masculinities and Shopping Spectacle', in Rob Shields (ed.), *Lifestyle Shopping: The Subject of Consumption*, Routledge, London, 1992, pp. 149–69.

Pringle, Rosemary, 'Women and Consumer Capitalism', in Cora V. Baldock and Bettina Cass (eds), *Women, Social Welfare and the State in Australia*, Allen & Unwin, Sydney, 1983, pp. 85–103.

Radway, Janice, 'Mail Order Culture and its Critics: The Book-of-the-Month Club, Commodification and Consumption, and the Problem of Cultural Authority', in Cary Nelson, Paula A. Treichler and Lawrence Grossberg (eds), *Cultural Studies*, Routledge, New York, 1992, pp. 512–30.

Reekie, Gail, 'Market Research and the Post-War Housewife', *Australian Feminist Studies*, no. 14, Summer 1991, pp. 15–27.

—— , 'Changes in the Adamless Eden: The Spatial and Sexual Transformation of a Brisbane Department Store 1930–90', in Rob Shields (ed.), *Lifestyle Shopping: The Subject of Consumption*, Routledge, London, 1992, pp. 170–94.

Rigg, Julie, 'The Loneliness of the Long-Distance Housewife', in Julie Rigg (ed.), *In Her Own Right: Women of Australia*, Nelson, Melbourne, 1969, pp. 135–49.

Roper, Michael, 'Yesterday's Model: Product Fetishism and the British Company Man, 1945–85', in Michael Roper and John Tosh (eds), *Manful Assertions: Masculinities in Britain since 1800*, Routledge, London, 1991, pp. 190–211.

Rosewarne, Stuart, 'The Political Economy of Retailing Into the Eighties – Part 1', *Journal of Australian Political Economy*, no. 15, 1983, pp. 18–38.

—— , 'The Political Economy of Retailing into the Eighties – Part 2', *Journal of Australian Political Economy*, no. 16, 1984, pp. 75–91.

Rowse, Tim, 'Heaven and a Hills Hoist: Australian Critics on Suburbia', *Meanjin*, vol. 37, no. 1, April 1978, pp. 3–13.

Ryan, Jenny, 'Women, Modernity and the City', *Theory, Culture and Society*, vol. 11, 1994, pp. 35–63.

Sanders, Matthew R. and Hunter, Allen C., 'An Ecological Analysis of Children's Behaviour in Supermarkets', *Australian Journal of Psychology*, vol. 36, no. 3, 1984, pp. 415–27.

Sharp, Geoff, 'Constitutive Abstraction and Social Practice', *Arena*, no. 70, 1985, pp. 48–83.

—— , 'Extended Forms of the Social: Technological Mediation and Self-Formation', *Arena Journal* (New Series), no. 1, 1993, pp. 221–37.

Shaw, Gareth, 'The Evolution and Impact of Large-Scale Retailing in Britain', in John Benson and Gareth Shaw (eds), *The Evolution of Retail Systems, c.1800-1914*, Leicester University Press, London, 1992, pp. 135–65.

Shields, Rob, 'Spaces for the Subject of Consumption', in Rob Shields (ed.), *Lifestyle Shopping: The Subject of Consumption*, Routledge, London, 1992, pp. 1–20.

Smart, Judith, 'Feminists, Food and the Fair Price: The Cost of Living Demonstrations in Melbourne, August–September 1917', *Labour History*, no. 50, May 1986, pp. 113–31.

Smith, G.W., 'The Market Place: Progress or the Erosion of a Social Institution?', *Architecture in Australia*, February 1969, pp. 74–9.

Snooks, Graeme, 'Manufacturing', in Wray Vamplew (ed.), *Australian Historical Statistics*, Fairfax, Syme & Weldon Associates, Sydney, 1987, pp. 37–45.

Spearritt, Peter, 'I Shop Therefore I Am', in Louise C. Johnson (ed.), *Suburban Dreaming: An Interdisciplinary Approach to Australian Cities*, Deakin University Press, 1994, pp. 129–40.

Stauth, Georg and Turner, Bryan S., 'Nostalgia, Postmodernism and the Critique of Mass Culture', *Theory, Culture and Society*, vol. 5, no. 2–3, June 1988, pp. 509–26.

Steedman, Carolyn, 'Culture, Cultural Studies, and Historians', in Cary Nelson, Paula A. Treichler and Lawrence Grossberg (eds), *Cultural Studies*, Routledge, New York, 1992, pp. 613–22.

Steward, Fred, 'Green Times', in Stuart Hall and Martin Jacques (eds), *New Times: The Changing Face of Politics in the 1990s*, Lawrence & Wishart/Marxism Today, London, 1989, pp. 65–75.

Tasker, Yvonne, 'Having it All: Feminism and the Pleasures of the Popular', in Sarah Franklin, Celia Lury and Jackie Stacy (eds), *Off-Centre: Feminism and Cultural Studies*, HarperCollins, London, 1991, pp. 85–96.

Trotter, David, 'Fiction and the Economy of Abundance', *Critical Quarterly*, vol. 34, no. 4, Winter, 1992, pp. 27–41.

Turnaturi, Gabriella, 'Between Public and Private: The Birth of the Professional Housewife and the Female Consumer', in Anne Showstack Sassoon (ed.), *Women and the State: The Shifting Boundaries of Public and Private*, Hutchinson, London, 1987, pp. 255–78.

Turner, Graeme, '"It Works for Me": British Cultural Studies, Australian Cultural Studies, Australian Film', in Cary Nelson, Paula A. Treichler and Lawrence Grossberg (eds), *Cultural Studies*, Routledge, New York, 1992, pp. 640–53.

—— , 'Discipline Wars: Australian Studies, Cultural Studies and the Analysis of National Culture', in Graeme Turner (ed.), *Fabrications: Journal of Australian Studies*, no. 50–51, University of Queensland Press, St Lucia, 1996, pp. 6–17.

Turner, Ian, 'The Life of the Legend', in Ian Turner, *Room For Manoeuvre: Writings on History, Politics, Ideas and Play*, Drummond, Melbourne, 1982.

—— , 'The Bastards from the Bush: Some Comments on Class and Culture', in E.L. Wheelwright and Ken Buckley (eds), *Essays in the Political Economy of Australian Capitalism*, vol. 3, Australia & New Zealand Book Co., Sydney, 1978, pp. 167–89.

Walker, Robin, 'Aspects of Working-Class Life in Industrial Sydney in 1913', *Labour History*, no. 58, May 1990, pp. 36–47.

Webb, Beatrice, 'The Discovery of the Consumer', in Percy Redfern (ed.), *Self and Society: Social and Economic Problems from the Hitherto Neglected Point of View of the Consumer*, vol. 1, Ernest Benn, London, 1930 (pamphlet).

Wilson, J.L.J. (ed.), *Current Affairs Bulletin: The Merchandising Revolution*, vol. 31, no. 11, 15 April 1963.

Wolfers, Howard, 'The Big Stores Between the Wars', in Jill Roe (ed.), *Twentieth-Century Sydney: Studies in Urban and Social History*, Hale & Iremonger, Sydney, 1980, pp. 18–33.

Theses and Unpublished and Audio-Visual Material

Born to Shop, Sarah Gibson (dir./prod.), Inside Outside Productions, Australian Film Commission/Australian Broadcasting Corporation, 1991.

Collins, Michael, 'The Rise and Fall of Woolworths 1924–1986', Australian Centre for Retail Studies (unpublished paper).

Humphery, Kim, 'New Worlds, Familiar Places: Supermarkets, Consumption and Cultural Critique', PhD thesis, University of Melbourne, 1995.

Lateline: Retailing the Future, Australian Broadcasting Corporation, aired on ABC television, Melbourne, September 1994.

Peel, Mark, 'Elizabeth: From the City of the Future to a Suburb With a Past', PhD thesis, University of Melbourne, 1992.

Spierings, John, 'Magic and Science: Aspects of Business Management, Advertising and Retailing, 1918–40', PhD thesis, University of Melbourne, 1989.

Taksa, Lucy, 'All a Matter of Timing: The Diffusion of Scientific Management in New South Wales, Prior to 1921', PhD thesis, University of New South Wales, 1993.

The Investigators (segment on the future of supermarket shopping), Australian Broadcasting Corporation, aired on ABC television, Melbourne, March 1994.

Index

Adorno, Theodor, W., 64
advertising, 26, 28, 44, 83, 229n.26
Arena, 170, 171
Arnott, William, 42
ASDA, 2
Ashbolt, Alan, 168
Ashbolt, Anthony, 171
Aspinall, Clara, 34
Associated Australian Warehouses, 150, 238n.33
Australian Supermarket Institute, 153, 239n.54
Alexander, David, 24
Appadurai, Arjun, 33
Australian Women's Weekly,109–10
autonomy
    consumption and, 22–3, 170, 206–7
    self-service and, 84, 94, 96, 99, 205, 207
    shopping and, 120, 180, 208
    supermarkets and, 180

Barr, Anetta, 124, 125, 128, 129, 135, 136–7, 182, 190, 197
Barthel, Dianne, 28
Baudrillard, Jean, 146–7
Benjamin, Walter, 64
Bolte, Henry, 108
Bon Marché, 25
Boorstin, Daniel, J., 72

Bottomley, David, 93
Bowlby, Rachel, 12, 25, 32
Boyd, Robin, 164–5
Bradbury, Bevan, 150
Bramley, Edna and Albert, 126, 127, 131–2
Brand, Edward, E., 71
Brett, Judith, 174
Brisbane Cash and Carry, 81
Britain
    co-operatives, 21–3, 29–30, 73, 227n.89
    cultural influence, 34–5, 36, 39–40
    food consumption, 26–7
    food manufacturing, 27
    grocery retailing, 29–32
    retailing, 23–5
    self-service, 73–4
    supermarkets, 2, 74–6
Brooke Bond, 27
Brown, Linden, 150–1
buying groups, 87–8
    see also voluntary chains

Cadbury, Edward, 39, 51
Cadbury-Fry-Pascall, 43
Cairns, Tom, 49, 127
car ownership, 107, 166
Carroll, John, 166
Casey, Gavin, 79

cash and carry, 46, 81, 221n.3
category killers, 154
Chadstone, 115–16
Chain Store Inquiry, 51–2
Challinger, Dennis, 99
Chermside, 115
children, 61–62 *see also* young people
Clairs, Reg, 156
class
    consumption and, 165, 168, 170, 171
    food consumption and, 26–7
    food manufacturing and, 29
    food shopping and, 181–2
    self-service and, 67, 73
co-branding, 154
Coles, Edgar, 103, 113–14
Coles, G.J. & Coy, 3, 36, 100–1,
        103–104, 108, 110, 111–12, 116,
        133, 144, 146, 147, 150, 151
Coles Myer, 2, 152, 153
Collins, Michael, 150, 156
comparison shopping, 149
Composite Buyers, 88, 150
consumer movement, 23, 85, 241n.2
consumer culture, 2, 6–7, 12–13, 14–15,
        96, 122–3, 139, 210
    commodification and, 8, 16, 38, 64–5,
        72, 77–8, 116, 164–6, 168
    everyday critique of, 11–12, 16,
        196–202
    fragmentation of, 145, 148, 152, 156
    globalisation and, 3, 8, 63, 72, 207
    as mundane, 26
    negotiation of, 5–6, 206
    packaged commodities and, 33
    postmodernity and, 146–7
    as spectacle, 25–26, 77–8
consumer society, 3, 6–7, 196–7, 201
consumption, 6, 13, 123–4, 214n.9
    Aboriginal cultures and, 159,
        217n.31
    as active process, 7–8, 9,169, 171,
        171–2, 209–1, 10–11, 12, 14
    ambivalence towards, 10–11, 14, 173,
        176, 196, 209, 211
    autonomy and, 22–3, 170, 206–7
    citizenship and, 157, 166
    and conformity, 168
    as cultural defeat, 163–6
    and desire, 32, 93–4
    and empowerment, 12, 199–201
    expenditure, 83, 107, 150, 229n.20

history of, 7, 25–6
    and manipulation, 198–9,
    men and, 95–96, 148–9,
    popular culture and, 14, 167–8,
        171–2
    production and, 170, 194
    suburbia and, 162–3, 165, 168, 169,
        173
    women and, 47, 72, 94–5, 169–70,
        198
convenience shopping, 149
convenience stores, 148
Conway, Ronald, 165–6
co-operatives, 21–3, 29–30, 51, 73,
        227n.89
Crichton, John, 135, 137, 138
Crofts Stores, 50, 52, 53, 87, 125, 130,
        133, 135, 136
cultural studies, 7, 8–9, 10–11, 12, 14,
        15, 147, 167, 172, 215n.17
Curthoys, Ann, 15
Cusack, Dymphna, 102
Cusson, Jean, 132
customer types, 55–7, 91–2, 157

Dandenong
    grocery stores, 125–30
    history of, 125
    immigrants, 130–2
    self-service, 133–5
    supermarkets 133, 136–9
Darwin, 2
Davis, Dorothy, 29
Davison, Graeme, 35
Debord, Guy, 77–8
delicatessens, 126, 131, 184
department stores, 25, 36, 81–2
desire, 32, 69, 93–4
discount department stores, 144
discount grocery stores, 148
Dichter, Ernest, 65, 92
Dickins, 82, 87, 110
Dipman, Carl, W., 68
display, 86–7
Docker, John, 163, 168, 171
domestic science, 47

Edison, Thomas, 67
EFTPOS, 151
elderly people, 182
employment, retail, 50, 70, 76, 89, 104,
        106–7, 152, 232n.22

Fiske, John, 171–2
Fraser, Hamish, 27, 32
Freeman-Greene, Suzy, 158–9
Friedan, Betty, 72
Foley, Gary, 159
food consumption, 26–7, 45, 83, 107, 150
food manufacturing, 27–9, 41–5, 83, 229n.23
Foodland, 88, 153
Foodplus, 148
Franklins, 2, 110, 144, 147, 150, 151
Fulop, Christina, 73

Game, Ann, 169–70
gender, *see* masculinity; men; women
Gill, Gerry, 170
globalisation, 63, 72, 207
Gollan, Anne, 41
Grace Brothers, 81–2
Great Atlantic and Pacific Tea
     Company, 32, 69, 71
grocers
    and buying groups, 87–8
    and conversion to self-service, 81–4, 133, 135
    and credit, 129–30
    and customers, 127–30
    and masculinity, 50, 55–8, 85, 90
    professional organisations, 46, 47
    and stock, 127–8
    training of, 48–9, 223n.52
    unions, 47
    working hours, 49, 51
grocery chains, 2, 3, 30–2, 51–3, 69, 73–6, 87, 111–14, 130, 150
    market share, 104, 113, 150
    percentage of grocery stores, 88
    store numbers, 51, 69, 71, 87, 113, 144, 151
    training schemes, 53
see also Coles; Woolworths, etc.
grocery stores, 39–41, 48, 103–4, 125–30, 213n.2
    female labour in, 50
    profit margins, 89,
    store numbers, 46, 80, 83, 110, 152, 227n.88
Groenewegen, Peter, 168

Hagstrom, Ingrid, 171
Harris, Max, 165

Hart, Dorothy, 132
Harvey, David, 107–8
Heinz, 43
Henry Jones and Company, 41
Hoadley, 44
Hodge, Bob, 171–2
Home and Colonial Stores, 31
home ownership, 35, 107
home shopping, 154, 155
Horkheimer, Max, 64
Horne, Donald, 163, 166–7
house brands, 147, 227n.75
Hussey, Fay, 130, 132, 135, 135–6, 137, 179, 194
Hutchinson, R.C., 45
Hutton, Nan, 109
hypermarkets, 77, 146–7, 237n.12

immigrants, 101–3, 130–1
inflation, 144–5

James, Florence, 102
Jameson, Fredric, 146,
Jarvis, Maurie, 129–30
Jefferys, James, 24
J. Kitchen & Sons, 42
Jobson, Sandra, 119,
Johnson, Lesley, 13, 94, 174
Johnston, George, 44

Keating, Paul, 153
Kellogg, 43
King Kullen, 68
Kingston, Beverley, 174
Kitchen, Ford, 84, 86
K Mart, 144
KraftWalker, 43, 44
Kroger, 32

Lake, Marilyn, 55
Laski, Harold, J., 22
Lebhar, Godfrey, 66
Lefebvre, Henri, 78, 108
Lipton, Thomas, 27, 30–1
Lee, Jenny, 42
Legge, Kate, 159
Lever Brothers, 42
Levett, Elizabeth, 21
Lightfoot, Jack, 130, 133, 135
living standards, 38
Lukacs, Georg, 64
Luker, Philip, 151

Mackay, Hugh, 157
Mac.Robertson's, 42, 203
McCalman, Janet, 174
McClelland, W.G., 63–4, 73
McEwan's, 132, 133–5
McGregor, Craig, 167–8
McVities, 27
Mack, Max, 54
Majik Market, 148
management, retail, 67, 76, 91, 105–6, 152
Marcuse, Herbert, 72
markets, 126–7, 185
market research, 92, 109, 230n.58
market share, 2, 70, 104, 113, 150, 153, 213–4n.4
Markin, Rom, 68
Marx, Karl, 64
masculinity
   consumption and, 168, 169
   grocery stores and, 55–8
   scientific retailing and, 37, 55, 58
   self-service and, 85
   shopping and, 150
   shopping centres and, 117–18
   supermarkets and, 105–6
Matthews, Glenna, 28, 29
Meanjin, 168
memory, 123–4
men
   and consumption, 95–6
   gay, 191–2
   and shopping, 5, 135–6, 148, 149–50, 186–9, 191, 214n.6
   and retail management, 5, 67, 76, 91, 105–6, 152
Menzies, Robert, 108
Midro, Lily, 131, 138–9
Miller, Michael, B., 25
Mitchell, Evelyn, 125–6, 127, 128
modernity, 7, 86, 94, 96, 108
   failure of, 151, 152
   gender and, 96
   retailing and, 24, 35, 52, 80, 96, 101, 103, 105, 207
   self-service and, 84, 90, 94, 96
   supermarkets and, 3, 61, 71, 75, 104, 112, 137
Moran & Cato, 51, 52, 53, 57, 125, 204
Morris, Meaghan, 10, 173–4
Mui, Hoh-Cheung and Lorna, 24
Myer, 115–16

nationalism
   commerce and, 34–5, 44, 103, 105, 108, 207
   and Empire, 34, 44
   manufacturing and, 44, 207
Nestlé, 42–3, 44
Neville, Richard, 159
New South Wales Inquiry into the Living Wage, 46
niche marketing, 153–4, 156
Norris, Muriel, 133, 135, 137, 137–8, 182, 190, 194
Northland, 116

optical scanning, 151, 155

packaging, 27–9, 33, 65, 87
Paton, Alex, 89
Patten, Simon, 28
Peek Freans, 27
Peters, 44
Piggly Wiggly, 66
pleasure, 75, 109, 114, 133, 152, 155
population, statistics, 35, 107, 220n.58
Porter, Hal, 39
post-Fordism, 145–6, 236n.9
postmodernity, 7, 146–7, 154
Powell, David, 73
Pratt, Ambrose, 44
Pratts Supermarkets, 112
Pringle, John Douglas, 165
Pringle, Rosemary, 169–70
products, numbers of types stocked, 71, 110, 151, 152

Quadrant, 165

rationing, 73, 83, 228n.16
Redfern, Percy, 22
Reekie, Gail, 5, 36, 47, 57, 92, 128, 148, 174
Reiger, Kerreen, 47
relationship marketing, 157
retail cultures, 5, 15
retail forms, 5
retailing
   in crisis, 154, 156
   critique of, 119–20
   history of, 23–5, 34–8
   revolutions in, 24–5, 89, 103, 154
   and science, 32–3, 37, 54–5, 58, 70–1, 85–6, 106, 207

training schemes, 53
Richards, Thomas, 25
Rigg, Julie, 163, 169
Robinson, J.C., 45
Roper, Michael, 90
Roselands, 117
Rosella, 41
Rosewarne, Stuart, 107
Ruthven, Phil, 154
Ryan, Jenny, 94
Rynsent, Kitty, 130–1

Safeway, 69, 71, 75–6, 108, 112–13, 144,
    146, 147, 203, 206
Sainsbury's, 2, 31, 73–4, 75
Sanitarium, 41
science and retailing, 32–3, 37, 54–5,
    58, 70–1, 85–6 106, 207
self–service
    and autonomy, 84, 94, 96, 99, 205,
        207
    and class, 67, 73
    critique of, 136
    emergence of, 3, 66, 73–4, 80–4,
        111–12, 133–5, 205, 207
    as impersonal, 63–4, 65, 84, 90
    as leisure, 90
    and psychoanalysis, 92–3
    and science, 85–6
    store numbers, 73, 80, 228n.4
    use of, 83–4, 89, 135–6
    women and, 85
semi-self-service, 84, 90–1
7 Eleven, 148
sex and supermarkets, 190–2
Sharmas, Carol, 24, 27
Shaw, Gareth, 24, 31
shopaholic, 159
shoplifting, 96–9
shoppers, in supermarket, 2, 151, 153,
    156
shopping, 9–10, 132–3, 149, 158–9,
    192–3
    arcades, 36
    and autonomy, 120, 180, 208
    children and, 61–2
    and coupledom, 190–1
    critique of, 193–6
    elaborated forms, 184–5
    as family activity, 71, 136, 193
    as impersonal, 150
    as leisure, 193–5

lists, 71
men and, 135–6, 148, 149–50, 186–9,
    191, 214n.6
as mundane. 143–4
and self-identity, 195–6
as social activity, 46, 157, 179–80,
    184–6
transformation of, 156–7
women and, 5, 29, 51, 67, 75, 120,
    135, 189–90
shopping centres, 9, 114–18, 173
    critique of, 119–20
    expansion of, 153
    number of, 116
    scientific planning of, 115
Simmel, Georg, 64
Smith, G.W., 119
social theory, 8, 10, 11
Southland, 116
space, 107–8
Staggart, Arthur, 111
Strasser, Susan, 27
Steedman, Carolyn, 15
Stretton, Hugh, 168
store numbers, 46, 51, 69, 71, 73, 80,
    83, 87, 110, 112, 113, 144, 151,
    152, 153, 227n.88, 228n.4
store size, 76, 77, 104
suburbanisation, 35, 37–8, 107, 109,
    117
suburbia, 161–2, 164, 167, 168, 172,
    174–6
Summers, Anne, 169
superette, 87
supermarkets
    critique of, 138–9, 150–1, 180–1,
        183–6
    decline of, 150–2, 207–8
    definition of, 213n.3
    emergence of, 3, 68–69, 104–5, 133
    future of, 154, 156
superstore, 146, 237n.14
Swallow & Ariell, 42, 126
symbolism of supermarkets, 72, 100–1,
    105, 108
Synott, Kevin, 125

Tedlow, Richard, 70
television, 108
Tesco, 2, 73, 74, 76
Tieck, Norman, 104, 109
Top Ryde, 115

Trade Practices Commission, 153
trading hours, 51, 83
trading stamps, 227n.84
trolleys, 69–70, 154
Turnaturi, Gabriella, 47
Turner, Graeme, 171–2
Turner, Ian, 168, 171

United States
    cultural influence, 35, 36, 43, 73, 86,
        101, 103, 104–5, 112–13, 164
    food manufacturing, 27–8
    grocery retailing, 32
    self-service, 66–7
    supermarkets, 62–3, 68–72
unemployment, 145
unions, 47, 50, 106–7

variety store chains, 36–7, 89, 144, 203
    see also Coles; Coles Myer;
        Woolworths
Veblen, Thorstein, 64
voluntary chains, 150

Webb, Beatrice, 22

Williams, Rosalind, 25, 28
White, Richard, 44
Whitwell, Greg, 37
women
    consumption and, 47, 72, 94–5,
        169–70, 198
    and desire, 93–4
    employment in retailing, 50, 70, 76,
        106–7, 152
    lesbian, 192
    and market research, 92
    and self-service, 85
    and shoplifting, 97–9
    shopping and, 5, 29, 51, 67, 75, 120,
        135, 189–90
    and space of supermarket, 76, 149
Woolworths, 2, 3, 36, 112, 144, 147,
    150, 151, 152–3, 156

young people
    and shoplifting, 97–9
    and shopping, 61–2, 121–2, 180,
        190–1

Zimmerman, Max, 100

DATE DUE

			Printed in USA

HIGHSMITH #45230